MARKETING KNOW-HOW

Your Guide to the Best Marketing Tools and Sources

Peter Francese

American Demographics Books
Ithaca, New York

A Division of American Demographics, Inc.
127 West State Street, Ithaca, NY 14850
Telephone: 607-273-6343

Executive Editor: Diane Crispell
Managing Editor: Nancy Ten Kate
Project Editor: Ellen Marsh
Publisher: Wade Leftwich
Associate Publisher: James Madden
Marketing Associate: Kevin Heubusch

Library of Congress Catalog Number:

Cataloging In Publication Data
Francese, Peter 1941–
Marketing Know-How

ISBN 0-936889-38-1

Book design and composition: Peter C. Krakow

Table of Contents

Chapter 1: Consumer Trends

Chapter 2: Marketing Information

Chapter 3: The Articles

Chapter 4: Private Sources

These sources provide a broad variety of data, from basic demographic
statistics to media use, purchase behavior, and attitudes. They provide
information in a variety of formats, from printed reports to sophisticated
electronic information systems.

Chapter 5: Federal Government Sources

Government data often get a bad name for being out of date, but their
timeliness is improving, they are statistically sound, and they are
sometimes the only available source. While the Census is the biggest
government producer of demographic data, other agencies collect and
publish information about everything from birth statistics to projections
of the veteran population.

Chapter 6: State and Local Sources

When it comes to getting the local scoop, local sources know best. Just be
careful to temper their occasionally optimistic numbers with a dose of reality
checks. This chapter directs you to sources of demographic, employment,
vital statistics, and education data in all 50 states and D.C.

Appendices

Demographic Dictionary:

Keyword Index to Sources:

Source Name/Telephone Index:

Preface

This book used to be called *The Insider's Guide to Demographic Know-How*. It is still an insider's guide, in that it has been compiled by a group of people with collective decades of experience with demographic and consumer data. But in this, its fourth edition, its title has become broader to reflect its increased coverage of the ever-expanding marketing information industry.

Following in the tradition of the previous three editions, *Marketing Know-How* opens with an overview of significant demographic and consumer trends in place as we approach the third millennium. Chapter 2 lists four key questions to ask about your customers and suggests a three-legged stool of databases you need to develop to understand them.

Chapter 3 offers an all-new and updated selection of articles from *American Demographics* and its new sister publication, *Marketing Tools*. These articles will help you target the mature mind, get to the grassroots, understand advertising options, geocode customer lists, respect privacy concerns, and more.

Chapters 4-6 are filled with descriptive listings of organizations that provide marketing data and solutions. These range from the huge Bureau of the Census to specialized consulting companies. Chapter 5 describes the colossal amount of data available from dozens of federal statistical agencies. Chapter 6 goes local with state and local sources, mostly government agencies, that provide demographic, social, and economic information for their regions.

Chapter 4 covers the most dynamic portion of the marketing information industry, and it is substantially more comprehensive than in past editions. It lists hundreds of private, academic, and nonprofit organizations that provide products and services to help marketers and others understand more about their customers and potential customers.

These organizations publish population projections, gather social and economic data, compile industry and market segment profiles, and sell samples and lists. They measure media use, purchase behavior, and attitudes and lifestyles. They offer custom research and consulting, as well as geographic analysis, database marketing, and other services. They can help you learn more about your customers and the consumer marketplace than you can possibly need to know. But their goal—and ours— is to help you determine just what it is you do need.

If you are like me, you may prefer to use the extensively cross-referenced keyword listings that start on page 307 to help you quickly locate the data or services you are seeking. But, if you are not adverse to technology, you will be able to accomplish more refined searches by using a companion electronic file, which contains a full-text database of all the source listings. The file may be downloaded from our Web site (http://www.demographics.com) or obtained on disk by calling our customer service center (800-828-1133). Whether you take the high-tech or low-tech road, this book aims to help you get where you want to be.

—Diane Crispell
executive editor, American Demographics

Introduction

Marketing Know-How is about how to get more customers. The more you know about your present and future customers, and the more you use that knowledge to serve them better, the more customers you will retain and the more prosperous your enterprise will become. The purpose of this book is to increase the value of your enterprise as well as the value of your work.

In today's hotly competitive marketplace, your business success depends on how well you keep up with changing customer needs. This fact is well known to the many businesses that provide goods and services directly to individuals and households. But other organizations, such as nonprofit or business-to-business firms can also gain important advantages by tracking changes in the consumer markets that ultimately support them. The rule is simple: focus on our customers' needs and make sure they are satisfied in some way by what you provide.

This rule sounds so obvious. Why doesn't everybody just do it? Why do you need a book about such a basic business principle? There are three good reasons.

First, most business enterprises don't follow the rule. Their managers follow the human tendency to focus on what they already do well, such as administration or product development, instead of on what their customers want or need. It is hard to talk to customers and listen to them complain. And, it's truly challenging to make your organization more like what those customers want it to be. If you take complaints personally, and many of us do, listening to customers complain is like listening to someone say that your baby is ugly. Nobody wants to hear comments like that.

Second, people who are at or near the top of an organization often forget the limits of their power. After years of exercising control in their firm, bosses often come to believe that they can control their customers, too. It is a blow to their ego to admit that it's those fickle, troublesome customers who are really in charge. Overcoming the basic human desire for comfort and control is always difficult. But everyone in an organization has to acknowledge that the customer is the boss before the organization can really change.

The third and most compelling reason to study your customers isn't personal. It is simply that the economic and social environment is vastly more complex than it used to be. The wants and needs of your customers are changing faster than ever before. In most industries, the customers are fragmenting into dozens or even hundreds of overlapping groups. You can't keep track of changes like these just by following your instincts. To know them, you need marketing information, software, and databases. The mission of *Marketing Know-How* is to help you find and use these tools.

The New Tools of Marketing

Successful marketing is harder these days because it is a lot more complicated than it used to be. Customers have more choices than they did a generation ago. The most sophisticated and affluent customers have access to a lot more information about their choices. Our population is aging as well, and this means that a higher proportion of customers are experienced and skeptical shoppers. Older customers have already heard most of the standard advertising claims. They won't be swayed by clever graphics or celebrity endorsements; they are more likely to find for themselves the price-to-value relationship for your product and make their own decisions.

Marketing is often called an art, probably because it involves so much creativity. But marketing is also a craft. Like weaving or fine woodworking, it requires the artful use of tools to create something that is at once beautiful and functional. Marketing also means closing the sale, delivering the goods, and making sure the customer is satisfied. To succeed in this complex endeavor requires learning about the new tools of marketing and how to use them creatively.

Developing marketing know-how does not come naturally to most people. For one thing, marketing involves asking your customers to help you by telling you about their wants and needs. Asking for help is not something most people want to do. Marketing also means hearing things you might not like to hear. If your spectacular new product idea is something people don't need or want, you'd better rethink things.

Yet marketing is more necessary today than ever before. If you're opening a new business or selling a new product, you'll find that the marketplace has become very tough. Every year there seem to be more competitors and more regulations. Your customers seem increasingly cynical and deal-oriented. These trends put the squeeze on profits. Meanwhile, each part of the marketing function has become more complex. There are more ways to conduct market research than ever before, and there are more places to advertise than we ever thought possible.

The good news is that every year the essential tools of marketing also become more powerful, more accurate, easier to use, and less expensive. Meanwhile, media options such as cable television and the Internet are more sharply targeted than ever before. *Marketing Know-How* shows you how to identify which of these media and marketing tools best fit your needs.

Marketing is one of the most important parts of starting a new business, but it is often overlooked. Most entrepreneurs open their shops with a firm idea of what they want to provide. Most of the time they do not have a lot of intimate knowledge of their potential customers. And all too often, they do not take the time to understand the size and viability of their market.

Successful marketing begins before opening for business or selling the first item, because market research is an essential part of the preparation. It involves identifying different groups of potential customers and then probing to find out how likely each group is to buy your product or service. This pre-launch research is the only way to know if enough customers will spend enough money regularly to make your product or service profitable.

In the excitement of starting a new service or inventing a new product, it is easy to believe that everyone in the world will be as excited by your idea as you are. Talking about it with friends doesn't help, because it is very hard to get negative feedback from friends. The almost-universal reply when somebody suggests a new business is "Wow, that sounds like a good idea!" Or, "This town has needed one of those for a long time."

Still, it's important to remember that not every good idea for a business is economically viable. We all need encouragement from our friends. But the real critical thinking about the size and economic viability of a customer base hardly ever comes from talking to family, friends, or acquaintances. It comes from objectively researching would-be customers or otherwise testing the market to see how many people will buy what you want to sell, how often they will buy it, and how much they will pay for it.

A Note on Business–to–Business Marketing

Marketing Know-How is for everyone in business, but it may also be useful to the new breed of entrepreneur who serves other businesses. One of the most important trends of the 1990s has been the explosion of personal enterprises. Millions of talented workers have left large corporations to work for themselves or in smaller firms. Among the reasons are the downsizing of corporations, the elimination of middle managers, and changes in technology that permit people to work at home with computers and modems.

It's popular to say that the growth of personal enterprise would not be possible without new technology. But another, equally important reason has gone largely unnoticed. In the last two decades, the U.S. has had a rapid increase in its proportion of college-educated workers. People with college experience are highly skilled, ambitious, and less likely to settle for an unsatisfying job. Moreover, they are more likely to have what it takes to strike out on their own. Freed from the regulations and bureaucracy of a large organization, they can quickly adapt their businesses to match the shifting realities of the market.

Many personal enterprises serve other businesses instead of serving consumers directly. Rather than hire employees to do various non-core jobs, large and medium-sized businesses are hiring independent contractors and small firms to provide services that range from emptying wastebaskets to developing high-tech software. Between 1987 and 1992, the number of businesses that provide services to other businesses increased 22 percent, according to the Census Bureau. In contrast, the number of retail stores increased less than 2 percent.

The fundamental rule in consumer marketing is to know the customer. Business-to-business firms must follow a slightly more complicated rule: they must know the customer and the customer's customer. If you provide a service or a product to another business, you can gain an advantage with your clients whenever you help them develop or improve a product or service for their customers.

Business-to-business firms face just as much competition as do ordinary retailers or restaurateurs, and failure for small firms can have a high personal cost. But the strategic use of market information can give struggling entrepreneurs an advantage. For example, a company that provides paper towels or janitorial services to fast-food restaurants might suggest diaper-changing stations in areas where births are high. Savvy business suppliers will find ways to deliver their services along with something extra: information that helps clients serve their customers better.

It doesn't take a lot of time or money to come up with good ideas about how to serve client's customers. Marketing information is usually not expensive, but a free statistic from the government can have a high perceived value if it brings knowledge. Even a one- or two-page report about the latest trends in customer satisfaction lets clients know that you are vitally interested in their success.

Business-to-business firms vary tremendously in size and type, but the fundamental rule of all business-to-business marketing is the same. Know the customer, and then know the customer's customer.

Chapter 1: Consumer Trends

The fundamental trends driving consumer markets in the U.S. have been evident for at least a decade. They are slowing population growth, an aging population, and the fragmentation of consumer markets. These trends continue unabated in the mid-1990s, and new variations are emerging. For example, the slowdown in population growth now extends to slow growth in other areas. Most markets are seeing little or no growth in household incomes, and the rate of growth in households has slowed considerably.

The fragmentation of markets is also evolving. A decade ago, most organizations could easily understand their customer segments in terms of demographic differences such as age and income. Demographics still play a vital role in marketing know-how, but today it is also important to understand the attitudes and lifestyles of customer segments. Customer segments have emerged around activities such as smoking, eating vegetarian, and riding motorcycles. Each of these activities implies a certain way of looking at the world.

The fact is that no American can be called "typical." There is no average family, no "living" wage, and no middle class as we once knew it. Every product or service has its own customer base that should be narrowly targeted and specifically served.

For several decades, business leaders have followed broad demographic trends to better understand their customer segments, because patterns of change in the general population are likely to affect individual market segments and alter consumer behavior. But as consumer markets become more complex, success in business will depend to a greater extent on also keeping up with the changing wants or needs of specific customer segments.

When it comes to targeting customers, you can think about them as individual economic actors who make their own purchase decisions, or you can think of them as families or other small groups that make collective decisions.

Targeting individuals usually makes sense if you're selling personal-care products, books, or clothing. But many other products and services have a primary buyer who is affected by the opinions of others in their household—automobiles and food come to mind *(See "Pulling the Family's Strings," p. 30)*. Targeting households also makes sense for obvious household items like furniture, appliances, or cable-television hookups.

To understand how individuals are changing requires tracking personal demographic and lifestyle change. For example, understanding the growth and buying patterns of different age groups can provide insight into how each generation will change consumer behavior as it moves through life. Trends in the labor force provide some understanding of how job and work changes affect people's attitudes and how they use their time. It's also important to look at educational attainment, which has an enormous effect on both income and purchase behavior.

Household consumer behavior is also affected by personal characteristics such as the income and education of the householder or other household members. But the life stage of the household has a big impact as well. Whether the household is a young married couple with small children, an older married couple with grown children, a single parent, or a single person living alone or with friends profoundly influences the type of dwelling they rent or buy, what they put into it, and how they landscape around it.

What follows are the most current available data on how U.S. population and households are changing and what they may mean for consumer behavior.

Age Group and Generational Markets

In 1996, the U.S. is home to 265 million people and 100 million households. About one in four persons (26 percent) are children under age 18, and one in eight (13 percent) are aged 65 and older. The remaining 61 percent are working-age adults.

By generational markets, this nation's people can be classified into four major groups: the baby boom and the next baby boom, at about three in ten each; the baby bust between them, at nearly two in ten; and the mature market, with one in four persons.

During the next decade, the U.S. population is projected to grow less than 1 percent per year. But even that low average masks wide variations in growth rates by age segments. The fastest growth will occur among people in their 50s (up nearly 50 percent); the fastest decline among people in their 30s (down 14 percent). Above-average growth will occur among teenagers, young adults, and those aged 75 and older.

In 1996, the median age of the U.S. population is 35. In 20 years, there will be about 290 million people in the U.S., and half of them will be past their 40th birthday. Since women generally live longer than men, an aging population means that women will be in the majority for the foreseeable future. Above age 65, for example, there are roughly three women for every two men.

Population By Age

age	population (in millions) 1996	% change 1996 - 2001	% change 1996 - 2006
0 - 9	38.96	-0.7%	-1.0%
10 - 17	30.42	+6.2	+10.4
18 - 24	24.62	+9.1	+16.0
25 - 29	19.00	-9.4	- 2.5
30 - 34	21.37	-8.6	-17.0
35 - 39	22.54	-3.8	-12.1
40 - 44	20.78	+9.4	+5.2
45 - 49	18.42	+10.4	+20.7
50 - 54	13.92	+30.2	+43.9
55 - 59	11.36	+19.5	+55.8
60 - 64	10.00	+9.2	+30.8
65 - 69	9.89	-5.2	+4.1
70 - 74	8.79	-0.9	-5.4
75 - 84	11.44	+8.9	+12.7
85+	3.75	+17.0	+35.5
Total	265.25	+ 4.4	+8.7
< 18	69.38	+2.4	+4.0
18 - 24	24.62	+9.1	+16.0
25 - 34	40.37	-9.0	-10.1
35 - 44	43.31	+2.5	-3.8
45 - 54	32.34	+18.9	+30.7
55 - 64	21.36	+14.7	+44.1
65 +	33.87	+3.1	+8.0

Source: Census Bureau

An aging population will have a profound impact on every business and market segment. The changes older adults demand will be both large and small. For example, a higher proportion of the population will require reading glasses in the future. More customers will have more difficulty reading small print on direct mail, restaurant menus, and packaging. Higher contrast between printed words and their background will be necessary to accommodate older eyes *(See "Vision in an Aging America," p. 35)*.

Redesigning packages is a fairly simple task, but an aging population will also bring more difficult challenges. Adults older than 40 will boost spending on health care because they are more likely to have arthritis, high blood pressure, and other chronic conditions. They may even force changes in traffic laws, because people's reflex times tend to slow with age.

The psychological changes that accompany aging will transform consumer markets as well. An older population is less likely to be fashion-conscious, and more interested in clothing that offers comfort and good value. In the broadest sense, older adults are more interested in having an interesting or meaningful experience than in acquiring consumer goods, according to author David Wolfe *(See "Targeting the Mature Mind," p. 40)*. This is another reason why the quality of customer service is of increasing importance.

The aging of America will be the dominant demographic trend of the next two decades, but it does not mean that all Americans will be getting old. There will always be millions of people who do not wear glasses or watch their blood pressure. Fortunes can still be made by serving the needs of children and young adults.

The Next Baby Boom

Between 1977 and 1994, baby boomers gave birth to a generation almost as large as their own. The annual number of births in the U.S. started increasing in 1977, when the childbearing years for baby boomers were just beginning. It stayed above 4 million a year between 1989 and 1993. In 1994, as the boomers' childbearing years drew near their end, births fell just below 4 million, and the next baby boom was over *(See "The Next Baby Boom," p. 45)*. Births are projected to decline slightly between 1995 and 2000.

Demographers have called this generation the "baby boomlet" or the "echo baby boom" to tie it to the original event. But it is the first generation to come of age after the end of the Cold War, so you could call it the "post-cold-war baby boom." It is the first generation to grow up in the age of global online information, so you could also call it the "Internet baby boom."

Whatever you call them, there are many differences between these children and the boomers who gave birth to them. The next boomers are the first generation to be brought up mostly in day care, because a majority of their mothers work full-time. They are the first multicultural generation: one-third of the next boomers are either Hispanic (14 percent), black (15 percent), or Asian/other nonwhite (5 percent), and this does not include the 2 million children who are of mixed race.

The next boomers are also the first generation to be totally comfortable with a new, looser definition of the American family. A high proportion of them have never lived in a conventional husband-and-wife family; they have been raised by single parents, stepparents, and grandparents. These facts will shape the attitudes and

Generation Gap

baby boom 1946-1964	next boom 1977-1994
Cold War	regional wars
nuclear threat	terrorist threats
mother's care	day care
"Father Knows Best"	father not present
TV dinners	low-fat food
network TV	cable TV
45s and LPs	CDs and MTV
Ma Bell	Internet and cellular phones
VW buses	minivans
free love	condoms

consumer behavior of young adults for the next two decades, until the next boomers give way to the generation making its entrance in the late 1990s.

The next baby boom is such a large group that it cannot be accurately described in a few short phrases. In the next decade, this generation will enter a labor force that is driven by savage global competition, little job security, and declining government assistance. But even if they never reach the heights of prosperity attained by the post-World War II generations, the huge numbers of the next baby boom will ensure that they have a major impact on U.S consumer spending for most of the 21st century.

The Baby Bust

About 45 million people were born in the U.S. between 1965 and 1976. That is a lot of people—more than the population of Argentina—but it was a big decline from the birth totals of the 1950s and early 1960s. Demographers called it a baby bust, in contrast with the earlier baby boom. The bust began when births sank below 4 million in 1965, and it ended when births began increasing again in 1977. The name stuck as the generation moved through life.

In 1996, people in the baby-bust generation are aged 20 to 31. As young adults, they acquired new nicknames of a derogatory nature, such as Generation X or slackers, because so many of them seemed cynical about the future. These stereotypes contained a grain of truth, but to portray young adults as lazy or spoiled would be completely unfair.

Many members of the baby-bust generation feel they have been dealt a bad hand. And why not? After all, there are fewer guarantees these days that hard work and sacrifice will buy the American dream. Young adults know that a college degree is no longer a guaranteed route to a good job. Many talented college graduates have settled for jobs that were previously held by those with high school diplomas or less *(See "The Generation X Difference," p. 52).*

The baby bust is also the first generation to be told that they probably will not live as well as their parents did. Some of them believe it, too. Young adults have suffered a dramatic decline in real wages over the past 15 years, a stark truth that lends credence to their gloomy outlook. About one-quarter of this smaller generation are already college graduates, and many are still college-aged. Many graduate with large student loans and other debts that hamper their ability to buy a car, get married, buy a home, or otherwise move up the social ladder.

The baby bust does have some advantages, however. They are entering their working lives at the dawning of the global information network, a major technological change that is creating significant business opportunity. Young adults who maintain their computer literacy are starting successful businesses and finding good jobs. They are also becoming well-informed, savvy consumers. Open forums on the World Wide Web provide many opportunities for brutally frank political or personal discussions, as well as a wide array of information about products and services.

Despite their smaller numbers, lower incomes, and higher debt, young adults have been the targets of millions of advertising messages. Perhaps the gap between the prices of goods and their meager ability to buy has made them more cynical about being consumers. But even if their incomes become much higher later in life, the cynicism toward marketing may continue.

The Baby Boom

Baby boomers are defined both by demographics and by attitudes. In demographic terms, they are Americans born between 1946, when the number of births rose dramatically, and 1964, the last year in the 1960s when births totaled more than 4 million. In 1996, the boomers are aged 32 to 50, and in 2000 they will be 36-to-54 years old.

The baby boom is a massive group of 77 million people, accounting for almost one in three Americans. They are notable and influential because their great numbers dictate consumer demand in broad terms. But the boomers are also distinguished by a unique set of attitudes that are by no means shared by other generations.

The leading authority on baby boomers is Cheryl Russell, author of *The Master Trend: How the Baby-Boom Generation Is Reshaping America.* One of her most important points is that boomers' attitudes and lifestyles are significantly different from those of previous generations. They are so different, in fact, that the closest you can come to predicting their behavior is to expect the unexpected. As the oldest boomers move into their 50s, they will redefine the mature market *(See "The Baby Boom Turns 50," p. 58).*

Despite the fact that they are moving into their peak earning years, many baby boomers appear to be facing serious financial difficulties. Most members of this group postponed marriage, children, and savings. Now, with the prospect of retirement moving closer, boomers want to save more. But a fast-track retirement plan isn't always possible for the millions of boomers who have moderate incomes and children who want to go to college, or for those who have aging parents in need of financial support. College tuition bills and ailing parents can become a major problem, particularly for those whose home equity declined when real-estate values slumped in the early 1990s.

Baby boomers in their 50s will almost certainly face rising medical bills, for two reasons. First, they will develop more health problems. But more significant is the fact that their parents will move into the final stages of life, when medical costs can be extremely high. In the next five to ten years, many billions of dollars from those peak earnings that would otherwise be spent on consumer goods will instead go toward education expenses, medical expenses, and savings plans.

The Mature Markets

The "mature market" has been defined as people aged 50 and older, probably because that is the age at which you can join the American Association of Retired Persons. But if we think of the mature market as anyone older than baby boomers, it is better to make the adjustment that will fit at the turn of the century and define them as anyone aged 55 or older. Also, there are really three mature markets: the pre-retired (aged 55 to 64), who came of age in the 1950s; the early retired (aged 65 to 74), who relate to World War II; and the elderly (aged 75 and older), who became adults during the Great Depression.

Many myths and misconceptions surround the mature markets. Some boosters suggest that they are a multi-billion-dollar consumer gold mine, a huge group of rich people just waiting for the right product pitch. Others suggest that most people in this age group are poor and probably curmudgeons as well.

As usual with sweeping generalities, there is some truth to both sides. But the real facts are more complicated and more interesting. It's true that there are more well-to-do older people in America than ever before, thanks to three decades of robust financial markets, generous expansion of pension plans, and federal benefits that have guaranteed nearly all older people a base income and freedom from huge medical bills.

Yet the median household income of those aged 65 and older is only about $18,000, which is 44 percent below the national average. Also, nearly four in ten householders aged 55 and older are single people, and the household income of this segment is below $15,000. The truth is that mature markets are so vast and complex that you can probably find statistics to support almost any assertion you want to make about them.

The youngest segment of the mature market, those aged 55 to 64, will grow the fastest in the next 15 years as the baby boom moves into it. This segment is also likely to change the most, as the boomers' unique styles make their mark. One likely change is an even more intense resistance to the idea of growing older. Think of boomers like Candice Bergen and Rod Stewart, both of whom will celebrate their 55th birthdays in the year 2001.

Another likely change is a surge in labor force participation. In 1996, about one-third of men and one-half of women in this age group are not in the labor force. But the financial pressures on baby boomers, combined with their lower asset bases, suggest that labor force participation rates of this group will rise over the next decade.

The middle segment of the mature segment, aged 65 to 74, has grown slightly faster than average over the past ten years, but no growth is projected for at least the next ten years. The vast majority of men and women in this age group are retired, and no significant change in that situation is expected in the near term. At the present time, household net worth peaks in this age group, with a median value of $94,000. Yet their household income is almost 30 percent below average. Despite their demographic stability, this group will also change its style over the next ten years. Their style leaders may include Woody Allen, Sophia Loren, and Dan Rather.

The oldest segment, people aged 75 and older, has been growing rapidly—about 2.5 percent a year—and it is likely to continue that high growth rate for the foreseeable future. The oldest Americans are by far the most dependent group of adults. Their household income is 44 percent below average. And despite Medicare and Medicaid, their health care bills consume 14.4 percent of their household spending, compared with 5.5 percent for all U.S. households. In the next decade, the 75-and-older group will absorb the men and women who served in World War II. Think of Bob Dole, Betty White, and Bob Hope.

One in three households is headed by someone aged 55 or older. Vast differences exist between various segments of this huge market. Each segment contains niche markets for a vast array of consumer services, such as household and yard work, everyday transportation, vacation travel, financial services, and the full spectrum of health care.

Labor Force Trends

About 132 million Americans are either employed or looking for work. That's about two in three civilians not living in group quarters (like dorms, prisons, and hospitals). Within this group, about 8 million are unemployed on average; 23 million work part-time; and about 8 million hold more than one job. Also, about 1 in 20 workers is defined as "contingent" by the U.S. Department of Labor. Contingent workers are temporary clerical workers, short-term technical experts, and those otherwise not on staff. Officially, they do not have an "implicit or explicit contract for ongoing work." They are the fastest-growing segment of the labor force *(See "Temps Are Here to Stay," p. 65).*

Clearly, the workplace is not as simple as it used to be. But Americans still work hard, and understanding their work patterns can offer important clues to their consumer behavior.

American Workers

Persons in civilian labor force, 1995 .... 132 million
    Self-employed .... 7.1 %
    Multiple job holders 6.0
    Men.. 53.9
    Women 46.1

By occupation:
    Professional, managerial...................................... 28.3 %
    Technical, sales, administrative support 30.0
    Service 13.6
    Production, craft, repair 10.8
    Equipment operators, laborers 14.5
    Farming, forestry, fishing 2.9

By industry:
    Agriculture, mining, construction 9.3%
    Manufacturing 16.4
    Transport and communication 7.0
    Retail and wholesale trade 20.9
    Finance, insurance, real estate........................... 6.4
    Services 35.2
        Business services 6.0
        (includes advertising, computers, etc.)
        Personal and entertainment services............. 4.5
        (includes hotels, recreation)
        Professional services 23.7
        (includes health care, legal, education)
    Public administration 4.8

Source: Census Bureau

The jobs Americans hold are changing, too. About one-third of workers are employed by a service industry, while only one in six works in manufacturing. But 25 years ago they were about equal, with one in four workers in each industry. About one in five persons at work in the 1990s is in retail or wholesale trade, virtually unchanged over the past 30 years. Fewer than 1 in 20 workers is employed by the government today; in 1970, it was 1 in 17 (about 6 percent).

All this suggests that the world of work is a far less orderly place than the old-fashioned world of 9-to-5 hours and one employer for life. It is no longer safe to assume your customers are prepared to buy, or what they will buy when they show up.

For the rapidly increasing number of Americans who own their own enterprises or work at home, the line between work life and home life has virtually disappeared. As a result, a small-time entrepreneur may be as likely to spend $500 on a fax machine or small mailing as on a vacation or clothes. If a person with flexible job hours has an extra afternoon, he or she may choose to earn a few more dollars rather than go out and play.

In millions of households, consumers have learned to think like businesspeople. They are both buyers and sellers of goods and services. This complicates your relationship with customers because it gives them more knowledge and power. People who have conducted commercial transactions themselves know how businesses operate. As a result, they are more likely to demand higher-quality goods and services at lower prices. They are also more likely to demand better customer service, because they know from their own experience how important it is to please the customer.

Education and Income

The link between education and income may be the strongest connection in consumer demographics. More than two-thirds of people who earn at least $50,000 a year are college graduates. Moreover, real income has continued to grow for those with a college education, while income for most Americans has either been declining or stagnant when adjusted for inflation.

The much-written-about gap between the haves and have-nots in the U.S. is really a widening gap between the more-educated and the less-educated. It is simply that in an information-based economy, the higher-paying jobs will most likely go to those with good analytical skills or specialized training.

The best way to see the connection between income, education, and experience is to look at income quintiles (five equally sized groups by income) and income by age. The vast majority of households in the top income quintile are college graduates. Income also rises with age, up to a point. It peaks for those aged 45 to 54, currently growing faster than any other group. Over the past ten years, income for all house-

Middle-aged Affluence

age of householder	households (in millions) 1995	median income 1994	% change income (1984-1994 constant $)
15 - 24	5.4	$19,300	- 3.6%
25 - 34	19.5	33,200	- 2.3
35 - 44	22.9	41,700	- 2.2
45 - 54	17.6	47,300	+ 4.9
55 - 64	12.2	35,200	+ 2.3
65 and older	21.4	18,100	- 1.1
all households	99.0	32,300	+ 0.7

Source: Census Bureau

holds has risen slightly. But income for younger households has fallen, while older households have generally seen their incomes increase.

Households and Families

Income trends are best understood in the context of households, because those who have income frequently share their wealth with children and other dependents who live with them. But in the next ten years, more and more Americans will live in households where they are accountable to no one but themselves. In March 1996, the number of households in the U.S. reached 100 million *(See "The 100 Millionth*

Nontraditional Family Gains

(numbers in thousands)

	1985	1995	% change 1985-1995
all households	86,789	98,990	14.1%
families	62,707	69,311	10.5
married couple, without related children under age 18	25,312	27,498	8.6
married couple, with related children under age 18	25,038	26,367	5.3
other family	12,357	15,446	25.0
nonfamily	24,082	29,686	23.3
male-headed	10,114	13,190	30.4
female-headed	13,968	16,496	18.1

Source: Census Bureau

Household," p. 70). Nationally, households are growing at a rate of 1.4 percent a year—but nonfamily households are growing at about 2.3 percent a year. Single-parent and other family households that are not headed by a married couple are growing even faster—about 2.5 percent.

The average household in the U.S. is still headed by a married couple, but this segment is barely growing. The number of couples with no children present has been increasing at about 1.2 percent a year. It should increase much faster in the next decade, as baby boomers say goodbye to their children. But the number of married couples with children is barely growing at all. There are just about as many married couples with children today as there were in 1970, when they were 40 percent of households.

The rise of nontraditional households has been a major factor in the disintegration of the mass market into hundreds of consumer segments. The household pie has been sliced into smaller and smaller pieces, just as changing lifestyles have created demand for products and services that did not exist 25 years ago.

The most recent example of a product breakthrough aided by household trends is the cellular phone. Millions of working mothers with children in day care have a cellular phone to make sure that they are never out of reach. These women also feel safer traveling with a phone in the car. Household trends clearly create consumer demand. The key task is to determine which kinds of households comprise your customers, what their specific needs are, and how they may be changing over time.

Trends in Housing

Americans spend enormous sums buying, maintaining, and decorating their homes. The average homeowner spends 28 percent of after-tax income on housing. That is roughly equal to the amount spent on food and transportation combined.

Of course, not everyone owns a home. In 1995, 65 percent of households were homeowners, slightly more than the 64 percent in 1985. Homeownership rates have actually declined slightly over the past decade for most age groups, with the exception of a rapid increase among householders aged 60 and older. More than three-fourths of householders aged 45 and older own their home. Among those aged 55 and older, fewer than half carry a mortgage.

For most older Americans, their home is their most substantial asset. Some equity-rich homeowners pay everyday expenses by taking out home-equity loans. Others hang on to their house as a way to finance their entry into a retirement or life-care community. But millions of older people simply choose to live under the same comfortable roof they have known for decades, not thinking much about its financial value.

It's a different story for younger homeowners. Their home equity has shrunk substantially over the past five years, for several reasons. Home values have declined in many markets, especially in California and the Northeast. And younger homeowners have also taken out home-equity loans to buy cars or pay college tuition, further reducing the value of their asset.

Why Follow Trends?

Tracking demographic trends can be as confusing as watching the world through a kaleidoscope. Customers are changing faster than ever. So is the competition, the technology that supports your business, and the government that taxes it. But the fundamental rule of creating a successful enterprise never changes: know thy customers and serve their needs.

You don't have to be big or rich to be an expert trend-spotter. One of the best I know is Dr. Charles Trautmann, executive director of a small nonprofit science museum in Ithaca, New York. He reads extensively, talks to other museum directors, and—most important—stays in constant touch with his customers through surveys, database marketing, and old-fashioned conversations on the museum floor.

Recently, Dr. Trautmann made a list of 20 trends that are vital to the future of his Sciencenter. Not all of the trends on this list will be relevant to you. But by reading the list, I hope you may be inspired to create one of your own. Here is Trautmann's top 20:

1. The need for science literacy continues to grow, even though there is currently a glut of scientists. The call for more research and development scientists has been replaced by a more sustained need for a population that can do basic math, solve problems, and communicate the results.

2. Exhibits are moving toward the process of science, with more in-depth investigation and understanding at each exhibit, less button-pushing, and simple demonstrations of a phenomenon.

3. Outside private science program providers will increasingly provide educational services that science museums once considered their primary turf.

4. Collaboration will become increasingly important as foundations, donors, and corporations seek to ensure that their dollars are not buying duplicate services.

5. Economic Development (read tourism) will be a primary justification for future state investment in science museums.

6. More organizations will look for capital funds. This will force donors to be more careful in selecting charities to support.

7. Nonprofits will be restructured along the lines of business and government: downsizing staff, and outsourcing more work.

8. A major nonprofit shakeout will occur.

9. Households will get older and wealthier as baby boomers mature.

10. Demand for youth services will increase.

11. Nationally, science-museum visitorship has declined 5 percent per year for the past three years after steady growth in the 1980s.

12. Federal funding is going away.

13. Unrestricted corporate giving is going away.

14. Local support is going away, and governments are looking for additional revenues from nonprofits.

15. Local schools are broke. Budget cuts are making it next to impossible for schools to support anything regarded as "extra."

16. Visitor competition will increase from nearby science facilities.

17. Staff burnout is a potential time bomb.

18. Volunteer patterns are changing, and demographic changes will continue.

19. Corporations will continue to reduce financial support.

20. Museums will have to make up for lost contributions with earned income.

Perhaps the next chapter of this book can help you make your own top-20 list. It is about marketing information, such as demographics, information on values and attitudes, and customer records. You'll see what kinds of data are vital to building marketing know-how. We will tell you the different ways these data are made available, and how to use them to fine-tune your enterprise

The consumer information industry is full of jargon, acronyms, and unfamiliar terminology. But there should never be any confusion about why we pay attention to trends and gather information about our customers. By knowing them better, we can serve them better and become more profitable.

Chapter 2: Marketing Information

You can't navigate in the high-tech world of business without a good education, and education is expensive. People spend years of their lives and many thousands of dollars to get a college degree. But a college degree is only the beginning. Your education must continue throughout your life, with a steady stream of reading, seminars, and other information about your field. It has to be this way because the good jobs today go to the most nimble minds: staying ahead intellectually is the best way to stay ahead financially.

Organizations also need a constant flow of new information to stay competitive. Their managers spend considerable time and money to decide which data are relevant, gather them in a timely and professional way, analyze them, consider the implications, and distribute the knowledge throughout the organization. This is not easy. Every college student knows how hard it is to absorb new knowledge while under severe financial and time pressures. These days, business managers know it, too.

The day-to-day basics of operating a business can take up more than 100 percent of anyone's working hours. It's hard to find the time to pay attention to statistics, especially when they describe demographic shifts or other changes that might affect your operation in a year or two. But the more successful managers make time to track the trends. Those who don't make the time are like the unfortunate young people who say, "I don't have time to go to college." Tracking trends, like going to college, teaches you to think strategically—and strategic thinking is what separates the economic winners from the losers.

Organizations that make intelligent investments in marketing information on a regular basis are more likely to reap big long-term benefits. But what information is relevant? Most of us suffer from information overload—the feeling that it is nearly impossible to digest enough information to be well-informed. Many organizations spend vast sums on data that are of only marginal value. Figuring out which marketing information is important is a vital first step.

When you're trying to find out which marketing data are relevant to your organization, it helps to follow the money. Ask yourself where your cash flow is coming from, and you open the door to many interesting questions. Here are four important questions to begin your search.

Four Questions

First, **who are your customers?** Specifically, what kind of people are your most loyal and profitable customers? Which folks represent the middle of your market—profitable to pursue, but not as good as the best? Which customers are marginally profitable, and who are the people who will never buy your wares?

Demographic characteristics such as age, income, education, or family status are often the best way to separate customers into these categories, even though the key traits of your customers may have nothing to do with demographics. That's because demographic data are easy to compare against each other, and because they are available for every city block and zip code in the country. Once you know the demographic characteristics of each customer segment, you can go out and look for other people with similar profiles.

But before you can find out who your customers are, it is vital to find out where they live. Retail stores, restaurants, and other storefront organizations gather their customers' addresses so they understand how far people will travel to buy from them. Address lists are just as important to nonretailers, for a different reason: people with similar characteristics tend to live in certain neighborhoods.

In many cases, simply knowing a customer's address can substitute for asking them direct questions about their demographics and lifestyles. Cluster analysis systems, which have been sold by marketing information companies for almost three decades, take an address and create a likely profile of the people who live there, based on census demographics and surveys of product use, media use, and attitudes. Cluster analyses have reached such heights of sophistication and detail that they can tell you the likely ages, incomes, hobbies, and politics of average people in every American neighborhood *(See "Understanding Cluster Analysis," p. 72).*

The second key question is, **what's on our customers' minds?** What are their attitudes regarding our products and services? How do they perceive our organization and its employees? Do they have firmly established product or brand preferences?

Simply knowing the intensity of the public's brand loyalty in your product category can tell you how difficult or easy it will be to persuade people to switch to your brand. For example, I am intensely fond of Fig Newtons, but not necessarily of their manufacturer. If someone offered me a fig-filled cookie that tasted better, I would probably switch brands. Do your customers value what you make or who you are? The industry term for this kind of information is psychographics.

Psychographics is frequently referred to as information on values, attitudes, and lifestyles. But the term "lifestyles" doesn't really belong with the other two, because it refers to a different but related type of information. It refers to the way people lead their lives and spend their time, not the way they think. Some people love to ride motorcycles or go rock climbing. Other people, perhaps even those with similar demographics, prefer to seek out art museums or collect stamps. Lifestyle preferences are related to values and attitudes because a lifestyle is often a manifestation of a way of thinking. All three things have a big influence on consumer behavior.

Getting reliable psychographic information is considerably more complex than collecting demographic information. Even the highest-quality psychographic surveys cannot compare with demographic surveys. As a result, it is often impossible to compare psychographic surveys against each other.

The most popular way to gather information about attitudes is through focus groups, in which a trained moderator gets a small group of people to share how they think or feel about a product, service, brand, place, or institution *(See "Using Focus Group Research," p. 84)*. Focus groups can give managers crucial insights into the strengths and weaknesses of their wares, but they have a significant disadvantage. They are anecdotal, which means that they do not ask a representative cross-sample of a market large enough to be statistically significant. As a result, a focus group does not necessarily reflect how the majority of customers feel.

Carefully worded questionnaires administered to a random sample of individuals or households can quantify customer attitudes. But even these have problems. The results of an opinion survey depend largely on how the questions are worded, whether the survey is conducted in person or by phone or mail, and how likely respondents are to give truthful answers. These are serious concerns, because Americans have an unnerving habit of saying one thing and doing something else. Many surveys have shown a widespread interest in more nutritional foods, for example, but hamburgers and french fries still vastly outsell carrot sticks. People sometimes say they want something when they have no real intention of buying it.

Research on customer values and attitudes can be a hall of mirrors, and the cutting edge of this field is extremely complex. Many of the brightest minds in this area are now working on more effective ways to measure customer satisfaction and loyalty. Many companies, after investing lots of time and money in efforts to enhance customer satisfaction, found to their horror that satisfied customers were just as likely as unsatisfied ones to switch to the competition. Today, the best research is moving toward measuring the three Rs: recruiting new customers, retaining existing customers, and regaining lost customers *(See "Measure for Measure," p. 87)*.

The third key question is, **where can I efficiently reach new customers?** The key word here is "efficiently." Other words, like "cluttered" and "splintered," are often used to describe the media environment facing most advertisers. Expert use of marketing information can precisely determine the media preferences of a customer segment, and this efficiency can counterbalance the chaos and jargon advertisers face when making media choices *(See "Bye Buy Blues," p. 91).*

Few things are harder to measure than the performance of advertising or promotions, but you can do it and it is well worth the trouble. For some businesses, advertising and promotion is a very large expense. The effectiveness of advertising and promotion, in fact, can be the difference between success and failure. Regularly obtaining information about the media preferences of your target audience can repay itself many times in lower marketing expenses.

However, it isn't enough just to choose the right radio station or the appropriate section of the local newspaper. You also have to make sure that the message cuts through the clutter and resonates with potential customers. To craft such a message requires further analysis of psychographic data. The goal is to understand what is on your customers' minds, so you can speak to them more effectively.

If you can develop a deep understanding of the real reason people buy from you instead of someone else, then your advertising and promotions can celebrate those reasons and positively reinforce the customer's choice. You need to make your customers feel good about choosing your store because they have an abundance of commercial establishments to choose from. America has too many stores in almost every retail category, and there are certainly more than enough catalogs in every mailbox.

Question four is, **what are they buying?** It's important to keep track of customers' purchase behavior so you can offer them incentives to buy more and expand their relationship with you. But it's just as important to stay informed about the general purchasing patterns of different consumer groups. This information gives you important clues about how to grow your business.

One of the most important ways to use purchase behavior is to monitor changes in consumer behavior over time. For example, industry surveys that show a general decline in household spending on women's clothing could help to explain why sales in your women's clothing store are down. If your store has not seen a decrease in sales, the survey could serve as a warning that such a decline is likely. It could also be a sign that something about your store is causing your business to run counter to the general downturn. If you're doing something right, knowing what it is could help you do even better.

Specific segments of each consumer market may be affected by overall trends in purchase behavior, but they also follow their own cycles. For example, the market for luxury vehicles or boats may be more affected by how well the stock market is doing than by increases or decreases in spending by average households. That's why it is vitally important to make links between patterns of purchase behavior and the demographics of your customers. The ultimate test of marketing efficiency is to measure sales performance against the sales potential of a specific marketplace.

Evaluating a market's potential sounds simple. It's a matter of multiplying the number of persons or households in a sales territory or trading area by the average amount spent by each person or household in your product or service category. Later in this chapter, you'll see how to do this by combining data on your customers with data that describe your marketplace.

Answering these four questions gives you the who, what, where, and why of your customers. Who are my customers? Why do they act as they do? Where should I reach them? What are they buying? All of the answers, working together, form the basis of your marketing know-how. The diagram below shows how the interaction of different consumer characteristics can answer the four key questions, build a knowledge base, and lead to efficient marketing.

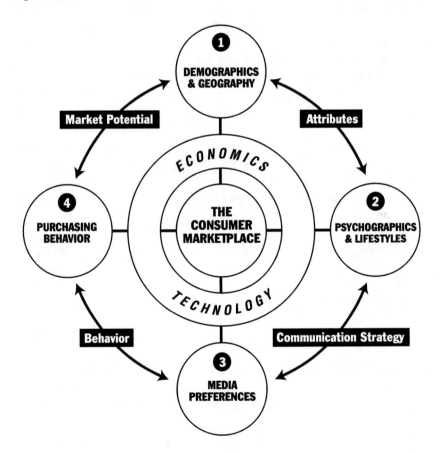

No product or service appeals to everyone, everywhere. The key to profitably marketing any product or service is to identify and locate key buyer segments, assess the size of those segments, and develop an appropriate communication strategy that includes a targeted message and media plan.

Building a Knowledge Base

The second section of this book lists and describes hundreds of databases, software products, and services that can assist your marketing efforts. The diagram on page 19 is like software for your mind: it describes the essential components of consumer knowledge. But the marketing tools listed in this book are not always presented in the form of that diagram. For example, you can build knowledge about purchase behavior by studying the known buying habits of your own customers, as contained in your own records. You can study the purchasing behavior of different customer segments by buying a syndicated survey from a data company, or by commissioning your own private survey of buying behavior. All three kinds of information are important, but they all have different uses.

It is all too easy, however, to become overwhelmed by an ocean of numbers. I prefer to start with just one or two key facts about customers and see if they predict anything about their buying behavior. It often helps to draw a diagram of the way facts such as age of customer might influence how much or how often they will buy. Once the value (or lack thereof) of any piece of data has been fully understood, more items can be added and tested to see if they increase your understanding of the customer's actions. The acquisition of demograpic, psychographic, media preference, and purchase data will be more effective if begun in a small way, tested in one or two places, then expanded as your budget and expertise grows.

Building a marketing knowledge base means understanding the need to answer the four questions posed above, as well as knowing what databases to create, buy, and maintain. For most organizations, marketing know-how rests upon a three-legged stool of databases. It's crucial to build knowledge and track changes in your customers, your marketplace, and your industry.

Customer Database

Remember coffee? Two decades ago, it came in two forms. You either went to the supermarket and bought a can of Folger's, Maxwell House, or some other well-known brand, or you went to a restaurant and bought a cup of whatever they brewed.

Today, the supermarket sells ground and whole-bean coffee in cans and foil bricks and things that look and act like teabags. Most supermarkets also sell hot brewed coffee at their deli counters. Or if you're really serious about coffee, you can buy beans and cups from specialty coffee shops in flavors too numerous to list here. At

Spending by Age

(average annual household expenditures by age of householder, 1994)

	all house- holds	25-34	35-44	45-54	55-64	65+
Food at home	$2,877	$2,663	$3,520	$3,493	$2,924	$2,347
Food away from home	1,811	1,844	2,143	2,413	1,962	1,069
Owned dwellings	3,492	2,709	4,963	5,069	3,691	2,307
Rented dwellings	2,194	3,262	2,209	1,954	1,562	1,425
Utilities etc.	3,072	2,856	3,536	3,483	3,274	2,864
Furnishings etc.	1,348	1,237	1,565	1,950	1,696	847
Apparel	1,644	1,748	2,054	2,262	1,586	873
Transportation	6,044	6,523	6,796	7,893	6,504	3,572
Health care	1,755	1,086	1,616	1,855	2,144	2,678
Entertainment	1,567	1,519	2,025	2,104	1,565	879
Reading and education	625	504	667	1,086	553	267
Contributions	960	381	788	1,436	1,292	1,419
Insurance and pensions	2,957	2,847	4,022	4,539	3,440	1,007
Miscellaneous	1,405	1,286	1,684	1,905	1,509	1,001
Total expenditures	$31,751	$30,465	$37,588	$41,442	$33,702	$22,555
Total households	102,210	20,606	22,825	17,812	12,015	21,500

Source: Bureau of Labor Statistics

Age of householder is one of the powerful determinants of desire and ability to buy consumer products. It is of particular interest that the fastest-growing age group for the next five years—45 to 54—is also the one with the highest level of overall household spending.

Households headed by people aged 45 to 54 spend 30 percent more than the average household. They spend 54 percent more than average on insurance and pensions and 74 percent more on reading and education.

the Short Stop convenience store near my office, a coffee drinker can choose from more than 25 fresh-brewed flavors, 24 hours a day, 365 days a year. Any of those flavors can be bought as beans, ground, or hot in a cup. You can even mix flavors in the cup to create nearly infinite varieties of your own personal coffee.

The explosion of consumer choice has transformed businesses in many ways. It has created significant inventory control problems, for example. And it has raised questions about how to compete when everyone, everywhere seems to be selling nearly everything—even when the product is something as simple as coffee. The answer, of course, lies in creating a dialogue with your customers.

The interaction of producers and consumers is moving from the relatively simple world of the one-way commercial message to the more complex, information-rich world of the two-way conversation. Rather than sending out advertising messages and waiting for customers to arrive with their money, more and more businesses are contacting customers in advance to find out what they want, when they want it, and how they want it wrapped. In most cases, this dialogue requires that the producer know how to send a specific message to one customer and respond to any reply. In the near future, that may mean knowing someone's e-mail address. Today, the key piece of information is the postal address.

Any customer database starts with a simple mailing list. For many businesses (like magazines) and nonprofit institutions (like colleges), mailing lists are a necessary by-product of the business. But restaurants, coffee shops, retailers, food stores, and many other businesses must make a special effort to obtain customer addresses.

People do not ordinarily give you their address or phone number without asking for something in return. As the public's concern for privacy and distrust of marketers increases, the price of those addresses goes up. You might offer a discount on a present purchase, or a promise of one on a future purchase. That's how supermarket shopper cards work. Or a restaurant might offer a free dessert on your next visit in return for filling out an address card. But once you have a customer's name, it is extremely important to avoid offending them by using it in a way they consider inappropriate.

One of the smartest observers of consumer attitudes toward privacy is Mary Culnan, a professor at the Georgetown University School of Business. Culnan recommends that businesses manage privacy concerns by remembering three words: knowledge, notice, and no. First, give your customers knowledge of how you will use personal information about them. Second, give them notice whenever you plan to share their names with another business. And finally, give them the chance to drop out of the process by saying "no."*(See "The Privacy Checklist," p. 100)*.

A collection of customer addresses is just a mailing list until you enhance it in some way with extra information. After that, it's a database. Probably the easiest and most valuable way to enhance customer addresses is to add a record of the indi-

Spending by Education

(average annual household expenditures by educational attainment of householder, 1994)

	all house- holds	high school graduate	some college	college graduate
Food at home	$2,877	$2,823	$2,904	$3,072
Food away from home	1,811	1,542	1,923	2,788
Owned dwellings	3,492	2,818	3,411	5,954
Rented dwellings	2,194	2,007	2,249	2,833
Utilities etc.	3,072	2,978	2,975	3,905
Furnishings etc.	1,348	1,066	1,346	2,271
Apparel	1,644	1,447	1,683	2,392
Transportation	6,044	6,130	6,157	8,046
Health care	1,755	1,717	1,607	2,077
Entertainment	1,567	1,406	1,701	2,387
Reading and education	625	389	742	1,194
Contributions	960	827	865	1,726
Insurance and pensions	2,957	2,467	2,935	5,168
Miscellaneous	1,405	1,354	1,443	1,662
Total expenditures	$31,751	$28,971	$31,941	$45,475
Number of consumer units	102,210	32,148	24,387	45,475

Source: Bureau of Labor Statistics

Total spending by college-graduate households is about 40 percent higher than for all households. They spend nearly twice the average on reading materials and education, and give 1.8 times the average in cash contributions. College graduates represent only 24 percent of households, but account for nearly half (45 percent) of aggregate charitable contributions.

vidual's purchases from your own files. This can answer such questions as, what have Mr. and Mrs. X bought? How much do they spend, on average, each time they visit? And how often do they make a purchase? Once you answer these questions, you can sort your customers into at least three categories: very profitable, somewhat profitable, and not profitable at all.

A database that tracks the buying habits of individual customers can also be designed to automatically alert you to any unusual customer activity. When a regular customer suddenly stops buying, an infrequent customer increases activity, or a small spender turns into a big one, a well-programmed computer can let you know about it. Timely, direct communication with customers who have recently changed their habits can make them feel more appreciated. The net result of paying attention to these details will be higher sales from existing customers, fewer customers deserting you for a competitor, and reduced expenses for new customer acquisitions.

One of the most valuable services provided by marketing information companies is called address coding, or geocoding. This exercise appends to each address a set of numerical geographic codes which tell you precisely where a particular address is located. Not all addresses can be coded in this way. Rural addresses, for example, are difficult to find. But geocoding gives you a fast, inexpensive way to place most of your customers within small neighborhoods, or at least within a zip code *(See "Match Making," p. 101).*

You have probably heard that birds of a feather flock together. Marketing information companies sell a slightly different version of that old adage: they tell you that most households in a single neighborhood probably have similar demographic characteristics. Marketing campaigns based on address coding depend on this assumption. In many cases, the campaigns also assume that people in similar neighborhoods will drive the same kinds of cars and eat the same kinds of foods. And for the most part, they're right.

Geocoding is most valuable when it identifies concentrations of profitable customers in a particular place. Armed with a demographic and lifestyle profile of this place, you can look for other places that have a similar profile. These should be the first places to target with advertising promotions or other marketing efforts, because they will be most likely to yield a lot of new customers.

A customer database with purchase data appended tells you the value of each customer. When it is geographically coded, such a database can assign a value to each unit of geography in your trade area. The higher the value, the more marketing effort can be justified to maintain or increase the sales from those units.

Think of it as if you were managing hot-dog vendors at a ballpark. Suppose that Section A contained a large group of children. Based on your previous sales records, you know that the demand for hot dogs in that section will be at least twice as great as in the average section. So you might assign twice as many vendors to that section.

Spending by Family Type

(average annual household expenditures by household type, 1994)

	all house- holds	husband/ wife only	husband/ wife/ children	single parents
Food at home	$2,877	$2,875	$4,081	$2,689
Food away from home	1,811	2,118	2,485	999
Owned dwellings	3,492	4,250	5,605	1,763
Rented dwellings	2,194	1,798	1,927	2,912
Utilities etc.	3,072	3,292	4,178	2,814
Furnishings etc.	1,348	1,746	1,948	689
Apparel	1,644	1,639	2,427	1,624
Transportation	6,044	6,929	8,770	3,246
Health care	1,755	2,555	2,049	884
Entertainment	1,567	1,786	2,272	1,057
Reading and education	625	604	987	383
Contributions	960	1,577	993	216
Insurance and pensions	2,957	3,561	4,605	1,326
Miscellaneous	1,405	1,468	1,762	1,070
Total expenditures	$31,751	$36,198	$44,089	$21,672
Number of consumer units	102,210	22,017	27,572	7,065

Source: Bureau of Labor Statistics

Married couples with children spend the most on food at home, as we would expect. But they also spend heavily on transportation, presumably carting the kids around. Single-parent households, with only two-thirds the income of average households, spend less on virtually every category except apparel and rent.

Or if you can't do that, you would at least provide the assigned vendors with twice as many hot dogs.

The same principle applies to zip codes, neighborhoods, and sales territories. It's a simple matter of knowing where your customers come from by attaching a simple kind of geographic software to your customer database. Some businesses, such as small-circulation publications, have no ties to any particular piece of geography. For them, the individual customer is the appropriate unit of analysis, and creating a customer database with purchase or other information attached to each customer record becomes the objective. Then customers can be grouped in categories of profitability to see which individual characteristics impact sales or profits.

Marketplace Database

How much business should you expect from each neighborhood or customer segment in your market? You may do business in ten different places, or with ten different customer segments. If place #1 accounts for 10 percent of sales, #2 for 5 percent, and #3 for 1 percent, is that the best you can do from each place? Or can you do better? A marketplace database helps you answer this important question.

There may be twice as much potential business in place #1 as in place #2. Or there may be just as much business in place #2, but you haven't found it yet. To find the answer, you must gather information about the market conditions in each place.

Start with your customer database. It might tell you that your most important customer segment is married couples with children and a median household income of $30,000 to $40,000 a year. Armed with this description, you can estimate the number of potential customers in each segment by counting the number of households in each segment that match this demographic description. If 10 percent of your potential business comes from place #1, then that place is meeting the demand of the marketplace perfectly.

But it rarely turns out that way. Instead, you will almost always find that individual segments are performing above or below expectations. Then you need to ask why. There is usually some logical explanation. One of the most common reasons is physical distance. Storefront businesses find it more difficult and expensive to serve customers who live further away, so it is not surprising to find below-expected sales in a distant neighborhood. Rating the performance of neighborhoods is a quick and easy way to determine the size of your trading area.

Another common reason for below-expected performance is competition. If someone sets up a shop near the edge of your trade area, you will probably lose some business from that sector. This technique gives you an idea of exactly how much business you're losing, and how important it is to do something about it.

Spending by Income

(average annual household expenditures by household income, 1994)

	all house-holds reporting income	$20,000-$29,999	$30,000-$39,999	$40,000-$49,999	$50,000-$69,999	$70,000 or more
Food at home	$2,939	$2,782	$3,060	$3,382	$3,815	$4,291
Food away from home	1,884	1,437	1,942	2,333	3,054	4,226
Owned dwellings	3,464	2,210	3,264	4,261	5,898	9,371
Rented dwellings	2,232	2,517	2,388	2,282	1,919	2,541
Utilities etc.	3,094	2,791	3,062	3,520	3,989	5,444
Furnishings etc................	1,399	972	1,338	1,823	2,172	3,507
Apparel............................	1,688	1,465	1,673	1,891	2,463	3,944
Transportation................	6,076	5,598	6,011	8,886	9,176	11,705
Health care	1,768	1,579	1,762	2,008	2,210	2,694
Entertainment.................	1,619	1,292	1,565	1,915	2,544	3,781
Reading and education....	640	378	469	695	867	1,678
Contributions	1,067	772	1,050	1,005	1,648	3,240
Insurance and pensions ..	3,404	1,986	3,207	4,514	6,264	10,612
Miscellaneous	1,488	1,263	1,685	1,786	2,159	2,472
Total expenditures	$32,762	$27,042	$32,476	$40,301	$48,178	$69,506
No. of consumer units	85,994	13,975	10,922	8,280	10,510	10,099

Source: Bureau of Labor Statistics

Total expenditures by the most affluent households ($70,000 or more annual income) are more than twice the national average. They contribute three times as much to charitable organizations and spend more than three times the average on personal insurance and pensions.

If sales are slow in a given area and the explanation is obvious, you may not have an opportunity to do anything about it. But if sales are below expectations and you can find no logical explanation, then an extra investment of marketing dollars in that area is likely to pay off. By measuring the potential of each sector of your market, you can precisely target your marketing efforts to where they will do the most good.

If your market is geographically defined—if it is a town or city or metropolitan area—then a marketplace database has another valuable use. It can help you customize your advertising or promotion to individual segments. For example, a neighborhood with a lot of children might be a good place to sponsor a new playground. Frito-Lay did this in the 1980s in Hispanic sections of Dallas. But if your market is a retirement community, perhaps it would be to your advantage to donate a minivan or other transportation to the local seniors' center.

Accurate, up-to-date data that describe neighborhoods and other small geographic areas can be easily purchased from private companies. Data from the decennial census are only collected once every ten years, but they are much less expensive. And it is sometimes possible to gather high-quality data on local areas from planning agencies, utility companies, or state governments. You just have to know where to look and what questions to ask *(See "How to Get to the Grassroots," p. 104)*.

Industry Database

Even if your knowledge of your actual and potential customers is masterful, industry trends can still have a serious impact on your operations. Different sectors of the economy have different business cycles. Industries are sometimes transformed at lightning speed by technological developments, consolidations, and competitive pressures.

Understanding your competition is the only way to really determine your own position in the marketplace. Whether you are the industry leader, the number-two player, or an also-ran will largely determine the kind of marketing strategy you should follow. Nobody writes about this topic better than Al Ries and Jack Trout, who began their writing career with the classic *Positioning: The Battle for Your Mind (1981)*. See also Jack Trout's *The New Positioning (1995)*.

Reis and Trout say that in almost any industry, some customers are being poorly or incompletely served. There are almost always niches that are not filled. Successfully establishing your place in a crowded field depends on finding and filling some of those niches. That is an important first step in growing a business.

Much has been written about how to obtain competitor intelligence *(See "How to Search for Market Information," p. 106)*. I prefer the simple and direct approach, which is to act like a customer and ask yourself: what is each competitor's unique selling proposition, and can we clearly differentiate ours from theirs? What the customer thinks of each supplier is more important than what those firms say about themselves in advertising or other public statements.

Creating a customer database, a marketplace database, and an industry database may seem like a daunting task best left to some far future time when things slow down. There is, of course, no such time. But by thinking about marketing information as a form of higher education that can be obtained one course at a time or one book at a time, it can become more manageable.

The key is to think first about the customers and make a list of what you would like to know about them that would be helpful in reaching them. The list will naturally grow into databases and subsequently a knowledge base that will make you more effective at marketing and more successful in your business enterprise *(See "Suitcase Savvy," p. 107)*.

The second section of this book is a list of organizations that provide data, software, research, and other services that can help you become a better marketer. Some organizations provide demographic data and some provide information on customer geography. Others specialize in psychographics, media preferences, or purchase behavior. There are also suppliers of customer database services such as geocoding, marketplace databases, as well as industry research services.

Some of the organizations on our list are very large. The Census Bureau, for example, has thousands of employees. Others consist of only one or two people. But size is not important. Somewhere in the second section, there are at least one or two firms that can provide exactly what you need to answer the four key questions, build the three-legged stool of databases, and acquire marketing know-how. Good luck!

Chapter Three: The Articles

Pulling the Family's Strings

by Robert Boutilier
August 1993
American Demographics

If you're selling refrigerators, it makes sense to think of the family as a single unit. But if you're selling shampoo, it makes more sense to think of families as collections of individuals. And if you're selling cars, you should define families as collections of people who may live in different households, and who may or may not be related.

Some businesses should market to families; others should market through families, using word of mouth within the family to influence the members who make the purchase. But most business leaders will need to use both strategies, sometimes to sell the same product.

Marketing efforts aimed at the family as a unit usually assume that family members make decisions jointly and use the product equally, especially if they live together. In contrast, marketing through families by having one family member influence another is more likely to involve relatives who live outside the immediate household. But both kinds of marketing have the same core strategy: to influence purchase decisions by enlisting the power of family relationships.

Academics have long studied how families make decisions. But their theories usually cover only a narrow range of family configurations, and much of their research defines families as households containing husbands and wives. Marketers must go beyond this definition, because their best market may be single-parent households or single people. They need a model of family decision-making that is general, applies to all types of families and households, and uses simple concepts to cover most of the factors involved in purchase decisions.

The model of family decision-making presented here builds on concepts used in marketing to individuals. Like individual marketing, family marketing should create a relationship between individuals and products. But family marketing goes beyond the purchase decision-maker to address the relationships between purchasers and consumers in families.

Family decision-making can be an enormously complex process. Consider a nuclear family that contains Mom, Dad, Sister, and Brother. Sister might initiate a product search by asking for a bicycle as a birthday present. In this case, the consumer has initiated the purchase but has only decided the product category, not the brand or model.

After Sister states her preferences, Mom and Dad might discuss the idea to confirm a price range. If Dad is the actual purchaser, Mom might function as a price-range watchdog, a nonconsuming purchase decision-maker whose main role is to veto or approve price ranges. Brother's self-appointed role is to constrain the duration and location of the shopping. In other words, he might threaten to throw a tantrum until he is taken to McDonald's. Thanks to Brother's influence, bicycle retailers who are distant from the restaurant will quickly fall off the shopping list.

Before venturing out with Brother, Dad may seek further information from Sister about cosmetic features such as color. But he will also impose additional criteria of his own, such as durability and safety, when choosing the final brand and model.

Family marketing must systematically consider these purchase scenarios, along with the distribution of consumer and decision-maker roles among family members. The distribution of roles often differs from one scenario to another. Building a marketing plan that reflects this complexity can be extremely profitable. It could also be costly. To keep the cost below the anticipated additional profit, the key is to reduce family complexity to the important relationships that affect marketing strategy and market only to those essential relationships.

When searching for the essential relationships, it helps to answer these key questions: Who's buying for whom? Which family members will consume the product, and which will participate in the purchase decision? How much overlap is there between the consumers and the decision-makers? Who are the principal characters? Who are current and desired consumers and purchase decision-makers? What are their demographic profiles? What kind of family structures do they live in? Are any relatives or others outside the household involved in the purchase? What's the plot for the purchase? What are the steps in a purchase? What initiates it? Do different people have different roles in the sequence? Who performs which functions? Is each step repeated with each purchase, or is there an abbreviated sequence for subsequent purchases? Is there a special scenario for changing brands? Who wants what when? What benefits do each of the players seek at each stage of the process? In addition to product-related costs and benefits, what family relationship outcomes do various influencers want from the purchase process? What can we assume? What do we know about family decision-making? How can consumer psychology and marketing simplify the planning process?

Answering these questions should reveal the outlines of a family marketing plan. But the questions above may not cover all possibilities, and not all of them will be relevant to every product. Any family can, and probably does, use variations of the model for different products. For example, ordering a home-delivered pizza is usually a joint decision, while buying vacuum-cleaner bags seldom involves discussions with other family members.

Ordinary marketing views the individual as both decision-maker and consumer. Family marketing adds three other possibilities. Some purchases have more than one decision-maker, and some have more than one consumer. And sometimes, the purchaser and the consumer can be different people.

The family marketing model contains 9 cells, each of which represents a different pattern of purchaser/consumer relationships. Purchase decision-makers can be a single individual, a subset of individuals in the family, or all the members of the family. Likewise, consumers can be one, some, or all family members. The product may be purchased for the buyer's use or for someone else. Some decision-makers may consume the product, while others may not.

Family marketing assumes that consumer preferences may not be directly expressed in marketplace purchases. For example, children who want sweetened breakfast cereal might not get it if Mom decides they shouldn't have it. But they may be able to influence her, especially if they accompany her to the food store. In either case, the consumers' (children's) preferences affect the purchase decision indirectly, because the purchase decision is made by another family member (Mom) who does not consume the product. In the case of sweetened cereal, Mom may buy the product even though she dislikes it.

When several family members make a purchase jointly, at least one of them often has a higher interest in the outcome than the others. To marketers, family members who are both consumer and purchaser are more important than those who play only a single role. If Mom and Dad are jointly buying an exercise bicycle for Mom, Mom typically would have more influence. The decision-maker who is going to consume the purchase has complete information about his or her own (i.e., the consumer's) preferences. The other decision-makers can only get that information if the consumer tells them. Understanding the distribution of consumer and decision-maker roles within a family is crucial to developing a family marketing plan. To develop this understanding, it's useful to put purchasers and consumers into three categories, based on the number of people who share the role: one, some, and all.

The family grocery shopper often plays the role of sole purchase decision-maker for other family members. In this "purchasing agent" role, the grocery shopper is a conduit to the marketplace for the real consumers' preferences. Like an agent or broker, the family grocery shopper can also use some personal discretion to modify the signal sent to the marketplace by his or her clients.

The family purchasing agent is analogous to an insurance broker in the business world. Insurance brokers can act as agents for several insurance companies. A broker may have a client who is bent on buying one particular brand of insurance simply out of ignorance about the competitive alternatives. If the broker finds another insurance company offering longer-term coverage for the same price, the broker may alter the client's choice when it comes time to book the policy.

Of course, relationships between family members are usually much more personal than are those between brokers and clients. Mothers who buy sugar-saturated cereal may have to pay higher dental bills down the road. As a result, family decision-makers are more likely than insurance brokers to change the consumers' preferences.

It is important to know how much input a sole decision-maker will accept from other family members before making the purchase. If the decision-maker receives no input, individual marketing will be appropriate. Yet there are relatively few products or services that are unaffected by the opinions of other family members. For example, Dad may not know as much as Mom about which clothing stores offer the best values, but he does have plenty to say about what kind of tie he wants to wear. In such cases, the goal is to motivate consumers to express their preferences for your product to the decision-maker. When some family members are decision-makers and others are not, unique psychological forces come into play. This combination includes scenarios like a grandfather and grandmother giving a gift to a grandchild. One decision-maker might specialize in discovering the consumer's preferences; for example, the kind of gift a grandchild wants. Another decision-maker might focus on finding the best value in the marketplace for that kind of product. Some decision-makers in the family may not be interested in the product, while others may have no knowledge of the product category. The possibilities are so numerous that these cases will always require specific research. The best place to start such research is to separate the decision-makers from the bystanders and determine whether the two groups share common demographic or psychological characteristics. The same job will be necessary when only some family members are consumers. For example, tricycles are only consumed by very young family members.

The family decision-maker has the most difficult task when everyone in the family is a consumer. She must acknowledge, if not satisfy, the diverse preferences of all family members. Products that offer interpersonal harmony as a benefit are likely to be popular when divergent preferences and tastes can embarrass or threaten the decision-maker. Blue Nun wine played this angle when it advertised itself as "the wine that goes with anything." Restaurant parties usually order a single wine, which can force some members to modify their menu choices to fit one wine type. Blue Nun leapt into the breach by offering a middle-of-the-road wine that would go with any menu choice. It also offered anyone playing "wine connoisseur" a convenient way to avoid displaying ignorance.

At special times of the year like Christmas and Thanksgiving, or when products have a high social component in their joint consumption (e.g., pizzas, holiday travel, amusements), the decision-making group is more likely to include the entire family. Market researchers Pierre Filiatrault and Brent Ritchie suggest that seven variables are associated with joint decision-making. In their view, families are likely to make decisions together when the perceived risk associated with the decision is high, when ample time is available for the decision, when the family places great importance on the decision, when there are no children in the family, when the family is middle-income, when the family is young, and when the family contains two spouses but only one breadwinner.

When all members of the family are also decision-makers, the family makes its consumer choice "as a family." In these cases, family myths and history are more likely to influence the process. At the same time, the need to find compromise products or decision strategies—such as coin tossing and turn taking—is greatest.

In the "traditional" family of the past, a full-time homemaker made most of the purchase decisions for the household, especially for small, frequent purchases of food and housewares. The breadwinner made the decisions about large-ticket items like cars. The children had no say in decisions for jointly consumed items and made only a few purchase decisions on their own.

Today's families rarely operate according to this simple model. As an increasing share of families contain two breadwinners, more family members are taking responsibility for their own purchases. A new generation of parents are giving their children far more influence in the marketplace, and children are becoming sophisticated consumers while they are still in elementary school. Meanwhile, grandparents and other nonhousehold members are increasingly likely to aid families with gifts of products and services.

Family members rarely make decisions for each other with no strings attached. Marketers who understand the web of family relationships can pull those strings with carefully targeted advertising and promotions. A well-designed family marketing program could make family life easier for consumers while boosting the company's bottom line.

Taking It Further: For more information on joint decision-making, see "Joint Purchasing Decisions: A Comparison of Influence Structure in Family and Couple Decision-Making," by Pierre Filiatrault and J.R. Brent Ritchie in the *Journal of Consumer Research*, 7, September 1980, pp. 131-140. A good analysis of husband-wife consumer relationships is in "Household Decision Behavior: The Impact of Husbands' and Wives' Sex Role Orientation," by William J. Qualls, *Journal of Consumer Research*, 14, September 1987, pp. 264-279. A special issue on "The Family as a Consumer" was published by *Psychology and Marketing*, Vol. 10, No. 2, March/April 1993. This article is excerpted from the book *Targeting Families: Marketing to and Through the New Family*, available from American Demographics's *Marketing Power* catalog; telephone (800) 828-1133.

Vision in an Aging America

by Patricia Braus
June 1995
American Demographics

Like it or not, baby boomers' eyes are getting weaker. Older eyes have trouble with small print, glare, and low-contrast color schemes. They are also more prone to a variety of eye diseases. Businesses that ignore the fuzzier world of older eyes may become invisible to a growing share of consumers.

When editors for the *Miami Herald* held focus groups in the late 1980s, readers made it clear that they didn't like what they were seeing—or rather, what they weren't seeing. "In every focus group we did, they said, 'Can you make the type larger?'" recalls Randy Stano, director of editorial art and design.

The *Herald* increased the type size and changed its style. "Readers noticed it immediately," says Stano. Now many of the readers in focus groups want the newspaper to change the type again to make it even easier to read.

The *Herald's* circulation area is rich with older Americans. In the future, more and more newspapers will find themselves in the same situation. As the population ages, the quality of the average American's vision will decline due to both normal age-related vision problems and an increase in diseased eyes, says Dr. George Bresnick, professor and chairman of the Ophthalmology Department at the University of Rochester Medical Center in Rochester, New York. "As you get a demographic shift to the aged, you're going to get more people with glaucoma, macular degeneration, and diabetic retinopathy."

Potential customers with limited vision may ignore advertisements they can't read because the type is too small. Products labeled with poorly contrasting colors or stored in cases that produce a glare may also be passed over. Fortunately, it is not usually difficult to make the changes that older eyes appreciate. "You're not going to make the blind see," says Mary Anne FitzGerald, a research manager for Age Wave, a market research firm in Emeryville, California. "But you can compensate for the lack of perfect vision."

As life expectancy has increased due to better health care and improved nutrition, the number and proportion of older Americans has grown dramatically. In 1960, 16.7 million Americans aged 65 and older accounted for 9 percent of the U.S. population. In 1990, the number had risen to 31 million and the share to 12 percent. By 2025, when most baby boomers will be elderly, the U.S. will have 62 million people aged 65 and older, accounting for nearly 18 percent of the population, according to Census Bureau projections.

These population trends are good news for manufacturers of eyeglasses, contact lenses, and other eye-related products. Wisdom may increase with age, but young people have better vision. "Blindness is highly correlated with age," says Fred Neurohr, a research assistant in the programs and policy research department of the American Foundation for the Blind in New York City.

Approximately one in five Americans aged 85 and older is severely visually impaired, according to a 1993 study by foundation researchers Katherine A. Nelson and Ganka Dimitrova. The study updated data from the government's 1977 Health Interview Survey Supplement on Aging and the 1984 Health Interview Survey to reflect current population trends. The study defines people as severely visually impaired if they cannot read newspaper print, even with corrective lenses.

Twelve percent of those aged 75 to 84 have severe visual impairments, compared with less than 1 percent of adults aged 18 to 44. The number of Americans of all ages with severe visual impairments in 1990 was 4.3 million, 1.7 percent of the total U.S. population. But an aging population means that this number should grow rapidly in the future, from 5.1 million in 2000 to 8.9 million by 2030, according to Neurohr's projections.

Severe impairment is uncommon, but virtually everyone suffers some loss of visual acuity by age 65. Many factors contribute to visual impairment, including a number of normal aging processes. The first to strike many individuals is the loss of focusing ability at close range, otherwise known as farsightedness. This typically occurs at about age 45 and is caused by weakening eye muscles. It occurs when the lens is no longer flexible enough to change shape properly when focusing on close objects, says Dr. Bresnick of Rochester.

The loss of focusing ability means that people aged 45 and older often have difficulty reading small print in telephone books, on packaging, and anywhere else it appears. They also may have difficulty reading complicated types of print.

To be legible for older readers, print size should be at least 12 or 13 points, according to Frank Conaway, president of primelife, Inc., a marketing and research firm that focuses on the mature market. If the print is not large enough, many potential customers will simply miss the advertisement. And simple type styles are more effective than ornate ones that tend to clutter the image. All upper-case lettering should also be avoided. "The whole issue is readability," says Conaway, who teaches a course in marketing to older people at the Fullerton campus of California State. "This audience says, 'I can't read it. I'm not interested in it.'"

Reduced flexibility of the aging eye also makes adjusting to changes in light and darkness more difficult. This is one reason why older drivers face greater challenges than younger drivers adjusting to oncoming headlights, says Charles D. Schewe, a professor of marketing at the University of Massachusetts in Amherst.

Schewe says that glare can be a particular problem in supermarkets. Older shoppers can't "see inside the fish counter because of the Plexiglas and fluorescent light combination," says Schewe, who is also a principle in Lifestage Matrix Marketing of Amherst. Food packaged in shiny wrappers was also a problem. To appeal to older customers, Schewe says that businesses should control glare with blinds, shades, or curtains on windows.

The lens of the eye yellows with age. This means that older people are less sensitive to colors at the blue end of the spectrum, making it difficult to see the difference between blues and greens. Age Wave's FitzGerald sometimes brings a strip of yellow laminated plastic for participants to place across their eyes so they can get a sense of what the yellowing of the lens feels like. "It's like when you put sunglasses on," she says.

Another normal physiological change that makes distinguishing between colors more difficult is the loss of cells in the retina, according to Bresnick. The retina is comparable to film in a camera. As retinal cells are lost, it is more difficult to see the contrast between two colors and to see in dim light.

To battle these limitations, marketers must avoid subtle color contrasts. Pink on red or red on pink is likely to be a difficult combination for many potential customers to see. The same goes for light brown and dark brown, says Conaway. The strongest color contrast, and the easiest to see, is black on white. Colors should have enough contrast for easy reading.

Including enough white space is also essential. "If you have a lot of letters packed together without white space, the eye gets tired," says FitzGerald. While this is good design strategy for all readers, it is particularly true for older readers whose ability to distinguish contrast and to read small letters is diminished.

Such messages may sound costly to businesspeople, but FitzGerald and others argue that the investment is a sound one in potential customers. "Obviously, it's difficult when advertisers are paying a premium for space," says FitzGerald. "They don't want dead space. But they need an effective use of space."

Normal developments in the aging eye often occur simultaneously with eye diseases or other abnormalities, compounding the chance that potential older readers will benefit from clear type and other visual aids. A common eye disease among older people is cataracts, in which a cloudy layer develops in the lens or eye capsule. About half of all individuals in their 80s have some degree of cataracts, says Bresnick. Untreated cataracts can cause blindness, but cataract surgery is common and has a high success rate.

Individuals with cataracts suffer from reduced visual acuity, which can include blurry vision or vision that gets worse in bright sunlight. Using larger type and bold contrasting colors increases the odds that people with cataracts will see advertising and other print material.

Another condition that afflicts older eyes is age-related macular degeneration, which results in blurred vision and can lead to blindness. About 1.7 million Americans have some visual impairment from this disease, according to the National Eye Institute in Bethesda, Maryland. The disease develops when blood flow to the macula, the central region of the retina, is restricted as the small blood vessels of the eye narrow or harden. There can be some leakage of fluid from the blood cells under the retina. Some types of macular degeneration can be treated with laser therapy if diagnosed quickly enough.

Diabetic retinopathy, an eye disease linked to diabetes, is more common in older diabetics. But about 40 percent of all diabetics have at least a mild case. The condition, which can be treated at almost any stage using laser therapy, occurs when blood vessels in the retina leak or produce abnormal vessels that bleed, says Dr. Bresnick. Diabetic retinopathy can lead to partial or total loss of vision.

Vision is also threatened by glaucoma, a condition in which pressure within the eye can cause blindness without timely treatment. Glaucoma, which most commonly strikes people in their 40s and 50s, can cause symptoms ranging from blurry vision to halos around lights to difficulty seeing in dim settings. But the most common type of glaucoma, chronic open-angle glaucoma, has few symptoms and presents a special threat to those who do not receive regular eye exams. About 3 million Americans have open-angle glaucoma, according to the National Eye Institute. Treatment for glaucoma through medication or surgery is usually effective when the disease is promptly diagnosed. But even during recuperation from surgery, visual acuity can be limited.

Some businesses have already responded to the challenge of aging eyes. *Reader's Digest* printed its first large-type edition in July 1973. The large-type edition is published by Reader's Digest Fund for the Blind, a not-for-profit organization established by the original *Reader's Digest.*

Due to the fund's relationship to the parent company, the magazine is not aggressively marketed and is not sold on newsstands. "I cannot compete with *Reader's Digest's* regular type," says Susan Olivo, general manager of the Fund for the Blind. Instead, subscriptions are sold through direct-mail solicitation. But she sees a bright future for the large-print edition, which currently has a circulation of just over half a million. "I imagine that as baby boomers age, there's going to be a large market for this product."

Some of the nation's largest publishing companies have been selling large-type editions of books for years, including Macmillan Publishing and Bantam-Doubleday-Dell Publishing. The Friendly's restaurant chain uses larger type in its menu for mature diners. A Swedish newspaper offers a small plastic magnifying glass to older readers. A variety of high-tech aids can help people read small print. These range from software that enlarges text on computer screens to electronic voice systems that read print aloud. Nonprint media are getting into the act, too. For those who don't want to bother with the fine print, many communities provide local radio reading services that broadcast news from newspapers and magazines.

The Lighthouse, a nonprofit organization in New York City, offers a catalog of products that "enhance the independence of older adults with impaired vision." A recent catalog features large-display and talking calculators, watches, and clocks, as well as lighting, telephone accessories, and writing supplies. But there's evidence that many companies are not paying attention to the declining visual acuity of the average American. "I don't think a lot in advertising and communication has been done yet," says Conaway of primelife.

One problem cited by many experts is the lack of sensitivity among those who develop advertising. "In advertising and merchandising, you have some very creative people," says FitzGerald. "You don't want to dampen their creativity. But often they are 25 years old and don't understand what it's like to lose visual acuity."

The situation may change in the future. With the first baby boomers turning 50, the eyesight of a huge and affluent consumer group has already started to fade. "Companies are seeing the baby boomers start to age," says FitzGerald. "At every point in their lives, they've changed history. Now they are going to reshape and influence how manufacturers are making their products. It's a matter of looking at your packaging and advertising with a different eye."

Taking It Further: The Lighthouse National Center for Vision and Aging offers a variety of publications, research, and education programs dealing with vision and aging; call (800) 334-5497 or (212) 821-9200. To contact the American Foundation for the Blind in New York City, call (212) 502-7600. Age Wave, Inc. of Emery, California, and primelife, Inc. of Orange, California, provide consulting services for marketers targeting mature consumers; telephone (510) 652-9099 and (800) 284-3140, respectively. To contact Lifestage Matrix Marketing of Amherst, Massachusetts, telephone (413) 256-0914.

Targeting the Mature Mind

by David B. Wolfe
March 1994
American Demographics

The cashier made an appreciative comment about her customer's elegant taste in clothing. "It's true," smiled the customer's wife. Looking at her husband, the message became clear to the cashier. The urbane older gentleman was, as the cashier said, "aged to perfection."

Funk & Wagnalls Standard Dictionary defines "mature" as "completely, highly, or thoroughly developed; perfected." "Aged to perfection" is often used to describe a good wine or fine cheese, and it is not uncharacteristic of many older people.

Various theories of developmental psychology have explored the relationship between aging and psychological change. Yet after a decade of talk about the aging of America, few businesses have considered the psychological differences between older and younger consumers.

The differences are profound. The journey toward maturity involves many changes, including changes in the way people think. The journey begins in childhood, when a person's thinking is largely subjective, heavily based on internally generated cues.

As people develop into adulthood, their thinking becomes more objective, and cues originate increasingly from the external world. Objective thinking reaches its zenith in early adulthood.

Around the onset of middle age, thinking patterns usually begin to draw once again from a subjective perspective, but are integrated with objective thinking. This multidimensional style forms much of the foundation of human wisdom. It is the balanced exercise of feelings and rational thought, fortified by experience.

Thinking styles influence consumer behavior far more than is commonly recognized in market research. If you're targeting mature consumers, you must understand how the mature mind differs from the mind of youth.

Subjective thinkers organize their perceptions of reality in a kaleidoscopic rather than a linear fashion. Their sensitivity to subtleties is keen, and the meaning of what they perceive is strongly influenced by the relationship between the object and the context in which it appears. Older minds are generally quite context-sensitive. They are also capable of seeing the forest, not just the trees.

Cynthia Adams, a Eugene, Oregon, psychologist who studies the cognitive styles of older people, has observed their uneasy responses to objective questions that don't allow for context-sensitive responses. When asked, "Are discounts important to you?" a younger, more objective mind might answer, "Yes." More mature people tend to prefer the answer, "It depends."

The cues that prod our minds to action—be they objectively or subjectively derived—emanate from a set of key underlying motivating values, or key values. In younger consumers, these values are concerned with objects, events and conditions in the outer world. In older consumers, these values are concerned with conditions in the inner psyche.

Five key values form the root motivations of older consumers. They are autonomy and self-sufficiency, social and spiritual connectedness, altruism, personal growth, and revitalization. Regardless of older people's rationalization for buying a given product, they will probably not buy it if it fails to respond to motivations generated by these values. That's because older consumers tend to be motivated by the capacity of a product or service to be a "gateway to experiences," and not by the attributes and direct functional benefits of a product. This rule of thumb is especially true when it comes to discretionary spending.

The following examples of successful marketing to older adults demonstrate how tapping into their key values can have a dramatic effect on their decisions.

Kimberly-Clark's promotion of Depends undergarments for incontinent women is based on the idea that a product can enhance autonomy and self-sufficiency. Its advertising shows a famous actress, June Allyson, playing golf, going to cocktail parties, and otherwise leading an active life unhindered by a physical problem.

Competing brands stress the product's functional qualities, such as moisture absorbency. This factual approach might work better on a younger adult whose thinking is more objective. But older people are ultimately more interested in how buying the product will contribute to self-enriching experiences. In any event, an older consumer's subjective way of appraising advertising tends to make them suspicious of claims about a product's functional attributes. For these reasons, Depends enjoys more than 50 percent of the market share for undergarments in supermarkets.

In an industry plagued by failure, the Freedom Group of Florida is one of the more successful developers of senior housing. When a development is 90 percent full, it symbolically emphasizes the freedom that autonomy brings at a special mortgage-burning party. The ceremony celebrates more than the community's emancipation from a lender; it also ushers in freedom from the worry that future financial problems might result in a mortgage foreclosure. Freedom Group residents also play a larger-than-normal role in community operations, thereby giving full-bodied substance to the idea of autonomy and self-sufficiency.

Contrary to common thinking, promises of indulgent service often work best on younger consumers. Hal Norvell of the AARP says older people can be repelled by promises that their travel hosts will offer detailed planning and extravagant service. Older people, he says, tend to travel more for enriching experiences than for ambient services. Too much service can compromise their need for autonomy and self-sufficiency.

Many mom-and-pop businesses are more successful than larger firms in reaching mature markets. Free of formal policies and procedures designed for managerial efficacy, small-business operators are often more flexible in responding to the idiosyncratic behaviors of mature personalities. Moreover, the sense of social connectedness between the product or service provider and the consumer tends to be stronger in smaller organizations.

Paul and Terry Klaasen run Sunrise Retirement Homes and Communities from an office in Arlington, Virginia. They design and operate senior housing with a heavy focus on its social and spiritual qualities. Rather than drawing on the "chain" model of U.S. hospitality service companies, Paul Klaasen, a second-generation Dutchman, chose European family-run hotels as his model. The architecture of Sunrise Communities reflects social connectedness in its huge wraparound porches. This makes a Sunrise building look more like a friendly boarding house than a hotel or apartment building.

For years, developers struggled against high market resistance to senior housing in the Washington, D.C. area. The Klaasens entered the market in the late 1980s and succeeded with seemingly effortless ease. Now they are the largest operators of senior housing in the area.

Mature minds see social and spiritual connectedness as part of the same cloth. The promotion of one promotes the other. This is reflected in older peoples' frequent comments that grandchildren enhance their sense of connectedness with eternal values and existence. Quaker Oats has tapped into this value with TV commercials and print ads featuring actor Wilford Brimley. The actor appears as a grandfatherly type dispensing wisdom about eating right to members of the younger generation.

Some companies that do intergenerational advertising depict older people being served or honored by others. Older consumers can perceive these kinds of scenes as patronizing and compromising their autonomy and self-sufficiency.

The desire to give something back to the world is a strong influence in many older consumers' lives. Thrifty Car Rental based a highly successful marketing program for older consumers on this value. In a survey of older consumers, the company found that only 11 percent of respondents said a 10 percent discount was a decisive difference in selecting a rental-car company. But 41 percent said an opportunity to donate the amount of a discount to a pool for buying vans for senior-citizen centers would be decisive. Thrifty then launched the successful "Give a Friend a Lift" program.

The most successful commercial in Shearson Lehman Brothers history shows an elderly attorney who is about to retire from his lucrative practice to run a school for blind children. His annual salary will decline to just $11,000. By managing his investments wisely, Shearson Lehman has made his altruistic career move possible.

Companies that seek to gain business by touting their social conscience should use caution, however. The sentiment has to be genuine. When socially conscious programs are merely marketing ploys, they are likely to bomb in the marketplace. The subjective, more astute feelings of older minds give them a special ability to see through sham.

Phoenix Systems, an advertising firm in Sioux Falls, South Dakota, developed a series of public-service-style announcements under the heading, "Tributes to Aging." The ads feature the later-in-life accomplishments of such famous people as Clara Barton, Grandma Moses, Benjamin Franklin, and Noah Webster. Companies buy rights to "Tributes" on a geographically licensed basis and add their own tag lines.

"Tributes" aren't used to sell products; rather, they position the social values of a company. The public response has been outstanding. One senior housing developer claimed that traffic increased more than 30 percent during the period the "Tributes" were on the air. Prudential is using "Tributes" as the foundation of a multimillion-dollar campaign for a new health-care product in California. "Tributes" shows that realistically portraying older people as still-developing human beings can produce strong positive responses. Yet even this can go too far. Commercials that show images such as a 90-year-old man on a surfboard, as one California HMO did, may be rejected as too outlandish.

Elderhostel, headquartered in Boston, offers perhaps the most famous example of personal growth values used in marketing. The organization offers travel in conjunction with educational programs at colleges and universities in every state in the U.S. and in more than a dozen foreign countries. Elderhostel had more than 290,000 participants in 1993.

Unlike younger people, who tend to seek out escapist activities in their leisure time, older people tend to integrate productive pursuits into activities designed to revitalize themselves. One man told me on the way to a nursing home where he and a friend worked as volunteers, "I really got my batteries charged this morning. Every Thursday morning, I go downtown to mentor students in math." The man's "work" is volunteering at the nursing homes. His "recreation" is mentoring inner-city youth. Capturing such images in advertising tells older consumers that your company really appreciates the unique human beings they are. As McDonald's can attest, the public's response to such advertising can be powerful.

The most powerful ads and commercials targeting older markets integrate all five key values. In fact, analyzing an ad, commercial, or brochure to ascertain the amount of key value content can predict the probable level of positive responses for older consumers.

McDonald's ran a commercial integrating all five values more than six years ago. The commercial still lingers in people's minds. In fact, it reportedly ranks among the all-time top ten in consumer recall. The ad, entitled "New Kid," depicts an elderly gentleman going to work at McDonald's.

"New Kid" was developed to show that even older people work at McDonald's. Not only did McDonald's continue to receive job applications from seniors, but patronage by older people increased. The commercial reflected all five key values systems that activate older consumers' hot buttons, readying them for a smart marketer's gentle touch.

On the other side of the Atlantic, British Airways has generally outperformed other airlines with its Privileged Travelers program. The program does not restrict when members may travel, thereby responding to their autonomy and self-sufficiency values. British Airways also demonstrates an understanding of the "gateway to experience" principle by offering such value-added features as English Walking Tours and London Study Days, which are noted for their lack of tour guides.

Alexander Hamilton Life Insurance Company decided to test the key value hypothesis in a direct-mail campaign. In a mail drop to 60,000 prospects, it tested its standard letter against two new letters. The standard letter opened with a direct (objective) appeal to the rational sides of consumers' minds. The other two letters centered on key values. One reflected the values of personal growth and autonomy and self-sufficiency. The other letter integrated all five values. The standard letter produced a typical 1.6 percent response rate. The two-values letter drew a 4.5 percent response rate. The five-values letter outperformed the standard letter by nearly 400 percent, with a 6 percent response.

The results of using key values in marketing can be measured, but their use is an art. It involves direct conversations with the subjective self, the most sensitive side of our being. Addressing these values with bold flourishes can offend the often shy and deferential nature of a subjective thinker, who often will respond more strongly to understatement than to the overstatements widely characteristic in advertising.

Another note of caution: it is not enough to integrate key values into marketing communications. You also need to avoid compromising them accidentally. These unintentional goofs frequently occur in marketing literature for retirement housing, where catered services are so strongly emphasized that potential residents can't perceive the possibilities of a truly autonomous lifestyle. Fears arise that social connectedness will be forced by "social" directors.

Key values do not operate at the top of the mind. They appear to originate—like appetites for food, drink, and making love—from deep within the psyche, below the levels of consciousness. The challenge of marketing to mature minds is to get through the gatekeeper of the unconscious. If you can do that, you're more than halfway home.

The Next Baby Boom

by Susan Mitchell
October 1995
American Demographics

The 72 million children of baby boomers form a huge generation that will come of age in the next five years. They will be the first generation to accept mixed races, "nontraditional" families, and gender-bending sex roles as mainstream. Unlike the original baby boomers, most will think their parents are cool. They will also cope with stark economic divisions based on high-tech skills.

Two-year-old Julie couldn't wait for Halloween.

"What are you going to be, Julie?"

"Geen powie anja! Geen powie anja!"

If you need a translator, you aren't a parent. Julie, like millions of her playmates, went trick-or-treating as the green Power Ranger.

The youngest Americans are opinionated consumers before they even learn to speak. Teenage Mutant Ninja Turtles, Barney the purple dinosaur, and now a multiracial fivesome of teenage boys and girls—the Mighty Morphin' Power Rangers—capture the imagination of young children and a huge quantity of their parents' dollars. Their teenage brothers and sisters already exert a heavy influence on music, sports, computers, video games, and dozens of other consumer markets. Yet the consumer power of today's children is just the first ripple of a huge wave.

Americans aged 18 and younger will form a generation as big as the original baby boom. Like the baby boom before them, their huge numbers will profoundly influence markets, attitudes, and society. Their true power will become apparent in the next five years as the oldest members come of age. Their habits will shape America for most of the 21st century.

Our country wasn't always on a demographic roller coaster. In the first half of the 20th century, the annual number of births in the U.S. remained fairly steady, at 2.7 million to 3 million a year. Then, about nine months after the end of World War II, the number of births began a quick, steep climb. It rose from 2.9 million in 1945 to 3.4 million in 1946 to 3.8 million in 1947. The boom continued for 19 years, with 4.3 million babies born in the peak year of 1957. Births remained above 4 million until 1965, when they dropped to 3.8 million. When it was all over, a grand total of nearly 76 million baby boomers had arrived.

Through the late 1960s and early 1970s, births remained well below 4 million a year, dipping to only 3.1 million in 1973. But in 1977, the beginning of the next baby boom, annual births began climbing again. Births topped 4 million in 1989 and continued at that high level through 1993. In 1994, however, the next baby boom finally came to a close, when births dipped just below 4 million, to 3,979,000.

The next baby boom is 72 million Americans, and their proportion of the total U.S. population rivals that of the original boom. Children and teens aged 18 or younger are 28 percent of the total population; the original baby boom, now aged 31 to 49, is 30 percent.

This new generation differs from the baby boom in significant ways. While the boomer generation was a relatively uniform group, the children of the next boom differ radically from each other in race, living arrangements, and socioeconomic class. The children of this generation also face much more serious problems than the boomers did when they were children. AIDS, crime, violence, and divorce cast long shadows over their world. As the children of working parents, they often have to assume adult responsibilities at an early age.

Members of the next baby boom may be more competent, confident, and wary than the original baby boom. If you could sum them up in one word, the word would be diverse.

In the 20th century, international migration and differing fertility rates have made each generation of Americans more racially and ethnically diverse than its predecessor. The original baby boomers are 75 percent non-Hispanic white, according to Census Bureau estimates. Eleven percent are black, 9 percent are Hispanic, and 4 percent are Asian or American Indian, Eskimo, or Aleut. The next baby boomers are only 67 percent non-Hispanic white; 15 percent are black, 14 percent are Hispanic, and 5 percent are Asian or American Indian, Eskimo or Aleut. Within this generation, younger cohorts are even more racially diverse. Only 64 percent of infants born in 1994 are non-Hispanic white. Sixteen percent of infants are Hispanic, 15 percent are black, and 5 percent are Asian or American Indian, Eskimo, or Aleut.

The Census Bureau's broad racial and ethnic categories tell only part of the diversity story. The next baby boom will be the first generation to seriously question all traditional racial categories. The reason is that many of today's children and teens are of mixed races. In 1990, there were nearly 2 million children under age 18 who were reported as being "of a different race than one or both of their parents," according to the Census Bureau. The largest group is children of black and white parents, but close behind are children of white and Asian parents. That translates into about 1 mixed-race child for every 35 members of the next baby boom.

The larger share of minorities in the next baby boom means that there is far more interaction between people of different races than there was for most of the baby-boom generation. The oldest half of the original boomers was born into a fully segregated society, with separate schools, neighborhoods, and public facilities for whites and blacks. The next baby boom is the product of a more integrated society.

Today, white kids have nonwhite playmates, a casual appreciation for "ethnic foods," and heroes of every race. Teens of all races listen to rap, hip hop, and Tejano music. "Minority teen culture has an incredible influence on white teens," according to Peter Zollo of Teenage Research Unlimited. "Everything from music to fashion to language seems to be adopted by a large number of suburban white teens."

One reflection of racial and ethnic diversity among children can be seen in the toy market. Mattel, Tyco Toys, and Playskool are just some of the big players that are responding to ethnic and racial diversity. "We have Dream Doll House families that are African American, Hispanic, Asian, and Caucasian," says Laurie Strong of Fisher-Price, a subsidiary of Mattel.

Zollo says the key is inclusion. "Advertisements, even those for large mainstream brands should be very inclusive," he says. That's why some marketers now shoot different versions of the same ad using rap, alternative rock, and even country music to reach all the different groups of teens and children.

Teens know their world is multicultural, even if grownups don't. Almost three-fourths of 12-to-17-year-olds say they receive too little information at school about Muslims, according to a 1991 poll by the George H. Gallup International Institute. About two-thirds say they receive too little information about "Africans before they came to this country" and about nonwhite women. Well over half feel that Asian Americans and Hispanics are given short shrift in school.

In addition, the majority of people aged 12 to 17 believe members of minority racial and ethnic groups receive too little respect. And reflecting their greater tolerance for diversity in all forms, 57 percent believe gays are also too little respected, according to the Gallup Institute.

While increased diversity might lead to greater racial tolerance, other signs point to further polarization among the races. Schools were successfully integrated decades ago, but many neighborhoods are as firmly segregated as ever. Race-related violence and organized racial "hate groups" are increasingly visible, and schools around the country report increased racial tensions among students.

For the original baby boom, racial issues were explosive and defining. Race will be just as important to the next baby boom, but in a different way. More of today's kids have first-hand experiences with integration, prejudice, and other race issues.

When the original boomers were children, new friends would often ask each other, "What does your father do for a living?" But for the children of the next baby boom, the question is more likely to be, "Does your dad live with you?" The next boomers' family arrangements are widely varied, and increasingly, they do not include a father.

In 1970, 85 percent of children under age 18 lived with two parents and 12 percent lived with one parent. By 1993, this had changed significantly. Only 71 percent of children have two parents present, and 27 percent live with a single parent, according to the Census Bureau.

Striking racial differences in family composition are driving the diversity of this new generation. In 1993, 77 percent of white children and 65 percent of Hispanic children live in two-parent families. Yet only 36 percent of black children have two parents present.

Since the 1970s, more children (and their families) have had to move into grandparents' homes for economic reasons. In 1991, 5 percent of all children lived in grandparents' homes, including 12 percent of black children, 6 percent of Hispanic children, and 4 percent of white children, according to the Population Reference Bureau. In about half of these cases, the mother also lives there. Both parents live with grandparents in 17 percent of these cases. In 28 percent of these households, neither parent is present and grandparents are solely responsible for their grandchildren. Even children in "intact" families may have an absent parent. Among children of the next baby boom who live with two parents, 16 percent live with a step-parent, according to the Census Bureau.

Children today are also far more likely to live with a never-married mother than boomers were. Among children living with one parent, 7 percent in 1970 and 31 percent in 1990 were living with a parent who had never married. Among single-mother families in 1993, 21 percent of white mothers, 35 percent of Hispanic mothers, and 55 percent of black mothers have never been married.

As the children of divorce, the next baby boomers will grow up determined to have strong marriages for themselves. Three-fourths of children aged 13 to 17 believe it's too easy to get divorced, and 71 percent believe people who have divorced did not try hard enough to save their marriages, according to a 1992 survey by the Gallup Institute. This could mean divorce rates will plunge in the next decade, as the next boomers work harder to save their new marriages. Or it could bring further delays in marriage, as the next boomers wait longer to take their vows.

When the original baby boom came of age, America was rocked by a huge clash of values between young adults and their parents. Much of that generation gap persists today, as attitude surveys show a solid demarcation between people younger and older than age 50. The major reason for the gap is higher educational attainment, which pits the boomer generation against their less-educated parents.

Today, there is little evidence of a comparable gap between the original boomers and their next-generation children. While many of the boomers' parents never finished high school, nearly nine in ten boomers did. This achievement should be realized again with the new generation. One-fourth of boomers completed college, and about the same percentage of their children are also expected to obtain college degrees, according to the Census Bureau.

Nearly half of children think their parents are "up to date" on the music they like, according to a 1993 study by *Good Housekeeping* and Roper Starch Worldwide. Few boomers could make the same claim of their parents when they were teenagers. The children surveyed also say their parents' opinions matter most to them when it comes to drinking, spending money, and questions about sex and AIDS. They even listen more to their parents than their friends about which snack foods to eat.

The next baby boom will not attach a stigma to young men and women who still live with their parents. On the contrary, they will seek close bonds with parents and other relatives as a way to find security in an uncertain world.

The next baby boom may also reject advertising that sells a product or service specifically to men or women. Calvin Klein has seen the future in "cK one," a unisex fragrance. Tomorrow's young men will be more likely to try hair color and jewelry, while women will be more likely to visit the hardware store.

The next baby boom is growing up in an era when the shifting sex roles of the 1970s and 1980s have become the new social norms of the 1990s. Young women already outnumber men at college, and they are making substantial headway in professions traditionally dominated by men, such as law and medicine. The women of the next baby boom will take these gains even further. Fifty-eight percent of young women and 44 percent of young men believe the women's movement has done a good job. Twenty-five percent of young men, but only 5 percent of young women, believe it has "gone too far," according to a 1991 Gallup Institute poll.

In fact, the young women of the next baby boom are taking the women's movement into new arenas such as sports and entertainment. Title 9, a federal law prohibiting sex discrimination at colleges, including college athletics, "has done a lot to make girls more prepared to take their place in new areas," says Irma Zandl, president of the Zandl Group in New York City. While they are gaining as athletes, young women are also gaining greater attention and status as musicians and entertainers.

But the battle between the sexes is still far from over. Young women are more likely than young men to believe that men do not understand the issues that concern women the most—62 percent of teenage girls believe this, compared with 56 percent of teenage boys. Yet 67 percent of teenage boys and girls believe that the gains women have made have not come at the expense of men, according to the Gallup Institute.

Most social scientists expect the daughters of employed women to have a positive view of having a career. But Peter Zollo of Teenage Research Unlimited found that teenage girls with stay-at-home moms expect to work for a slightly different reason. "What's driving young women to want to have their own careers is that divorce rates are so high they don't want to rely on any man," he says. Even their fathers are pushing them to make sure they can be self-reliant and not dependent on a husband.

In 1959, at the peak of the first baby boom, 27 percent of children lived in poverty. In 1993, a smaller percentage—23 percent—of children under age 18 were poor. But the finances of the next baby boom are far from secure. In fact, their situation is getting worse.

From 1950 until 1969, the average family's economic situation was improving. The poverty rate for children dropped from 27 percent to 14 percent. During the 1970s, the proportion of children in poverty fluctuated between 14 and 17 percent. For the next baby boom, however, the years of their birth have coincided with steadily increasing poverty among children, with rates rising from 16 percent in 1977 to 23 percent in 1993.

Even more significant for this generation is the racial difference in poverty rates. While 18 percent of white children are poor, 46 percent of black children live in poverty. For black children, the proportion of poor children has not been lower than 40 percent since 1959, when the Census Bureau first measured childhood poverty rates.

The rapidly changing nature of the workplace makes it more difficult for some people to escape poverty. Even the lowest-paid jobs are increasingly dependent on high-tech equipment, such as computerized cash registers and inventory systems. Children who have little or no experience with technology early in life may have little comfort or facility with it as adults. Unfortunately, the next boomers are divided into haves and have-nots according to their access to technology and the ability to build important skills early in life.

This technology gap worsens the existing socioeconomic divisions among children and teens. The poorest members of the next baby boom are the least likely to have access to up-to-date technology. Two-thirds of households with personal computers in the home are headed by college graduates earning over $50,000, according to a 1994 survey by The Times Mirror Center for The People & The Press. But computers are present in only 15 percent of homes where the householder did not graduate from college and has earnings of less than $30,000. Half of college-educated parents say their children use PCs at home, compared with only 17 percent of parents with a high school diploma or less.

Changes in the computer market may eventually narrow this gap. "A lot of kids say they only have an old computer or access through a friend or someone else," says Zollo. "The gap in access may decrease as technology becomes more affordable and kids have more opportunities to use up-to-date technology at school."

Regardless of access, the next baby boom is convinced that computers are cool. Sixty-two percent of those aged 12 to 19 say online computing is 'in,' but only about 13 percent have been online in the past month, says Zollo. "That gap represents a huge opportunity."

Education is still the ticket out of poverty, and members of the next baby boom value education even more than their parents did. In 1971, 60 percent of college-bound boomers were motivated by a desire to gain a general education, and 69 percent wanted to "learn more about things that interest me." In 1993, 65 percent were interested in education in general, and 75 percent wanted to learn more about things of interest, according to the Higher Education Research Institute at the University of California, Los Angeles.

The freshman class of 1993 sees a dual role for education: it is a worthy goal in itself, and also the key to financial success. In 1971, 74 percent of boomers indicated they decided to go to college to get a better job, and 50 percent cited the desire to make more money. Among 1993 freshmen, 82 percent said they were going to college to get a better job, and 75 percent wanted to increase their earning power.

Twenty-four years ago, baby boomers were noted for their self-confidence. Yet the freshmen of 1993 are even more confident of their abilities than were the freshmen of 1971. One-third of baby-boomer freshmen rated themselves above average in leadership, mathematics, popularity, and intellectual and social self-confidence. In 1993, 43 percent of entering students rated themselves above average in these areas.

The next baby boom will need all the confidence it can get. Their parents, the original boomers, experienced social turmoil during their childhood and young adulthood. But many of the issues facing today's young adults are far more frightening. They live in a world where violence and infectious diseases compete for attention with savage economic competition and rapid technological change.

As a new century begins, the next baby boom will enter the adult world and begin struggling with these problems. But their place in the record books is already secure. They may one day surpass their parents to become the largest and most influential generation in U.S. history.

Taking It Further: *The Official Guide to the Generations* (New Strategist, 414 pp., $69.95) defines and profiles the original baby boom and other generations, with some information on the next baby boom. It is available from American Demographics's *Marketing Power* catalog; telephone (800) 828-1133. *The American Freshman* survey has been conducted annually by the Higher Education Research Institute of the University of California-Los Angeles since 1966; telephone (310) 825-1925. The Gallup Organization is in Princeton, New Jersey; telephone (609) 924-9600. More information on the 1993 *Good Housekeeping* survey of parents and children is available from Roper Starch Worldwide in New York City; telephone (212) 599-0700.

The Generation X Difference

by Nicholas Zill and John Robinson
April 1995
American Demographics

A new generation of young adults has higher college attendance rates, but their graduation rates are unchanged and incomes are down. They are more interested in the visual arts, less active in sports or sex, more scarred by divorce, and more likely to live with parents. Their lives are defined by education, insecurity, and a slow transition to adulthood.

Some of them wear their baseball caps backwards. Some put safety pins through their nipples and rings through their noses. But are today's young people really all that different from the young adults of 10 or 20 years ago? Do they merit labels like "Grunge Kids," "Slackers," or "Generation X"?

A few years ago, American newspapers and magazines were filled with stories about a peculiar new generation that faced terrible employment prospects, exhibited perverse tastes and behavior patterns, and was even more politically apathetic than its predecessors. Then researchers found that some of the characteristics the media attributed to Xers contradicted each other. Other Xer labels were not supported by trend data, and still others applied to a minority of young adults. The media began running articles like *Newsweek's* cover story, "The Myth of Generation X: Seven Great Lies About Twentysomethings." That story concluded, "There are only two generalizations we can make about them with any degree of certainty: they are Americans, and they are in their 20s."

Sweeping generalizations about any generation are bound to be incorrect. But so too is the notion that there is nothing different or noteworthy about today's young adults. In fact, trend data from national surveys such as the Current Population Survey and the National Endowment for the Arts' Survey of Public Participation in the Arts demonstrate that the current crop of 18-to-29-year-olds differs from its predecessors in several important regards. Their economic situations and prospects are different, as are their educational enrollment and attainment patterns. Their media and recreation habits are different, too. Even their relationships with their parents are different than were those of baby boomers. Taking a close look at these facts is the best way to separate the truth about today's young adults from the media-fueled hype.

When young adults complain about their dim financial prospects, many older adults accuse them of being whiners. A *Washington Post* headline proclaimed: "Grow Up, Crybabies. You're America's Luckiest Generation." The critics seem not to have noticed the slide in young workers' wage rates. Between 1983 and 1992, the median weekly earnings of young men aged 16 to 24 who were full-time workers fell 9 percent, from $314 per week to $285 per week in constant 1992 dollars. Over the same period, inflation-adjusted earnings of young women in the same age group slipped 4 percent, from $277 to $267 per week. The earnings of men aged 25 and older also declined during this period, but only by 6 percent. Wage rates for women aged 25 and older increased by 6 percent.

The reasons behind wage declines are familiar, but that doesn't make them any easier for young workers to live with. They include a loss of high-paying manufacturing jobs due to automation, foreign competition, and shifting of jobs to countries with lower labor costs. In contrast, service industries are creating masses of low-paying jobs that offer meager benefits. In addition, technological changes have put a premium on workers possessing the high-level skills needed to read and understand abstract prose, operate computers and complex machinery, and easily adapt to rapidly changing work environments. That is good news for the twentysomethings who have grown up computer-literate. But it is bad news for the large number of young people whose reading and math skills never advanced beyond the eighth-grade level and whose only familiarity with microprocessors comes from hanging out in video arcades.

Given the need for technical skills and education credentials to earn decent wages, it is hardly surprising that today's young adults are flocking to two- and four-year colleges at record rates. The percentage of 18-to-24-year-olds currently enrolled in college or having completed one or more years of college was 54 percent in October 1992, up from 43 percent a decade earlier, according to the Current Population Survey.

Baby busters may be the most college-bound generation ever, but they aren't necessarily the best-educated. As of March 1993, 24 percent of adults aged 25 to 29 had bachelor's degrees, not much different from the 22 percent with such degrees in

1982. So while today's young adults may be eager for college credentials, many have not attained these passports to higher earnings. Furthermore, the proportion of young adults who attain college degrees is only half as large among blacks as it is among whites.

Perhaps it's natural that young people of the post-television era seem moved more by the visual image than by the written word. The percentage of 18-to-24-year-olds who read any novels, short stories, poetry, or plays in the previous 12 months fell from 60 percent in 1982 to 53 percent in 1992, according to the arts survey. Over the same period, literature reading declined 2 percentage points among middle-aged adults and held its own among adults aged 50 and older. The survey also found that 41 percent of today's young adults did not read a single book not required for school or work in the last 12 months, and 60 percent had read fewer than four.

While the proportion of young adults who read literature regularly has been on the decline, the proportion who go to art museums or galleries has been rising. Twenty-nine percent of 18-to-24-year-olds in 1992 reported attendance at an art museum or gallery during the previous 12 months, compared with 23 percent in 1982. The percentage of young adults who say they would like to go to art museums or galleries more often showed an even larger increase, from 32 percent in 1982 to 42 percent in 1992. The proportion who watched a television program or video about artists, art works, or art museums in the last 12 months also increased, from 18 percent to 26 percent.

Some of the increase in fine-arts attendance may reflect the greater availability of art in traveling shows, videos, and cable, as well as the more effective packaging and promotion of art by museum officials. But it also seems likely that the pervasive media environment in which today's young adults have grown up has helped to nurture their awareness of and interest in the graphic arts.

Young adults' increased interest in the visual arts has occurred despite the decline of formal art education in childhood. The proportion of 18-to-24-year-olds who have ever taken lessons or classes in visual arts such as sculpture, painting, printmaking, photography, or film dropped from 41 percent in 1982 to 24 percent in 1992. The decline is probably attributable to a downgrading of arts instruction in the nation's public schools, a deemphasis now apparently in the process of being reversed in many school systems. On the other hand, the proportion of young adults who had taken a class in art appreciation or art history did not decline during the 1980s: it was 22 percent in 1982 and 27 percent in 1992, and the apparent increase is not statistically significant.

Young adults spend much of their time with the omnipresent visual form of the late 20th century. Eighteen-to-24-year-olds report watching three hours of television on an average day, according to the arts survey. This makes them no different from young adults of the previous decade. Stereotypes portray baby busters transfixed by MTV, but the reality is that, like their elders, young adults are far more likely to be watching top-rated shows on network television. In spring 1994, the most popular TV programs among 18-to-29-year-olds were "Seinfeld," "Roseanne," "Home Improvement," and "Coach," also among the top-drawing programs for viewers of all ages.

The big differences in television viewing patterns are found not between busters and boomers, but between adults under age 50 and those aged 50 and older. The latter are far more likely to be tuned in to shows such as "60 Minutes" and "Murder, She Wrote." It remains to be seen whether this age gap will shift when boomers enter their 50s in the next decade.

When young adults do get off the couch and out of the house for entertainment, they're probably going to the movies. Eighty-two percent of 18-to-24-year-olds reported attending a movie in the last 12 months, according to the 1992 arts survey. This was down slightly from the 87 percent of the same age group who reported film attendance a decade earlier, but was still considerably higher than the 59 percent movie attendance rate among adults of all ages.

The proportion of young adults who attended films in 1992 surpassed the proportions who attended amusement or theme parks (68 percent), amateur or professional sports events (51 percent), arts or crafts fairs or festivals (37 percent), or historic parks or monuments (33 percent). And it greatly exceeded the proportions who went to stage plays (13 percent) or live performances of jazz (11 percent) or classical music (10 percent).

Young adults like to exercise their eyeballs with art, TV, and movies, but they are less fond of exercise for the rest of their bodies. Perhaps the most perplexing trend involving young adults is the decline in their levels of physical activity. Medical science continues to find evidence of the benefits of an active, vigorous lifestyle over a sedentary one. Yet compared with their counterparts of a decade ago, baby busters are less likely to engage in sports and outdoor activities.

According to the arts survey, the proportion of 18-to-24-year-olds who engaged in sports such as softball, basketball, golf, bowling, skiing, or tennis in the last 12 months declined from 66 percent in 1982 to 59 percent in 1992. The proportion who went camping, hiking, canoeing, or took part in other outdoor activities fell from 51 percent to 43 percent over the same period. The share who reported jogging, lifting weights, walking, or engaging in other regular exercise did not change significantly, from 70 percent in 1982 to 67 percent in 1992. But the overall proportion of adults who exercised regularly increased during this time period from 51 percent to 60 percent.

The decline in physical activities among young adults is documented even more dramatically in a detailed survey of 22 fitness activities conducted by the National Center for Health Statistics. Based on samples of more than 30,000 adult respondents nationwide, the 15 percent decline in fitness activities between 1985 and 1990 for those under age 30 was almost twice as large as the decline for older Americans.

The drop has been particularly pronounced for young women. Women under age 30 took part in fitness activities at 61 percent the rate of young men in 1990, compared with a 75 percent gender ratio for older women and men. This suggests that women may fall further behind men in fitness in the years ahead.

Today's young adults are also less involved in sexual activity. The authors of *Sex in America* (1994) found that the youngest adults report levels of sexual intercourse that are closer to people aged 50 to 59 than to those in their 30s. While that may be due in large part to their being single rather than married, young adults also report lower rates of masturbation.

Both the divorce rate and the percentage of children born outside of marriage in the U.S. doubled between 1965 and 1977, the years in which today's young adults were born. As busters grew up, the divorce rate leveled off and even declined slightly, but it remains much higher than it had been before the mid-1960s. The percentage of children born to unmarried parents also continued to rise, reaching 30 percent in 1992. As a result, more than 40 percent of today's young adults spent at least some time in a single-parent family by age 16.

These events left their marks on young-adult psyches. The National Survey of Children, a longitudinal study of people born in the late 1960s, found that 26 percent of these busters had received psychological treatment for emotional, learning, or behavior problems by the time they reached adulthood. The share who had been in therapy was twice as high among those whose parents had divorced as it was among those whose parents had not, 41 percent versus 22 percent.

Young adults whose parents divorced are twice as likely as others to have poor relationships with their parents, especially their fathers. Two-thirds of young adults whose parents divorced report poor relationships with their fathers, and one-third with their mothers. By comparison, among busters whose parents did not divorce, 29 percent have poor relationships with their fathers and 13 percent with their mothers.

In some respects, however, relations between busters and their parents are more harmonious than were those between baby boomers and their parents. In particular, there seems to be less of a generation gap with respect to tastes in music. Large majorities of busters and their parents like oldies rock and roll. Three-fourths of 18-to-29-year-olds and 40-to-59-year-olds say they like oldies, according to the 1993 General Social Survey from the National Opinion Research Center in Chicago.

There is more generational discord regarding heavy metal and rap, although it is not absolute. Five percent of 40-to-59-year-olds say they like heavy metal, while 81 percent dislike or hate it; the remainder have mixed feelings. The pattern is similar for rap; 8 percent like it, and 71 percent don't. However, these music forms also have minority followings among the baby-bust generation itself. One in four 18-to-29-year-olds likes heavy metal, while half dislike or hate it. Thirty percent like rap, but 45 percent don't.

It is a good thing that busters and their parents agree on some musical matters, because young adults are spending more of their lives bunking with Mom and Dad. The proportion of women in their 20s living in their parents' homes rose from 17 percent in 1977 to 24 percent in 1993, according to the Current Population Survey. Young men the same age are even more likely to remain in or return to the parental nest (35 percent in 1993, up from 30 percent in 1977).

One reason why many busters have not left home is because they are marrying later. The share of women aged 25 to 29 who had never married tripled from 11 percent in 1970 to 33 percent in 1993. The share of men in their late 20s who have never married climbed from 19 percent to 48 percent during the same period. Another factor underlying the "long goodbye" phenomenon is the high cost of housing. Coupled with busters' diminished earning power, living rent-free may be the only feasible way of saving enough for an eventual down payment on a house or condo.

When young adults do leave home, they are likely to wind up in a legal marriage. But the chances are greater that they will live with a partner before marrying that person or someone else. The number of unmarried-couple households rose from 500,000 in 1970 to 3.5 million in 1993. At the same time, the ratio of unmarried couples to married couples rose from 1 per 100 to 6 per 100. In about half of these non-traditional households, one or both partners are under age 30.

Young adults are almost twice as likely as older adults to have tried microbrewed beer in the last year, according to a recent national survey. This could eventually turn out to be one of the hallmark activities that identifies Generation Xers in the years ahead—not because it involves beer, but because it may signify a trend toward seeking out local, specialized products with a distinctive flavor. Busters may favor beer over wine because they prefer its informality. Many of them may find the specialized vocabulary of wine appreciation intimidating and potentially embarrassing.

Besides preferring visual to physical exercise, twentysomethings of the 1990s are clearly not the same as young adults of the past. In many ways, they are more diverse and complex, yet they exhibit a few unifying traits. The first is insecurity. Today's young adults are less confident than their predecessors about the stability of jobs, earnings, and relationships. This may be good news for companies that want to hire twentysomethings for modest wages and minimal benefits. It also means that busters may be looking beyond salaries for jobs that offer meaningful opportunities for skill building and advancement.

A second unifying theme is the critical importance of education in shaping the life chances of today's young adults. Busters appreciate the value of education, but many are frustrated about their inability to achieve the schooling they would like.

As they move through the work world, they will be an eager market for adult education and job-related training. Although their focus will be practical for some years, they may later seek the arts, humanities, and even spiritual instruction lacking in their earlier schooling. They will probably prefer to learn about these subjects through multimedia avenues rather than traditional books.

The third theme that distinguishes busters from previous generations is how long it is taking them to fully enter the adult world. In the book *Childhood and Society*, Erik Erikson described adolescence as a psychological stage between childhood and adulthood. Now it seems that a new pre-adult life stage has emerged. This isn't to say that people in their 20s are merely overgrown children. It's more that they are understandably hesitant to take on some of the tasks at which they have seen their elders fail. Busters will undoubtedly make their own mistakes in life, but they don't want to repeat ours.

Taking It Further: The 1992 Survey of Public Participation in the Arts interviewed a national sample of 12,736 adults aged 18 and older about their arts participation and leisure activities. The interviews were conducted throughout 1992. About three-fourths of the interviews were conducted by telephone and one-fourth in person. The response rate was over 80 percent. A similar survey was conducted in 1982. There were 1,390 respondents in the 18-to-24 age range in the 1992 survey and 2,851 in the 1982 survey. For information about reports based on the arts surveys and copies of public-use data files, contact the Research Division, National Endowment for the Arts, 1100 Pennsylvania Avenue NW, Washington, DC 20506; telephone (202) 682-5432. For similar information about the Current Population Survey, contact the Public Information Office, Bureau of the Census, Washington, DC 20233; telephone (301) 457-2794.

The Baby Boom Turns 50

by Cheryl Russell
December 1995
American Demographics

The 50th birthday of the oldest baby boomer is just a media event. But boomers' midlife crises are real, and they will create huge business opportunities. Freed from the responsibilities of their 40s, boomers will create an adventurous life stage called "midyouth" that will push traditional ideas of a "mature market" into oblivion. "Power Players," "Fun Seekers," and "Matriarchs" will typify boomers in their 50s.

The first baby boomer will turn 50 on January 1, 1996. This will surely become the biggest made-up story since the mainstream media invented the yuppie in the early 1980s. Major articles in national newspapers and magazines have already trumpeted the event. In the next month, we can expect live reports from birthday celebrations, jokes about graying hair and expanding waistlines, and plenty of pundits telling us what it all means. Through it all, businesses serving the "mature" market will sharpen their knives and prepare to carve up the boomers.

But when the first 7,745 of 78 million baby boomers turn 50 on January 1, nothing will happen. By the end of 1996, 3.4 million baby boomers will have turned 50, and still nothing much will have happened. The 50th birthdays of the oldest boomers are a media event, not a watershed for businesses.

There are several reasons why the baby boom's 50th birthday celebrations don't matter very much. Even though the oldest boomers will cross the quasi-official threshold that defines the "mature" market, boomers will account for a small share of the market for the next decade. Not until 2005 will boomers become a majority of those aged 50 to 74.

A more important reason to use caution when celebrating is that boomers will never be part of the "mature" market as we know it today. Baby boomers are entirely unlike older generations of Americans, both in attitudes and lifestyles. Businesses that ignore the gulf between boomers and older Americans do so at their peril. Attempts to lump boomers into the "mature" category simply because they are in their 50s will be either ignored by boomers or greeted with hoots of contempt.

Rather than join the mature market, boomers will create a new and vibrant midlife marketplace over the next few decades. As they do so, they will push the threshold of the traditional "mature" market into older and older age groups. Consequently, the very idea of a "mature" market will age with the older people the concept currently defines. Ultimately, the idea will fade away with the generations that precede the baby boom.

These facts won't stop the media onslaught, however. Stories about boomers turning 50 are sure to attract a big audience of boomers, who are always happy to hear about themselves. Unfortunately, they will also confuse anxious marketers and advertisers who are always wondering what's next. Those who are convinced that the 50th birthdays of boomers are a watershed face two dangers. They could write off the generation because it has matured beyond their products and services, thereby ignoring millions of customers. Or they could mistakenly assume that boomers can now be targeted with products and services popular among the traditional mature market.

Businesses that write boomers off because of their preconceptions about fiftysomething consumers will be giving up the single most lucrative consumer segment in the nation. Householders in their late 40s and early 50s are the most affluent group, and they are also the biggest spenders.

Businesses that try to market to boomers as they did to the "mature market" will see their sales plummet, because the baby boom's wants and needs are different from the wants and needs of previous generations. Boomers are a well-educated generation. This makes them more demanding and sophisticated consumers than people in the current mature market. Boomers are also highly individualistic, which makes them independent and self-indulgent. These are qualities rarely seen in the 50-plus crowd today. The best position businesses can take is to prepare for radical change among midlife consumers.

Middle age is a difficult stage of life when job and family responsibilities mount relentlessly. The years surrounding age 50 are a time of frustration and even crisis for many people. Profound things happen in midlife, and profound events will shake millions of baby boomers as they enter their 50s.

Businesses are already serving the wants and needs of baby boomers as they pass through difficult transitions. Sales of skin creams, suntan lotions, hair coloring, cosmetics, vitamins, and nutritional supplements are surging as millions of boomers join the battle against aging. Self-help books have become so popular that the *New York Times* publishes a separate best-seller list for them. Spirituality, if not traditional religion, is seeing a rebirth as the burgeoning middle-aged population searches for life's meaning.

There is plenty of anecdotal evidence to sketch out the midlife crises of baby boomers, but the evidence goes far beyond office gossip. The 1994 General Social Survey (GSS), conducted by the National Opinion Research Center of the University of Chicago, has statistically documented midlife crisis. GSS interviewers asked a nationally representative sample of Americans whether they had experienced any trauma in the past 12 months. Overall, 40 percent said they had. This proportion is lowest (27 percent) among people in their early 30s. It is highest among the middle-aged, rising to 49 percent among people in their late 40s and peaking at 53 percent among 50-to-54-year-olds. Invariably, the crises of midlife revolve around the things that are most important—families, jobs, and personal health.

The death of a parent is one of the traumatic events most people experience during their late 40s or early 50s. Today, most baby boomers have yet to experience the death of a parent. In ten years, most will have had to cope with this experience. The proportion of people with living mothers falls from 74 percent among 40-to-44-year-olds to just 34 percent among 55-to-59-year-olds. The proportion with living fathers drops even faster, from 57 percent among 40-to-44-year-olds to 31 percent among 45-to-49-year-olds. The death of a parent awakens people to their own mortality. It can also mean added responsibilities at a time of emotional distress. Newly orphaned boomers will need a lot of hand holding.

Last summer's death of cultural icon Jerry Garcia upset many boomers more deeply than can be explained by the loss of a popular rock musician. Garcia's death at the relatively youthful age of 53 raised the specter of their own mortality. Many people experience their first serious illness in their late 40s or early 50s as the prevalence of chronic illness rises. Arthritis, high blood pressure, hearing problems, and heart disease are among the most common ailments. As chronic conditions emerge, people spend more on health-care products and services. Expect boomers to be avid consumers of quick fixes and magical cures.

For boomers in their late 40s, the siren song of career no longer sounds so sweet. Many find it hard to believe they will have to work another 15 or 20 years before they can even think about retiring. Most boomers say they sometimes or always feel burned out by their jobs or used up at the end of the workday. With the heady days of rapid promotion and pay increases behind them, people in their 40s know exactly what the future holds—and this predictability can feel like a prison sentence. Work is important to many boomers in midlife, but to others it's just a job. One-third of workers say they would quit working if they had enough money to live comfortably for the rest of their lives. The proportion is 42 percent among 45-to-49-year-olds, according to the 1994 GSS. It peaks among 55-to-59-year-olds, at 50 percent.

With so much responsibility on their shoulders, life's excitement wanes for people in their 40s. The percentage of Americans who say their life is exciting drops below 50 percent among those in their 40s, according to the GSS. The daily tedium experienced by millions of fortysomething baby boomers may account for the wild popularity of *The Bridges of Madison County*, in which a middle-aged woman breaks free from her humdrum existence, if only for a few days. The proportion of Americans who agree that extramarital sex is always wrong falls below 70 percent among people in their 40s. This is the lowest level among all age groups except the youngest (18 to 24). The proportion of Americans who admit to ever having an extramarital affair peaks in the 45-to-49 age group, at 22 percent. Boomers are looking for ways to escape the tedium.

Baby boomers in the midst of midlife crises need to be reminded that adventures await. In contrast to people in their 40s, half of those in their 50s report that their life is exciting. Advertisers who want to participate in the next consumer revolution should prepare for the excellent adventures of midlife boomers.

Expect the unexpected. Baby boomers will be unlike any previous generation of older consumers. The best advice is to scrap all the conventional wisdom about older consumers and start from scratch.

In 1950, over three-fourths of people aged 55 or older did not have a high school diploma. The share with a high school diploma did not pass the 50 percent mark until

1980. It was during those 30 years, from 1950 to 1980, that businesses created the "mature market," a concept that helped them target poorly educated and unsophisticated Americans. Now all that is about to change.

Among the oldest baby boomers, fully 87 percent are high school graduates. More than one in four are college graduates, and over half have some college experience. The increased educational level alone will revolutionize the midlife market. Add to that working women, divorce, individualistic attitudes, small families, and dual incomes, and you've got the recipe for a new consumer market.

If you're having a hard time shedding your preconceptions about the mature market, think about it this way. Three decades ago, baby boomers created the youth market. In the next decade, they will recreate that youth market among consumers in their 50s. After all, the only reason the baby boom's wants and needs were called the "youth market" is because the baby-boom generation at that time was young. Now in middle age, boomers still have many of those same wants and needs. The youth market is the boomer market, no matter what the age. With the boomers entering their 50s, many so-called "youthful" products, services, lifestyles, and attitudes will become common among midlife consumers. Boomers will create the new "midyouth" market.

Three segments of this market bear watching. Power Players, Fun Seekers, and Matriarchs will set the trends for other boomers to follow.

The Power Players: People in their 50s are at the peak of their power. This is the age at which people finally achieve the top posts in government and business. It is also when they earn and spend the most money. While 42 percent of older baby boomers would quit their jobs if they had enough money to live comfortably, 56 percent would still go to work. Those are the achievers, who are about to reap the rewards of decades on the job.

In the next few years, baby boomers will take over the reins of power in the corporate world and at most levels of government. The consequence will be rapid—even revolutionary—change in the workplace. Finally, the nation will be run by those who understand the lifestyles necessitated by the modern economy. Many of today's leaders do not have this understanding.

This was documented by *The Wall Street Journal* in a 1993 survey of the CEOs of 76 of the nation's top-100 industrial companies. The survey revealed that 95 percent of the CEOs had wives who stayed at home while their children were young. Not one had ever had to put his children in day care outside the home. Fully 87 percent had never experienced child-care issues that caused a hardship for the family. Most of today's political leaders have led similarly insulated lifestyles. This may be why so many Americans say the nation's political leaders are out of touch. They really are out of touch with the needs of Americans under age 50. Baby-boom leaders will bring with them a visceral understanding of today's workers and citizens.

The Fun Seekers: It can't be said enough: boomers just want to have fun. The baby boom's lifelong search for a good time springs directly from its strong sense of individualism. Fun is something you do for yourself, and it is in short supply in the lives of today's fortysomething boomers.

By now, baby boomers know all too well that middle age is a time of duty, obligation, and responsibility. It is a time of doing for others rather than for yourself. Boomers have been doing their duty, and they miss the good times. They want them back, and they will be looking for fun as they emerge from the crises of their middle years.

Fun cannot be emphasized enough as the best way for businesses to reach boomers. Yet there is nothing fun about the way products and services are now marketed to older Americans. In part, this is because people currently in their 50s and 60s are duty-bound and always will be. That's not the case with boomers. What else explains the surprising success of tiny upstart Ben & Jerry's Ice Cream, which capitalizes on the boomers' sense of humor with ice cream flavors such as Wavy Gravy and Cherry Garcia? What else accounts for the broad appeal of "The X-Files," "Seinfeld," and other supposedly "youthful" television programs? The only thing youthful about such programs are the television programmers and advertisers behind them. They assume boomers are too old to love wacky and offbeat humor. Businesses that direct their traditionally dour mature-market advertising campaigns at midyouth boomers will not just be ignored—they will be loathed.

Starved for fun, midyouth boomers will be the best thing that ever happened to the travel and entertainment industries. Their search for fun will shape other industries as well, such as automobile manufacturers. It won't be long before empty-nest boomers abandon their stolid minivans and look for something with style and energy. Middle-aged consumers are already the biggest spenders on new cars and trucks. Fiftysomething baby boomers will be a huge market for sporty, stylish cars. Perhaps this time around, American car companies can beat the Japanese to this baby-boom-inspired lifestyle shift.

The Matriarchs: The fierce, new-found energy of independent baby-boom women in their 50s will turn markets upside down. For years, boomer women have been suppressing their individualistic natures as they raised children—often single-handedly. With their children grown, they can satisfy their pent-up demand to think about—and spend on—themselves again.

One thing baby-boom women may do for themselves is divorce. We might expect a surge in midlife divorce as women who have long worked a second shift at home finally get to tell their husbands to take a walk. If they do, many more women may head their own households and become the matriarchs of far-flung families consisting of grown children and stepchildren, grandchildren, in-laws and ex-laws, nieces and nephews, and close friends.

The adult children of baby-boom women will be an important focus of their lives. While some children will be away at college, many others will still live at home. Almost one in four households headed by 45-to-64-year-olds includes adult children. This proportion has been rising because today's young adults are slower to leave home than were baby boomers in their youth. Many midyouth boomers will welcome the emotional and economic support of their ever-changing, multi-generational households.

As baby-boom women begin to spend on themselves again, businesses that have long ignored older women may begin to pay attention. Perhaps even the apparel industry will finally wake up to the facts. Householders aged 45 to 54 spend more than any other age group on women's clothes. Though this household segment is expanding rapidly, apparel spending may be falling partly because designers and retailers are hawking clothes to teens and young adults while snubbing their best customers.

The moral of this story is that businesses ignore midyouth boomers at their peril. By 2000, householders aged 45 to 54 will account for the largest share of spending on most categories of goods and services. So when you tune in to the 50th birthday celebrations of the boomers, enjoy the show. But remember, the real drama is just beginning to unfold as the baby-boom generation reinvents yet another lifestage— this time, middle age.

Taking It Further: *The Official Guide to the Generations*, by Susan Mitchell, is a business reference book that examines the lifestyles and attitudes of four generations of American adults: Generation X, baby boomers, the Swing generation, and the World War II generation. *The Master Trend: How The Baby Boom Generation Is Remaking America*, by Cheryl Russell, examines how the strong sense of individualism of the baby-boom generation is changing American society. *The Official Guide to American Attitudes* is a book based on trends in the General Social Survey. All three books may be ordered from American Demographics' *Marketing Power* catalog; telephone (800) 828-1133. For questions about the General Social Survey, contact the National Opinion Research Center at (312) 753-7877.

Temps Are Here to Stay

by Jan Larson
February 1996
American Demographics

E stimates of the number of people with temporary work situations vary tremendously, but researchers agree that outsourcing is one of the hottest branches of the labor force. Contingent workers enjoy variety and flexibility, but they usually get lower earnings and benefits. Most would prefer "regular" jobs, but employers aren't hiring. The result is unmet demand for health insurance and other things temps need.

The term "temp" brings to mind a replacement receptionist who answers phones and sorts the mail while a salaried employee is on vacation or medical leave. But this is only one of many ways of describing today's contingent work force. The term describes millions of people who, for whatever reason, do not have a sense of permanence about their jobs.

Estimating the size of the nation's contingent work force is like asking a group of scientists when and where the next California earthquake will hit. It all depends. "There is no agreement among scientists about what constitutes a contingent worker or how many there are," says Heidi Hartmann, author of a number of studies on contingent workers and director of the Washington, D.C.-based nonprofit Institute for Women's Policy Research.

The job may be tough, but researchers are scrambling to find the answers. They are counting the number of contingent workers, describing their varied life and work situations, and assessing employee attitudes toward contingent work. Managers are eager for this information because the use of temporary workers, also known as "outsourcing," is one of the hottest trends in business. Two-thirds of surveyed executives of large corporations expect to use more temporary help in the next three years, according to a 1995 study conducted by the staffing service Office-Team in Menlo Park, California. The reason is that more managers are using temporary workers as a competitive tool, rather than a simple means of cost control.

Outsourcing such tasks as building maintenance or fleet management is relatively common. But according to a survey by the global accounting firm Arthur Andersen & Company, a growing number of companies are hiring outsiders to take care of central business functions like tax, payroll, and pension management. "Companies are recognizing the need to focus relentlessly on their core competencies," says Dennis Torkko of Andersen's contract services practice. Contingent workers can take care of non-core but essential business functions, he says. As this trend grows, more business managers will view skilled labor as something they can lease with an option to buy.

The word "contingent" is fraught with uncertainty. The term has been used to describe a variety of employment situations, including part-time work, self-employment, employment in the business services industry, and work situations of a tenuous nature. Depending on the definition and data used, contingent work force estimates range from less than 2 percent of the working population to an impressive 16 percent-plus. That's a difference of between 2 million and 19 million workers.

The lowest estimate is published by the Federal Reserve Bank of Chicago, at 1.9 million. The Bureau of Labor Statistics (BLS) publishes three estimates based on the results of a first-time supplement to the bureau's monthly Current Population Survey conducted in February 1995. The lowest number (2.7 million) derives from a narrow definition that includes only wage and salary workers who had been in their jobs one year or less and who anticipated those jobs would last an additional year or less.

The second BLS definition adds self-employed and independent contractors who consider their jobs less than long-term, which bumps up the tally to about 3 percent of workers (3.4 million). The third and broadest BLS estimate includes any worker who considered his or her job temporary, resulting in a total of 5 percent, or 6 million.

Some observers consider the numbers low; they say that the BLS definitions are too narrow. Hartmann's 1995 study of the economic impact of contingent work on women and their families found that in 1990, more than 19 million workers, or 16 percent, held contingent jobs. This number was based on the Census Bureau's 1987 and 1990 Surveys of Income and Program Participation.

The number of contingent workers grew 5 percent between 1987 and 1990, according to Hartmann's study, compared with an overall work force gain of less than 4 percent. One easily identifiable portion of contingent workers, those employed by the personnel-supply services industry, is clearly outpacing other industries. Personnel services employment increased 25 percent between 1990 and 1993, compared with 1 percent for total employment, according to BLS data.

Whatever their numbers, contingent workers are no longer limited to clerical duties. They include pink-, blue-, and white-collar workers, according to Lewis Segal and Daniel Sullivan, senior economists at the Federal Reserve Bank of Chicago. Their research focuses on the personnel-supply industry—the largest employer of contingent workers—and is based on BLS and 1990 census data, which show that approximately 2 million workers are currently employed in the personnel-services industry.

Nationally, manufacturing employment has been declining. But the share of temporary workers who hold blue-collar jobs grew from 9 percent in 1983 to 23 percent in 1993. This indicates that manufacturers have moved away from periodically hiring and laying off workers, and toward filling more of their variable employment needs with contingent workers on a routine basis. The number of white-collar professional temporary workers has also grown. But the faster gains in blue-collar employment mean that white-collar temps have lost share, from 34 percent in 1983 to 27 percent in 1993.

The share of temp workers in "pink-collar" or clerical jobs has remained stable, at about one-third. Women continue to dominate this portion of the industry, but men are entering it at a faster rate and gaining share. In 1993, 38 percent of all personnel-supply service workers were men, up from 25 percent in 1983, according to Segal and Sullivan. Data from the National Association of Temporary and Staffing Services (NATSS) in Alexandria, Virginia, confirm that male participation in the temp work force is growing.

The temporary work force is aging along with the total labor force; 52 percent of contingent workers were aged 35 or older in 1994, up from 43 percent in 1989. Yet they remain much younger than the overall work force. Between 31 and 42 percent of all types of contingent workers were aged 16 to 24 in 1995, according to the BLS estimates, compared with 14 percent of noncontingent workers. And between 12 and 14 percent of contingent workers aged 25 to 64 are not high school graduates, compared with 10 percent of noncontingent workers. The share of temporary workers with a high school diploma or less increased from 18 percent in 1989 to 27 percent in 1994, according to NATSS.

Youth and lack of higher education would appear to explain part of the wage gap between contingent and noncontingent workers. But contingent workers tend to earn less than their permanent counterparts even after adjusting for age, sex, race, and education, according to Segal and Sullivan's research. Pink-collar temporary workers earn 10 percent less than comparable permanent workers. The wage differential is even greater for blue-collar workers, who earn 34 percent less in contingent jobs than in permanent ones. The exception is among white-collar contingent workers, who earn 2 percent more than noncontingent workers. Highly skilled professionals, executives, and technicians who work as consultants on a project basis can often command fees well in excess of staff salaries.

Contingent workers worry about things that "regular" employees take for granted. Dave Reichard, a contract worker for a technical services firm in Escatawpa, Mississippi, worries about health insurance. His firm offers access to group health insurance, but Reichard says it's "pretty expensive." He and his wife have four children, one income, and a monthly insurance tab of $145. Reichard would like to start his own computer services business, but doesn't know where he'd find affordable insurance. "I have to be concerned with my insurance, because I would be on my own," he says.

Insurance isn't Reichard's only concern. He's wondering if he'll ever be able to retire. By the time he pays for insurance, rent on his home, and other daily living expenses, there's not much left.

The proportion of contingent workers with health insurance from any source ranges from 57 to 65 percent, according to the BLS, compared with 82 percent of noncontingent workers. And contingent workers who do have health insurance are much less likely to get it through an employer. This indicates a growing need for affordable private options, says Audrey Freedman, an economist and management consultant based in New York City, who coined the term "contingent workers" in the mid-1980s. "Nobody is really specializing in portable benefits that workers can carry from employer to employer. If entirely self-financed, health insurance is portable, but it's also high-priced," says Freedman.

The same problem exists in the area of financial planning. Contingent workers don't have access to standard employer-provided pension plans, so they have to do it themselves. Businesses that can help people plan their retirement will be tapping into a growing market. So will those that help workers plan their work lives.

Child care is the top concern for women employed as contingent workers, says Hartmann of the Institute for Women's Policy Research. She has found that one in four women contingent workers has young children, compared with 16 percent of women who work full-time for a single employer. One explanation is that contingent workers tend to be younger.

Flexibility is a key advantage for hiring contingent workers, but the workers themselves also need flexibility from those who provide them with services. Pay-by-the-day, drop-in day care can offer a sense of security to parents whose erratic work schedules prevent them from taking out long-term contracts.

What many contingent workers really want is to become noncontingent. For four weeks in 1994, Joyce Hall, a home-health-care worker in Fresno, California, was a contingent worker in the temporary-services industry. When her temporary employer offered to make the position permanent, Hall eagerly made the switch. She increased her earnings and gained health benefits and a 401K plan. "The benefits are really important, as well as the pay," says Hall.

She is not alone. Over half (54 percent) of NATSS survey respondents say they took temporary work because they were between jobs and needed the money. Fifty-six percent of the personnel-supply workers studied by Segal and Sullivan say they took a temporary job for economic reasons. The BLS estimates that between 56 and 64 percent of contingent workers would prefer a more permanent arrangement.

Employers may be reluctant to end contingent arrangements, says consultant Freedman. She insists that the contingent arrangement is the natural evolution of businesses seeking new ways to remain competitive in a demanding environment. But the arrangement may be less attractive to workers. Fewer than one-third of the temporary workers Segal and Sullivan studied were still in temporary positions a year later; more than half had gotten permanent positions.

Some temps like the arrangement. For college students, semi-retirees, and those free of financial worries, contingent work may be the optimal choice. Thirty-one percent of those responding to the 1994 NATSS survey say they like the "diversity and challenge of working on different assignments," and the same share say they work as temps because it gives them "the flexibility and time to pursue nonwork interests."

Maureen Briggs lives and works in Honolulu. Although her primary occupation is teaching English as a second language, Briggs has worked as a temporary employee for nearly three years. In 1995, NATSS named her national temporary employee of the year. "Working as a temp fills in the gaps in my teaching schedule," says Briggs, who is a contract instructor for Hawaii Pacific University. Briggs pursued temporary work when she moved to Hawaii to finish her college education.

Previous career experience as a public relations and retail marketing director in the banking industry has helped Briggs land a number of temporary jobs with law firms and stock brokers. She enjoys the constant change of pace, but has been pleased when firms invite her back for other assignments.

Briggs works as a temp because it fits her lifestyle. She enjoys traveling and doesn't want a full-time job to stand in the way of her teaching career. She has turned down many full-time job offers and the retirement and health benefits they'd provide. "For me, it's a matter of weighting your priorities," she says.

Despite the many pros for both employers and employees, contingent employment as a business strategy may have a less certain future than proponents suggest. While the average annual growth rate in personnel-services employment charted by Segal and Sullivan of the Federal Reserve Bank of Chicago between 1973 and 1994 was 11 percent, it has fluctuated from a decline of 10 percent in 1982 to a high of 30 percent in 1984. "It's a fast-growing part of the work force now," says Segal. "But it's a little risky to say it's going to become the modal type of employment." In fact, Segal suggests that this type of arrangement is a cyclical trend. Currently, it is on an upswing, but it's bound to fluctuate in the future.

William Bridges, author of *JobShift*, sees promise in the "de-jobbing" of America. He sees a society in which people are not tied to restrictive job descriptions but enjoy the freedom to simply get the work done. At the other extreme, the April 1994 issue of *Reason* magazine decries the "myth of a contingent work force" as one invented "to advance the political agenda of unions."

Most Americans probably don't care whether it's called a job, or whether the arrangement benefits employers, unions, or anyone but themselves. As long as it provides them with the wherewithal to keep a roof over their heads, put food on the table, and pay the bills, workers will adapt to their surroundings and do whatever they have to do. But if employers no longer provide them with health insurance or a regular schedule, workers have to change their habits when they become consumers. That shift will create opportunities for many businesses.

Taking It Further: The Bureau of Labor Statistics published data from its February 1995 supplement to the Current Population Survey in *Contingent and Alternative Employment Arrangements,* Report 900; available by calling (202) 606-6378. Lewis Segal and Daniel Sullivan's analysis of the personnel-supply services industry appeared in the March/April 1995 issue of *Economic Perspectives*, published by the Federal Reserve Bank of Chicago; single copies are available free by calling (312) 322-5111. For more information about the National Association of Temporary and Staffing Services, contact Bruce Steinberg, NATSS, 119 South Saint Asaph Street, Alexandria, VA 22314-3119; telephone (703) 549-6287. The Institute for Women's Policy Research is at 1400 20th Street, NW, Suite 104, Washington, DC 20036; telephone (202) 785-5100. Audrey Freedman & Associates is at 111 Broadway, New York, NY 10006; telephone (212) 406-2148.

The 100 Millionth Household

by Peter Francese
March 1996
American Demographics

Diversity continues to define the American "family," even as baby boomers create a return to the past. By the middle of March, the U.S. will have 100 million households, according to Census Bureau estimates. But what will be the new household that puts the nation over that threshold? It could be college students sharing an apartment, a young couple moving into their first house, or a divorced man moving into a condo.

The odds are that Americans will live in their own homes, since two-thirds of U.S. householders own their homes. There is a slightly better than even chance that the average household will be headed by a couple, because 55 percent of households consist of married couples with or without children. The odds are also good that it is headed by someone aged 45 or older, as are 52 percent of households nationwide. And chances are that the average householder is not a minority, because three in four U.S. householders are white non-Hispanics.

Beyond these suppositions, we can only speculate about the 100 millionth U.S. household. About one in four households contains a couple with children under age 18, while 29 percent are couples without children and 16 percent are other types of families. The other 30 percent are not families at all. Of the four census regions, the South dominates, with 35 percent of households. The other three regions share the remaining two-thirds more or less equally, ranging from 20 percent in the West to 21 percent in the Northeast and 24 percent in the Midwest.

The number of U.S. households has almost doubled in less than 40 years, from 53 million in 1960. At the same time, household size has shrunk from an average of 3.3 persons to 2.6 persons. The share headed by married couples has fallen from 74 percent to 55 percent. The share headed by nonwhites has risen from 11 percent to 17 percent.

In one way, however, today's households strongly resemble those of yore. The age structure of households in 1995 is more like that of 1960 than of the 1970s and 1980s. During the 1970s and 1980s, baby boomers distorted the young-adult portion of the age distribution. Today they are roughly the same age their parents were in the 1960s—that is, in their 30s and 40s. Furthermore, the share of householders aged 55 and older is identical to its 1960 level. In fact, despite longevity gains, the proportion of mature householders is actually lower than it was in 1970 and 1980, because the smaller cohort born during the Depression is currently aged 57 to 66. Both parallels between 1960 and 1995 will be short-lived, however, as aging boomers boost the mature market above any historic level.

Youthful boomers in the 1970s and 1980s boosted household formation rates far beyond the norm. Although middle-aged boomers will continue to form new households in a small way, it is unlikely that the next decade or two will see the same growth rate that has brought us to the 100 million mark. Most projections forecast an annual growth rate of about 1 percent. At that rate, none of us will live long enough to see 200 million U.S. households.

More information on 1995 households is available from the Census Bureau by calling (301) 457-2465, or checking the bureau's Internet home page at http://www.census.gov.

Understanding Cluster Analysis

April/May 1994
Marketing Tools

I. What Is Cluster Analysis For?
by Peter Francese

Have you ever gone to a party and felt like there was no way you would ever fit in? Was it hard to chat with the other guests because they were so different from your friends and neighbors? Did the whole experience make you uncomfortable? If so, you were probably out of your cluster.

For two decades, market researchers have been trying to quantify consumers' comfort levels. They use a statistical technique called cluster analysis to manipulate data from the decennial census, syndicated surveys, and other sources. Their efforts result in systems that classify U.S. neighborhoods by their residents' demographics, attitudes, purchase behavior, and media habits.

"Geodemographic" cluster systems compare and sort U.S. neighborhoods on the basis of their median household incomes, the educational attainment and occupations of residents, homeownership rates, family types, age groups, and dozens of other characteristics. They assign neighborhoods with similar characteristics to a common category, or "cluster." Through a continuous process of "smoothing"—a statistician's term for rounding off similar numbers until they appear the same— market researchers usually settle on a system that uses several dozen cluster categories to describe all U.S. neighborhoods.

Some companies have invested a lot of time and effort to build in-house cluster systems that describe only their customers. But most marketers use one of the systems developed by marketing information companies for their clients. Off-the-shelf systems typically use catchy names to make each cluster instantly understandable. For example, MicroVision 50 from Equifax National Decision Systems has a cluster called "Upper Crust," and it's easy to imagine who they're talking about.

These systems are not perfectly accurate, but they're not meant to be. Their purpose is to predict consumer behavior more precisely than by mere chance, thereby giving users a competitive edge. And to a large extent, they work. Neighbors do tend to live in similar dwelling units, drive similar vehicles, and eat similar foods. Because of this fact, a good cluster system can roughly predict consumer expenditures and media preferences.

Cluster systems assign their consumer categories to small units of geography such as census tracts or zip codes, so it's easy to assign a category to any address.

This is how the respondents to syndicated media surveys, such as the ones sponsored by Mediamark Research Inc. (MRI) and Simmons Market Research Bureau, are categorized by cluster type. The survey-cluster connection is how we know which cluster types drive Chevrolet Blazers and which ones drive Ford Explorers.

One of the original and best uses of cluster systems is for direct mail. If some zip codes from a specific cluster group respond strongly to a mail offer, marketers can concentrate on other zip codes that have similar characteristics and ignore those that don't perform. When done well, this technique allows marketers to mail fewer pieces and get higher response rates by cutting waste.

One advantage cluster systems have over traditional mass-marketing efforts is that their results can be measured. You can't build a good cluster system without good statisticians, and high-quality statistical techniques generally produce better cluster systems. But the systems can be judged entirely on how well they work. This can be very comforting if you don't know the difference between a regression analysis and a skewness test.

Another good use of cluster systems is easing communication with people who don't understand statistical methods. Explaining the interactions between age, income, and homeownership to a media buyer can be next to impossible; it is much easier to say that the desired audience belongs to a cluster of middle-class, middle-aged homeowners, and that same cluster reads a particular magazine. If the customers for a product and the readers of a publication are from the same clusters, the buyer will get the most benefit from advertising in that publication.

Attempting an in-house cluster system requires bravery, lots of time, and deep pockets. Most market researchers lack at least one of these qualities, so they turn to a marketing information company for help. The demographic experts who build Claritas's PRIZM, Strategic Mapping's ClusterPLUS 2000, and other systems are continually refining their efforts, for one simple reason: any improvement in their system's ability to predict consumer behavior will give their company a competitive edge when they seek your business. And when they find an edge, the results show up on your bottom line.

Below, Michael Mancini of Claritas describes how his company's cluster system was used to build a comprehensive marketing campaign. An explanation of the nuts and bolts of cluster systems by demographer Barbara Clark O'Hare follows, and the article concludes with specific information about the systems offered by major marketing information companies. We hope that our coverage will give you fast, permanent relief from confusion and other cluster headaches.

II. Putting the Pieces Together
by Michael Mancini

It's easy to spend lots of money pushing your product. Unfortunately, marketing and advertising campaigns aren't considered successful unless their cost is exceeded by the revenue they generate. Companies succeed at marketing by meeting two goals. First, they control their marketing costs through targeting. Second, they measure the effects of their efforts by linking marketing data to sales.

Building a successful marketing campaign is a matter of answering a series of complex questions. Who are your customers? Who could become a customer if you asked them? Who will never become a customer? Where does each group live? What advertising and promotional messages will work best on each group? Where are the best media choices for those ads? Each question, when answered, provides one piece of the puzzle.

Cluster analysis can help you put these pieces together quickly and efficiently. The following article shows how a group of college students used cluster analysis to solve the puzzle for Chevrolet Blazer dealers in the Washington, D.C. area.

Sales of Blazers were declining in the Washington area, while sales of the Ford Explorer were growing rapidly. Chevrolet dealers in Washington needed a campaign that would persuade more potential buyers to stop by for a test drive. They also wanted to establish the S-10 Blazer as a leader and pioneer among sport-utility vehicles in the minds of their potential customers.

According to Webster's, the word "blaze" means "to lead or pioneer in a direction or activity." The word "blazing" means having "outstanding power, speed, and intensity." To associate these images with the Blazer, the student group came up with the slogan "The Power to Blaze." They also decided that their advertising needed to stress the theme of leadership.

After settling on the general theme, it was time to find the puzzle pieces and put them together. Here's how the students created a profile of actual and potential Blazer buyers, designed advertising that spoke to the attitudes and values of each target group, identified the print and television media choices of the target groups, and ran a promotional campaign to attract potential customers.

The student group's first job was to understand sport-utility-vehicle owners in general and Chevy S-10 Blazer owners in particular. The group conducted focus groups and mail surveys to get a picture of the typical Blazer-owning household. The result was a portrait of "Bill and Barb Blazer," a married couple with children who live in an outer suburb of Washington, D.C. Bill and Barb are in their mid-30s, and each has a professional job. They own two vehicles, a Pontiac Bonneville and a Chevy S-10 Blazer. Bill uses the Blazer on weekdays to commute to his job in Crystal City, a nearby Virginia suburb, while Barb uses it on the weekends for grocery shopping and other errands. They like their Blazer for three main reasons: the safety of driving a larger car with a driver's seat positioned above other traffic, providing greater visibility; the security of four-wheel drive and anti-lock brakes; and the power of a large engine. The three key words are safety, security, and power.

Bill and Barb's demographics are similar to thousands of Washington-area couples, so the students turned to a cluster system to find more detailed information about Blazer owners. PRIZM combines demographic data from the Census Bureau with consumer-purchase data from syndicated surveys to classify neighborhoods into demographically and behaviorally distinct "cluster" types. The geographies classified by PRIZM include zip codes, census tracts and block groups, and even zip+4 areas. The PRIZM model used by this group consisted of 40 clusters—it has since been replaced by an updated version with 62 clusters.

The group found S-10 Blazer buyers in the Washington and Hagerstown, Maryland ADIs (Areas of Dominant Influence) by using 1991 truck registration data from the R. L. Polk Corporation. The Polk database is geocoded, meaning a PRIZM code can be (and in this case was) attached to it.

The Polk data confirmed the students' survey finding that Blazer owners tend to be middle-class, while-collar families. The strongest PRIZM clusters for Blazers have names like Young Suburbia and God's Country. But they also found potential in middle-class, blue-collar, small-town clusters like Blue-Collar Nursery and Coalburg and Corntown.

Forty clusters are too many to target, so the group further consolidated the PRIZM clusters into eight target groups. Five of the groups buy Blazers at rates near or above the market average. Groups that are more likely than average to buy Blazers are Young Urban Families, Smalltown/Rural Families, and Blue-Collar Satellites. Groups near the market average are Affluent Suburban Families and Urban Gentry. These five account for 83 percent of Blazer buyers and 65 percent of Washington-area households. Naturally, these groups received most of the marketers' attention.

The PRIZM profile revealed that Ford Explorers had become more popular than Blazers among the key Affluent Suburban Families segment. One of the campaign's main objectives, then, was to make inroads into this group. One Blazer stronghold was outer-ring suburban areas filled with Young Metro Families, but Explorers were also popular in these areas. In more remote, mid-scale, blue-collar satellite suburbs, Blazer ownership was well above average, while Explorer ownership was far below average. Chevrolet needed to maintain its market dominance in the more rural target groups.

Another group, the Urban Gentry, presented Chevrolet with a unique opportunity to maintain Blazer sales and generate new growth. While smaller than the other target groups in size and number of sales, this group showed sales rates 6 percent above the market average. All other sport-utility vehicles, including the Explorer, had below-average sales for this segment.

The next step was finding the neighborhoods in the Washington, Baltimore, and Hagerstown areas that had concentrations of the target groups. Using PRIZM, the students generated a map showing where target clusters were prevalent. Then it was time to answer the next question: What are the customers' lifestyles?

Probably the most important target group was Affluent Suburban Families, for two reasons: First, these households tend to be innovators and opinion leaders, and second, they can afford nearly any vehicle they want. When people in this cluster do buy an S-10 Blazer, they tend to get the upscale "Tahoe" version. A fully loaded Blazer matches their lifestyle of foreign travel, golfing, and sailing. Like other affluent adults, they are not heavy television viewers, but they are heavy readers. They have a special fondness for business publications such as *The Wall Street Journal* and *Forbes.*

Young Metro Families are tomorrow's Affluent Suburban Families. They are college-educated, have white-collar jobs, and are either newly married childless couples or couples with younger children. They are heavy users of a variety of consumer products, and they lead health-oriented, active lifestyles. They also prefer reading over television, and they subscribe to such publications as *Money* and *National Geographic.* The specialty segment Urban Gentry is related to this group: it consists primarily of college-educated black families with mid- to upper-level incomes.

Like Young Metro Families, Blue-Collar Satellites and Smalltown/Rural Families tend to have school-aged children. But the breadwinners in these households are more likely to be employed in skilled crafts, manufacturing jobs, or agriculture. Their lifestyles center around outdoor activities such as power boating, camping, and fresh-water fishing: in other words, they like to get dirty on purpose. They are heavy users of television and other broadcast media. These groups constitute the largest proportion of current Blazer owners. They are the core of the Blazer's market.

The next step was to develop targeted print advertising. The students decided to develop three newspaper and magazine ads aimed at three separate target markets. Each ad defined the word "blaze" in ways that correspond to the lifestyle of the target audience. The ads were mostly done in black and white, but each featured a bright-red Blazer to catch the reader's attention. The slogan "The Power to Blaze" was featured in each ad.

The ad for Affluent Suburban Families showed a woman architect standing next to her four-door Tahoe Blazer at a Washington-area construction site. The ad conveyed her professional leadership in a city with one of the highest rates of labor force participation for women. The ad copy emphasized the Blazer's pioneering spirit; its leadership position in safety, on-the-fly four-wheel drive, and anti-lock brakes; and the Tahoe's luxurious "car-like" features, such as leather seating and a CD player. It was designed to run in several local print media favored by affluent suburbanites. These included *Washingtonian* magazine, the Friday *Washington Post,* and the *Washington Times.*

The ad for Young Metro Families shows a family on its way to a beach vacation. They are using a four-door standard edition S-10 Blazer ostensibly because of its affordability, versatility, and reliability. The ad features a father with his two children and speaks to his concern for his family's well-being and safety. It emphasizes the security he feels when driving a Blazer with anti-lock brakes and four-wheel drive. This ad was to be placed in the Washington regional issue of *Redbook* magazine, the *Washington Post,* and the *Washington Times.*

The last print ad, aimed at the small-town clusters, stresses the Blazer's power, speed, and intensity. It shows a two-door Blazer owned by a firefighter from Winchester, Virginia. The ad says that the man enjoys his Blazer because it is powerful, rugged, and reliable—just like him. It was designed to be placed in the *Washington Post* and a regional edition of *Field & Stream* magazine.

The choice of specific media options like *Field & Stream* or *Redbook* was not left to chance. Mediamark and Simmons data, which are included in PRIZM, show that *Washingtonian* is one of the most effective local magazines for reaching Affluent Suburban Families. *Redbook* is one of the few family-oriented publications with a regional insertion capability, and *Field & Stream* has broad appeal among white men in the Blue-Collar Satellite and Smalltown/Rural Families groups. Because these targets are already likely to choose a Blazer, the group recommended using *Field & Stream* only if the dealer's budget allowed it.

Another source used to make media choices was Scarborough Research, which conducts local readership surveys for magazines and newspapers in the top 55 markets nationwide. The marketers used Scarborough to evaluate how well the *Washington Post* and its competitor, the *Washington Times,* reached the target groups.

The *Washington Times* has a smaller, more upscale reader profile than the *Post.* It outperformed the *Post* among the Affluent Suburban Families and Young Metro Families clusters, so it was chosen for the architect and family-vacation ads. The *Post* is the clear choice of small-town, blue-collar readers, so it got an exclusive on the firefighter ad. But the *Post's* circulation is four times as large as the *Times's,* so the group decided to use it for all three ads. To save money and get a tighter focus, different ads were placed in zip-code zoned editions, according to the cluster composition of each zone, as freestanding inserts. With this tactic, each ad could reach its target with an appropriate message.

Weekly suburban newspapers are another way to reach affluent suburban households. The group selected 14 suburban papers in the region that matched various target groups and planned to run ads in each weekly paper according to the cluster characteristics of its circulation area.

The next step was to design and place television advertising. Careful targeting of media is essential in this area, because of the great expense of producing and placing television ads. The group designed an ad that shows different models of sport-utility vehicles driving around Thomas Circle, a well-known Washington landmark. A Blazer enters the group and then leaves the circle; the other vehicles follow it up Massachusetts Avenue.

"BLAZE," says the announcer. "To lead and pioneer in some direction or activity. In the confusing world of sport-utility vehicles, there are ONLY two choices. You can EXPLORE where others have been, or BLAZE where others will follow. Chevrolet S-10 Blazer . . . the power to BLAZE!"

The TV ads displayed only 12 Chevy dealer locations at a time. But with a targeted television campaign, the group was able to rotate the 12 dealers based upon the target group composition of the dealer's trade area and the placement of the television spot.

To further refine their television media buys, the students examined the local television viewing habits of each target audience. The group identified shows on broadcast networks that had high viewership among the groups they wanted to reach. But they saw added potential in cost-effective targeting by analyzing the reach and composition of Washington-area cable-TV audiences. Using syndicated survey data from Simmons, the students examined viewership of various cable networks by their target groups. They examined viewership by target group for 14 of the largest commercial cable networks.

Two of the target groups—Affluent Suburban Families and Young Metro Families—are not heavy users of television. Their cable viewing habits tend to center around informational channels like CNN, ESPN, CNBC, and A&E. However, Blue-Collar Satellite Families and Smalltown/Rural Families are heavy users of all forms of television. Unlike the white-collar groups, these groups tend to watch entertainment channels like MTV, Nickelodeon, and WTBS. Finally, Urban Gentry households are heavy television viewers. Not surprisingly, they are the most likely of the four targets to watch Black Entertainment Television (BET). They also prefer VH-1 over MTV, although they watch both of these channels at above-average rates. Nearly all of the cable networks fare well within this target.

Using the Simmons profiles, the students created "network packages" for each target group—for example, buying time on A&E, CNN, ESPN, and CNBC/FNN to reach Affluent Suburbans. Each package was allocated a certain number of ads per week. When dealing with local cable systems, they placed the network packages appropriate to each cable system's franchise area. In this way, the "Power to Blaze"

TV campaign was slated to reach over 725,000 households, the vast majority of which are within the desired targets.

Carefully targeted print and television ads will raise awareness of the S-10 Blazer and position it as an alternative to the Ford Explorer. But the ultimate objective of the students' marketing campaign was to get prospects into Chevrolet dealerships for a test drive. To complete the puzzle, the group had to answer one last question: what kind of promotional campaign will draw shoppers into the showrooms?

The group created a contest that would send 20 winners on "Blaze Away" weekend packages, including the use of a Blazer for three days. People who showed up for test drives would also get a T-shirt printed with "The Power to Blaze" slogan.

To promote the contest, the group turned to one of cluster analysis's greatest strengths: creating a highly targeted mail campaign. They generated a mailing list of families in the target groups who live near Chevy dealerships and who own three-to five-year-old vehicles, making them the most likely targets for a new-vehicle purchase. Each mail package is a more detailed version of the architect, family, and fireman print ads, and the appropriate ad could be mailed to appropriate groups.

Now that the pieces were all together, it was time to tally up the bill. The group envisioned a four-week campaign under a low-budget and high-budget scenario. The low-budget option would cost $453,000; the higher scenario, $608,000. In the low-budget version, 43 percent of the cost goes to television to increase awareness and enhance the Blazer's image, 23 percent goes to print media that increases awareness and promotes the sweepstakes, and 31 percent supports a sweepstakes designed to get people into the showroom.

Here's how the specific costs break down. Television commercial production: $40,000. Television spot buys: $110,000, yielding a total GRP (Gross Ratings Points. Ratings points reflect the viewing audience for a particular show; GRP is the total number of ratings points produced by a given media buy) of 422 for the entire television viewing area and a GRP of 657 among target groups. Local cable buys: $45,000 to reach 725,000 homes, 90 percent of which are in target audiences. Print advertisement production: $12,000. Placement in two magazines: $20,000. *Post* and *Times* newspaper placements: $52,000. Suburban newspaper placements: $36,000. Promotion: $85,000, including independent auditor. Direct-mail campaign: $55,000 for 50,000 pieces.

The "targeting" budget for this campaign constituted a small fraction of the entire expense: approximately $15,000 (three Polk PRIZM profiles: $3,000 to $4,000; maps: $1,200; TV ratings data linked to PRIZM: $3,000 to $4,000; Simmons or MRI profiles and customer target analysis: $5,000). This figure is based on service bureau (pay-as-needed rather than licensed) data and analysis from Claritas.

This "investment" spending, however, helps ensure that the dealer group gets the biggest bang for its marketing buck. By identifying and understanding the key target groups, the dealerships could obtain tightly focused media buys and higher frequency within the targeted households. It's simply smarter to get higher GRPs within proven target groups. Also, targeting helps ensure more effective promotional themes and creative elements directed at specific consumer types.

The moral of the story: a small investment in behaviorally based lifestyle targeting can boost the power and effectiveness of any marketing budget-providing, you might say, the power to blaze.

III. The Art of Clustering
by Barbara Clark O'Hare

Cluster analysis depends as much on art as it does on statistical science. It's really a generic term for a number of statistical techniques that rely on numeric measures of similarity between units to classify the units into homogeneous groups. The first applications of these techniques came in the biological sciences, as researchers tried to merge hundreds of plant and animal specimens into categories that made sense. More recently, clustering has been dominated by marketers who try to merge diverse specimens of consumers into easily targeted groups.

The art of clustering requires the user to select appropriate characteristics and compare them across units. Cluster artists must also select appropriate measures of similarity to classify their units, and they must settle on an appropriate "cluster solution," or number of clusters, for a practical application.

Unlike a science, each cluster solution depends on the assumptions of the people who build it. It is no wonder, then, that competitors who all begin with the same U.S. census data have developed such varying systems. If you're shopping for a cluster system, you should have a good understanding of its uses before you buy it. You should also have a working knowledge of the technical differences between different systems, because so many marketing decisions will ultimately depend on the assumptions behind the system.

The first step in choosing a cluster system is to look at the needs of potential users. The users could include marketers, sales staff, planners, personnel managers, and any technicians or analysts who may work on the system after you buy it. Some users will want the system to help them more efficiently reach customers. Others will want to produce reports that make sense to time-pressured clients and top executives who have little grounding in statistics. And some users will demand that the system is technically sound and does not depend on unreliable assumptions, small sample sizes, or other statistical pitfalls.

Cluster systems condense thousands of data variables into just a few categories, so developing them requires a lengthy process of trials and reviews. For example, census data provide counts of individuals by 31 age groups and by 25 income breaks. What are the best measures of age and income for your system? It depends on who's asking the question.

A statistician may come up with an equation that does a wonderful job of discriminating units from one another but is incomprehensible to everyone else. A marketer may come up with a system that appears to describe consumer characteristics in razor-sharp detail, but depends on sample sizes too small to be trusted. Tom Hryniewicz, a research statistician for Strategic Mapping Inc.'s ClusterPLUS 2000, says that technicians often favor data elements that create tidy clusters but have few marketing applications. Marketers, he says, often insist that certain elements such as income be included in the system to provide an intuitive level of confidence.

A good cluster system should include data that are updated regularly, so the system can be re-examined on a frequent basis. But remember: every time a data element is added or thrown out, the characteristics of the final system will change.

Although a statistician can use many statistical means to arrive at a cluster solution, all clustering techniques do have common characteristics. There are two basic approaches to developing a cluster solution. In the first, the "hierarchical agglomerative method," units are compared in stages. Each unit starts in its own "cluster." Then the two most similar units are combined, creating one less cluster of units. The process continues, gradually combining similar clusters and reducing the number of clusters in the solution. This process continues until all units have been assigned to one of two clusters. The analyst must then decide what number of clusters is most appropriate for the intended use of the cluster solution.

The second basic approach to clustering is through an "iterative partitioning method." In this method, the number of clusters in the solution is specified before the analysis begins. The units are then assigned to clusters, and the relative homogeneity of each cluster is examined. Units are gradually reassigned to clusters to make each cluster more homogeneous, like oranges of different sizes being thrown into sorting bins. The process is repeated until the clusters are as homogeneous as possible and as distinct as possible from each other.

Each of these two methods depends on subjective judgments to find the appropriate number of clusters. The final cluster solution needs to provide sufficient differentiation of units, but it can't contain so many clusters that it becomes difficult to use. The clusters must be distinctive, and the distinctions must be easy to recall.

Some cluster systems sidestep this dilemma by taking broader categories of units and breaking them down into smaller clusters. In a geodemographic system, this may mean that a cluster of middle-income suburban households might be further differentiated into "subclusters" of different types of middle-income suburban households.

As they develop the system, analysts carefully examine the impact of individual data items, the measures of similarity, and the differing techniques. Their goal, according to Doug Haley of Yankelovich Partners, is to see "what is driving the cluster." Finally, each cluster in the final solution must stand up to the tests of the end users and the system developers.

The marketing information companies that sell cluster systems are always searching for an edge on their competition. Recently, some of them have begun pushing their systems to describe smaller and smaller units of geography. Although detailed "sample" census data are only available down to the block group level, new techniques, including the blending of census and household-specific databases, are being examined to develop systems to target at the block group or even the household level.

Another trend is the development of tailored segmentation systems that focus on specific consumer characteristics. The "readership clusters" recently developed by Mediamark and Yankelovich are two examples of classification systems that differentiate consumers based on specific behaviors.

Some marketing information companies have also developed industry-specific cluster systems. "Different aspects [of a cluster system] are important to different industries," says Dave Miller of Claritas. For example, life-insurance companies are particularly interested in family structure and how it changes over time. Financial-services companies are keenly interested in household income, and advertising agencies must have good data on magazine reading and TV viewing.

Specialized cluster systems are now offered for the financial services and automotive industries, while advertising agencies can use systems from Mediamark and Yankelovich that link magazine readership with purchase behavior. Other available systems key on the Hispanic market and TV viewers.

The move toward industry-specific segmentation systems has a natural limit, says Miller. That is because a system is only useful if it can be linked with other information to enable the user to reach the potential consumers. If your system can't be linked with other databases that develop mailing lists or help you buy media, it has few marketing uses.

Cluster systems are continually being upgraded to offer a finer and finer-grained picture of your customers. But they will always depend on a few simple statistical techniques, and their developers will always use a mixture of art and science.

IV. Where to Buy Cluster Systems
by Claudia Montague

There are four neighborhood-level and two household-based consumer market segmentation systems. The first four listed below are general-purpose cluster systems that have been developed by consumer information companies. They are based on the 1990 census and enhanced with lifestyle data or other consumer information from syndicated consumer studies or demographic updates.

The other two cluster systems use the household as their basic unit of analysis. They were created by direct-marketing firms and are used primarily for list selection and enhancement purposes.

Neighborhood-based cluster products:

ACORN: This system has 40 residential clusters with vivid names, ranging from "Top One Percent" to "Distressed Neighborhoods." For more information, contact CACI Marketing Systems, 1100 North Glebe Road, Arlington, VA 22201; telephone (800) 292-2224.

ClusterPLUS 2000: This system offers 60 neighborhood cluster designations, with letter/number identifiers from the top echelon (S01) to the bottom (C57). Each of the 60 clusters is further divided into 8 sub-clusters. For more information, contact Strategic Mapping Inc., P.O. Box 120058, 70 Seaview Avenue, 5th Floor, Stamford, CT 06912; telephone (203) 353-7270.

MicroVision 50: This system contains 50 general-purpose clusters, ranging from "Upper Crust" to "Urban Singles." There are also 95 working clusters for doing industry-specific segmentation. For more information, contact Equifax National Decision Systems, 5375 Mira Sorrento Place, Suite 400, San Diego, CA 92121; telephone (800) 866-6510.

PRIZM: Next Generation: PRIZM, one of the oldest lifestyle cluster segmentation systems, was first introduced 20 years ago. It has recently been updated to include 62 segments for different industrial applications, compared with the previous 40. Cluster names reflect lifestyles, degrees of affluence, and other distinctions from "Blue Blood Estates" to "Public Assistance." For more information, contact Claritas, 201 North Union Street, Alexandria, VA 22314; telephone (800) 284-4868.

Household-based cluster products:

Cohorts: This system has 33 segments, each of which is identified by a pair of names that reflects the type of people ("Margot and Elliott," "Clyde and Opal") who belong to it. For more information, contact National Demographics and Lifestyles (NDL), 1621 Eighteenth Street, Denver, CO 80202; telephone (303) 292-5000.

Niches: A general-purpose segmentation system with 26 clusters reflecting consumers from "Already Affluent" to "Zero Mobility." The clusters themselves are divided into five categories according to income range. For more information, contact Polk Direct, 6400 Monroe Boulevard, Taylor, MI 48180; telephone (313) 292-3200.

Using Focus Group Research

by William Weylock
July/August 1994
Marketing Tools

You hear a lot about focus groups these days—at cocktail parties, in business meetings, and even on television sitcoms. You also read a lot about focus groups—in national magazines, in business journals, and even in college-level textbooks.

On the positive side, you hear that focus groups have helped political campaigns, increased sales of faltering products, raised customer satisfaction levels, and helped build award-winning advertising campaigns. Some accounts make it sound as if focus groups are an almost magical technique, working marketing miracles with little help from human beings.

On the negative side, you hear that groups are unscientific voodoo—a crutch for lazy and irresponsible marketers. Pointing out correctly that groups are easily misused, detractors go on to damn the entire approach as pseudo-research.

I make a lot of my living from focus groups, so you won't be surprised that I come down on the positive side. It's my contention that if focus groups are used when appropriate, and if they are properly designed, conducted, and analyzed, they are extremely valuable.

On the other hand, I agree that if they are used for inappropriate tasks, if they are designed carelessly or run by unskilled moderators, and if they are not analyzed carefully by a professional, they can be dangerously misleading.

Many people have the idea that focus groups are an alternative to surveys and other quantitative research. This notion is simply not true, and it causes a lot of trouble for both marketers and marketing researchers. In fact, focus groups and surveys are ideal partners.

Groups can generate questions to be asked in surveys. They generate hypotheses that can be tested quantitatively. They can also help phrase survey questions properly, in language that really speaks to respondents.

Jerry is a political campaign manager in a Senate race. He needs to market his client to the broadest possible audience and avoid offending as many people as possible. He needs research into the public's opinion on issues facing the state.

He can conduct a survey asking how many people approve of this or disapprove of that, but he wants something more useful. He wants to know what kinds of things his candidate should be saying in response to these problems.

He needs to know what different points of view there are on the key issues, how many people hold each opinion, how firm their positions are, what might change them, and what kinds of programs seem appealing in response.

His first problem is that he doesn't really know how to ask questions about some of the issues. They are complicated, and he doesn't want to use language that the public will not understand. He also wants to be careful not to bias the responses by inadvertently using inappropriate language to describe them.

Jerry convenes several focus groups of frequent voters and opinion leaders (important, because who wants to hear from people who won't play a role in the election?). The groups discuss the issues in general and provide many insights into how voters talk about things among themselves, how the various issues interrelate, what differences of opinion there are, and how concerns might be met.

Jerry then does a survey to find out how many people in the state feel each issue is important and how they feel it should be addressed. His candidate emerges with live ammunition to use in the campaign.

Groups can also be used to probe issues that emerge in quantitative studies. Let's suppose Jerry's candidate is being hammered in the polls. His credibility goes way down, and surveys reveal that voters "don't relate well" to him.

Focus groups can pull together people who say they "don't relate" to the candidate. Under careful moderation, they can discuss what it is about Jerry's candidate that rubs them the wrong way. They can watch commercials and television appearances and point to key moments:

"There! When he shifts his eyes like that. You can tell he doesn't believe what he's saying."

"It always seems as if he's angry at the reporters. They're just doing their job."

"I don't like the way he crosses his legs."

All of those things are changeable. Since the numbers show that the problem is real and not just the cranky opinion of a few picky people, it is probably worth Jerry's while to coach the candidate on public behavior.

For another example, an advertising agency sends three test television commercials out for audience response analysis. The agency's favorite commercial scores low on persuasiveness. Of course, the client has no interest in producing a commercial that has tested poorly. The agency believes in the approach, but does not understand what to do in order to make a more persuasive commercial.

Focus group respondents can look at the three commercials and discuss them among themselves, going deeply into the reactions they have to various elements and sharing their views. The moderator can suggest ways in which the commercial might be altered to make it more persuasive, and the panel can give feedback on which changes might be effective.

It is fairly easy to see why the match of focus groups and surveys works well. It may not be quite so easy to see why using only one method has risks.

If Jerry does a survey on the issues without doing the focus groups, he may not ask the right questions. Or he may not ask the questions in the right way—and if questions are not very carefully phrased, they can bias answers. If some people misunderstand the question, even slightly, they may be providing incorrect answers. Later, when Jerry and his team look to the survey results for guidance, they may be misled.

If Jerry merely accepted the results of the other survey and didn't do focus groups to follow it up, he might conclude that the candidate should smile more, kiss more babies, or trot out his family. None of those things would work, because the key problems would not have been identified.

If Jerry does the focus groups without the survey, he runs an even greater risk. The campaign may respond perfectly to a concern that is shared by only a few people who happened to come to the focus groups. They may waste precious media dollars that could be spent on issues that concern a much broader segment of the public.

If the candidate responds to one or two focus groups without any polls to indicate that he's in any kind of trouble, he might stop crossing his legs, start chatting with reporters, and stare directly into the camera at all times. In fact, these may not have been problems at all, and the wider public might lose their identification with him as his "personality" changes in public appearances. ("Why has he started sucking up to the press?")

For some reason, when surveys are proved wrong, people question the skill of the pollsters. When focus groups are misused or presented as completed research without supporting quantitative data, groups get blamed for being "unscientific" or "misleading." Focus groups are quite "scientific." They are simply not a substitute for statistical sampling techniques.

Surveys, by the way, are not all "science." There is considerable art to constructing appropriate questions and putting them in the appropriate order. There is also a great deal of intuition required for constructing the questionnaire and performing the analysis.

These general rules should be helpful, but knowing what kind of research to perform for what kind of marketing issue is an art in and of itself. It's one of the main things a research consultant, familiar with various techniques and options, can provide. At least, you should be better prepared to approach a researcher, and should have a better sense of why you need to.

Measure for Measure: Market Research in the 1990s

by David G. Bakken
April/May 1994
Marketing Tools

Look around at a typical corporate marketing research department, and you might notice that, compared with a few years ago, there are fewer people doing more work. Marketing research was not spared from the pressure of downsizing. Look more closely, and you'll notice that in addition to a leaner team, there have been some profound changes in the content of marketing research.

Customer satisfaction measurement, the growth sector in the research industry, is the most visible manifestation of a trend that is changing the way companies view and use customer-focused information. Research has gradually shifted from "studies" that try to comprehend the buyer's psyche at a level that might rival psychoanalysis to "measurement systems" that monitor a few select indicators managers can use to determine appropriate courses of action. Researchers and users of research must understand the requirements they will be expected to meet as this trend gathers momentum.

In 1981, when I began my career as a marketing research professional, the trendy tools were strategic marketing theories championed by the Boston Consulting Group (remember Cash Cows, Rising Stars, and Dogs?) and other gurus. Researchers mastered perceptual mapping, market segmentation, conjoint analysis, and simulated test markets such as BASES and ASSESSOR. Marketing strategy focused on matching a customer's desires with a firm's core strengths, and much corporate energy and person-hours were expended identifying those core strengths and writing mission statements. Niche marketing emerged as we realized that money could be made by selling premium-priced products to smaller, homogeneous and price-insensitive groups of customers. Product positioning was a big concept. Psychographic and geodemographic segmentation services emerged, promising new ways of identifying consumers' hot buttons.

At least three major trends that are now reshaping the industry started about the same time. While most users were collecting frequent-flyer miles to watch focus groups or do brief mall interviews, the seeds of a research revolution were being sown in supermarkets around the country. Information Resources, Inc. leveraged a new technology and more or less invented electronic point-of-purchase data collection. The result was data on consumer behavior that were both timely and sensitive to the impact of price, in-store promotion, couponing, and advertising. Brand managers suddenly had access to information that revealed the effectiveness of the tools they were using to influence consumers. Moreover, the scanner data provided diagnostic information. Scanner panels made possible the application of existing analytic methods, such as brand-switching models, that previously had been limited to academic investigation.

Outside of the consumer packaged-goods world, business-to-business marketers and service organizations, many of which had been primarily sales-driven or product-driven, were discovering marketing and the benefits of marketing research. The concept of customer satisfaction really emerged in these organizations as they began to realize the importance of maintaining repeat business.

A third trend began with changing ideas about the use of information in managing a business. Total Quality Management, or TQM, placed a premium on gathering information that would aid specifically in improving processes within the organization. This has been accompanied by a back-to-basics movement, as companies appear to place less emphasis on vision and more on actually running their businesses.

Finally, many managers looked at the mountains of computer printouts and research reports being generated from survey data and threw up their hands in despair. There was no shortage of data. But information, especially information that could be acted upon, was in short supply.

As these trends converge, a greater proportion of research expenditures and energy will be directed toward managing the three Rs of marketing: recruiting new customers, retaining existing customers, and regaining lost customers. This research will focus on cause-and-effect relationships between actions that management can take and the behavior of customers. Once cause-and-effect relationships have been determined, usually in a benchmarking study, systematic measurement systems will be employed to monitor the causal factors and predict changes in customer behavior. "Exploratory" and "descriptive" studies—especially those that seek to understand what is going on in the customer's mind—will be commissioned much less frequently. In hindsight, the reason for this shift appears obvious. If the knowledge gained from old-fashioned research can't sharpen the tools marketers have to work with, the research is of little use.

A closer look at each of the three Rs will provide some insight into the tools that both marketers and marketing researchers will need to thrive into the next decade.

Researchers devote far more effort to acquiring customers than to retaining existing customers or regaining lost customers. Advertising tracking surveys, market segmentation, and multi-attribute product positioning models are all designed to match buyers to the right products and services. If the purpose of marketing is to match the benefits a firm has to offer with the benefits that customers seek, then marketing research should naturally focus on that matchmaking process. The major shortcoming of such studies is that they provide little understanding of the impact of specific marketing actions on customer behavior. They also offer no understanding of the interactions between those different actions, such as increasing ad spending while decreasing the size of the sales force.

Research that helps a firm acquire new customers must focus on a much more complex set of factors, including distribution channels, sales contact, word of mouth, previous experience with the firm's products and services, the actions taken by competing companies, advertising and sales promotions. In the past, "marketing mix" decisions often involved allocations among different advertising and promotional vehicles. A few leading-edge manufacturers and service companies have now realized that the marketing mix consists of all the resources the firm can commit to the challenge of acquiring customers.

Researchers will need to use causal models that predict customer choice. These might include logistic regression and multinomial logit, as well as techniques such as discriminant analysis and log-linear modeling. A typical model will sort out the relative importance of direct sales, advertising weight, brand image, and satisfaction with the current brand to a consumer's purchase decision. Different customers have different experiences when facing different products, so the models will be more sophisticated than we might have seen in the past.

The ability to communicate clearly about one's modeling efforts will be another required skill. Researchers will succeed by translating the complex interrelationships they find in a dataset into actions that management can take.

For their part, users must recognize the need to cover all marketing resources in the research effort. They must also have the ability to understand and appreciate interrelationships between these resources. Greater integration of sales, marketing, and distribution functions within the user organization may be necessary to realize the benefits of the new information.

In some respects, customer satisfaction measurement is the original key indicator measurement system. As companies began to realize the financial value of retaining existing customers, they sought a measure that would reveal a firm's success in satisfying its existing customers. The situation becomes more difficult when the goal is understanding why customers are satisfied or dissatisfied. Current customers, former customers, competitors' customers, and prospective customers can provide valuable information on the experiences that contribute to satisfaction.

Customer retention research will require similar modeling skills, with an emphasis on linear regression, path analysis, or structural equation modeling. Users will place a premium on satisfaction measurement systems that clearly prioritize problems so they can allocate resources effectively.

Of course, modeling the determinants of customer satisfaction is only one step toward the goal of retaining customers. Predicting which customers are likely to become ex-customers is equally important. Customer databases, especially those that are transaction-based, will provide new ways of identifying events that are most likely to lead to customer defection. For example, an office-equipment manufacturer might determine that a rise in the frequency of service calls precedes cancellation of a service contract on a piece of equipment. The firm might also determine that cancellation of a service contract is often associated with the purchase of a new machine, usually from a competitor. A database could be designed to flag customers that exhibit the pattern associated with defection so that some action can be taken.

By now it may be apparent that recruiting new customers, retaining existing customers, and regaining lost customers are not three separate problems with different solutions. The information gained in the service of the first two Rs should help manage the third. The modeling techniques mentioned above will also help to distinguish those who leave from those who stay. Communication tools, such as Pareto analysis, will be useful here as well.

Where is the research industry right now? Many companies have implemented key indicator measurement systems to aid in retaining existing customers. The services offered by research consultants are similarly focused on retaining customers through customer satisfaction measurement. A few firms have implemented measurements to understand the root causes of defections.

In the near future (if it has not happened already), some major manufacturer or service organization is likely to roll out an integrated key indicator measurement system covering all three Rs. This system will provide those bits of information that are critical for choosing between alternative actions and allocating resources across each of the three Rs as well as to different actions within each objective on an ongoing basis.

Potential customers, existing customers, and former customers will be included in this comprehensive program. The analysis will be complete within a month of data collection, and the interconnections between acquisition, retention, and winback will be displayed graphically on a mere handful of slides (key indicators only!) at quarterly management meetings.

Marketers will continue to ask questions and require information that can be provided only by ad hoc descriptive and exploratory research. But key indicator measurement systems are likely to command the lion's share of marketing research resources as we approach the new millennium.

Bye Buy Blues: Understanding Advertising Options

by Katy Bachman
July/August 1995
Marketing Tools

L ocal media salespeople. They come to your office with a shoeshine and a smile. They speak an incomprehensible dialect, using words like "huts," "puts," "cumes," "rotations," "insertions," and "showings." Each one claims to be representing the number-one choice among affluent, upscale adults aged 25 to 54 with an index of something or other above 120—and has a set of figures to "prove" it.

"What has this got to do with getting customers into my store?" you ask yourself.

Advertising is one of the basic tools of the retail business. The premise: tell people who you are, where you are, what products or services you offer, and why you offer a better value. The goal: get paying customers into your store. The problem: which ad media to invest in, and how much to spend?

This article won't answer all your questions. Every market, every advertiser is different. What it will do is provide you with the questions to ask so that you can pry the answers out of the parade of media salespeople who are knocking on your door, presentation in hand.

The four major "mass media" options we'll explore are newspapers, television (both broadcast and cable), radio, and outdoor. Each has its own strengths and weaknesses.

Most cities today are one-paper towns. The combination of rising costs and a declining readership base has pushed marginal papers over the brink or forced morning and afternoon competitors to merge operations. Despite tough times on the operations side, however, more advertising dollars in local markets go to newspapers than to all the radio and TV stations combined.

One of the biggest strengths of a newspaper ad is that it is so tangible. You can cut out your full-page ad and post it on a placard. You can see a stack of newspapers at a newsstand and know that every one has your ad in it. And a tear sheet is the easiest way to verify your ad schedule when it's time to collect your co-op dollars. All these attributes are a big edge that savvy newspaper account executives use to their advantage.

What is newspaper best at? Price item advertising. Every day or every week, a newspaper can put a catalog of the goods and services you have to offer in the hands of potential consumers. Your ad can have even more impact when it's placed in a relevant special section, such as those devoted to automotive, fashion, food, or entertainment. (But don't let the newspaper rep tell you that everyone who reads the newspaper reads every section—ask to see their section readership information.)

Even as it nears the half-century mark, television is still the most glamorous of the local media options. There are TV news shows about TV shows and TV stars. There are even TV specials about TV commercials. It's not for nothing that print ads for mail-order gadgets boast "as seen on TV."

In terms of ad dollars, television stations are the second biggest ad medium. In most cities, you typically have three to four commercial stations to chose from—several network affiliates (stations who agree to carry programming and advertisements originating from ABC, CBS, NBC, and, lately, Fox) and an independent. In the last year, new networks like Paramount and Warner Brothers have signed on a lot of formerly independent stations as affiliates. Networks are a great vehicle for national advertisers, but by soaking up commercial slots on formerly independent stations, the emergence of new networks has so far meant that local advertisers end up paying more for the spots that are left over.

Television is best at covering a market. If you expect to draw customers from all over your market, TV makes sense. Just about every home in your city has a TV (98 percent is typical) and at least one person who watches it at least once a week. If your appeal is more localized, be sure to base your cost efficiencies solely on the area of the market you're concerned about. (Ask the TV station for audience figures broken out by counties or groups of zip codes.)

Another TV strength is building brand identity. When the big packaged-goods advertisers launch a new consumer product, TV advertising is at the top of their list. Done correctly, no other medium can establish an identity the way TV can. Don't scrimp on your commercial, however. Your ad could run next to a slick Toyota or AT&T spot and wind up looking like a "Saturday Night Live" parody by comparison. Nothing will ruin the impact of your TV advertising like poor technical quality and low "production values." With new TV technology, creating an effective TV spot doesn't have to cost a small fortune; even so, this is definitely not the place to cut corners.

Don't think you've got to buy the top-rated programs or just the top station to have an impact. Running more commercials on lower-rated programs is the ideal way to establish your identity in the minds of your customers. Be sure to stick to a consistent theme and message if you run more than one version of your commercial.

Cable looks like television to the viewer, but for the local advertiser it's very different. While viewers are watching the cable networks (ESPN, MTV, Nickelodeon), a local advertiser buys time in between the programs from the local cable system, the company that strings the coaxial cable and collects the subscription fees.

Local cable systems are relative newcomers to the advertising game. While the radio and TV broadcast outlets can reach everyone in the market, cable gets into fewer than seven in ten homes nationwide—and the rate in individual markets can vary from as low as 40 percent to as high as 90 percent. What's more, even the viewers in cable homes are likely to spend much of their time watching the standard broadcast stations; the typical local cable audience for any one network like MTV or ESPN isn't very large. On the other hand, cable advertising costs less than that of its over-the-air cousin, meaning you can run your spot more frequently for less money. A good many local advertisers wouldn't be on the tube at all if it weren't for the relatively modest cost of cable advertising.

Local cable is best at delivering the cachet of television, at a fraction of the cost of traditional TV advertising. However, there may be two or more cable systems in your market. And since cable audiences are so fragmented, you can't use cable instead of broadcast television if you're looking to cover the market or build an image quickly. The geography that a cable system covers is a key factor to consider.

You can also treat individual cable channels like sections of the newspaper. Run spots on ESPN if you're a sporting-goods store, MTV and VH1 if you're a record store. Cable seems to have a channel for just about every interest. However, don't think that every cable subscriber watches every cable channel all the time. Audiences for any individual cable channel are very small, but you can be sure the viewers you do get will be the right prospect for your product or service.

Radio is probably the most underrated ad medium. Just about everyone has a radio or two, or even three or four. And radio is the medium that can reach people while they drive to and from work and while they are working in the office.

In a typical market, there are more radio stations than TV stations, cable systems, and newspapers combined. At first glance, that makes buying radio advertising seem like a time-consuming and complicated business for a local advertiser. But hidden in this diversity is radio's strongest sales point—the ability to target a specific lifestyle or consumer group.

Today's radio stations focus their programming and promotions to reach a very carefully defined audience. The rock station always plays rock, the classical station always plays classical music, the all-news station only provides news. That means, more than any other medium, radio can be used to target a specific kind of consumer. Whatever your marketing goal, there's almost certainly a radio station or two to deliver the kind of audience to whom you want to sell your product or service.

The process of buying radio time has been made even less complicated by the emergence of a new trend in the business: so-called "duopolies." Until recently, federal law sharply restricted the number of radio stations that could be owned by any one entity. Today, one party can own several stations in one market, bringing efficiencies in operation to the owner and simplicity for buying advertising to the retailer while still preserving the diversity of programming that makes radio an interesting option.

Radio is best used for promotions and events tied to your advertising goals. A typical radio station has more flexibility in its on-air programming than television or newspaper. The on-air personalities can make your Fourth of July sale part of the programming by talking up the prize you are contributing to the station's contests or by broadcasting direct from your store. Contests at radio stations are more a part of the programming than they are in newspapers or TV.

Radio commercials are inexpensive to produce. The simplest spots require little more than a script and a tape recorder. If you want something more elaborate or creative, the radio station can put its studios and music library at your disposal to create an interesting and effective commercial for very little investment on your part. And local radio personalities who have loyal fans make great spokespersons for your store.

Like newspaper, outdoor advertising tends to be a one-supplier medium in most markets. The biggest advantage of billboards is that they can reach an audience without conscious effort on the part of the target (i.e., picking up a newspaper or tuning into a specific station). Also, like radio, outdoor is an "out of home" medium, an ideal way to reach consumers when they are on the go. And you can place your billboards where you need them, within the trading area from which you draw your customers.

Use billboards to reinforce a message or an image that you've established with other media. With the right creative, a billboard can extend the impact of your newspaper, TV, or radio campaigns. If you decide to go with outdoor, be prepared to go for the long haul. Most outdoor contracts require a commitment of six months to a year. It can take as long as a month to produce your billboard; don't expect to be able to change your ad as quickly as you can with newspaper, TV, or radio.

If your advertising message is simple and to the point, it's possible to get by on billboards alone. "Kids Eat Free" is about as complicated a message as you want to put on a poster that might get no more than seven to ten seconds of viewing time. Be sure your graphics are just as simple, bright, and bold as your message.

Given all the advertising options for a local retailer, how do you know if you're getting your money's worth? The key to judging the value of your ad schedule is in understanding the jargon those media salespeople speak when they knock on your door.

When you buy advertising, what you are really paying for are impressions. You pay for each time a pair of eyes looks at your ad or a pair of ears listens to it, whether or not those eyes (or ears) have seen (or heard) the spot before. That's why TV stations and radio stations are in the business of getting bigger ratings and newspapers strive for bigger circulation. It's not just bragging rights that these media are after; it's more eyes and ears to sell to you, the advertiser.

Advertising has a unit price just like the cost per pound you see on the price tag for prime rib. Instead of by the pound, advertising is sold based on its cost per thousand impressions or cost per rating point, which is another way to count impressions.

If the basic unit of advertising is the impression, then the basic question you need answered is how many impressions you are buying for your money. Newspapers tend to talk about their circulation in easy-to-understand numbers like 100,000 readers, or 75,000 readers per issue. Figuring impressions per expenditure is easy—simply multiply the number of readers per issue by the number of issues in which you run your ad.

Radio, TV, and outdoor sales reps will almost always talk in terms of ratings. A rating is simply 1 percent of the people in the category you are trying to reach. If a TV station says that its early news show delivers a 6 rating among Adults 25-54, the station means that 6 percent of all the adults aged 25 to 54 in your market watch that station's early news show. To find out how many impressions one ad in the early news will generate, simply calculate 6 percent of the total number of adults aged 25 to 54.

If you run five spots throughout the week in that station's early news show, then you have generated 5 times 6 ratings points, or 30 gross ratings points. If there are 550,000 Adults 25-54 in your market, then your five-spot schedule has generated 165,000 impressions (5 x .06 x 550,000) among Adults 25-54.

Stretching the butcher shop analogy just a bit, you can buy your prime rib as one big roast, or carve it up into a half dozen rib-eye steaks. It's up to you to decide whether you want to serve six people all at one dinner, or serve two people prime rib on three different occasions.

That's the idea behind the advertising concepts of reach (how many people am I reaching?) and frequency (how often am I reaching them?). Your 165,000 impressions can be 82,500 people reached twice, or 41,250 people reached four times. How often you need to reach people with your message depends on the amount of competition in your category. The more competition you face, the more frequently you need to rise above the clutter and make a favorable impression on your target consumers.

All these definitions lead us back to our basic measures of advertising's efficiency:

Cost per point. If you spend $400 per spot on an early news show that reaches 6 percent of Adults 25-54, you are paying $67 per ratings point ($400 divided by 6).

Cost per thousand. That same spot on the early news generates 33,000 impressions (.06 x 550,000). At $400 per spot, you are paying $82.50 per 1,000 impressions.

A word of caution: while cost per point or cost per 1,000 is one way to judge the value of an advertising schedule, don't use that as the only criterion, especially when comparing one medium to another. You wouldn't skip the prime rib just because potatoes cost less per pound. Like a balanced meal, each medium can play an appropriate role in getting customers to your store.

One final tip: If you are buying your ad schedule directly from the station or publication, ask for the traditional 15 percent agency commission as a discount. You just might get it!

For more information:

Industry Associations: Industry associations promoting a particular medium have all prepared handy guides for retailers and advertisers. While each unabashedly touts its advertising option as the best solution, all the guides have a wealth of information that can help you understand your local media options and use them properly once you've made your decision.

Billboards and Outdoor: Outdoor Advertising Association of America; telephone (212) 688-3667; fax (212) 752-1687.

Television: Cable Television Advertising Bureau, Inc.; telephone (212) 751-7770; fax (212) 832-3268. Television Bureau of Advertising; telephone (212) 486-1111; fax (212) 935-5631.

Radio: Radio Advertising Bureau; telephone (212) 387-2100; fax (212) 254-8713.

Newspaper: Newspaper Association of America; telephone (703) 648-1000; fax (703) 620-4557.

Professional Associations: Retail Advertising and Marketing Association International; telephone (312) 251-7262; fax (312) 251-7269.

Media Measurements Services: If you want to get your own copies of the local ratings report, you can go directly to the measurement companies that conduct the surveys. Prices for local retailers are affordable for the basic market report, and all are willing to help you understand the information you've purchased. Caution: ratings reports don't come with handy executive summaries about your customers; the books are page after page of numbers. Expect to spend time with them to get the most out of your investment.

Television and Cable: Nielsen Media Research; telephone (212) 708-7500; fax (212) 708-7795.

Radio: The Arbitron Company; telephone (212) 887-1300; fax (212) 887-1390.

Newspaper: Scarborough Research Corporation; telephone (212) 789-3560; fax (212) 789-3577.

Outdoor: Traffic Audit Bureau; telephone (212) 972-8075; fax (212) 972-8928.

Local Market Profiles: Media Audit; telephone (713) 626-0333; fax (713) 626-0418.

Huts, Puts, Purs, and Grps
A Glossary of Very Basic Media Terms

RATING: The audience expressed as a percentage of the total population. A rating of 5 equals 5 percent of all the people in the market.

SHARE: The percent of those listening to radio (or watching TV) who are listening to a particular radio station (or watching a particular TV station).

GROSS IMPRESSIONS: The total number of exposures (not total audience) to a commercial schedule. One person who sees your ad three times counts as three exposures.

GROSS RATING POINTS (GRPs): The sum of all ratings delivered by a commercial schedule, or the gross impressions expressed as a percentage of the population being measured.

COST PER POINT (CPP): A measure of the medium's efficiency. The cost to deliver 1 percent of the people in a demographic category.

COST PER THOUSAND (CPM): Another measure of the medium's efficiency. The cost to deliver your spot to 1,000 people or homes.

REACH: The number of different people who are exposed to a commercial schedule. Reach can also be expressed as a rating (percentage of the population being measured).

FREQUENCY: The average number of times a person is exposed to a commercial.

CUME: The total number of different people who are exposed to a schedule of commercials.

HUT: Households Using Television. The percent of households using television at a particular time of day.

PUT: Persons Using Television. The percent of people (in a particular category) using television at a particular time of day.

PUR: Persons Using Radio. The total of all listening in a market including listening to commercial, noncommercial, and unidentified radio stations.

DEMOGRAPHIC: Measures for each medium are often expressed in terms of age and sex. For example, Adults 25-54 is a demographic, as are Women 18-49 and Teens 12-17.

—*Claudia Montague*

We're Number One (among insomniac adult males aged 18 to 34 on alternate weekends between October and May)
A Quick Guide to Media Research

Of all the mass media, newspaper is the most straightforward when it comes to answering the question: How many people? The basic measure of newspaper's power as an ad medium is its circulation. It's the easiest number to track (number of papers printed less returns); most papers certify their circulation figures through the Audit Bureau of Circulation.

Finding out what kind of consumers these readers are is trickier. For that, newspapers use syndicated research services like Scarborough Research and Media Audit.

Scarborough Research surveys consumers in 58 markets. The company asks randomly selected consumers about their socioeconomic profiles, their shopping habits, what newspapers they read, the radio stations they listen to, and the kinds of TV programs they watch. Media Audit is a similar service profiling much the same information in 55 markets.

The value of Scarborough and Media Audit information is that these ratings services talk about a "Nordstrom shopper" or a "True Value shopper," describing that consumer in terms of income, occupation, the other stores they patronize, as well as the radio and TV stations they tune to and the newspapers they read. Unfortunately, their information isn't detailed enough to help you plan a schedule of television or radio spots, or to make decisions on prices.

The only way local television stations can know the size of their audience is to subscribe to the Nielsen ratings. The television research giant has attached the famous black boxes to a random sample of TV sets in the 30 largest markets, giving those stations and their advertisers a fix on the size of the TV audience 365 days a year. For the rest of the cities across America, the ratings firm sends out diaries to homes selected at random. These diaries are mailed out in February, May, July, and November (which is why all the good movies are on during those months!). Willing TV families keep the diaries for one week, writing down who is watching what broadcast or cable channel. The diaries are mailed back to Nielsen's processing center in Dunedin, Florida.

What comes back four times a year is a printed report on the size of TV audiences, defined primarily by the age and sex of the viewers. Socioeconomic information is very limited, and there are no comparisons to other media. For the local advertiser, combining TV ratings with information from qualitative services like Scarborough or Media Audit gives you the best picture of your customers and the media they use most often.

Unfortunately, TV jargon doesn't give a new-to-TV advertiser any easy way to understand how many people a TV spot in the afternoon news show will reach. Most TV ad sales folks talk about ratings, shares, HUTs, and PUTs (see the preceding glossary). However, all those terms can be translated into simple numbers like newspaper circulation figures. Don't bother to reach for your calculator. Ask the TV sales rep to do the conversions for you.

Like television, radio stations must subscribe to a ratings service to find out how big their audiences are. The leading radio research service is Arbitron, which measures radio station audiences in more than 260 markets. The company recruits households at random and then sends a diary to each person aged 12 and older. The diary is a simple booklet that people fill out for one week, noting when they listen to radio, the station they listen to, and where they are—at home, in the car, or at work. (Have you ever wondered why all the big money giveaways on radio stations are held on Thursday morning? Thursday is the first day of the Arbitron survey week.)

The diaries are mailed back to Arbitron's research and technology center in Columbia, Maryland for processing. In the top 94 markets, Arbitron issues audience reports every quarter with monthly updates in between. In the smallest markets, Arbitron issues reports covering the spring survey (April, May, and June) once a year in July. Medium-sized markets are measured twice a year: one in spring and one released in January, covering the fall survey (October, November, December).

Like television ratings reports, radio stations receive a printed report that details the size of their audiences for specific demographic breaks such as women aged 25 to 54, men aged 18 to 24, teens aged 12 to 17, and the like.

Again, radio sales reps tend to lapse into the same sort of jargon as their TV counterparts, speaking in terms of shares, cumes, and PURs (see the preceding glossary). Make them do the math for you, so you know in plain numbers exactly how many people you are reaching with your ad schedule.

—Katy Bachman

The Privacy Checklist for Database Marketing

by Mary J. Culnan
October 1994
American Demographics

In the long run, ensuring a customer's privacy can improve a company's prof-itability. Privacy is really about earning the customer's trust, and trust is a cen-tral component of relationship marketing. Consumers of many different kinds of products are attracted to firms with strong privacy policies, according to a 1993 Lou Harris poll conducted for the newsletter Privacy & American Business.

Anyone who uses personal information to target customers can stay on top of the privacy issue by writing a formal privacy policy. If you need to create a policy or review your old one, here are some basic guidelines:

Remember "knowledge, notice, and no." Tell your customers how you will use their personal information. If you plan to share the information with a third party, tell your customers and give them a chance to drop out of the database. Even if you don't sell your customer lists, tell them so. The practice of renting customer lists has become so widespread that a customer may assume you share your lists unless you explicitly tell them otherwise.

Look before you cross-market. Do your customers believe that personal infor-mation collected for one purpose is being used for a different unrelated purpose without their consent? If so, improve your communication with them. Be sure the "knowledge, notice, no" rule applies to both your internal cross-marketing and your frequent-buyers programs, especially if these programs involve unrelated products. Consumers may not know that responding to one of your offers may trigger subse-quent offers. The customer should never have to ask anyone, "How did you get my name?"

Don't be tempted by incidental information. Information about a transaction typ-ically passes through many hands. Credit-card companies, insurance companies, and others usually serve as brokers for transactions between consumers and other businesses. If this is your role, take care to protect the content of that transaction. In 1991, public opposition forced AT&T to abandon its plans to sell lists of con-sumers based on the 800-numbers these individuals called.

Exercise conscience and common sense. So far, few legal restrictions apply to the gathering and use of personal information by the private sector. That's why privacy is more about "should" than "must." Clearly, some medical, financial, and lifestyle data are more sensitive than others. Apply a "sniff test" to any proposed reuse of your customer database. Would you be comfortable sending a member of your family the same offers that you propose to mail to your customers? If your company is identified as a sponsor of this mailing, will your 800-number be clogged with complaints?

Match Making: Geocoding Your List

by Susan Krafft
July/August 1994
Marketing Tools

When people talk about geocoding, they are usually talking about taking a list of names and addresses and assigning them to a geographic unit like a census block group or latitude and longitude. This is a type of geocoding called address matching. "If you look at an address, there is a hierarchy of geographic specificity," says Peter Van Demark, technical manager-desktop mapping for Caliper Corporation in Newton, Massachusetts. "You can work from the bottom line up, getting more and more specific—state, then city, then zip; street, house number, apartment number, and person name." Although all this information is desirable on an envelope, Van Demark figures a house number and zip+4 alone is sufficient to get a piece of mail delivered. "Increasingly specific numbers to identify a point. That's geocoding."

Simple idea, hard to do. "The computer coding is overwhelming," says Suzanne Shepherd, a geographer in the Geography Division, Bureau of the Census. "We've had this in development for 25 years. It's very sophisticated programming."

The first step is to organize all the information in any possible address into logical fields. Called parsing, this process takes the address line and separates it into seven fields. So 129 West 12th Street NW, Apt. 43, would have a piece in each field—the house number field, prefix direction, name, type, suffix direction, multi-unit type, and multi-unit value.

"Picking apart the address is the hardest problem," says Matt Jaro, president of MatchWare Technologies, Inc. of Silver Spring, Maryland. "We've been working to take very complex addresses and get the components out. We use pattern recognition routines, so we can keep adding new patterns as we encounter problem addresses." There are some confusing addresses floating around on American envelopes, like "123 1 st St. St. 56." The computer sees three street abbreviations in a row, when the actual address should read, 123 First Street, Suite 56.

Once the pieces are identified, each piece brings the process closer to a match—sometimes. "If every street type in the file was a Street," says Jaro, "and there were no Roads or Avenues, then Street wouldn't help to distinguish between records. In Knoxville, there is just one Square. Someone could really make a major mistake in the address, and we could still get the right match."

One of the ways to predict the probability of getting a correct match is to conduct a frequency analysis of the fields. The rarer the value in the field, the better. As in the case of Knoxville, if there's only one Square in town, you don't have to worry about matching an address to the wrong one.

It would take too long to match all the records in an address database to all the records in a geographic database. For example, two small databases of 1,000 records each would have 1,000,000 possible combinations. If the databases themselves have several million records, the number of combinations has too many zeros for this writer to count. Building an index allows you to use subsets of the files and compare them. One common subset is zip code.

"When you're matching interactively using a database management system, you can't retrieve every record and look at it," says Jaro. "You need to restrict the search to certain key fields, called blocks. Soundex is one option. It's a technique to get a group of candidates that are probably related." Soundex was developed in the 1920s. It takes a word, like a street name or last name, and turns it into a 4-character code that represents the sound of the word. It retains the first letter, ignores vowels, and groups consonants. For example, Rockingham Street, in Rochester, New York, becomes rcng (or, in the original notation, r252 where numbers represent groups of letters). Rochester has 7,000 streets, but only one with a Soundex code of rcng.

"It's the oldest algorithm," says Jaro, who uses this technique, "and its sloppiness allows us to group a lot of candidates together." It usually takes a couple of passes to match the majority of records. If there's an error in a blocking field, that address won't match anything in the geographic database. A second pass (with different blocking fields) may pull up that candidate. The first pass usually matches around 80 percent of records, according to Donald F. Cooke, president of Geographic Data Technology, Inc. (GDT) in Lyme, New Hampshire. Then, additional passes continue to winnow down the residual, unmatched records.

Once the file is broken down into subsets, the fields in each subset are compared. The program compares fields to the geographic database. If it can't find JFK Boulevard in zip code 11233, it will look for aliases, like John F Kennedy, JF Kennedy, or just Kennedy. (Punctuation is taken out of the address early on.) "The program should also provide the facility to go through one by one and check manually," says Cooke.

Each field is given a number, called the weight, describing how close it comes to a perfect match. This is a statistical representation of the likelihood of a correct match. A good match gets a positive number; a bad one gets a negative number. The lower the overall score for a record, the worse the match.

Each field has two properties: reliability and probability of accidental agreement. The reliability factor describes the likelihood that a mistake was made in the original address, like Main Avenue instead of Main Street. The lower reliability, the less confidence you have that a match is truly correct.

Accidental agreement is the likelihood that a field agrees by accident. For example, you might not think that two John Smiths with different addresses were actually the same person. But two Leonid Brezhnevs would make you suspicious. "You need to know the most popular names by doing a frequency analysis to calculate the probability of accidents," explains Jaro.

All the statistical justification in the world won't guarantee perfect matches. But it does mean the user will know how much confidence to have in the final match. Some systems allow interactive analysis so the user can adjust the match cutoff weight and see how much of the file can be matched at a high level of confidence.

Matching the last 10 percent of the file takes 99 percent of the time and money. "Almost all geocoding is by machine," says the Census Bureau's Suzanne Shepherd. "We have some money for clerical research. When we did the economic census, we looked at the 40,000 employers that did not geocode. We tried to take the most important. But when the money is gone, you do the best you can with the last line (city, state, and zip code)."

There are still many places that are very difficult to geocode. "I'm ungeocodable," confesses GDT's Don Cooke. "I'm RR 141, Box 3." (Not his real address.)

But there are reasons to be optimistic. As the 911 emergency response system takes hold in more rural areas, rural routes are being replaced by easier to code street names. And "people are getting a lot better about recording addresses," he says.

A thorough service bureau will first geocode a file by machine, matching most of the address. Then a person will look at the records to try to match them logically. Then if necessary, the person will consult local authorities, directories, and maps to try to make a match.

This article has primarily looked at address matching, which is a subset of geocoding. And geocoding is just one type of record linkage. There are three ways to use record linkage. The first matches two databases of individual records like voter registration and motor-vehicle registration. The second matches an individual record like an address to a geographic database like a TIGER (Topologically Integrated Geographic and Encoding Reference file: a complete boundary file for the U.S.) map that has codes for each street segment; this is address matching. The third is a much broader application of record linkage—matching a file to itself to clean up duplication.

Whatever the application, the more accuracy and the larger the database, the more expensive the matching system will be. "Most users tend to be painting with a broad brush or they are working on small areas with which they are familiar," says John Haller, vice president of technology and founder of MapInfo in Troy, New York. So they don't need the highest levels of matching software.

Desktop systems like Caliper, Claritas, ESRI, MapInfo, and Strategic Mapping have geocoders built into the GIS. GDT and MatchWare offer separate systems for users who need a higher level of control.

How to Get to the Grassroots

by Judith Waldrop
May 1989
American Demographics

Cities and counties change rapidly as neighborhood populations shift, often in just a few months. One of the best ways to keep up with local population is to go to the source.

While many federal agencies generate small-area statistics, local sources frequently have more up-to-date and detailed data. The variety of local sources can be overwhelming, however. Here's a guide to navigating the bureaucracy.

If you're interested in several localities in one state, start by calling the state data center's lead agency. These agencies serve as clearinghouses for Census Bureau data. State data centers can give you census data for the areas you're interested in, as well as information from more recent surveys. Some data centers produce estimates and projections of cities within their state, and many also distribute local data collected by other state agencies.

Other state agencies that might be useful in your quest for local information are state departments of health, vital statistics, and education. In some areas, interstate agencies also have valuable information. Some examples of these agencies are the Tennessee Valley Authority, the New York Port Authority, and the Metropolitan Washington Council of Governments.

At the local level, city or county planning departments are most likely to collect demographic data and track development. They may also aggregate building-permit data and generate population and employment forecasts. The planning departments in larger cities will do more data collection and compilation than those in smaller cities. Locate the agency that handles transportation planning in your area. These agencies must develop and maintain sophisticated databases.

Once you've investigated what data the local planning departments have, check with the building departments, housing authorities, health departments, employment offices, board of realtors, industrial and downtown development boards, and school boards for additional information. If you plan to visit an area, call ahead and make appointments. A few telephone calls will direct you to the most knowledgeable experts.

The best source of information on an area is firsthand experience. A lot of construction in an area means investors are committed to growth. But find out if developers are building on speculation or with contracts. At public meetings, pay attention to what people say about local development, and take note of who's making the most noise.

Local experts are the most knowledgeable about local developments. But be aware that boosterism is commonplace among people intensely involved in their community. Be sure you know the methodology behind local estimates. Gather data from as many different sources as possible. Then evaluate those data in light of what you know about the community.

Look for clues to back up your assumptions. If you're interested in children, for example, school enrollment figures provide a good proxy. Data on the number of children in each grade by race and sex may be available from the school board. Remember to take private-school enrollment into account. Large private-school enrollments in a district can selectively remove students from public-school rolls.

Utility-company data can help you estimate an area's overall population growth, and traffic counts can approximate daytime populations. Employment figures can help you identify economic change that can affect migration patterns. These sources of information have their problems, however. Make sure the area for which data are collected coincides with the area in which you are interested, and take seasonal variations into account.

Watch out for annexations, which can inflate growth and mask demographic change. In Tampa, Florida, for example, a 1985 test census showed a 2 percent population gain since 1980. On closer examination, however, city planners discovered much of the growth was due to annexation. If Tampa had not added new areas to its territory, its increase would have been just 1 percent.

Annexation can affect other statistics, as well. When suburban neighborhoods are added to urban areas, for example, minorities shrink as a share of the total population. Both annexations and de-annexations are common in incorporated areas. Don't confuse geography with a little change in demographics.

Data collection at the local level can be as simple as a telephone call. Private consultants can provide you with detailed local data, tailored to your needs. Or you can spend weeks collecting and sorting through data provided by dozens of public agencies. Which route you take depends on the number of local areas you need to analyze, your analytical skills, and the time and money you want to invest. The more involved you are in the data-collection process, however, the more you'll learn about the local market.

How to Search for Market Information

by Katherine S. Chiang
September 1993
American Demographics

Online databases have two layers: individual records that make up the database, and search software that picks out the record that you want from the thousands or millions the in the database. Think of search software as an idiot that works at the speed of light. If you type in a word or phrase, the software will find every occurrence of that word or phrase in the database, exactly as you typed it and regardless of context. The system will respond with the number of records in the database that match your search.

Say you are interested in mentions of the president's home. A search of the phrase white house might retrieve 45 records—14 that pertain to 1600 Pennsylvania Avenue, 4 on the coffee brand, 1 on Marin County (an area known for the predominantly white color of its houses), and 26 from the White House Publishing Company in New Delhi, India.

Reading irrelevant articles is an expensive waste of time. But virtually all online systems allow you to cut the waste by fine-tuning your search. By combining several concepts, using shortcuts in typing and connecting words like AND, OR, and NOT, and limiting the search to particular parts of the record, you can hit the center of the target.

If you are interested in the travel business in the Caribbean, retrieving articles about the political situation in Haiti or Jamaican exports is not helpful. To avoid these, you can narrow your search by looking for articles that have the words travel AND Caribbean.

But what about an article on the cruise market in Bermuda? The above search phrase might not uncover it. Try keying in a set of synonyms for each keyword, such as: (travel OR tourism OR cruises OR Bermuda OR Jamaica OR Virgin Islands OR

St. Thomas). This can be tedious at the beginning, but yield much more useful information in the end.

With the NOT command, you can eliminate dreaded "false drops"—citations that match your search requirements but have nothing to do with the topic you want. An article about a man who sued a cruise line after suffering an allergic reaction to Bermuda onions can be eliminated by adding the qualifier, "NOT Bermuda onion" to your search.

You can further refine your search by looking at specific fields in the records. For example, you can limit your search to articles published in a specified year. You can search for articles about an author, rather than articles by that author. Some databases even use standard codes or phrases that automatically broaden searches. Instead of having to think of every synonym for hotels, you may be able to search on SIC code 7011, which includes hotels, auto courts, bed and breakfast inns, cabins, cottages, casino hotels, motels, resorts, and lodges.

The actual syntax of each statement depends on the database's search software. Think of automobiles: they all have windshield wipers and reverse gears, but the specifics vary depending on the model. Depending on the online system, the command for a search of records with the word "demographic" in their titles might look like: demographic/ti, demographic.ti, demographic in ti, or [ti]demographic.

Several software vendors offer more than one type of search software. They may have a simple menu-driven version for more serious users. Some larger vendors even have ways to search across groups of databases simultaneously.

Savvy researchers view searching as a multi-stage process. They start by searching for exactly what they want, but they are prepared to broaden or narrow their searches based on initial results.

Suitcase Savvy: A Database Marketing Case Study

by Shelly M. Reese
June 1995
Marketing Tools

U sing a database for direct marketing is like using a computer to type a letter—it's basic, efficient, and it doesn't even come close to exploiting the tool's power. As with computers, many firms have trouble moving beyond the basics of using a database. They track their customers, approach them, and—hopefully—make a sale. End of story. But for the Denver-based Samsonite Corporation, the world's largest luggage manufacturer, that's just the beginning.

Because Samsonite sells its luggage through retail outlets, the most common application for a database—direct marketing—would put it in competition with its dealers. Rather than jeopardize those crucial relationships, Samsonite is exploring ways to use its database to enhance them, starting from the premise that dealers and manufacturers are in the same business: serving customers' needs.

As a manufacturer, Samsonite uses purchaser information to determine what customer needs are and how to design products that meet them. As a supplier to retailers, it passes the information on so dealers can better understand their customers and tailor their luggage departments to meet customer needs. Samsonite can tell dealers who their customers are, what they want, and perhaps most importantly, what a dealer needs to do to attract them.

"What it's done, basically, is give us a noticeable advantage in our dealings with vendors," says Robert Bengen, Samsonite's director of direct marketing and research. "Samsonite can't always be the low-cost vendor, but we can give an additional advantage to our vendors that goes beyond raw product and deal making." When a dealer works with Samsonite, it's buying more than luggage: it's buying information.

Samsonite tracks customer information through three independent but overlapping databases. The first and largest system is maintained by National Demographics and Lifestyles in Denver. Developed in 1990 from product registration cards mailed in at the time of purchase, the database includes demographic, lifestyle, and purchase data on 1.5 million customers. Samsonite encourages purchasers to return the cards by giving them a chance to win free luggage. About 320,000 registration cards are mailed in monthly, according to associate director of marketing Kay Greenlee, who oversees database management on a day-to-day basis. A second, smaller database was developed from calls to Samsonite's 800 number. The 800 number is included in all Samsonite advertisements. Potential customers are told to call if they'd like additional information about Samsonite products or are interested in finding a Samsonite vendor in their city. So far, about 60,000 people have called the company and been added to a database maintained by TMP Worldwide in Mt. Olive, New Jersey.

Lastly, Samsonite collects customer information through "bingo" cards: magazine inserts readers mail in if they want to receive additional information on a particular advertiser. Developed three years ago and maintained by TMP, the bingo card database includes more than 80,000 names.

Because integrating the databases would cost hundreds of thousands of dollars, Samsonite merges them only occasionally. This year it plans to merge the systems quarterly to study their overlap, says Greenlee.

Maintaining a three-pronged system hasn't been a problem, Greenlee adds, because Samsonite isn't sending out mass mailings where overlapping systems would result in duplicated mailings. Instead, Samsonite uses its separate databases for specialized tasks that support the company's marketing, market research, and sales efforts.

Like most companies, Samsonite uses its system to identify customers. But once it has captured that information, it moves on to the tougher issues: What do the customers like? What *don't* they like? What is Samsonite failing to deliver that is causing them to purchase other brands?

By taking the process a step further, Samsonite can move from the basic issue of identifying customers to the far more complex and potentially lucrative one of anticipating their needs.

To some, the data Samsonite collects might seem like minutiae. In addition to the standard questions regarding income and product usage, Samsonite asks a number of lifestyles questions. "Which, if any, of the following do you plan to do in the next 12 months: Get married? Have a baby? Buy a house?" "Please indicate the interests and activities in which you or your spouse/partner enjoy participating on a regular basis: Flower gardening? Grandchildren? Home decorating?" Questions about hobbies and interests go so far as to ask what type of reading material a purchaser enjoys and whether they purchase pre-recorded videos.

From that laundry list of seemingly unrelated information, Samsonite is able to draw composite sketches of its customers: Not just which colors men prefer, what type of trim women like, and how old purchasers of a particular style are likely to be, but subtle differences. For example, although two older Americans might fancy the same lightweight style of wheeled luggage, one might favor a line that includes a matching cover for his golf clubs while the other would prefer a cosmetics case that will fit under her airline seat. Samsonite's database enables it to understand these customers' differing needs quickly so it can modify products "on the fly," as Bengen says.

Similarly, the database helps Samsonite identify gaps in its product lines. In a recent case, Samsonite used consumer preference data to determine a product's color. A department-store client approached the manufacturer about expanding an existing line, recalls Diane Pryor, manager of national accounts. The retailer already carried the line in black, which men favored, and green, which sold well with both men and women. The retailer thought the addition of a third color in a more feminine shade would help it capture additional sales among women.

After failed experiments with shades of mauve, Samsonite turned to its database. Using that information, Samsonite was able to show female purchasers were more likely to favor a neutral color rather than a feminine shade. Based on that, Samsonite introduced the line in navy blue.

"The result so far has been overwhelming," Pryor enthuses. Samsonite expects to sell almost $4 million worth of navy luggage to the retailer this year—about $1.5 million more than it would have been able to sell if it marketed the same line in mauve, she says.

While the database serves as a good empirical tool for making decisions, it meets a more basic and equally important need: it lets Samsonite talk to its customers. Twice a year Samsonite conducts a consumer satisfaction survey, calling about 200 customers from its primary database and asking them how they like their luggage and whether Samsonite's service has met their demands. The survey serves two purposes: it lets customers know Samsonite cares about their purchase experience, and it gives Samsonite valuable feedback.

In addition, the luggage maker conducts a quarterly survey on a particular issue. By calling about 100 owners of a specific type of bag, Samsonite can determine if travelers use a particular feature or like a change the manufacturer has made in the line.

For example, Samsonite's Oyster line of luggage originally included a detachable tote/sport bag inside. Samsonite considered eliminating the feature as a way of reducing the price to the consumer, but first had to determine whether consumers were using the feature or not.

After interviewing users, the manufacturer discovered that men tended to use the sport bag less than women. That finding led Samsonite to develop two versions of the piece. One included the tote, sold at the original price, and was targeted toward women. The other did not include the tote, was priced lower, and was targeted toward men.

While the interviews require calling people at home and infringing on their time, Greenlee believes that customers don't mind the calls. "As long as you're not absurd and don't call at 10 p.m., it's OK," she says. "People are pretty helpful. They love to talk about their luggage and their travels."

Consumers aren't the only constituents Samsonite needs to communicate with. Vendors—the manufacturer's intermediate customers—are equally important. Because Samsonite and its vendors are working toward the same end, the manufacturer indirectly shares its database with retailers in a variety of ways.

"The sales department is probably one of the best users of the database," says Greenlee, "because they show people the effect carrying Samsonite can have on their business. When people see a way to increase their sales dollars, they grab hold of it."

At the executive level, Samsonite's top brass uses the database to show executives at major retail accounts the type of customers Samsonite is bringing into their stores. "We can go to a retailer and say, 'This is what the customer looks like who buys Samsonite at your store'," says Greenlee. "We show it to them. We leave it there. We don't hide anything. That's pretty powerful stuff when you walk in and share information about that retailer and their customers that they don't have from any other sources."

Similarly, sales reps in the field can use the information to help dealers develop a business plan for their luggage departments. If they want to attract more of a particular type of shopper or achieve a certain level of inventory turns, a Samsonite sales representative can help them select the lines that best fit their needs.

Samsonite sales representatives can also use the database to garner add-on business and/or prevent lines from being dropped. Because Samsonite manufactures dozens of different types of bags and is constantly developing more, vendors are sometimes inclined to drop an existing line in favor of a similar new model. Using information developed through the databases, Samsonite reps are able to demonstrate that while two lines may resemble each other, they may attract different customers.

Pryor recalls using information from the database to convince a retailer to add a new product to its selection, rather than substitute it for an existing line. By showing the retailer that the lines attracted two different customers, Pryor says she was able to sell an additional $1 million worth of luggage.

Samsonite's database doesn't just profile customers, however. It also describes dealers. Because the database includes purchase information, Samsonite can tell dealers who their primary luggage customers are and what types of luggage sell the best at their outlet.

"We have a very high-end profile," says Greenlee. "We can show dealers what type of customer will come into their stores if they have Samsonite."

Equally important, Samsonite can identify the type of customer a dealer is conceding to the competition by refusing to carry Samsonite. That argument goes a long way toward helping Samsonite place its products in new stores.

"The database takes some of the guesswork out of the buying and selling business today," says Pryor. "Retailers today want to know who's shopping in their stores. We have an exceptional competitive advantage because we can tell them."

Profiling customers also helps Samsonite and its vendors avoid costly mistakes. Bengen recalls a department-store chain that wanted to upgrade its Samsonite lines. By studying the product registration database, Samsonite could see the store's customers were unlikely to purchase a higher-end product. The chain, which represented a multimillion-dollar account, was adamant. The deal took on an all-or-nothing character until Samsonite showed profiles of the retailer's existing Samsonite customers and customers who bought the higher-end line. Because there was little overlap between the two, the retailer agreed the more expensive line wasn't appropriate for its customers and Samsonite retained the account. In that case alone, the database "paid for itself from the beginning of time," jokes Bengen.

While the database is an invaluable tool for developing business strategies, Samsonite and its vendors use it for much simpler purposes as well.

One of the most basic and effective ways of developing new business is through referral. People who call Samsonite's 800 line are often anxious to buy luggage and are looking for places to purchase it. By calling Samsonite, they can receive a list of vendors in their area. Because the customer has made contact with Samsonite even before he or she has made contact with a retailer, that list plays an important role in the customer's decision about where to buy.

Consequently, it is to a vendor's advantage to be included on the list. To qualify, however, vendors have to routinely carry a certain amount of Samsonite stock. This condition ensures the retailer will have inventory on hand when a referred customer walks in the door, and it bolsters Samsonite's dealer sales. This is a powerful tool for the sales force, says Greenlee, who estimates 3,000 customers call Samsonite for referrals every month.

Because Samsonite can see which referrals resulted in sales, it can measure the benefits of its 800 number. Other benefits of the database are harder to calculate.

"Someone like L.L. Bean, that lives or dies by their direct sales, can measure their success," says Greenlee. "They can send out a catalog and say, 'Was this successful? Was that successful?' They can go through and see what sales were generated. We can't do that. We have to infer a lot."

Inferences are based on anecdotal information—a lot of it. Greenlee surveys Samsonite's sales reps to find out how they are using the database and passes their stories on through word of mouth and sometimes through the company's weekly newsletter. "It's a constant sales job," she says. "The problem is getting the word out" to the sales force about the database's potential use.

Still, Greenlee must be succeeding. Although Samsonite won't reveal the return on investment in the database, Bengen says it's "double digit," and use of the system is on the rise. "We're very practical," he says. "If all of these things hadn't paid for themselves, we wouldn't be talking about them."

Even as Samsonite quietly appreciates what its database tactics have already accomplished, plans are being laid for exploiting its uses even further. The company is constantly evaluating new ways to use the information. Among the experiments: limited direct marketing and partnering with its vendors.

Twice in the past two years, Samsonite has used limited direct marketing to inform specific customers that the lines they owned were being modified. That notice, which didn't include any sales or promotional information, let users know that if they wanted to complete their sets, they needed to do so quickly. Without engaging in direct selling, Samsonite was able to produce returns of between 50 percent and 80 percent from the outreach—and reduce markdowns, Bengen says.

Encouraged by the results, Samsonite is considering expanding its "reminder" marketing program.

"I think there's a tremendous amount of untapped opportunity for communicating with customers by letting them know about new products or closeouts or holidays: 'Don't forget about Mother's Day' or 'Don't forget about graduation','" says Greenlee. "There are plenty of ways—without direct selling—to increase communications."

Samsonite is also experimenting with letting vendors use the database to contact customers. The company began exploring partnering opportunities last year, permitting dealers to use its database to notify area Samsonite owners of a sale. By hiring an outside firm to process the information, Samsonite is able to share information with its retail partner, yet maintain its proprietary customer list.

So far the programs have been successful for both Samsonite and its vendors. Bengen says Samsonite plans to expand them.

Ambitious as their near-term goals may be, Greenlee and Bengen say they still haven't come close to unlocking the database's potential uses. Among the myriad of functions Samsonite has toyed with: Tracking calls to the company's 800 number to measure the effectiveness of advertising and media placement, and using the database to improve customer loyalty by developing programs in conjunction with the consumer service department. By merging information from the database and the service department, the manufacturer could better track its service record and find ways of improving customers' perception of Samsonite.

Those possibilities are just a sampling, says Greenlee: "I think there are opportunities we haven't begun to touch."

Chapter 4: Private and Nonprofit Sources

3D Software Services

Keywords: computer services; survey software

David Cushman Griffis, President
1015 E. Hillsdale Boulevard, Suite 206
Foster City, CA 94404

Phone: 415/574-0178
Fax: 415/574-0164
E-mail: griffisd@aol.com

3D Software Services provides interview center software for surveys and telemarketing called TELEPROMPT. It runs on DOS, Windows, MacIntosh, Novell, and UNIX. The software includes sample management, setup and interview screens, import/export dialogs, and reports.

A. C. Nielsen

Keywords: buying behavior; market research; retailing

Elliot Bloom, Vice President, Public Relations & Advertising
150 N. Martingale Road
Schaumburg, IL 60173-2076

Phone: 708/605-5881
Fax: 708/605-2570
E-mail: ebloom@nielsen.com

A. C. Nielsen provides a wide range of services that help consumer packaged-goods manufacturers and retailers screen, plan, test, and evaluate individual brands and marketing programs. The company provides manufacturers and retailers with comprehensive insights on sales volume, shares, trends, pricing, promotions, distribution, and inventory levels. Nielsen also offers a full range of scanner-based services, from comprehensive national analyses to local markets and individual household buying patterns.

About Women, Inc.

Keywords: consulting; market research; women

Michelle LeBrasseur, Marketing Services Manager
33 Broad Street
Boston, MA 02109

Phone: 617/723-4337
Fax: 617/723-7107

About Women, Inc. reports exclusively on the women's marketplace. It provides compiled market research in formats ranging from a monthly business-to-business newsletter to topical reports to customized marketing consulting. Each issue of *Marketing to Women* provides 15 to 20 executive summaries taken from major research studies on the women's market. Topics covered include demographics, advertising, buying behaviors and influences, consumer behaviors and influences, consumer attitudes, media preferences, gender gap, health, technology, and more.

ACCRA Cost of Living Index

Keywords: cost of living; local and market information

Skip Kasdorf
4232 King Street
Alexandria, VA 22302-1507

Phone: 703/998-0072
Fax: 703/931-5624

The American Chamber of Commerce Research Association (ACCRA) Cost of Living Index provides quarterly cost-of-living comparisons for about 300 voluntarily participating urban areas. ACCRA provides a composite index plus six component indexes for grocery items, housing, utilities, transportation, health care, and miscellaneous goods and services. It also has average prices in each urban area for each of the 59 specific items surveyed.

Advanced Marketing Solutions, Inc.

Keywords: analytical services; computer services; statistical software

Emil D. Morales, Vice President, Custom Applications
One Corporate Drive, Suite 506
Shelton, CT 06484

Phone: 203/925-3038
Fax: 203/925-3009

Advanced Marketing Solutions, Inc., a subsidiary of NFO Research, offers a full range of Windows-based software. Its Expert Report Systems produce graphic and narrative reports of business information and research data. The AMS SmartSystem Suite is designed to address the needs of marketing professionals engaged in the analysis and output of concept tests, product tests, or tracking studies.

Advanced Media Systems

Keywords: local and market information; media research

Ellen Weinstein, Vice President, Sales & Marketing
114 West 47th Street
New York, NY 10036

Phone: 212/719-0100
Fax: 212/730-7479

Advanced Media Systems offers CableTrack, a database of more than 52 million cable homes that can receive local insertion advertising. CableTrack data can be accessed and analyzed through the following software packages: Compass/ CableTrack, a geodemographic mapping system; CableTrack Directory, a PC product that analyzes spot cable inventory by zip, town, county, state, and DMA; CableTrack Pre-Buy System, a PC product that analyzes multi-market, multi-system cable schedules and efficiencies; CableTrack Sysfile, a cable system file of unique identification codes, traffic and payable addresses, contacts, and fax numbers, accessible through Donovan Data Systems and Datatrak Systems, Inc.

Advanced Software Applications

Keywords: analytical services; consumer segmentation; database marketing; statistical software

Donna Bartko, Director of Marketing
333 Baldwin Road
Pittsburgh, PA 15205

Phone: 412/429-1003
Fax: 412/429-0709

Advanced Software Applications (ASA) provides automated data analysis tools based on hybrids of advanced technologies and statistics. Users can conduct predictive modeling, clustering, and segmentation. ModelMAX creates virtually any type of predictive model including response, profitability, cross-sell and up-sell, attrition, and LTV. dbPROFILE automatically clusters data revealing natural groupings and relationships within databases. ASA also offers consulting services and training.

Advertising Research Foundation

Keywords: advertising research; market research; media research

Carol A. White, Office Services Manager
641 Lexington Avenue
New York, NY 10011

Phone: 212/751-5656
Fax: 212/319-5265

The Advertising Research Foundation (ARF) is the only organization whose principal mission is to improve the practice of advertising, marketing, and media research in pursuit of more effective marketing and advertising communications. ARF conducts research projects ranging from assessing the validity of research measures to pinpointing the contribution of advertising in a specific situation. It maintains a highly active and continuing program of conferences and workshops. ARF constantly develops and distributes new guidelines, criteria, position papers, and other publications of value to the industry. ARF''s membership includes major advertisers, advertising agencies, media, research firms, educational institutions, and other industry associations.

ADVO, Inc.

Keywords: customer profiling; database marketing; desktop mapping/GIS; local and market information; market research

Barbara Shapiro, Director, Micromarketing
One Univac Lane
Windsor, CT 06095

Phone: 203/285-6100
Fax: 203/285-6348

ADVO, Inc. is a direct-marketing company that reaches more than 57 million households every week through services provided by 80 sales offices and 22 production facilities. It targets at all geographic levels, from entire markets to individual, with expertise in developing efficient trading areas. ADVO works with a combination of geographic, cartographic, and consumer information, including customer databases.

Affordable Samples, Inc.

Keywords: Canada; demographics; ethnic markets; market research

James Sotzing, President
312 Sound Beach Avenue
Old Greenwich, CT 06870

Phone: 203/637-8563
Fax: 203/637-8569
E-mail: 72672.1327@compuserve.com

Affordable Samples, Inc., founded in 1991, provides a wide range of samples for survey research applications. It specializes in narrowly targeted selections including exact age, gender, income, new mothers, ethnic groups, businesses, executives by title, tract/block groups, radius, Canadian, and many low-incidence categories such as consumer product users, smokers, online users, and a variety of census demographics. Samples are shipped in electronic or printed form within 24 to 48 hours.

Age Wave, Inc.

Keywords: analytical services; census data; market research; mature market

Rebecca Chekouras, Vice President
1900 Powell Street, Suite 800
Emeryville, CA 94608

Phone: 510/652-9099
Fax: 510/652-8245

Age Wave is a marketing services company that focuses on the current and future mature U.S. population. It provides demographic expertise for marketing and health care applications and offers a full range of services, from primary and secondary analysis to projections and forecasts. Its library includes all recent census, Current Population Survey, Bureau of Labor Statistics, and National Center for Health Statistics data sets, as well as market research reports, newsletters, and periodicals. It can also supply online data retrieval.

All China Marketing Research (ACMR)

Keywords: China

Yingli Liu
120 Cedar Grove Lane, Suite 126
Somerset, NJ 08873

Phone: 908/873-8836
Fax: 908/873-1424

All China Marketing Research (ACMR) is the consulting arm of China's State Statistical Bureau, with access to the bureau's nationwide data/survey network and focus-group facilities. Its services and products include surveys, quantitative/qualitative research, Statistical Yearbook, Monthly Statistics, demographics, and industry reports/directories.

America Online, Inc.

Keywords: online; travel and tourism

Kathy Johnson, Communications Specialist
8619 Westwood Center Drive
Vienna, VA 22182

Phone: 703/448-8700 x1948
Fax: 703/918-2002

America Online, Inc. offers more than 4 million worldwide subscribers a wide variety of services including electronic mail, conferencing, software, computing support, interactive magazines and newspapers, and online classes, as well as easy and affordable access to the Internet. Founded in 1985, AOL has established strategic alliances with dozens of companies, including Capital Cities/ABC, Viacom, IBM, Compaq, and American Express. Personal computer owners can obtain America Online software at major retailers and bookstores or by calling 800/827-6364.

America's Research Group

Keywords: crime; focus groups; market research; retailing; sales and marketing; trends

Chris L. Cooper, Vice President
1941 Savage Road
Charleston, SC 29407

Phone: 803/571-0225
Fax: 803/571-1336

America's Research Group, Ltd. is a full-service consumer behavior survey research company. The company utilizes both quantitative (survey) and qualitative (focus groups) research. It works with clients in developing marketing strategies. The National Crime Study is a source of information on public attitudes toward crime and its effects on retailers.

American Association of Retired Persons

Keywords: mature market

Philip Jones
601 E Street, NW
Washington, DC 20049

Phone: 202/434-2277
Fax: 202/434-2588

The American Association of Retired Persons (AARP) is the nation's leading organization for people aged 50 and older. It serves their needs and interests through legislative advocacy, research, informative programs, and community services provided by a nationwide network of local chapters and volunteers. AARP also offers members benefits including *Modern Maturity* and the monthly *Bulletin*.

American Business Information, Inc.

Keywords: business to business; database marketing; market research; sales and marketing

Tony Sgroi
5711 S. 86th Circle
Omaha, NE 68127

Phone: 402/593-4593
Fax: 402/331-6881
E-mail: online@abii.com

American Business Information, Inc. provides business lists and company profiles for more than 11 million businesses. Selection is based on type of business and size of business for any geographic segment in the U.S. and Canada. Information is available online and is updated monthly.

American Dialogue

Keywords: computer services; focus groups; market research; online

Andrew Watt
180 Maiden Lane, 38th Floor
New York, NY 10013

Phone: 212/804-1170
Fax: 212/804-1200
E-mail: adialogue@aol.com

American Dialogue is the world's first market research facility in cyberspace. Under an exclusive agreement with America Online, it has access to the 3 million people who currently log onto AOL. The firm offers online focus groups, one-on-one interviews, dyads, triads, and e-mail polls, customized to meet clients' specific needs. For focus groups and interviews, pre-recruited respondents enter a "virtual research room" at a specified time and answer whatever questions the moderator poses. American Dialogue is a sister company of Yankelovich Partners, Inc.

American Digital Cartography, Inc. (ADC)

Keywords: desktop mapping/GIS; international; Russia

Drew Fleck, Product Manager
3003 W. College Avenue
Appleton, WI 54914

Phone: 414/733-6678
Fax: 414/734-3375
E-mail: worldmap@adci.com

American Digital Cartography, Inc. produces ADC WorldMap, a comprehensive 1:1,000,000 scale vector map of the entire world. Designed to work with MapInfo software, ADC WorldMap features political boundaries, populated places, roads, railroads, utilities, airports, rivers, lakes, and elevation information on 4 CD-ROMS. The Whole Earth data set, minus elevation information, is available on a single CD-ROM.

ADC World Map Russia provides geographic and demographic data for business, education, and science in the former USSR. MapInfo software can display contours, railroads, utilities, airports, major roads, and other information throughout Russia. The dataset includes Oblast (state) and Rajon (county) internal boundaries. With corresponding demographic data for 8 major categories and 75 subset categories, users can thematically display data on age, education, first and second language, and much more.

American Marketing Association

Keywords: education; market research

Pat Goodrich, Director, AMA Marketing Research Division
250 S. Wacker Drive
Chicago, IL 60606-5819

Phone: 800/262-1150
Fax: 312/648-5625
E-mail: http://www.ama.org

The American Marketing Association (AMA) is a professional society of marketers with nearly 50,000 members in 92 countries. The AMA assists in personal and professional career development among marketing professionals and advances the science and ethical practice of all marketing disciplines.

The AMA conducts seminars, workshops, and more than 25 national conferences across the country on topics such as attitude research, behavior research, and applied research methods. Its quarterly *Journal of Marketing Research* covers the latest marketing research techniques, methods, and applications. The quarterly *Marketing Research: A Magazine of Management and Applications* covers legislative and regulatory issues, management tools, research trends, and new technology. The AMA also published the results of a joint study conducted by the AMA and the Advertising Research Foundation on the marketing research profession.

American Opinion Research

Keywords: customer satisfaction; environmental
research; market research; media research

Tony Casale, President
707 State Road, Suite 102
Princeton, NJ 08540

Phone: 609/683-4860
Fax: 609/683-8398

American Opinion Research is a full-service research company with divisions focusing on media research, the environment, customer satisfaction research, and commercial studies.

American Sports Data, Inc.

Keywords: fitness and sports; health care; market
research; media research

Harvey Lauer, President
234 North Central Avenue
Hartsdale, NY 10530

Phone: 914/328-8877

American Sports Data, Inc. publishes American Sports Analysis, an annual study of U.S. sports participation, and the Athletic Footwear Monitor, a tri-annual study of the U.S. athletic footwear market. It also publishes the Health Club Trend Report, Sports Brand Intelligence Report, and Sports Media Index.

Analytical Computer Software, Inc.

Keywords: market research; statistical software;
survey software

Jerome Madansky
640 North LaSalle Drive
Chicago, IL 60610

Phone: 312/751-2915
Fax: 312/337-2551

Analytical Computer Software, Inc. develops market research software. ACS-QUERY is a PC-based CATI and CAPI system that features questionnaire setup, sample management, quota control, and interviewer productivity and disposition reports. WINCROSS is a PC windows-based crosstab package.

Angoss Software International

Keywords: consumer segmentation; database
marketing; market research

Hugh Rooney, Director of Marketing
430 King Street West, Suite 201
Toronto, ONTARIO M5V 1L5

Phone: 416/593-1122
Fax: 416/593-5077
E-mail: www.angoss.con

Angoss Software International provides Knowledgeseeker, a data analysis/decision support tool that analyzes enterprise data to expose relationships and patterns using statistical methodologies.

Answers Direct Mail, Ltd.

Keywords: business to business; health care; mailing lists; sales and marketing

Gary Sawyer, National Sales Manager
434 Marietta Street, Suite 304
Atlanta, GA 30313

Phone: 800/257-5242
Fax: 404/523-8111

Answers Direct Mail provides mailing lists and market analysis for direct marketers. It specializes in physician recruiting, insurance/financial services leads, and business-to-business marketing, as well as regional/national residential lists.

Apian Software, Inc.

Keywords: survey software

Sales Department
P.O. Box 1224
Menlo Park, CA 94026

Phone: 800/237-4565 x379
Fax: 415/694-2904

Apian Software offers flexible solutions to mail survey needs. Survey Pro for Windows streamlines survey research with integrated questionnaire design, data entry, database management, and report generation. Key Collect allows flexible data entry with verification at one or several sites. LAN licenses are available.

Applied Information for Marketing, Inc. (AIM)

Keywords: advertising research; buying behavior; computer services; market research

Jose Anstey, President
15 Ketchum Street
Westport, CT 06880

Phone: 203/226-0316
Fax: 203/227-8969

Applied Information for Marketing, Inc. provides software for planning and evaluating marketing and promotional expenditures. Businessmax, Promomax, Pricemax, and Couponmax are based on continuously updated models of consumer response to activity based on integrated data from manufacturers and scanner data vendors.

Arbitron Company (The)

Keywords: consulting; focus groups; local and market information; media research

Stephen B. Morris, President
142 West 57th Street
New York, NY 10019

Phone: 212/887-1300
Fax: 212/887-1401

The Arbitron Company is a media research firm providing information services that measure and refine local marketing strategies of the electronic media, advertisers, and agencies. Arbitron measures local radio audiences and offers access to data through printed reports, computer tape, and software applications. Through

Scarborough Research, a joint venture between The Arbitron Company and VNU Business Information Services, Arbitron provides syndicated measurement of local market media, consumer, and retail behavior in 58 top markets. RetailDirect is Arbitron's local market integrated audience measurement service for television stations, radio stations, and cable systems in small- to medium-sized markets. Arbitron New Media offers survey research, consulting, and methodological services to the cable, telecommunications, direct broadcast satellite, online, and new media industries.

Argus Technologies Corporation

Keywords: census data; desktop mapping/GIS

Bruce H. Rampe, Executive Vice President
One Speen Street
Framingham, MA 01701-4644

Phone: 508/875-5551
Fax: 508/875-5545
E-mail: bhrampe@interenetmci.com

Argus Technologies Corporation develops geographic data visualization tools for the client/server and desktop environments. ARGUS 4.0 is a data visualizer and geographic mapping tool for client/server applications, providing SQL direct-read and direct-write capabilities compatible with all relational databases. Argus recently announced the capability to interface directly as a graphical front-end for Oracle Corporation's MultiDimension spatiotemporal RDBMS add-on for the Oracle7 RDBMS. Argus also markets ARGUS Census Map USA, a self-contained CD-ROM version of the ARGUS data visualization software, bundled with key demographic variables from the 1990 census.

ASI Market Research, Inc.

Keywords: advertising research; media research

Bill Moult, President and CEO
1 Stamford Plaza, 263 Tresser Boulevard
Stamford, CT 06901

Phone: 203/328-7000
Fax: 203/323-6698
E-mail: bmoult@asiresearch.com

ASI Market Research, Inc. provides advertising research including copy testing, advertising tracking, advertising response and market mix modeling, and interactive media research, including "Anywhere Online," a joint venture with Nielsen and Yankelovich.

Asian Marketing Communication Research

Keywords: Asian-American market

Felipe Korzenny, PhD
1301 Shoreway Road, Suite 100
Belmont, CA 94002

Phone: 415/595-5028
Fax: 415/595-5407
E-mail: korfel@aol.com

Asian Marketing Communication Research (AMCR) conducts qualitative and quantitative research in most major Asian languages in the U.S. and Asia. It provides full-service qualitative and quantitative research, and conducts copy testing, motivational discovery, product design and evaluation, and cultural analysis for positioning products and services to Asians. AMCR also conducts focus groups, in-depth interviews, CATI surveys, and tracking studies. Psycho-socio-cultural Asian research is its approach to understanding the diversity of the Asian markets. It has facilities in the San Francisco-San Jose Bay area. (AMCR is a division of Hispanic & Asian Marketing Communication Research, Inc.)

Association of Public Data Users

Keywords: census data; economic data

Susan Anderson, Executive Director
87 Prospect Avenue
Princeton, NJ 08544-1002

Phone: 609/258-6025
Fax: 609/258-3943

The Association of Public Data Users (APDU) is an organization of users, producers, and distributors of public data. Through monthly newsletters, an annual conference, and numerous mailings during the year, APDU strives to keep users informed of the availability of a wide variety of public data products, as well as federal information policy that affects the collection and dissemination of public data. It also keeps major federal statistical agencies informed about the needs and concerns of public data users.

Audit Bureau of Circulations

Keywords: circulation data; demographics; media research

Evelyn A. Hepner, Director, Circulation Data Bank
900 N. Meacham Road
Schaumburg, IL 60173

Phone: 708/605-0909
Fax: 708/605-0483
E-mail: http://www.accessabc.com

Audit Bureau of Circulations (ABC) maintains the world's foremost electronic database of audited circulation information. ABC audits paid and nonpaid business, consumer, and farm periodicals, as well as daily and weekly newspapers in North America. The ACCESS ABC product line delivers circulation data and analysis tools to members on CD-ROM. ACCESS ABC: Periodicals combines Publisher's Statements replicas for business, consumer, and farm publications with analysis tools for business and consumer publications. Also included are DMA/MAS data for 200-plus consumer and farm titles. ACCESS ABC: Newspapers contains circulation data for all 1,100-plus ABC-audited U.S. newspapers that provide zip-code analyses. Circulation data are combined with four sources of household data (Claritas/NPDC, National Decision Systems, Strategic Mapping, and U.S.P.S.), allowing the calculation of percent coverage. ABC also provides a wide range of diskette, reference report, and custom report products.

Audits & Surveys Worldwide, Inc.

Keywords: customer satisfaction; market research; media research; retailing

Jack Richman, Public Relations/Marketing Manager
The Audits & Surveys Building, 650 Avenue of the Americas
New York, NY 10011

Phone: 212/627-9700
Fax: 212/627-2034
E-mail: jrichman@audits.surveys.nyc.ny.us

Audits & Surveys Worldwide is a full-service international marketing research firm serving commercial, industrial, legal, institutional, governmental, and academic clients in more than 60 countries. It assists clients in developing marketing, advertising, and investment strategies, and as part of legal proceedings. Services include continuous retail sales measurement, product/service distribution, test marketing, in-store promotion testing, consumer and industrial surveys, customer satisfaction studies, qualitative research, financial research, demographic research, media research, and government and litigation research.

Bamberg-Handley, Inc.

Keywords: business to business; census data; consumer segmentation; demographics; desktop mapping/GIS

Ed Glaser, Vice President & General Manager
3377 Forsyth Road
Winter Park, FL 32792

Phone: 407/677-9292
Fax: 407/677-9519
E-mail: gis1info@aol.com

Bamberg-Handley, Inc. (BHI) provides a wide range of demographic information from the 1990 census as well as current-year and five-year projections for zip codes, census tracts, block groups, blocks, and 100th-of-a-degree x 100th-of-a-degree grids. In addition, BHI provides 17 business demographics (current year) at all of the above geographic levels.

Behavioral Analysis Inc. (BAI)

Keywords: business to business; customer satisfaction; database marketing; focus groups; international; market research

Kate Permut, Vice President, Marketing
580 White Plains Road
Tarrytown, NY 10591

Phone: 914/332-5300
Fax: 914/631-8300
E-mail: adamsrk@aol.com

Behavioral Analysis Inc. (BAI) is a full-service marketing research firm. Through BAI International, the company offers global research services. Custom research specialties include market sizing and segmentation analyses, customer satisfaction studies, new product/service development, business-to-business research, and qualitative research. Programs and syndicated products include: Mail Monitor direct-mail response tracking for credit-card acquisition programs; Inside Track direct-mail response tracking for credit-card retention and usage programs; The Performance Monitor program to evaluate training implementation and service quality; and On Target to analyze behaviors in response to direct-marketing programs and determine the corrective actions to be taken to improve bottom-line results.

Bernan Press

Keywords: demographics; local and market information

Don Hagen, Director
4611-F Assembly Drive
Lanham, MD 20706

Phone: 800/274-4447
Fax: 800/865-3450
E-mail: query@kraus.com

Bernan Press publishes *The 1996 County and City Extra*, a sourcebook of local-area information. The 1996 edition includes 204 statistics each for states, counties, and metropolitan areas, 151 for cities with populations of 25,000 or more, and 53 for congressional districts. It covers land area, population characteristics, employment, education, industry, and more.

Bernett Research

Keywords: computer services; consulting; customer satisfaction; focus groups; survey software

Andrew R. Hayes
230 Western Avenue
Boston, MA 02134

Phone: 617/254-1314
Fax: 617/254-1857

Bernett Software develops and markets Windows programs targeting the qualitative arena. FOCUSREPORTS software provides focus-group analysis. CODING ANALYST manages verbatim responses from telephone and mail surveys. INTERVIEW MANAGER facilitates the capturing, documenting, and analyzing of in-depth surveys. Bernett can also manage projects and build in-house custom programs.

Beta Research Corporation

Keywords: consulting; focus groups; market research; media research

Gail C. Disimile, Exec. Vice President, Sales & Marketing
6400 Jericho Turnpike
Syosset, NY 11791

Phone: 516/935-3800
Fax: 516/935-4092

Beta Research provides national coverage for consumer and business-to-business media surveys. Its services include mail, telephone, mall, and in-person interviewing; new product/concept research; and omnibus surveys of consumers, business executives, and physicians. It provides rapid turnaround with in-house data processing/statistical analysis/CRT interviewing. Focus-group facilities are in New York City and Los Angeles.

BiblioData

Keywords: academic research; online

Ina Champ Steiner
P.O. Box 61
Needham Heights, MA 02194

Phone: 617/444-1154
Fax: 617/449-4584
E-mail: 74722.2645@compuserve.com

BiblioData publishes *Fulltext Sources Online*, a directory for people who know which periodicals they need access to, but aren't sure which online vendors carry them in full text. This resource also provides comparative information about online products. It is available in printed form (updated twice annually) and on disk (updated four times a year).

Bibliodata also publishes *The CyberSkeptic's Guide to Internet Research*, a monthly newsletter that targets business librarians and researchers who need to find substantive information via the Internet.

BMDP Statistical Software, Inc.

Keywords: analytical services; statistical software

Leon DilPare, Sales Manager
12121 Wilshire Boulevard, Suite 300
Los Angeles, CA 90025

Phone: 800/238-2637
Fax: 310/207-8844
E-mail: sales@bmdp.bmdp.com

BMDP Statistical Software, Inc., offers a full range of data-analysis products for researchers including statistical software, data visualization and exploratory data analysis software, and structural equation modeling software.

Book Industry Study Group

Keywords: book industry; packaged goods

160 Fifth Avenue
New York, NY 10010

Phone: 212/929-1393
Fax: 212/989-7542
E-mail: 4164812@mcmail.com

The Book Industry Study Group tracks and projects book sales for the U.S. It also conducts an annual consumer market research survey on book buyers, available as a published report.

BPA International

Keywords: circulation data; international; media research

Jeffrey Yacker, Communications Manager
270 Madison Avenue
New York, NY 10016-0699

Phone: 212/779-3200
Fax: 212/779-3615

BPA International provides worldwide circulation marketing intelligence. Its members include about 1,700 business publications and special-interest consumer magazines as well as 2,500 advertisers and advertising agencies. BPA designs and executes circulation audits for member publications once a year, and issues biannual or annual circulation statements to advertisers, advertising agencies, and publishers.

Field auditors examine circulation trends and help members interpret and use circulation marketing intelligence. In addition, BPA provides training workshops and seminars, Business TRAC International and Consumer TRAC International trend reports, and The Center for Market Comparability, which helps members determine the recipients of particular publications.

Bruskin/Goldring Research

Keywords: attitudes and opinions; computer-assisted surveys; consulting; market research

Joel Henkin, Senior Vice President
100 Metroplex Drive
Edison, NJ 08817

Phone: 908/572-7300 or 800/634-5773
Fax: 908/572-7980

Bruskin/Goldring Research is a full-service company that offers custom designed research and an economical consumer omnibus survey. OmniTel is a weekly study of a nationally projectable sample of 1,000 adults. Interviews are conducted every weekend, and data are available on Tuesdays. A new custom overnight service provides 24-hour turnaround for up to 1,000 regional or national interviews. The company has WATS and CATI facilities across the U.S. It has expertise conducting surveys for industries including: automotive, computer, food, financial, health care, and broadcast media as well as surveys of businesses and executives, and international research.

BRX/Global, Inc.

Keywords: advertising research; brand equity; market research; packaged goods

Joel N. Axelrod, President
169 Rue de Ville
Rochester, NY 14618

Phone: 716/442-0590
Fax: 716/442-0840

BRX/Global measures the value of a brand to a customer using Brand Equity Systems to determine how much more a customer would pay to obtain one brand rather than a functionally equivalent alternative. This measure of brand loyalty is used to assess the viability of line extensions, the effectiveness of advertising and packaging alternatives, the optimum price, and to make decisions on budget allocation among alternative marketing strategies. This service is offered on a global basis. Within the strategic framework of Brand Equity Systems, each study is custom-designed.

Burke, Inc.

Keywords: analytical services; consulting; customer satisfaction; international; market research

Nancy Bunn, Director of Corporate Communications
805 Central Avenue
Cincinnati, OH 45202

Phone: 513/684-7509
Fax: 513/684-7717
E-mail: nbunn@burke.com

Burke, Inc. is comprised of four operating divisions. Burke Marketing Research provides custom marketing research and consulting for consumer product and service companies to help them understand marketplace dynamics. Research services include advertising testing, brand equity research, pricing research, market segmentation, and strategic research. Burke Customer Satisfaction Associates provides customer satisfaction measurement and consulting services dedicated to helping manufacturing and service firms improve productivity, competitiveness, and profitability by assessing customer needs and expectations. The Training and Development Center offers educational seminars on marketing research and analysis. Infratest Burke International Services is a partnership that creates a worldwide network of experts in custom marketing research.

Burke Institute (The), a division of BBI Marketing

Keywords: consulting; market research

B. (Sid) Venkatesh, President
50 E. Rivercenter Blvd.
Covington, KY 41091

Phone: 800/543-8635 ext. 6089
Fax: 606/655-6064
E-mail: burkeInstitute@bases.com

The Burke Institute is a marketing research training organization covering all aspects of marketing research. Seminars currently include marketing research methodology, including qualitative and quantitative approaches; communication of marketing information to decision makers; marketing research management; marketing research applications including segmentation, advertising research, product/service evaluation and customer satisfaction measurement; and marketing data analysis and interpretation. Many seminars have been adapted to meet the needs of specific industries. Three programmed series of seminars culminate in certificates of achievement–The Certificate of Achievement in Marketing Research Methodology and Applications, The Certificate of Proficiency in Qualitative Research, and The Certificate of Proficiency in Quantitative Analysis.

Business Location Research

Keywords: demographics; geographic boundary files; local and market information

Kevin Painter, Vice President
1820 East River Road, #110
Tucson, AZ 85718

Phone: 520/577-3772
Fax: 520/577-1675

Business Location Research (BLR) specializes in designing and developing advanced GIS data products. Formed in 1991, BLR offers a wide variety of geographic, demographic, and location databases, including Traffic Volumes, a single-source national database of traffic count information; MajorRoads, a metropolitan geographic reference; and the recently released StreetNetwork 5.0, a multilayered data file.

Business Trend Analysts, Inc.

Keywords: business to business; consulting; international; market research

Charles Ritchie, Executive Vice President
2171 Jericho Turnpike
Commack, NY 11725

Phone: 516/462-5454
Fax: 516/462-1842

Business Trend Analysts (BTA) is a business information and research firm. The company and its Leading Edge Group compile and publish analytic industry studies, as well as offer proprietary research projects on a contract basis. BTA and Leading Edge reports provide statistics, forecasts, and analysis. Historical and current sales trends are outlined on a product-by-product basis, along with projections for the coming decade. Typical areas of investigation include new products and technologies, market share, pricing, distribution channels, marketing strategies, foreign trade, end-use markets, factors affecting demand, industry economics and cost structure, and profiles of major competitors. Geographic areas covered vary and include the U.S. (region and state data), North America, and the world. Industries tracked include food and beverage, specialty chemicals, industrial equipment and supplies, machinery, consumer products and services, home and office furnishings, electrical and electronic equipment, as well as technology-sensitive industries and emerging markets.

CACI Marketing Systems

Keywords: consumer segmentation; demographics; desktop mapping/GIS; international; local and market information; projections

Kristine Tuazon, Marketing Manager
1100 North Glebe Road
Arlington, VA 22201

Phone: 800/292-CACI
Fax: 703/243-6272

CACI's Marketing Systems division maintains its European headquarters in London, England, and its U.S. headquarters in Arlington, Virginia. The scope of CACI Marketing Systems includes demographic data, consulting, consumer classification, market research, site evaluation, sales forecasting, direct-mail profiling, comprehensive CRA geographic analysis, and custom demographic and economic research.

It maintains an extensive data library that includes census data, forecasts, and consumer surveys with information on population, age, sex, Hispanic origin, race, income, housing, and consumer expenditures. Data are available in census, postal, media, and customized geographies and are available in outputs such as customized reports, sourcebooks, diskettes, CD-ROM, or maps.

Its Gold Standard Solution with Scan/US combines current-year demographics and five-year forecasts with geomarket analysis and mapping software. ACORN Consumer Classification groups households into geographic, socioeconomic, and demographic segments based on neighborhood or residence. CACI's Customer Profiling allows for geocoding and assignment of geographic location code, demographic data, and ACORN codes to address records.

California Retail Survey

Keywords: California; local and market information; retailing

James B. Vaughn, President
5303 Nyoda Way
Carmichael, CA 95608-3082

Phone: 916/486-9403

California Retail Survey publishes an annual analysis of retail sales trends in over 500 local markets throughout California's $180 billion retail market. Using sales data for each of the 325,000 retail establishments in California, the survey tracks, ranks, and analyzes market trends for each local market. It includes sales and outlet counts for the past 11 years, broken down into 45 retail categories. The publication also contains 16 analytical measurements for each market, allowing users to identify short-term and long-term retail performance trends for each market.

Cambridge Reports/Research International

Keywords: attitudes and opinions; consulting; consumer confidence; environmental research; international; market research

Ted Byers, President and CEO
955 Massachusetts Avenue
Cambridge, MA 02139

Phone: 617/661-0110
Fax: 617/661-3575
E-mail: creports@world.std.com

Cambridge Reports/Research International provides decision-makers in both the public and private sectors with consumer and public opinion research and business information. Cambridge Reports offers both custom research and syndicated research covering such topics as opinions on health-care reform, environmental issues, and consumer confidence.

CAP Index, Inc.

Keywords: crime; desktop mapping/GIS; local and market information; market research; risk assessment

Ricci J. Levy, Vice President, Director of Operations
20830 Valley Forge Circle
King of Prussia, PA 19406

Phone: 610/354-9100
Fax: 610/783-7825

CAP Index, Inc. offers consistent crime-risk information for all sites in the United States. Historical, current, and five-year projections of crime risks are available for homicide, rape, robbery, aggravated assault, burglary, larceny, and auto theft. The data are available in custom-printed reports and maps, and in tape, disk, and CD-ROM format.

Carol Wright Consumer Promotions

Keywords: database marketing; market research; mature market; retailing

Victoria James, Executive Vice President - Retail
70 Seaview Avenue
Stamford, CT 06902

Phone: 203/353-7111
Fax: 203/353-7175

Carol Wright Consumer Products Promotions (formerly Donnelley Marketing) provides direct-marketing co-op media and sampling programs through ten monthly mailings to 30 million consumers each year (excluding July and December).

Cartesia Software

Keywords: desktop mapping/GIS

Josh Brock, Customer Service
P.O. Box 757
Lambertville, NJ 08530

Phone: 609/397-1611
Fax: 609/397-5724

Cartesia Software provides MapArt, a series of digital map collections. MapArt images can be modified with popular graphics programs like Adobe Illustrator or Freehand, and are royalty-free for printed reproduction. Its collections include everything from complete world views to U.S. maps with counties and highways.

CAS, Inc.

Keywords: analytical services; business to business; customer profiling; database marketing; demographics

Kent Stormberg, President
616 S. 75th Street
Omaha, NE 68132

Phone: 402/393-0313
Fax: 402/390-9497

CAS specializes in database-marketing services. Specific services include demographic overlay, list rental, telephone number appending, modeling, merge/purge, lettershop, penetration analysis, NCOA, business demographics, and list order fulfillment.

Center for Applied Research in the Apostolate (CARA)

Keywords: attitudes and opinions; buying behavior; focus groups; religion

Gerald H. Early, Executive Director
Georgetown University
Washington, DC 20057-1033

Phone: 202/687-8080
Fax: 202/687-8083
E-mail: froehleb@guvax.georgetown.edu

The Center for Applied Research in the Apostolate (CARA) does social-science-based studies with particular emphasis on church or religious communities and ethical issues. CARA operates nationwide and works with clients from the religious and not-for-profit area, as well as from the private sector and government.

Center for Continuing Study of the California Economy (CCSCE)

Keywords: California; consulting; consumer segmentation; local and market information; projections and forecasts

Nancy Levy, Marketing Director
610 University Avenue
Palo Alto, CA 94301

Phone: 415/321-8550
Fax: 415/321-5451
E-mail: calecon@aol.com

CCSCE provides information on current and future trends in California markets. Market segments are presented through detailed analysis and projections of population and households by age, ethnic group, income, and family status. Publications include: *California Population Characteristics, California Economic Growth, and California County Projections.*

Center for Human Resources Research

Keywords: employees/labor force

Steve McClaskie, Coordinator, NLS Public Users Office
921 Chatham Lane, Suite 200
Columbus, OH 43221-2418

Phone: 614/442-7300
Fax: 614/442-7329

Since 1966, the Department of Labor and Ohio State University have been following thousands of men and women through the National Longitudinal Surveys of Labor Market Experience (NLS). Longitudinal data are valuable because they track individuals over time, uncovering the experiences of different groups of people throughout their work lives.

The Survey of Older Men studies the withdrawal from the labor force of more than 5,000 men aged 45 to 59 in 1966. Data were collected from 1966 to 1983, and again in 1990. The Survey of Mature Women tracks more than 5,000 women aged 30 to 44 in 1967. Pension data were collected in 1989.

The Surveys of Young Men and Young Women tracked more than 10,000 adults aged 14 to 24 in 1966 (men) and 1968 (women). Data for men are available through 1981 and for women through 1991. A new panel of nearly 13,000 young men and women was added to the NLS in 1979, and blacks and Hispanics were oversampled in this National Longitudinal Survey of Youth (NLSY). Data for 1979 through 1994 are available. In 1986, 1988, 1990, and 1992, children of NLSY women were interviewed on various cognitive, socioemotional, and physiological measures.

NLS data sets are available on computer tape, and the NLSY is also available on CD-ROM. The *NLS Handbook* is free and lists the publications, services, and data sets available.

Center for Mature Consumer Studies (CMCS)

Keywords: buying behavior; consulting; database marketing; market research; mature market

George P. Moschis, Director
Georgia State University, University Plaza
Atlanta, GA 30303

Phone: 404/651-4177
Fax: 404/651-4198

The Center for Mature Consumer Studies, a university-based research center, conducts national and regional studies, both proprietary and generally available, on purchasing and consumption behavior of older Americans. The Center specializes in measuring consumer response to specific products, advertisements, and sales promotions. It generates data and helps companies translate information about older adults into marketing strategies.

Center for Social & Demographic Analysis

Keywords: analytical services; census data; demographics; economic data; New York

Stewart E. Tolnay, Director
Social Science 340, Univ. at Albany, State Univ. of NY
Albany, NY 12222

Phone: 518/442-4905
Fax: 518/442-4936
E-mail: st716@cnsibm.albany.edu

The Center for Social & Demographic Analysis (CSDA) is a research facility within the College of Arts and Sciences at the University at Albany, State University of New York. Its primary clientele are faculty researchers who require access to large data files such as the U.S. census, Current Population Survey, and General Social Survey. Because CSDA is an affiliate of the New York State Data Center, it also answers inquiries about the social, economic, and demographic characteristics of the state and nation. CSDA's annual Capital District Telephone Survey has been conducted since 1990 and tracks basic demographic information, economic satisfaction, and residential satisfaction among Capital District residents.

Center For The People & The Press (The)

Keywords: attitudes and opinions; elections; media research; political polling

Carol Bowman, Director of Research
1875 Eye Street NW, Suite 1110
Washington, DC 20006

Phone: 202/293-3126
Fax: 202/293-2569

The Center For The People & The Press conducts public opinion surveys on media issues and social and political values. Demographic data include sex, age, education, income, and region. The nationwide surveys cover the years 1985-95 and are available in published reports free of charge.

Central Statistical Office

Keywords: economic data; United Kingdom

Archie Lang, Press Officer
Government Office, Great George Street
London, ENGLAND SW1P 3AQ

Phone: 011-44-171-270-6357
Fax: 011-44-171-270-6019

The Central Statistical Office is a government agency that provides macroeconomic data for the United Kingdom (England, Scotland, Wales, and Northern Ireland), including inflation rates, GDP, GNP, and trade data. It publishes Regional and Social Trends publications with data from the UK Government Statistical Service. Most data are national, but some are broken down by standard regions. Most data are available from 1948 through the present.

Channel Marketing Corporation

Keywords: business to business; consulting; desktop mapping/GIS; market research

David M. Goldstein, President
17400 N. Dallas Parkway, Suite 105
Dallas, TX 75287

Phone: 214/931-2420
Fax: 214/931-5505
E-mail: channel@ix.netcom.com

Channel Marketing Corporation specializes in precision sales and marketing. Its specific focus is in consumer and business-to-business product marketing and sales. Divisions include: Market Research Group, which provides custom-designed research ranging from focus groups and customer satisfaction surveys to in-depth channel audits; Geographic Information Systems Group, which develops targeted approaches to business using desktop mapping; and Consulting Services Group, which develops plans and strategies for new products, channel introductions, and the improvement of existing programs.

Child Research Services (Division of MSW)

Keywords: advertising research; youth and children

Arlyn Brenner, Vice President, Director Client Services
235 Great Neck Road
Great Neck, NY 11021

Phone: 516/482-0310
Fax: 516/482-5180 or 3228

Child Research Services, a division of McCollum Spielman Worldwide (see separate listing), focuses on youth and family research. Standardized and custom services are available. KID*COM offers commercial testing; CAPS involves child/parent interaction studies; and ACCU*TRACK does advertising tracking. Child Research Services offers screening and testing of concepts, premiums/promotion, product, and package as well as attitude usage, focus groups, custom surveys, and more.

Chilton Research Services

Keywords: business to business; consulting; focus groups; market research

Barbara A. Nuessle, Senior Research Project Director
201 King of Prussia Road, Third Floor
Radnor, PA 19089-0193

Phone: 610/964-4694
Fax: 610/964-2942

Chilton Research Services, founded in 1957, provides a full range of market research and consulting services. Specializing in consumer, business-to-business, and multimedia research, Chilton has a staff of more than 200 professionals supported by a group of full-time statistical analysts and programmers.

Claritas, Inc.

Keywords: consumer segmentation; database marketing; demographics; desktop mapping/GIS; local and market information; market research; projections

Kathleen Dugan, Public Relations Officer
1525 Wilson Boulevard, Suite 1000
Arlington, VA 22209

Phone: 703/812-2700 or 800/284-4868
Fax: 703/812-2701

Claritas develops national target marketing databases and software systems designed to meet the marketing needs of various consumer industries. Claritas, an information firm of VNU Marketing Information Services, Inc., has five offices in the U.S.

The company's Compass package is a PC-based targeting system for product development and profiling, site location, strategic planning, media planning, and direct marketing. The system combines and analyzes clients' customer information files, cartographic data, syndicated surveys, demographic indicators, and Claritas's PRIZM and P$YCLE segmentation systems. Compass links directly to several GIS systems and is available in a Windows platform with mapping, data retrieval, and analysis functions. PRIZM classifies U.S. households into 62 neighborhood types.

Claritas offers several products specifically for the financial services industry. P$YCLE is a segmentation system, and LifeP$YCLE is an insurance consumer database. Claritas also offers The Market Audit database, an annual consumer survey of financial services.

Claritas also produces annual demographic estimates and five-year projections for small geographic units. The firm taps 1,600 local sources to annually update its small-area data.

Cognetics, Inc.

Keywords: business to business; employees/labor force

David Birch, President
100 Cambridge Park Drive
Cambridge, MA 02140

Phone: 617/661-0300
Fax: 617/661-0918

Cognetics, Inc. provides targeted marketing services for business-to-business applications. Its software program, Growth Facts, forecasts employment growth for 273 markets and 1,776 submarkets in the U.S. for the next five years.

Compusearch Micromarketing Data & Systems

Keywords: Canada; census data; consumer segmentation; consumer spending; demographics; desktop mapping/GIS; projections

Ian Caminsky
330 Front Street West, Suite 1100
Toronto, ONTARIO M5V 3B7

Phone: 416/348-9180
Fax: 416/348-9195

Compusearch Micromarketing Data & Systems provides demographic and marketing data, including census data, current estimates and projections of households and income, consumer spending potential, PSYTE (Compusearch's new cluster system), taxfiler data, location data for businesses, stores, health-care providers, and shopping centers, plus boundary files, centroid files, streets, and highways available in all popular GIS formats.

CompuServe Incorporated

Keywords: business to business; computer services; online

Russ Robinson, Manager, Public Relations
5000 Arlington Centre Boulevard
Columbus, OH 43220

Phone: 614/457-8600
Fax: 614/457-0348
E-mail: 70006.101@compuserve.com

The CompuServe Information Service provides its worldwide membership with databases and services to meet both business and personal interests. Additionally, CompuServe Incorporated provides frame relay, wide and local area networking services, electronic mail, and business information services to major corporations worldwide.

Computers for Marketing Corporation   Keywords: analytical services; survey software

Leif Gjestland, President   Phone: 415/777-0470
547 Howard Street   Fax: 415/777-3128
San Francisco, CA 94105

Computers for Marketing Corporation (CfMC) has developed software for market
and survey research for more than 25 years. SURVENT (CATI) and MENTOR
(Tabulation) run on PCs, either DOS or UNIX, stand-alone or networked, HP3000,
S/900, S/800 and IBM RS6000 minicomputers. Sound-SURVENT plays commercials during CATI to respondents, and records their open-end responses. CfMC also
operates tabulation bureaus in Denver and San Francisco.

Conference Board (The)   Keywords: consumer confidence; consumer spending

                                                   Phone: 212/759-0900
845 Third Avenue   Fax: 212/980-7014
New York, NY 10022-6601

The Conference Board is a nonprofit membership organization whose Consumer
Research Center conducts ongoing analysis of demographic, social, and economic
changes in the consumer market and of consumer spending. The monthly *Consumer
Confidence Survey* newsletter reports the results of a nationally representative
survey of 5,000 households. The newsletter also reports regional data and buying
intentions for high-ticket items. *The Consumer Market Watch* newsletter carries
current income, employment, expenditure, and price data. The Consumer Market
Guide, which is updated continuously, is a statistical compendium of consumer data.
The center provides annual updates of consumer spending patterns based on the
government's Consumer Expenditure Survey. It also produces crosstabulations of
households and income from the Census Bureau's annual demographic file of the
Current Population Survey.

Conway/Milliken & Associates   Keywords: analytical services; Hispanics; market research; media research

Roger Ehle, President   Phone: 312/787-4060
875 N. Michigan Avenue, Suite 2511   Fax: 312/787-4156
Chicago, IL 60610   E-mail: cma-mkt@interacess.com

Conway/Milliken & Associates is a marketing and research firm providing a full
range of qualitative and quantitative projects for marketers of consumer products
and services. CMA offers experience in new-product development, concept testing,
product testing, tracking, and stategic studies. Special methodologies include:
Super Group ideation and concept development; Q2 Sort multi-item screening; RSM
product optimization; conjoint-based concept optimization; and advanced Discrete

Choice Modeling. The company's CMA Latina division is a Hispanic research group. TV commercial testing and business-to-business research is carried out by Communications Workshop, Inc., a recently acquired CMA company.

Council of American Survey Research Organizations

Keywords: education; market research

Diane Bowers, Executive Director
3 Upper Devon
Port Washington, NY 11777

Phone: 516/928-6954
Fax: 516/928-6041
E-mail: 76103.1407@compuserve.com

The Council of American Survey Research Organizations (CASRO), formed in 1975, now serves as the national trade association for more than 150 survey research companies, representing about 85 percent of U.S. research revenues. CASRO members are dedicated to promoting and ensuring research quality. It provides communication among its members, educates members about research methods and new technology, and safeguards the confidentiality of information gathered from the public in pursuit of clients' research goals.

Creative Research Systems

Keywords: computer services; consulting; survey software

Lisa Bacon
140 Vista View, Suite 100
Petaluma, CA 94952-4729

Phone: 707/765-1001
Fax: 707/765-1068

Creative Research Systems provides The Survey System, a comprehensive PC system for analyzing market research, public opinion, customer satisfaction, and employee attitude surveys. It produces tables and charts from personal, phone, scanner, disk-by-mail, and computer interviews as well as imported data files.

Creative & Response Research Services, Inc.

Keywords: advertising research; consulting; customer satisfaction; focus groups; market research; youth and children

Chris deBrauw, Executive Vice President
500 N. Michigan Avenue
Chicago, IL 60611

Phone: 312/828-9200
Fax: 312/527-3113

Creative & Response Research Services, Inc., (C&R) is a full-service custom research and consulting company that provides strategic studies, customer satisfaction, new-product development, brand imagery and positioning research, concept and advertising testing, research among children (KidSpeak), and concept development using a panel of creative individuals (Idea Team). C&R conducts approximately 1,000 group interviews a year, as well as 1.7 million mail, telephone, and mall intercept interviews.

Customer Insight Company, A Metromail/R.R. Donnelley & Sons Company

Keywords: advertising research; customer profiling; customer satisfaction; database marketing

Andrew J. Kamlet, Manager, Marketing Communications   Phone: 800-ANALYTX
6855 S. Havanna Street, 4th Floor   Fax: 303/643-1535
Englewood, CO 80112

Customer Insight Company provides database marketing systems to large companies for performing targeted direct marketing, profitability analyses, strategic planning, and customer retention and acquisition.

Customer Loyalty Institute (The)

Keywords: brand equity; consulting; customer profiling; customer satisfaction; market research

David L. Stum, President   Phone: 313/769-6868
210 East Huron Street   Fax: 313/769-0611
Ann Arbor, MI 48104-1913   E-mail: dstum@aol.com

The Customer Loyalty Institute is a nonprofit firm that provides research, consultation, education, and assessment to help organizations maximize the economic value of their customer base. The Institute conducts customized research using the Customer Loyalty Advantage Survey (CLAS) model to study consumer behavior and determine the factors and conditions that lead people to remain loyal to an organization or switch suppliers.

D.K. Shifflet & Associates Ltd.

Keywords: buying behavior; consumer spending; demographics; lifestyles; local and market information; travel and tourism

Dennis P. Dijak, Marketing Coordinator   Phone: 703/902-0012
6715 Whittier Avenue, Suite 200   Fax: 703/902-0075
McLean, VA 22101-1721   E-mail: dpd@dksa.com

D.K. Shifflet & Associates conducts syndicated and proprietary research and consulting in the travel and tourism industry for hotels, destinations, and a wide variety of travel-related businesses. It maintains the DIRECTIONS database, which can be segmented by traveler demographics, behaviors, and origin/destination locations. In addition, all data can be linked to PRIZM coding to provide lifestyle profiles and in-depth media and product usage data for specific traveler segments. The DIRECTIONS system provides census-balanced projections for all travel by continental U.S. residents. Data are available by census region, state, county, DMA, metropolitan area, city, and zip code. Lodging data are available since 1989, destination performance data are available since 1991, and destination awareness data are available since 1993.

Dakota Worldwide Corporation

Keywords: Canada; consulting; demographics; desktop
mapping/GIS; market research; Mexico

Tom Mach
4801 W. 81st Street, Suite 105
Minneapolis, MN 55437

Phone: 612/835-4505
Fax: 612/835-4461

Dakota Worldwide Corporation provides market analysis, consumer research, GIS mapping, visual databases, and demographic information to portray a complete picture of clients' North American markets. Customizing services to meet individual client needs, it offers research packages, supplies data, and offers the option of leasing its programs. GIS mapping provides direction in making target marketing and/or positioning decisions based on customer behavior and demographics. While market analysis demonstrates current or future sales potential, consumer research identifies consumer needs and satisfaction.

Danter Company

Keywords: housing and real estate; local and market
information

Terry Hall, Vice President, Director of Marketing
30 Spruce Street
Columbus, OH 43215

Phone: 614/221-9096
Fax: 614/221-4271

The Danter Company provides apartment occupancy and rent data for a significant number of metro areas nationwide, as well as proprietary survey data on upscale apartment renters. It also publishes an apartment industry newsletter, *Apartment Resources*. The Danter Company tracks rental housing demand by metro area and county on a nationwide basis.

Data Group (The), Over 40 Marketing Division

Keywords: baby boomers; consulting;
health care; market research;
mature market; trends

Jeff Ostroff, Vice President
114 Chatham Place
Wilmington, DE 19810

Phone: 302/475-8040, or 215/619-4900
Fax: 302/529-1103, 215/619-4999

The Over-40 Division of the Data Group specializes in helping businesses identify and seize opportunities created by aging baby boomers, mature consumers, grandparents, and the elder-care market. Its services include consulting, keynote presentations/seminars, promotion/publicity, and market research.

Data Mapping Services Corporation

Keywords: demographics; desktop mapping/GIS

Bob Sullivan, President
P.O. Box 1548
Akron, OH 44309-1548

Phone: 216/929-1353
Fax: 216/929-1393

Data Mapping Services Corporation installs customized desktop mapping systems for clients. It also acts as a service bureau to create custom maps. It is a reseller of MapInfo desktop mapping software.

Database America Companies (The)

Keywords: business to business; database marketing; demographics; ethnic markets

Sheila Rees Foster, Vice President,
Advertising/Marketing Communications
100 Paragon Drive
Montvale, NJ 07645-0416

Phone: 201/476-2300
800/223-7777
Fax: 201/476-2405

Database America (DBA) provides business and consumer marketing information and data processing services, focusing on the needs of direct marketers and market researchers. DBA compiles, maintains, and markets a database of more than 11 million businesses, including number of employees; sales volume; contact names by title, gender, and ethnic surname; as well as a complete range of geographic selections. A consumer database of more than 88 million households (160 million individuals) is also available offering such household and individual selection options as age and income ranges, presence and age range of children, gender of head of household, marital status, homeowner vs. renter, ethnic surname selection, mortgage information, and more than 20 other selection criteria. Formats include labels, tape, diskettes, and CD-ROM. The company also offers a full range of data processing services including database creation and maintenance; merge/purge; business and consumer enhancements and statistical modeling; NCOA, NCOA NIXIE, and DSF processing; and list rental fulfillment.

Database Marketing Resource Services, Inc.

Keywords: consulting; database marketing; market research

Bernice Grossman, President
333 Seventh Avenue, 20th Floor
New York, NY 10001

Phone: 212/465-0814
Fax: 212/465-8877
E-mail: dmrsbtg@aol.com

Database Marketing Resource Services, Inc. (DMRS) is an independent consultancy specializing in the design and development of marketing databases. It assists marketers in the vendor selection process as well as filling the project-facilitator position during marketing database projects. DMRS offers marketing database consulting for operational needs assessment and RFP development and administration; technical administration and systems integration; vendor evaluation, selection, contract review, and out-sourcing; due diligence for mergers/acquisitions; expert witness testimony; research, analysis, and modeling; and workshops and seminars.

Datamap Electronic Mapping

Keywords: Canada; desktop mapping/GIS; mailing lists; sales and marketing

Blago Simenov, President
56 Oakmeadow Boulevard
Scarsborough, ON M1E 4G1

Phone: 416/287-3240
Fax: 416/287-3476
E-mail: blago@io.org

Datamap Electronic Mapping provides mapping software, data, and consulting services. It acts as a broker for MapInfo and other software vendors (including training), provides Canadian and U.S. street maps, sells conventional map products, and offers digitizing/scanning services.

Decision Demographics

Keywords: consulting; demographics; mature market; projections and forecasts

Stephen J. Tordella, President
5510 Columbia Pike, Suite 204
Arlington, VA 22204

Phone: 703/931-9200
Fax: 703/931-9201
E-mail: tordella@cpcug.org

Decision Demographics specializes in custom demographic analysis and consulting. Market forecasts for any age, race, household, or family segment can be created. It provides detailed strategic planning reports that project consumer market potential using demographics, survey research, and custom projections. Decision Demographics is also developing a comprehensive database on older Americans.

Decisionmark Corporation

Keywords: attitudes and opinions; business to business; demographics; desktop mapping/GIS; mailing lists; statistical software

Sarah Caldwell, Marketing Representative
200 Second Avenue SE, Suite 300
Cedar Rapids, IA 52401-1214

Phone: 800-365-7629
Fax: 319/365-5694

Decisionmark's Proximity software has information mapping, analysis, and presentation capabilities. The product includes more than 800 population, housing, economic, and agricultural census attributes at the state, county, five-digit zip code and/or census block group level, plus current-year estimates and five-year projections for more than 20 key census attributes at the state and county level. Proximity includes a Data Resource Catalog featuring the leading compilers of consumer and business lists, demographics, psychographics, cartographic data, and specialty databases that may be used within Proximity. Data come map-, graph-, and table-ready. All data come with an installation program so users do not require assistance to access data.

Delphus, Inc.

Keywords: projections and forecasts; statistical software

Hans Levenbach, President
103 Washington Street, Suite 348
Morristown, NJ 07960

Phone: 201/267-9269
Fax: 201/285-1228
E-mail: 74242.1020@compuserve.com

Delphus, Inc. provides Peer Planner for Windows, an integrated forecasting and planning system for sales/marketing, inventory, and production applications. It handles large numbers of items by region and product groupings. Its software is applicable globally.

Demo-Detail

Keywords: demographics; local and market information

Richard Irwin, Director
2303 Apple Hill Road
Alexandria, VA 22308

Phone: 703/780-9563

Demo-Detail provides annual population estimates for all counties in the U.S. by age, sex, and race for 1970 to 1995. Race groups are white, black, American Indian, and Asian. Age groups are in five-year increments to 85 plus, with single years for ages 13 to 19.

Demographics Laboratory (The)

Keywords: consumer segmentation; international; projections and forecasts

Donald B. Pittenger, Director
2065 Lakemoor Drive, S.W.
Olympia, WA 98512

Phone: 360/352-3039

The Demographics Laboratory provides overseas and U.S. demographic market segment estimates and forecasts for nations and subareas such as counties and provinces. Data items include total population and households by type, age of head, and income group. Besides standard data sets, custom output is available for income groups, currency (dollar, yen, etc.), and demographic and household change.

DemoMetrics Corporation

Keywords: consulting; consumer spending; local and market information; market research; retailing

Charles R. Hammerslough
1117 White Street
Ann Arbor, MI 48104

Phone: 800/648-3366
Fax: 313/747-6276
E-mail: 71762.204@compuserve.com

DemoMetrics Corporation specializes in analysis of retail market potential and consumer expenditure. It produces Market Potential Reports for any type of census geography or custom market areas. Customers use Market Potential Reports to inform site selection, determine local market share, and value existing businesses. DemoMetrics' newest product is Market Opportunity Reports that simultaneously evaluate supply and demand within markets to find opportunities. The firm also furnishes custom consulting services.

Demosphere International, Inc.

Keywords: computer services; desktop mapping/GIS; international; local and market information

Kent Hargesheimer, Vice President
2735 Hartland Road, Suite 302
Falls Church, VA 22043

Phone: 800/949-9440
Fax: 703/560-0402

Demosphere International specializes in the development of geo-demographic databases for international markets. It provides GIS-compatible data for the world's most promising markets, including Mexico, Japan, and India.

Direct Marketing Association, Inc.

Keywords: database marketing

1120 Avenue of the Americas
New York, NY 10036-6700

Phone: 212/768-7277 x1155
Fax: 212/768-4546

The Direct Marketing Association (DMA) offers members online services and publications through its Library and Resource Center. Its seminars, conferences, and special-interest councils are places for meeting and learning from fellow professionals. DMA addresses direct-marketing concerns in the marketplace, in the media, and in government.

Disclosure

Keywords: advertising research; business to business; financial services; international

Krista Wilhelm, Marketing Associate
5161 River Road
Bethesda, MD 20816

Phone: 301/951-1300
Fax: 301/951-1753
E-mail: http://www.disclosure.com

Disclosure, a subsidiary of Primark Corporation, provides financial and business information on public companies worldwide. It serves professional, reference, and consumer markets with value-added databases, applications, and source documents. Information is delivered via CD-ROM subscription, online information services, the Internet, magnetic tape lease, and microfiche.

Dow Jones News/Retrieval - Dow Jones & Company, Inc.

Keywords: financial
services; online

P.O. Box 300
Princeton, NJ 08543

Phone: 800/522-3567

Dow Jones News/Retrieval is a comprehensive online source of business and financial news and information. It is the exclusive provider of full text of *The Wall Street Journal* and same-day editions of The New York Times News Service, the *Financial Times,* and the *Los Angeles Times.*

The Dow Jones Text Library includes more than 1,800 business, trade, and general publications, and more than 250 regional newspapers. The system offers an electronic clipping service, drawing information from all resources in the Text Library.

News/Retrieval also offers five real-time Dow Jones' newswires: Dow Jones News Service; Dow Jones International News Services; Capital Markets Report; Emerging Markets Report; Professional Investor Report; and Federal Filings. The full text of major press release wire services, which include PR Newswire, Business Wire, Canada Newswire, and Japan Economic Newswire are also available. The system also provides financial and statistical information on 10 million U.S. and international companies, as well as Dow Jones current, real-time, and historical stock quotes and averages.

Dun & Bradstreet

Keywords: business to business; database marketing;
financial services

Phone: 212/593-6800

299 Park Avenue
New York, NY 10171

Dun & Bradstreet Information Services maintains a database of 20 million businesses worldwide. D&B Information Services produces business information reports and company credit ratings. Dun's Financial Profiles are based on balance sheet and income data. This information is available in print and online.

DYG Inc.

Keywords: consulting; market research

Madelyn Hochstein, President
555 Taxter Road
Elmsford, NY 10523

Phone: 914/347-7200
Fax: 914/347-7415

DYG is a research-based consulting company. It conducts studies and advises clients in the areas of consumer trend identification, marketing planning and strategy, corporate communications, public opinion analysis, and public policy issues management. In addition to proprietary studies, including market segmentation, conjoint analysis, corporate image, and public opinion, the company offers DYG SCAN, a trend-identification program.

EastGate Services

Keywords: China

Elizabeth Homes, Vice President
1226 East Main Street
Stamford, CT 06902-3546

Phone: 203/323-9140
Fax: 203/323-9271

EastGate Services, a subsidiary of Management Counsellors International, provides a large database on Chinese firms. The companies represent 90 percent of the revenue and fixed assets of China's industrial sector and account for more than two-thirds of China's nonagricultural economy. The data are classified by industry code, province, and assets to help locate potential customers, suppliers, or joint venture partners. EastGate's database can be segmented to provide customized industry reports and contact lists. Also available is the Chinese Business Directory, a comprehensive 3-volume work covering 90,000 of the largest Chinese firms and 5,000 major retail and distribution companies.

ECA Windham LLC

Keywords: cost of living;
housing and real estate; international

Gary L. Parker, Managing Director
55 Fifth Avenue
New York, NY 10003

Phone: 212/647-0550
Fax: 212/647-0548
E-mail: 102015.204@compuserv.com

ECA Windham LLC is a membership organization that provides corporations with information and data to use in designing international assignment packages in more than 150 countries. Integrated services include compensation, benefits, cost-of-living, and housing data.

Election Data Services, Inc.

Keywords: desktop mapping/GIS;
education; mailing lists

Kimball W. Brace, President
1225 I Street, NW, Suite 700
Washington, DC 20005-3914

Phone: 202/789-2004
Fax: 202/789-2007
E-mail: kbrace@aol.com

Election Data Services, Inc. is a political consulting firm that provides redistricting and mapping services to public and private organizations. It also offers redistricting software and several geographic and election data products. These include polygon files of congressional and state legislative districts; ZIP+DISTRICT data files and address-matching services linking congressional and state legislative district boundaries to U.S. Postal Service ZIP and ZIP+4 Codes; and county-level election returns from primary and general elections since 1988. District polygon files and ZIP+DISTRICT files are available nationwide or for individual states. Redistricting (database construction) and custom mapping services make use of TIGER/Line geography and census demographic data.

Electronics Industry Association

Keywords: database marketing;
local and market information

Michelle Bing
2500 Wilson Boulevard
Arlington, VA 22201

Phone: 703/907-7751
Fax: 703/907-7769

The Electronics Industry Association's research service uses its customized databases as well as thousands of specialized sources to find electronics industry data. It provides current electronics market information on topics such as consumer electronics, cyberspace, interactive television, sales and trends, demographics, and forecasts.

Elrick & Lavidge

Keywords: consulting; focus groups;
international; market research

Jim Langendorfer, Senior Vice President
1990 Lakeside Parkway, 3rd Floor
Tucker, GA 30084

Phone: 404/938-3233
Fax: 404/621-7666

Elrick and Lavidge is a full-service research company providing quantitative and qualitative marketing research techniques and solutions. Consulting services for new product development and international research capabilities are available.

Employee Benefit Research Institute

Keywords: employees/labor force;
health care; mature market

Laura Bos, Director of Education
2121 K Street, NW, Suite 600
Washington, DC 20037

Phone: 202/659-0670
Fax: 202/775-6312

The Employee Benefit Research Institute's research studies examine trends in health-care plan design, insurance coverage, and cost reduction as well as the financial aspects of pension plans, tax policy and employee benefits, retirement income security, and more. *Employee Benefit Notes* and *EBRI Issue Briefs* are monthly newsletters that evaluate employee benefit issues and trends. EBRI also publishes *EBRI Outlook* three times a year, the *Quarterly Pension Investment Report*, the monthly *Washington Bulletin*, a series of Special Reports, and a variety of books.

Empower Geographics

Keywords: desktop mapping/GIS;
market research; sales and marketing

John H. Hoffman
Continental Office Plaza, 2340 River Road, Suite 416
Des Plaines, IL 60018-3225

Phone: 708/299-6952
Fax: 708/299-6990
E-mail: jhoff@empowergeo.com

Empower Geographics provides maps, demographic data, sales and marketing analysis, as well as custom and embedded applications. It is an authorized partner with MapInfo and Microsoft Excel's DataMap software.

Environmental Research Associates

Keywords: environmental research

Tony Casale, President
707 State Road, Suite 102
Princeton, NJ 08540

Phone: 609/683-0187
Fax: 609/683-8398

Environmental Research Associates (ESRI) provides custom research on environmental issues such as ad tracking, packaging, and community and employee image studies. It publishes *The Environmental Report*, a syndicated study of attitudes toward the environment and their impact on consumer behavior.

Environmental Systems Research Institute

Keywords: consulting; desktop mapping/GIS

Arun Rajavao, Product Marketing
380 New York Street
Redlands, CA 92373

Phone: 909/793-2853
Fax: 909/793-5953
E-mail: @esri.com

Environmental Systems Research Institute (ESRI) provides geographic information system (GIS) software and related services to clients worldwide. In addition to its core GIS software, ARC/INFO, ESRI develops and markets several other related software packages, including ArcView, a geographic data query, display, and output tool for the desktop. ESRI also offers GIS consulting services, including user needs assessment, system design, database design, data automation and conversion, training, and application design and development.

EPS Essential Planning Systems Ltd.

Keywords: desktop mapping/GIS

Alison Malis, Marcom Manager
6772 Oldfield Road, Suite 200
Victoria, BC V8M 2A2

Phone: 604/658-8895
Fax: 604/658-8896
E-mail: amalis@eps.bc.ca

EPS Essential Planning Systems, Ltd. provides PAMAP GIS, an integrated raster/vector PC-based system, which provides full workstation functionality plus an easy to use, customizable Windows graphical user interface. It is an ideal product used in a natural resource/environmental land management applications.

Epsilon

Keywords: analytical services; consulting; database marketing

Natasha Lopoukhine, Marketing Communications Manager
50 Cambridge Street
Burlington, MA 02142

Phone: 617/273-0250
Fax: 617/270-4162

Epsilon is a full-service database-marketing company. It provides strategic marketing consulting and direct-marketing services, and has expertise in a variety of industries.

Equifax National Decision Systems

Keywords: business to business; census data; consumer segmentation; demographics; desktop mapping/GIS; local and market information

5375 Mira Sorrento Place, Suite 400
San Diego, CA 92121

Phone: 800/866-6520
Fax: 619/550-5800

Equifax National Decision Systems offers more than 60 marketing databases; industry-focused expertise; and computer technology for data access, analysis, planning, and targeting. MicroVision is a consumer segmentation and targeting system. Infomark for Windows is a desktop PC system for market analysis, planning, and targeting that provides immediate, unlimited access to any or all of the company's information resources. Sparta is a PC-based software and data package that provides access to a number of business applications, including site evaluation, trade area analysis, CRA analysis, and market optimization. On-CD is a CD-ROM product line providing census demographics, consumer, and business data for places to the census-tract level.

Erdos & Morgan

Keywords: consulting; international; market research

Irene Ochs-Lilien
116 East 27th Street
New York, NY 10016

Phone: 212/685-9393
Fax: 212/685-9629

Erdos & Morgan is a full-service market research company offering experience in national and multi-national, proprietary, and syndicated research for corporate, media, agency, and association clients.

Etak Information Group

Keywords: business to business; demographics; desktop mapping/GIS; local and market information; market research

Nina Pruitt, Market Analyst
214 Carnegie Center, Suite 110
Princeton, NJ 08540

Phone: 800/810-6010
Fax: 609/452-1128

Etak Information Group (EIG) is a division of Etak, Inc., developed to provide mapping software and data to the business geographics marketplace. EIG offers mapping software, demographic data, geocoding services, and business information for the entire U.S.

Euromonitor

Keywords: consumer segmentation; international; market research; projections and forecasts

Katy Beesley, Marketing Assistant
60-61 Britton Street
London, ENGLAND EC1M 5NA

Phone: 011-44-171-251-8024
Fax: 011-44-171-608-3149

Euromonitor provides global consumer market intelligence. It publishes about 600 reports, journals, handbooks, and directories every year. Euromonitor's consultancy division designs and conducts customized research projects and global market information databases for individual clients. The company's research is worldwide with particular focus on the Americas, Western Europe, the Far East, and Southeast Asia. Euromonitor's customers include consumer goods manufacturers, retailers, service providers, advertising and marketing agencies, management consultancies, financial institutions, government departments, libraries, and academic institutions.

Euromonitor International, Inc.

Keywords: business to business; consulting; consumer segmentation; food; health care; international; retailing; travel and tourism; trends

Renuka Sastri, Marketing Executive
122 S. Michigan Avenue, Suite 1200
Chicago, IL 60603

Phone: 312/922-1115
Fax: 312/922-1157

Euromonitor, established in 1972, provides international market analysis and data. It specializes in researching consumer markets including food, beverages, household durables, leisure goods, retailing, travel and tourism, cosmetics and toiletries, and consumer health care. It publishes reports and conducts projects covering Europe, the Americas, the Pacific Rim, and Asia. Euromonitor also provides a research consulting service.

European Society for Opinion & Marketing Research

Keywords: consulting; Europe; market research; media research

Kathy Joe, International Relations Manager
J. J. Viottastraat 29
Amsterdam, NETHERLANDS 1071JP

Phone: 011-31-20-664-21-41
Fax: 011-31-20-664 2922
E-mail: email@esomar.nl

The European Society for Opinion and Marketing Research (ESOMAR) provides market research industry statistics, the International Research Prices Study, International Directory of Market Research Institutes, Reports on European Readership, and TV and Radio Measurement. ESOMAR holds seminars, regional conferences, and an annual congress. It also publishes International Codes and Guidelines Glossary of Technical Terms.

European Union, Delegation of the European Commission

Keywords: demographics; economic data; Europe

Barbara Sloan, Head of Public Inquiries
2300 M Street, NW
Washington, DC 20037

Phone: 202/862-9500
Fax: 202/429-1766
E-mail: www.cec.lu/en/comm/eurostat/eurostat.html

The 15-nation European Union, headquartered in Belgium, is a major source of demographic data for its member countries–Belgium, Denmark, France, Germany, Greece, Ireland, Italy, Luxembourg, the Netherlands, Portugal, Spain, Austria, Sweden, Finland, and the United Kingdom. The organization's most important compendium of demographic data is its annual yearbook, *Demographic Statistics*. This contains data on age, sex, region, vital statistics, migration, and life expectancy, as well as indicators such as age at first marriage. Data for the United States are often included for points of comparison. Current statistics for member countries are published in the monthly *Eurostatistics: Data for Short-Term Economic Analysis*, and include aggregate data on population, labor force, and employment. An annual publication, *Basic Statistics of the Community*, has demographic data on population change and density, and household size. The Statistical Office also publishes occasional reports of demographic interest. Publications are available from UNIPUB, 4611-F Assembly Drive, Lanham, MD 20706; telephone (800) 274-4888.

EXIMEX

Keywords: Mexico

Homero Reyes
503 Beacon Place
Chula Vista, CA 91910-7503

Phone: 619/585-1327
Fax: 619/585-8799

EXIMEX offers market research, feasibility analysis, and data-information gathering for Mexico, as well as direct home/business delivery of preprint inserts, flyers, catalogs, directories, and bulk mailings.

FIND/SVP

Keywords: business to business;
consulting; market research

Andrew P. Garvin, President
625 Avenue of the Americas
New York, NY 10011

Phone: 212/645-4500
Fax: 212/645-7681
E-mail: postmaster@findsvp.com

FIND/SVP is a publicly held worldwide consulting, research, and advisory firm. It operates four integrated service divisions: the Quick Consulting & Research Service, FIND/SVP Publishing, the Strategic Research Division, and the Customer Satisfaction Strategies Division.

First Financial Response

Keywords: business to business; computer services;
computer-assisted surveys; mailing lists

Steve Butler, President
587 N. Ventu F-231
Newbury Park, CA 91320

Phone: 805/339-2539
Fax: 805/496-7157

First Financial Response provides mailing-list management and brokerage services, with more than 60 lists under management and list research/segmentation, including business-to-business and direct-mail response, to narrow the focus of any targeted campaign.

FMP Direct Marketing Group (The)

Keywords: database marketing; mailing lists

Gayle Compton Huff, Vice President & Director
1019 West Park Avenue
Libertyville, IL 60049

Phone: 847/816-1919
Fax: 847/816-1969

The FMP Direct Marketing Group is a full-service direct-marketing organization specializing in targeted consumer and business mailing lists, and data processing, including response analysis and enhancement, full creative agency services, and promotional/incentive programs. It has an understanding of list compilation and database operations.

Food Institute (The)

Keywords: consumer spending; food;
projections and forecasts

Ivy Ellenberg, Marketing Coordinator
28-12 Broadway, P.O. Box 972
Fair Lawn, NJ 07410

Phone: 201/791-5570
Fax: 201/791-5222

The Food Institute is a nonprofit trade association providing information on the food industry. It publishes *The Food Institute Report*, a weekly trade publication covering industry issues and trends including consumer, legislative, and market information. The annual *Food Retailing Review* includes information on consumer food spending, performance of the grocery store and food service industries as well as current industry issues (ECR, Supercenters, Private Label, etc.).

The Demographics of Consumer Food Spending is a recent review of household food expenditures in 27 commodity categories segmented by income, age, household size, household composition, and region. The study also examines food spending for 23 major metropolitan areas and points out changes in age and racial/ethnic distribution projections through the year 2020.

Food Marketing Institute

Keywords: buying behavior; Canada; Europe; food; international; Mexico

Margo Cella, Director, Research
800 Connecticut Avenue, NW
Washington, DC 20006

Phone: 202/429-8286
Fax: 202/429-4589

The Food Marketing Institute conducts a wide variety of studies of consumer behavior as it applies to the supermarket industry. An annual survey has examined consumer food shopping habits and attitudes about nutrition and food safety in the U.S. since 1974. Reports are also available for Canada, Mexico, Europe, and Australia. Other consumer-focused studies include a look at how consumers shop at the supermarket, how they evaluate service, and how they make decisions about meal preparation. FMI studies how health concerns affect consumers' food choices and publishes reports on how to use primary and secondary data for better consumer marketing.

FMI also conducts studies of supermarket industry operations, distribution and logistics, strategic management, financial results, store development, and information systems and technology. Many studies are conducted on an annual basis and track trends in the industry.

Fulton Research, Inc.

Keywords: housing and real estate

George A. Fulton, President
12600 Fair Lake Circle, Suite 260
Fairfax, VA 22033

Phone: 703/802-4706
Fax: 703/803-3022

Fulton Research offers a variety of research and consulting services for those involved in real estate development, such as market area analysis, specific site analysis, planned unit development studies, and pricing and consumer studies. The firm also conducts a national survey of more than 2,000 home shoppers and provides its findings on a national and regional basis.

Futures Group (The)

Keywords: analytical services; business to business; international; projections and forecasts

Lorraine S. Wetstone, Senior Consultant
80 Glastonbury Boulevard
Glastonbury, CT 06033

Phone: 203/633-3501
Fax: 203/657-9701
E-mail: futures@tfg.com

The Futures Group provides emerging markets analysis to help companies identify and prioritize opportunities in new areas of the world. Its Business Intelligence exercises allow executives to make informed decisions about the external business environment, including the larger political, economic, and social forces at work in the world today. The Futures Group Market Information Modeling and Forecasting techniques integrate external information such as consumer demographics with internal corporate data.

FutureScan

Keywords: demographics; lifestyles; trends

Roger Selbert, Editor & Publisher
2118 Wilshire Blvd., #826
Santa Monica, CA 90403

Phone: 310/451-2990
Fax: 310/828-0427

FutureScan is a four-page biweekly newsletter that reports on economic, social, political, technological, demographic, lifestyle, consumer, business, management, work force, and marketing trends. Editor and publisher Roger Selbert is also available for keynotes or other presentations.

Gallup Organization (The)

Keywords: attitudes and opinions; political polling

Leslie C. McAneny, Editor, *Gallup Poll Monthly*
47 Hulfish Street, P.O. Box 628
Princeton, NJ 08542

Phone: 609/924-9600
Fax: 609/683-9256

The *Gallup Poll Monthly* has been published monthly since 1965. The magazine expands upon the Gallup Poll findings from weekly reports released to newspapers and its polls for CNN/*USA Today*. It provides detailed commentary on political, social, and economic issues of the day, drawing on trend data developed over half a century of public-opinion polling. The publication includes tabular material that provides complete breakdowns by demographic groups such as sex, age, race, education, occupation, income, religion, political affiliation, geographic region, and city size. It also features occasional special articles on methodological experiments and in-depth analyses on special topics.

GENESYS Sampling Systems

Keywords: demographics; geocoding; market research; survey samples

Amy W. Starer, Vice President
565 Virginia Drive
Fort Washington, PA 19034

Phone: 215/653-7100
Fax: 215/653-7114

GENESYS Sampling Systems is a full-service research sample provider. In addition to custom samples, it offers the GENESYS Sampling System, including the GENESYS database, a compilation of geodemographic information organized on the basis of telephone area code/exchange combinations. For each of approximately 37,000 area code/exchanges, the GENESYS database provides demographic estimates, PRIZM cluster codes, and geographic designations down to the census-tract level. It can be used for imputing demographic variables for incomplete survey data, appending geographic codes for data analysis, and creating geodemographic profiles from a variety of data sources including ANI, warranty card, or customer database information.

GeoDemX Corporation

Keywords: database marketing; demographics; market research

Larry Brophy, President
17117 West Nine Mile Road, Suite 708
Southfield, MI 48075

Phone: 800/569-3939
Fax: 810/569-1841
E-mail: 76631.1745@compuserve.com

GeoDemX Corporation is a subsidiary of American List Corporation. It manufactures and distributes GeoWizard, a PC-Windows-based, CD-ROM-delivered, focused marketing tool. GeoWizard provides names, address, and phone numbers of prospects within defined geographic areas. GeoWizard integrates software and data from MapInfo (desktop mapping), Claritas (demographic data), Donnelley Marketing (national directory lists), and Qualitative Marketing Software (address standardization). National coverage is updated quarterly.

Geographic Data Technology, Inc.

Keywords: desktop mapping/GIS; geocoding; geographic boundary files

Molly Hutchins, Marketing Manager
11 Lafayette Street
Lebanon, NH 03766

Phone: 800/331-7881
Fax: 603/643-6808
E-mail: sales@gdtl.com or http://www.geographic.com

Geographic Data Technology continuously updates its nationwide street database, which forms the foundation for a range of products: Dynamap/1000, Dynamap/2000, and 5-Digit ZIP Code boundaries; and Address Geocoding Service and Matchmaker/2000 for Windows geocoding software. The company is a major supplier of geographic data to all major GIS and desktop mapping vendors.

GEOQUEST Information Technologies, Inc.

Keywords: census data; computer services; demographics; desktop mapping/GIS; local and market information; projections

Larry Reynolds, Director of Marketing
529 E. Kettle Avenue
Littleton, CO 80122

Phone: 303/730-2818
Fax: 303/727-6778

GEOQUEST is a broker of mapping and demographic software and data sets from a variety of industry sources. It covers all levels of geography, from states to census blocks. Data are available for 1990 census, current-year estimates, and projections.

GEOQUEST provides initial set-up/installation, training, and consultation. GEOQUEST also offers needs assessment, providing guidelines to select the best mapping and demographic data configuration, as well as mapping services, providing full-service presentation-quality maps.

Global Business Opportunities

Keywords: buying behavior; demographics; international; projections and forecasts

Paul M. Seever, Principal
17 Shad Road West
Pound Ridge, NY 10576-2321

Phone: 914/764-4398
Fax: 914/764-0342
E-mail: vcsc02a@prodigy.com

Global Business Opportunities specializes in helping companies better understand and plan for market opportunities around the world, particularly in developing countries, through the use of economic, social, and market data. Typical projects include gathering, organizing, and patterning data; projecting possible futures and developing scenarios for planning; analysis, modeling, and projecting income and consumption distributions; sizing and projecting consumer markets in developing countries; and analysis and projection of household consumption patterns as related to purchasing power parity surveys.

Gordon S. Black Corporation

Keywords: business to business; customer satisfaction; financial services; health care; market research

Robert C. Kallstrand, Vice President - Research
135 Corporate Woods
Rochester, NY 14623-1457

Phone: 716/272-8400
Fax: 716/272-8680

Gordon S. Black Corporation is a full-service market-research firm. Its staff determines/prioritizes key factors driving customer satisfaction for clients in industrial, health care, education, consumer, insurance, banking, and service industry segments. Gordon S. Black specializes in loyalty/retention modeling, new-product development, and market share/potentials.

Group 1 Software, Inc.

Keywords: elections; geocoding; geographic boundary files; mailing lists; statistical software

Delaine Smith, Marketing Analyst
4200 Parliament Place, Suite 600
Lanham, MD 20706-1852

Phone: 800/368-5806
Fax: 301/731-0360

Group 1 Software, Inc. provides Political Coding System software, which enables users to identify individuals' elected representatives by cross-referencing zip+4 codes with political districts. CODE-1 Plus adds, corrects, and confirms 5-digit zip codes; adds carrier route, zip+4, and delivery point codes; and standardizes street, city, and state fields according to USPS standards. StreetRite lets PC users verify, correct, and standardize address data before mapping it. ModelMax is a predictive modeling application that identifies patterns of behavior to determine such things as single and multiple-purchase customers, and lifetime value of a customer. Generalized Selection Plus permits users to target markets by demographics and other zip code directory information and matches and/or merges files and records. dbPROFILE is a clustering and data visualization package. Geographic Coding System adds census-based geocodes, latitude and longitude information, and MSA codes to files in either an online or batch environment. Demographic Coding System contains comprehensive geographic and demographic data that users can append to customer files.

Harte-Hanks Data Technologies

Keywords: analytical services; computer services; database marketing; statistical software

James McNulty, Director
25 Linnell Circle
Billerica, MA 01821

Phone: 508/663-9955
Fax: 508/667-7297

Harte-Hanks Data Technologies, a division of Harte-Hanks Communications, provides marketing database preparation services and develops applications software. Its batch services can process marketing data for use in the relationship between two people in a household, strategic planning, site location analysis, and direct marketing. Software includes modules for query access, predictive modeling for direct mail, and profitability calculation. The software runs on IBM PCs and compatibles, Sun SPARC, IBM RS6000, and DEC Alpha services. Clients include the banking, insurance, retail, automotive, business-to-business, utilities, and mutual fund industries.

Harte-Hanks Direct Marketing/Market Research

Keywords: business to business; database marketing; desktop mapping/GIS; market research

Harte-Hanks National Sales Organization, Inc.
2950 Robertson Avenue
Cincinnati, OH 45209-1266

Phone: 513/458-7701
Fax: 513/458-7666

Harte-Hanks Direct Marketing, a division of Harte-Hanks Communications, maintains four data centers. Data services include cleaning data, NCOA, demographic profiling, database building/management, and mapping. Mapping capabilities include demographic selection, site selection, radius selections, and profiling. Another division, Harte-Hanks Market Research, conducts both consumer and business-to-business research.

Health Service Demand Forecast

Keywords: census data; health care; local and market information

Joe Witherington, President
8606 McKenna Way
Louisville, KY 40291

Phone: 502/239-7800
Fax: 502/239-7800

Health Service Demand Forecast provides health service demand estimates and projections for hospitals, emergency rooms, outpatient clinics, doctors' offices, home health care, and hospice cases at the ICD9 level down to zip code level. It provides statistical data on hospitals, Medicare, patient origin, and destination. Data are available in GIS, dbase, or report format. The information is generated from the latest available survey information linked with geographic census data.

Healthdemographics

Keywords: desktop mapping/GIS; health care; local and market information

Rich Zinne, Vice President, Business Development
4901 Morena Boulevard, Suite 701
San Diego, CA 92117

Phone: 619/581-3400
Fax: 619/581-3495

Healthdemographics provides market planning information, analytical tools, and data for the health-care industry. Clients can obtain information about population, health-care providers, and demand for health-care service specific to their unique market anywhere in the U.S. Delivery options include multiple media formats. HealthPacs are standarized information packages that contain the variables and categories of care most often requested.

Higher Education Research Institute, UCLA Graduate School of Education & Information Studies

Keywords: attitudes and opinions; education; youth and children

Linda J. Sax, Associate Director, or Kit Mahoney
405 Hilgard Avenue
Los Angeles, CA 90025

Phone: 310/825-1925
Fax: 310/206-2228

The Higher Education Research Institute conducts the Cooperative Institutional Research Program (CIRP), established in 1966 at the American Council of Education. CIRP is an empirical study of higher education, involving data on 1,300 institutions, more than 8 million students, and more than 100,000 faculty members. The annual report *The American Freshman: National Norms* provides national normative data for first-time, full-time college freshmen. The report includes information on academic skills and preparation, demographic characteristics, high school activities and experiences, education and career plans, and student attitudes and values. The American Freshman: Twenty-Five-Year Trends provides the same information for the 1966 to 1990 period.

Hispanic Market Connections, Inc.

Keywords: California; Hispanics; Latin America; New York

M. Isabel Valdes, President
5150 El Camino Real, Suite D-11
Los Altos, CA 94022

Phone: 415/965-3859
Fax: 415/965-3874

Hispanic Market Connections, Inc. (HMC) offers Hispanic cultural and marketing expertise to corporations, nonprofits, and government agencies. To describe and measure the Hispanic market, HMC has developed and tested Hispanic market-specific qualitative and quantitative research tools and methodologies. It conducts annual syndicated studies in New York, Chicago, and southern and northern California. HMC also offers marketing and research consulting services in all Latin American countries.

Hispanic Marketing Communication Research

Keywords: Hispanics; Latin America

Felipe Korzenny, PhD
1301 Shoreway Road, Suite 100
Belmont, CA 94002

Phone: 415/595-5028
Fax: 415/595-5407
E-mail: korfel@aol.com

Hispanic Marketing Communication Research (HMCR) conducts Spanish and Portuguese language marketing research in the U.S. and Latin America. It provides full-service qualitative and quantitative research. Its services include copy testing, motivational discovery, product design and evaluation, and cultural analysis for positioning products and services to Hispanics. HMCR also conducts focus groups, in-depth interviews, CATI surveys, and tracking studies. Psycho-socio-cultural Hispanic research is used to understand the diversity of the Hispanic market. It has facilities in the San Francisco-San Jose Bay area and conducts a quarterly Hispanic Omnibus. (HMCR is a division of Hispanic & Asian Marketing Communication Research, Inc.)

Hope Reports, Inc.

Keywords: employees/labor force; market research; media research

Mabeth S. Hope, Vice President
58 Carverdale Drive
Rochester, NY 14618-4004

Phone: 716/442-1310
Fax: 716/442-1725

Hope Reports, Inc. provides national and international statistics, history, market trends, and forecasts for the visual communications technologies, equipment, productions, and information on production company and media unit salaries. Data cover 1970 to 1995, with forecasts to 2000. Hope Reports provides printed reports and custom consulting.

ICR Survey Research Group

Keywords: computer-assisted surveys; consulting; youth and children

Sharon J. Roberts, Vice President/Managing Director
1450 E. American Lane, Suite 1400
Schaumburg, IL 60173

Phone: 708/330-4465
Fax: 708/330-4463

ICR is a full-service custom research firm conducting consumer and business-to-business surveys via telephone, mail, intercept, fax, and diskette. Services include EXCEL, a twice-weekly telephone omnibus, Teen EXCEL, multivariate analysis, customer satisfaction, continuous tracking studies, and automated graphics.

INFO ZERO UN

Keywords: statistical software; survey software

Maurice Beauregard, Commercial Director
1134 Ste-Catherine W., Suite 301
Montreal, QUEBEC H3B 1H4

Phone: 514/861-9255
Fax: 514/861-9209

Info Zero Un offers Interviewer software for CATI surveys on PC networks, as well as CAPI and self-administered surveys. Its TeleAction multi-users telemarketing system includes all Interviewer features and supports various output formats. The Stat XP multi-user statistical system performs descriptive and complex analyses in batch and interactive modes, as well as graphic functions. The Tab XP Windows-based add-on module provides desktop-quality table output.

INFocus, Inc.

Keywords: database marketing; direct marketing; market research

Lois Kaufman, President
707 State Road, Suite 102
Princeton, NJ 08540

Phone: 609/683-9055
Fax: 609/683-8398

INFocus, a national marketing communications firm, offers marketing services ranging from direct marketing to public relations, marketing materials, and marketing planning.

InfoLink

Keywords: advertising research; buying behavior; market research

Janet Gotkin, President
P. O. Box 306
Montrose, NY 10520

Phone: 914/736-1565
Fax: 914/736-3806
E-mail: jgotkin@aol.com

InfoLink provides on-demand business-information retrieval services. Information specialists access a wide range of sources including computer databases, investment reports, market research reports, industry and government experts, editors, and libraries to answer questions relating to all aspects of marketing.

Information Decision Systems

Keywords: demographics; local and market information; mailing lists; retailing

Terry Munoz, President
12770 High Bluff Drive, Suite 215
San Diego, CA 92130

Phone: 619/793-4151
Fax: 619/793-4160

Information Decision Systems (IDS) provides demographic, business, and retail expenditure information on a site-by-site basis for any radius, standard unit of geography, or by specific drive time. The Zip Code Express dataset includes more than 34,000 residential and residential post office zip codes in the U.S. and allows users to select from over 100 variables to create custom databases. All IDS data are current-year information, and they include key variables such as population, households, income, race, retail sales, and daytime population.

Information Resources, Inc.

Keywords: analytical services; buying behavior; consulting; market research; packaged goods

Robert Bregenzer, Vice President, Corporate Communications
150 North Clinton Street   Phone: 312/726-1221
Chicago, IL 60661   Fax: 312/726-0360

Information Resources, Inc. provides a variety of information, software, and consulting services with a particular focus on the consumer packaged-goods industry. IRI's services include proprietary databases, advanced analytics, and software application products to assist clients in testing, executing, monitoring, and evaluating sales, marketing, and distribution programs. Products include InfoScan, InfoScan Census, BehaviorScan, Apollo, and the Partners.

Inforum, Inc.

Keywords: consulting; health care

Frank Condurelis, Senior Vice President - Sales   Phone: 800/829-0600
424 Church Street, Suite 2600   Fax: 615/742-0908
Nashville, TN 37219

Inforum integrates historical patient (or claims) record data, proprietary PULSE research, demographics, PRIZM lifestyle segmentation, and a wide variety of other databases and modeling methodologies into Expert systems, geared to the specific needs of health-care providers and MCOs. Inforum also offers consultation services to assist hospitals in optimizing Disproportionate Share reimbursement. Inforum is currently transitioning all of its products to a Windows-based MediExpert software platform.

Institute for International Research/Marketing Institute

Keywords: business to business; international; market research

Denise Tortora,General Manager   Phone: 212/661-3500
708 Third Avenue, 4th Floor   Fax: 212/661-6677
New York, NY 10017-4103   E-mail: us002506@interramp.com

The Institute for International Research offers business information conferences geared to high-level marketing executives across industries. It promotes interaction between delegates and speakers. Conferences cover topics such as trade promotion, niche marketing, market research and pricing, sales promotion, international marketing, and database-driven marketing. It has put on events discussing specific demographic markets, such as the 50-plus market, kids, and college.

Institute for Social Research, University of Michigan

Keywords: consumer confidence; economic data; elections; lifestyles

Office of the Director
P.O. Box 1248
Ann Arbor, MI 48106

Phone: 313/764-8365
Fax: 313/763-9831

The Institute of Social Research (ISR), University of Michigan, conducts the Panel Study of Income Dynamics. This survey has followed the same households since 1968, providing a unique source of ongoing information about changes in Americans' lifestyles and economic status. ISR has also conducted the National Election Surveys since 1977, and the Surveys of Consumers, which measure people's economic expectations, since 1946.

Instituto Nacional de Estadistica, Geografia e Informatica

Keywords: demographics; desktop mapping/GIS; economic data; Mexico; travel and tourism

Alejandro Del CondeUgarte, Director
Av. Heroe de Nacozari Sur No. 2301,
Edificio de Atencion A Usuarios
Aguascalientes, MEXICO 20270

Phone: 011-52-18-22-32
Fax: 011-18-22-32
E-mail: webmaster@ags.inegi.gob.mx

The Instituto Nacional de Estadistica, Geografia e Informatica provides Mexican demographic, economic, geographic, social, commercial, financial, and tourist information in print for 1990, available for the country, state, municipalities, and census tracts. Many of the data are available on magnetic and optical media.

Integrated Database Technologies, Inc.

Keywords: database marketing; desktop mapping/GIS; statistical software

Tony Clemente, Vice President, Marketing
4100 Main Street, 4th Floor
Philadelphia, PA 19127

Phone: 215/487-4420
Fax: 215/487-3110
E-mail: idtmktg@intedatatech.com

Integrated Database Technologies, Inc. (IDT) provides a PC-based query system known as the DataStation. IDT can integrate numerous sources of internal and external customer and prospect data. The DataStation is a customized desktop database management and ad-hoc/standard reporting system supporting database marketing activities. Reporting capabilities include multidimensional statistical analyses, crosstabulations, profiles, lists, counts, labels, and maps for use in customer and prospect segmentation/profiling/targeting/tracking, response tracking, geodemographic/mapping analysis, customer lifetime value analysis, sales territory alignment, tracking and forecasting sales, identification of cross-selling opportunities, and site and distribution point analysis.

Intelligent Charting, Inc.

Keywords: demographics; desktop mapping/GIS; local and market information; projections and forecasts

Daniel G. Olasin, President
RR 3, Box 78R
Wellsboro, PA 16901

Phone: 717/724-6200
Fax: 717/724-7394

Intelligent Charting, Inc. (ICI) provides custom mapping and data analysis services. Its databases cover the entire U.S., including state, county, zip code, census tract, block group, and metropolitan area. ICI's maps are designed to each customer's specifications and can range from a local street-level area to a map of the entire U.S.

Inter-university Consortium for Political & Social Research

Keywords: attitudes and opinions; census data; consulting; international

Richard Rockwell, Executive Director
P.O. Box 1248
Ann Arbor, MI 48106-1248

Phone: 313/764-2570
Fax: 313/764-8041
E-mail: icpsr_netmail@um.cc.umich.edu

The Inter-university Consortium for Political and Social Research (ICPSR) is a membership-based organization with headquarters and central staff located in the Center for Political Studies at the Institute for Social Research (ISR), University of Michigan. Members include more than 325 colleges and universities in the U.S. and Canada and several hundred additional institutions served by national memberships in Europe, Oceania, Asia, and Latin America.

ICPSR functions as a repository and dissemination facility for computer-readable data for research and instruction in the social sciences and related areas. ICPSR provides access to tens of thousands of data files, including two centuries worth of U.S. census data and a wide range of public opinion and media polls. The data holdings are relevant to a broad spectrum of disciplines including demography, political science, sociology, economics, history, and social psychology, as well as more specialized fields such as crime deviancy, law and criminal justice, aging, public health, urban affairs, and international relations. ICPSR's Gopher facility and Homepage on the Internet provide search tools to query data holdings. Data are available to member institutions at no extra charge beyond the annual membership fee and to nonmembers for an access fee. They are supplied on a variety of media, including magnetic tape, tape cartridge, diskette, CD-ROM, and FTP (File Transfer Protocol). The annual Summer Training Program in Quantitative Methods of Social Research provides instruction in quantitative research skills. ICPSR also provides consultation in applying computer technology to research and instructional uses.

Interactive Market Systems, Inc.

Keywords: computer services; local and market information; market research; media research

Alison A. Porter, Marketing Manager
11 West 42nd Street
New York, NY 10036

Phone: 212/789-3600
Fax: 212/789-3636
E-mail: www.imsusa.com

Interactive Market Systems, Inc. (IMS) provides access to more than 600 databases and studies, including syndicated and proprietary, media and marketing, consumer, trade, domestic, and international data. IMS's Windows-based software integrates data and systems, providing comprehensive software solutions to meet the information needs of advertisers, agencies, and print and broadcast media.

Interpretive Software, Inc.

Keywords: automotive; computer services; health care; market research

Stu James, President
1932 Arlington Boulevard, Suite 107-109
Charlottesville, VA 22903

Phone: 804/979-0245
Fax: 804/979-2454
E-mail: 70401.2062@compuserve.com

Intrepretive Software, Inc. offers marketing simulations including PharmaSim, a brand-management simulation for the pharmaceutical industry, and AutoSim, which provides an overview of the small-car segment of the U.S. auto industry. Both products are compatible with a variety of operating systems. Each simulation can also be customized to the individual needs of the user or administrator.

Intersearch Corporation

Keywords: customer satisfaction; financial services; focus groups; health care; international; market research; packaged goods; telecommunications

Bruce Shandler, President
410 Horsham Road
Horsham, PA 19044

Phone: 215/442-9000
Fax: 215/442-9040

Intersearch is a full-service international survey firm with six offices in the U.S. Intersearch focuses on research for information technology, telecommunications, pharmaceutical, health care, scientific instrumentation, financial services, insurance, and consumer packaged-goods clients. The types of research performed include new-product development, customer satisfaction and quality measurements, positioning/strategy/tactical research, segmentation studies, pricing research, and tracking studies. A Service Quality Group provides consultation and ongoing research in support of total quality initiatives and satisfaction and quality information programs. A Health Science Group offers managed care and pharmaceutical/medical products research. An Advanced Methods Group offers consultation and development of research methodologies. The data collection methodologies include depth interviews, focus groups, teleconferences, mall intercept studies, personal interviews, and telephone interviewing through six CATI-equipped interviewing centers that have 500 WATS stations.

Irwin Broh & Associates, Inc.

Keywords: database marketing; lifestyles; market research

David Waitz, Executive Vice President
1011 E. Touhy Avenue
Des Plaines, IL 60018

Phone: 708/297-7515
Fax: 708/297-7847

Irwin Broh & Associates conducts Marcom, a quarterly national consumer omnibus survey of 50,000 households. Its Leisure Time Tracking Study is a quarterly study of how people allocate their time. The firm also conducts custom market-research surveys.

J. D. Power & Associates

Keywords: automotive; customer satisfaction; financial services; international; market research; sales and marketing

Steve Goodall, Senior Partner
30401 Agoura Rd
Agoura Hills, CA 91301

Phone: 818/889-6330
Fax: 818/889-3719
E-mail: jdpa@aol.com

J.D. Power & Associates is an international market research firm that measures and analyzes consumer opinions and behaviors including customer satisfaction. The firm conducts syndicated and proprietary studies in the telecommunications, automotive, office products, airline, and financial services industries. The firm is headquartered in Agoura Hills, California, with branch offices in Detroit; Westport, Connecticut: Torrance, California; Toronto; Tokyo; and London.

Journal of Business Forecasting

Keywords: market research; projections and forecasts; sales and marketing

Chaman L. Jain, Editor
P.O. Box 159, Station C
Flushing, NY 11367

Phone: 718/463-3914
Fax: 718/544-9086

The *Journal of Business Forecasting* contains articles dealing with how to prepare and use forecasts in a business environment. The *Journal* also provides forecasts of key economic variables of 47 different countries. Readers are primarily practicing forecasters of large corporations worldwide.

Jupiter Communications, LLC

Keywords: computer services; consulting; media research; online

Dennis Cedeno, Marketing Assistant
627 Broadway
New York, NY 10012

Phone: 212/780-6060
Fax: 212/780-6075

Jupiter Communications, LLC, is a research, consulting, and publishing firm specializing in emerging consumer online and interactive technologies. Its research reports, newsletters, multi-client studies, and industry seminars provide clients and customers with focused research and strategic planning support as they develop interactive products and services.

KidFacts Research

Keywords: advertising research; entertainment; market research; media research; youth and children

Lisa Adelman, Director of Marketing Research
34405 West Twelve Mile Road, Suite 121
Farmington Hills, MI 48331

Phone: 810/489-7024
Fax: 810/489-7056

KidFacts Research designs, conducts, and analyzes qualitative marketing and advertising research with children, teens, and parents. It has worked with a variety of industries including toys and games, food and beverages, apparel, computer software, CD-ROM, television, entertainment, and advertising research.

Knight-Ridder Information, Inc.

Keywords: academic research; business to business; Europe; health care; online

Sharyn Fitzpatrick, Sr. Director, Marketing Communications
2440 El Camino Real
Mountain View, CA 94040

Phone: 415/254-7000
Fax: 415/254-8093

Knight-Ridder Information, Inc., formerly Dialog Information Services, is a comprehensive source of electronic information for scientific and business research. Serving information searchers since 1972, DIALOG and its sister service DataStar (acquired in 1993) offer one of the largest collections of digital information in the world, including news, industry analysis, and market research, as well as coverage of European companies and industries. It provides scientific and technical information, from biomedicine, pharmaceuticals, and health care to chemistry, engineering, and computer science, as well as a collection of intellectual property data. All databases are available online, and more than 75 titles are now available on CD-ROM.

Knowledge Source

Keywords: customer satisfaction; Europe; health care; international; local and market information; market research

John E. Santilli, President
137 Wood Avenue
Stratford, CT 06497

Phone: 203/377-0883
Fax: 203/381-9801

Knowledge Source provides a variety of custom market intelligence services, including MarkeTrack, which tracks competitors, customers, and industries; EuropeWatch, focusing on European issue and industry analyses; and SatisFacts, providing customer satisfaction surveys. It also publishes *Regional HealthCare Digest*, a custom-tailored report that integrates regional and metropolitan market information and covers topics such as the demographic, cultural, and media influences that form local attitudes and opinion.

Langer Associates, Inc.

Keywords: focus groups; lifestyles; market research; trends

Judith Langer, President
19 West 44th Street
New York, NY 10036

Phone: 212/391-0350
Fax: 212/391-0357

Langer Associates, Inc. specializes in qualitative studies of social and marketing issues. The firm conducts focus groups, personal and telephone depth interviews, and offers consulting services on trends. The *Langer Report* is a syndicated newsletter on changing values and lifestyles. TrendSpotter studies identify emerging trends.

Latin American Demographic Centre (CELADE), United Nations

Keywords: demographics; Latin America; projections and forecasts; women

Reynaldo F. Bajraj, Director
Casilla 91
Santiago, CHILE

Phone: 011-56-2-210-2023
Fax: 011-56-2-208-0196
E-mail: rbajraj@eclac.cl

CELADE offers a variety of publications and software regarding the demography of Latin America. *Population Abstracts* scan current literature on the topic (bibliographic citations in English); Spanish-language books cover related subjects; and bilingual *Demographic Bulletins* provide population projections for Latin-American countries by urban/rural, age, economic status, and so on. Bulletin data are also available on diskette. A variety of software programs produce estimates and projections of populations and vital statistics. REDATAM-Plus stores, provides access to, and does crosstabulations of census and survey data; and DOCPAL CD-ROM is an annual compilation of bibliographic materials on Latin-American demography.

Leisure Trends, Inc.

Keywords: entertainment; fitness and sports; lifestyles

James Spring
3004 Arapahoe Avenue, 2nd Floor
Boulder, CO 80303

Phone: 303/786-7900
Fax: 303/786-9009

Leisure Trends, Inc., a licensee of the Gallup Organization, conducts a quarterly survey of how Americans spend their leisure time. Data include demographics and geographics, and profiles time-starved and time-rich Americans. Users receive customized versions of the activities Americans participate in during their leisure and activities they prefer doing by day, week, season, and annually from 1990 to the present.

LEXIS-NEXIS

Keywords: attitudes and opinions; business to business; online; trends

Tom McElroy, Market Manager
9443 Springboro Pike
Miamisburg, OH 45342

Phone: 800/227-9597 x5365
Fax: 513/865-1780
E-mail: thomas.mcelroy@lexis-nexis.com

LEXIS-NEXIS provides NEXIS, a premier database containing more than 4,000 sources of national and international news, financial, industry, and marketing information. Because of the continuity of database design, researchers can use similar search logic in a wide variety of databases. Highlights include the Roper Center's Public Opinion Poll dating back to 1935, several consumer trends publications, and Lexis-Nexis's Predicasts. The new Market Quick & Easy product helps marketing professionals easily find information essential to their work–competitors' marketing strategies, industry forecasts, brand and product category analysis, pricing information, new-product introductions, and more.

Lifestyle Change Communications, Inc.

Keywords: database marketing; lifestyles; market research

Tracy Finley, Director of Marketing
1700 Water Place, Suite 150
Atlanta, GA 30339

Phone: 770/984-1100
Fax: 770/984-8111
E-mail: lccatlanta@aol.com

Lifestyle Change Communications, Inc. (LCC) founded and incorporates the concept of synchographics, a marketing technique factoring time into the direct-marketing equation. When people go through life transitions like having a baby or moving, they want and need to buy lots of products and services, often during a brief window of opportunity.

LCC offers direct-media programs such as co-op mailing envelopes, ride-alongs, hand-alongs personally delivered to the consumer, and package inserts. Many of these programs make traditionally elusive markets easier to reach. LCC also features blow-in and bind-in media options in consumer magazines.

LCC provides a way to identify prospects through the Omnibus Telephone Survey. American Purchase Diary (APD) is a proprietary database with 93 million records available for precise targeting, enhancement, and modeling. World Savings Network (WSN) is a customized savings club for added benefits, enhancements, or incentive programs. Clients can create their own program from a varied selection of benefits tailored to suit their customers.

LIMRA International, Inc.

Keywords: consulting; financial services; international; sales and marketing

LIMRA InfoCenter
300 Day Hill Road
Windsor, CT 06095

Phone: 203/285-7767
Fax: 203/298-9555

LIMRA is a trade association for the financial services industry that supports and enhances the marketing function of its member companies around the world through original research, products, and services. LIMRA compiles data facets of the insurance industry. Through periodic and one-time research projects, LIMRA monitors, evaluates, and predicts trends and developments, and builds tools and services to improve marketing management and sales effectiveness. LIMRA houses a comprehensive library of financial services-related information.

LINK Resources Corporation

Keywords: analytical services; Asia; entertainment; Europe; market research; media research

Andy Bose, Group Vice President
79 Fifth Avenue, 12th Floor
New York, NY 10003

Phone: 212/627-1500
Fax: 212/620-3099

LINK Resources is a market research consulting firm for the electronic services industries. LINK assists technology vendors and service suppliers in capitalizing on opportunities emerging from the convergence of the communications, computing, information, and entertainment industries, and tracks trends in work-at-home and home-based entertainment. It also conducts multi-client surveys of consumers and business markets in the U.S., Europe, and Asia/Pacific region. LINK is a division of International Data Corporation.

Louis Harris and Associates, Inc.

Keywords: attitudes and opinions; focus groups; political polling; trends

David Krane, Executive Vice President
111 Fifth Avenue, 8th Floor
New York, NY 10003

Phone: 212/539-9600
Fax: 212/539-9669
E-mail: dkrane@lha.gannett.com

Louis Harris and Associates, Inc. conducts national public opinion surveys. It also publishes *The Harris Poll*, which provides trend data on a wide variety of subjects.

M/A/R/C Group

Keywords: consulting; database marketing; international; market research; survey software

Pete Bogda, President, M/A/R/C Consulting Group
7850 N. Belt Line Road
Irving, TX 75063

Phone: 214/506-3434
Fax: 214/506-3505

The M/A/R/C Research Company provides full service, custom marketing research for domestic, Hispanic, and international clients. Targetbase marketing provides database marketing programs including design, database management, creative, and execution. The M/A/R/C Consulting Group specializes in the preparation of strategic and tactical marketing plans. Its Automated Custom Research System (ACRS) is a fully integrated package designed by researchers to automate questionnaires, sampling, data collection, data preparation, and tabulation.

M/S Database Marketing

Keywords: business to business; customer profiling; customer satisfaction; database marketing; focus groups; online

Robert McKim, Partner, Strategic Marketing
10982 Roebling Avenue, Suite 101
Los Angeles, CA 90024

Phone: 310/208-2024
Fax: 310/208-5681
E-mail: http://www.rmckim@msdbm.com

M/S Database Marketing business services include database marketing, online/interactive, and decision support systems for both consumer and business-to-business industries. It also offers market segmentation, customer profiling, lifetime value estimates, satisfaction surveys, and focus groups.

MacFarlane & Company, Inc.

Keywords: international; risk assessment

Ian MacFarlane, President
Suite 450, One Park Place, 1900 Emery Street, NW
Atlanta, GA 30318

Phone: 404/352-2290
Fax: 404/352-2299

MacFarlane & Company, Inc. distributes more than 500 titles in hard copy and CD-ROM on international marketing, international business, and Business Environment Risk Intelligence. Publications include three multi-client study directories, all Euromonitor publications, all Datamonitor reports, all Kompass directories published worldwide, Marketing Survey for Industries, Marketsearch, Findex, and many others. MacFarlane also conducts international marketing research and consulting studies on a proprietary basis.

Macro.AHF Marketing Research and Consultancy

Keywords: advertising research; business to business; computer-assisted surveys; consulting; market research; projections and forecasts

Beryl L. Levitt, President
100 Avenue of the Americas
New York, NY 10013

Phone: 212/941-5555
Fax: 212/941-7031
E-mail: ahf@escape.com

Macro.AHF Marketing Research and Consultancy provides full-service, custom-designed qualitative/quantitative research. It conducts small-scale tests to full-scale national studies as well as consumer, executive, business-to-business research; concept and copy testing, positioning, segmentation and tracking studies; research (claim substantiation or challenge/expert testimony and representation at court/jury selection). Macro.AHF Marketing Research and Consultancy provides full multivariate skills; LoMACAST MODEL for new-product forecasting, 200-station in-house CATI telephone facility with predictive dialing or personal outside interviewing.

Macro International Inc.

Keywords: computer-assisted surveys; customer satisfaction; focus groups; international; market research

Sheila Paterson, Vice President
805 Third Avenue
New York, NY 10022

Phone: 212/888-4141
Fax: 212/888-0140
E-mail: paterson@macroint.com

Macro International provides full-service market research in more than 80 countries worldwide. Macro owns and operates offices in New York City, Washington, D.C., Atlanta, and Burlington, Vermont, as well as Moscow, Warsaw, Budapest, Prague, Jeddah (Saudi Arabia), and Cairo. Macro's Burlington office has a 99-station CATI center, and Macro-AHF in New York City offers a 100-station CATI system. All of Macro's U.S. and Eastern European offices also offer full-service focus groups.

Mailer's Software

Keywords: consumer segmentation; database marketing; local and market information

William Carter, Marketing Manager
970 Calle Negocio
San Clemente, CA 92673-6201

Phone: 714/492-7000
Fax: 714/492-7086
E-mail: mailers@netcom.com

Mailer's Software provides software-based solutions for reducing postal costs. Its nationwide software and database products help mailers maintain lists, standardize information, and mail more efficiently.

Management Horizons, a Consulting Division of Price Waterhouse LLP

Keywords: attitudes and opinions; buying behavior; consulting; market research; projections and forecasts; retailing

Peter Doherty, Principal Consultant
41 South High Street
Columbus, OH 43215

Phone: 614/365-9555
Fax: 614/365-7010

Management Horizons, a division of Price Waterhouse LLP, is a management consulting and market research firm specializing in the retailing and consumer-goods distribution industries. Management Horizons' proprietary consumer database contains results of national shopping behavior surveys conducted since 1986.

Management Horizons conducts strategy development, including market positioning, new concept development, retail merchandising and operating strategies, and retail growth and expansion planning. It also provides strategic information systems planning, package system selection, and custom system development and implementation. Its Retail Intelligence System is a subscription service that offers conferences, critical issue reports, economic forecasts, and the national consumer database.

MapInfo Corporation

Keywords: desktop mapping/GIS; geocoding; geographic boundary files; international

One Global View
Troy, NY 12180

Phone: 800/327-8627
Fax: 518/285-6070
E-mail: sales@mapinfo.com or http://www.mapinfo.com

MapInfo Corporation develops desktop mapping software solutions for data visualization and geographic analysis. Applications run on multiple platforms (Windows, Macintosh, Sun, Hewlett-Packard). An array of international maps, as well as market and statistical data, is available. Remote client/server data access via SQL DataLink and customized vertical applications with the MapBasic Development Environment allows users to intuitively analyze data and explore "what-if" scenarios. MapInfo has international offices in Tokyo, Sydney, Hong Kong, Beijing, the United Kingdom, and Germany.

MapPix

Keywords: desktop mapping/GIS; Europe; sales and marketing

Richard Miller, General Manager
1800 Sherman Avenue, Suite 200
Evanston, IL 60201

Phone: 708/492-3400 or 800/8-MAPPIX
Fax: 708/864-6378
E-mail: mappix@mappix.com

MapPix provides custom maps and reports for business applications, including sales force management, target marketing, service area analysis, site selection, and more. Capabilities allow for quick and accurate data processing, economical high-volume printing, and large-format output. Maps can be of any U.S. geography from the national level to the neighborhood level (some European geographies available).

Maritz Marketing Research Inc.

Keywords: customer satisfaction; international; market research

Phil Wiseman, Marketing Director
1297 North Highway Drive
Fenton, MO 63099

Phone: 800/446-1690
Fax: 314/827-8605
E-mail: wisemapl@maritz.com

Maritz Marketing Research is a nationwide firm that conducts custom and syndicated studies in the U.S. and abroad. It specializes in customer satisfaction measurement and offers full-service research in key areas: qualitative, tactical (tracking; attitude, trial, and usage, etc.), and strategic (product positioning, market segmentation, etc.).

Mark Clements Research, Inc.

Keywords: advertising research; attitudes and opinions; cost of living; market research; media research

Mark Clements, President
516 Fifth Avenue
New York, NY 10036

Phone: 212/221-2470
Fax: 212/221-7628

Mark Clements Research, Inc. is a full-service research firm that provides marketing management, sales, product, and attitude research for manufacturers, media, advertising agencies, and industry associations. It conducts individually designed quantitative and qualitative custom studies and tracking programs.

Market ACTION

Keywords: analytical services; computer
services; consulting; market research

Betsy Goodnow
2222 Westerland #250
Houston, TX 77063

Phone: 713/789-0652
Fax: 713/789-0652
E-mail: betsygood

Market ACTION provides DOS and Windows versions of statistical software for perceptual mapping of relationships among categories in crosstabulations. It is appropriate for demographic, economic, media, and other survey data. Uses include identifying needs, describing regions, tracking changes, segmenting populations, comparing institutions, and evaluating progress. The software generates a CGM (symbol) for presentations, and positions categories on axes to represent multivariate relationships.

Market Analysis and Information Database, Inc. (Corporate Profound)

Keywords: business to business;
financial services; market research; online

John M. O'Brien, Director of Marketing
655 Madison Avenue
New York, NY 10021

Phone: 212/750-6900
Fax: 212/750-0660

Market Analysis and Information Database, Inc., provides Corporate Profound, an online business service that offers comprehensive business, news, and research databases. The service features news from more than 4,000 newspapers, periodicals, and news wires, more than 40,000 full-text research reports, as well as financial reports and research on millions of companies. In addition, thousands of industry and company briefings can be accessed, along with current prices on stocks and commodities. The service offers an unlimited number of end users per site, immediate access to research upon publication, and a sophisticated customization feature that automically searches for pre-defined data.

Market Development, Inc.

Keywords: consulting; ethnic markets;
Hispanics; Latin America

Roger Sennott, Vice President, General Manager
1643 Sixth Avenue
San Diego, CA 92101

Phone: 619/232-5628
Fax: 619/232-0373

Market Development, Inc. is a full-service research company that provides transcultural consumer and marketing research. It conducts qualitative and quantitative research in Latin America and among U.S. Hispanics. Services include custom studies, Hispanic COPY-TRAC (standardized copy-testing of Spanish-language commercials), Hispanic OMNIBUS (shared-cost U.S. Hispanic quarterly survey), and the Latin American COMPASS (syndicated psychographic survey of major Latin American markets). MDI publishes two newletters, *Hispanic Perspective* and

Latin America Perspective. Telephone interviewing services are available through its subsidiary, MDIIS. It has branch offices in New York City, Mexico City, Sao Paulo, Buenos Aires, and Santiago.

Market Facts, Inc.

Keywords: advertising research; brand equity; market research

Tom Payne, President
3040 West Salt Creek Lane
Arlington Heights, IL 60005

Phone: 708/590-7000
Fax: 708/590-7010

Market Facts is a nationwide marketing research organization that conducts custom studies to solve specific marketing problems relating to consumer goods and services, such as health care, automotive, and industrial markets. Its mail survey panel consists of more than 450,000 households.

Market Opinion Research

Keywords: automotive; customer satisfaction; financial services; focus groups; health care; international; market research; utilities

Pete Haag, Vice President
31700 Middlebelt Road, Suite 200
Farmington Hills, MI 48334

Phone: 810/737-5300
Fax: 810/737-5326

Market Opinion Research (M.O.R.) specializes in strategic research and planning, market analysis, customer satisfaction, and advertising testing. M.O.R. provides information services for the automotive, consumer, health care, financial, advertising, media, government, and utilities industries. M.O.R. offers 190 networked WATS-line interviewing stations and state-of-the-art focus-group facilities.

Market Segment Research & Consulting

Keywords: consulting; ethnic markets; Latin America; market research

Gary L. Berman, President
1320 South Dixie Highway, Suite 120
Miami, FL 33146-2911

Phone: 305/669-3900
Fax: 305/669-3901

Market Segment Research & Consulting is a full-service research and consulting firm specializing in the Hispanic, African-American, Asian, and Anglo markets in the United States. The range of its work encompasses economic, demographic, social, political, and marketing studies. The firm has affiliates throughout Latin American.

Market Statistics, a Division of Bill Communications

Keywords: consulting; consumer segmentation; demographics; desktop mapping/GIS; projections and forecasts; retailing

Frank Pinizzotto, Vice President, Sales and Marketing
355 Park Avenue South
New York, NY 10010

Phone: 800/685-7828
Fax: 212/592-6259
E-mail: http://marketstats.com

Market Statistics is a 66-year-old data company whose core products are derived from the production of geodemographic information for a variety of industries and applications. Market Statistics provides an economic framework for much of its data, including Effective Buying Income (disposable income), Buying Power Indexes, and actual retail sales for communities and other small-area geographies such as zip codes. Market Statistics helps companies understand the economic environment of their distribution networks. In addition, Market Statistics publishes the Survey of Buying Power, Study of Media and Markets, and the Demographics USA series of books. Market Statistics has its own data reporting and analysis software, DART, which is a database management program that delivers comprehensive zip code, city, and county data. Market Statistics has also partnered with Scan/US, Inc. to develop a marketing information system that bundles data, boundaries, and software together in an easy-to-use mapping and analysis tool. This latter series of products is marketed under the MarketIntellect trademark.

Market Strategies, Inc.

Keywords: attitudes and opinions; focus groups; health care; market research; media research; political polling; survey software

Alex Gage, President, Politics & Policy Group
2000 Town Center, Suite 2600
Southfield, MI 48075

Phone: 810/350-3020
Fax: 810/350-3023
E-mail: http://www.mktstrat.com

Market Strategies, Inc., is a survey research and consulting firm organized into four strategic business units: Information & Technology (high tech, communications, media); Energy Utilities Research & Consulting; Health Care; and Politics & Policy. MSI conducts public opinion surveys and focus groups, both national and international. It also offers the Perception Analyzer Interactive Research System software for focus groups, meetings, and educational markets.

Marketing Evaluations/TVQ

Keywords: advertising research; entertainment; market research; media research

Steven Levitt, President
14 Vanderventer Avenue
Port Washington, NY 11050

Phone: 516/944-8833
Fax: 516/944-3271

Marketing Evaluations/TVQ provides national syndicated consumer surveys in five specific categories: TVQ program ratings, sports Q ratings, performer Q ratings, product Q ratings, and cartoon Q ratings. Q ratings measure familiarity and appeal or popularity. All studies are conducted by mail using the company's "People Panel" of 60,000 cooperating households.

Marketing Intelligence Service, Ltd.

Keywords: food; international; packaged goods

Thomas R. Vierhile, General Manager
6473D Route 64
Naples, NY 14512

Phone: 716/374-6326
Fax: 716/374-5217

Marketing Intelligence Service publishes a variety of newsletters that report the introduction of new packaged goods. Titles include: *Product Alert* (published 51 times a year); *International Product Alert* (published twice monthly); *Category Report* (published monthly in Foods; Beverages; Health & Beauty Aids; Household, Pet & Miscellaneous Products editions); and *Lookout Foods* and *Lookout Nonfoods* (both published twice monthly), which discuss new product innovations.

Marketing Masters

Keywords: online; survey software

Jodi Smits, Marketing Manager
P.O. Box 545
Neenah, WI 54957-0545

Phone: 414/788-1675
Fax: 414/788-1675
E-mail: jsmits@masters.atw.fullfeed.com

Marketing Masters has survey software for all computer-based environments. Survey Said for Windows does survey administration, data collection, and analysis on stand-alone or networked PCs. Add-on modules allow data to be collected non-Windows PCs and through the mail. Survey Said for Networks and for the Web perform similar functions on local area networks and through Internet Worldwide Web sites.

Marketing Research Association, Inc.

Keywords: consulting; market research

Maureen Blake, Staff Manager, Publications & Marketing   Phone: 860/257-4008
2189 Silas Deane Highway, Suite 5   Fax: 860/257-3990
Rocky Hill, CT 06067   E-mail: aamra@aol.com

The Marketing Research Association, Inc. (MRA) is a national association with approximately 2,300 members. The association promotes excellence in marketing and opinion research, providing members with a variety of opportunities for advancing their marketing research and related business skills. MRA also acts as an industry advocate with appropriate government entities, other associations, and the public. It publishes a variety of tools for researchers (including the *Blue Book, Research Services Directory*) and holds two annual conferences.

Marketing Science Institute

Keywords: academic research; consulting

Marni Clippinger, Director of Communications   Phone: 617/491-2060
1000 Massachusetts Avenue   Fax: 617/491-2065
Cambridge, MA 02138

The Marketing Science Institute is a nonprofit research organization established in 1961 as a bridge between business and academia. The Institute's mission is to create knowledge to improve business performance. It does this by stimulating, supporting, and publishing academic research that addresses topics specified by its sponsoring corporations. The Institute brings together corporate executives with researchers from approximately 100 universities worldwide. Its activities are supported by member corporations and research grants from other sponsoring organizations.

Marketing Techniques

Keywords: consulting; customer satisfaction; information technology; market research

Sharman Egan, President   Phone: 404/892-8838
75 Fourteenth Street, Suite 2410   Fax: 404/892-8622
Atlanta, GA 30309   E-mail: 75317.2341@compuserve.com

Marketing Techniques provides product marketing consulting and market data for information technology companies. It conducts studies and advises clients in the areas of product planning and strategy, market segmentation, market size projections, target audience identification, and competitive strategy. Services include qualitative research, customer satisfaction surveys, and online computer-based research.

Marketing to KIDS Report (The)

Rena Karl, Executive Editor
3364 Country Rose Circle, 2nd Floor
Encinitas, CA 92024-5709

Keywords: youth and children

Phone: 619/756-5446
Fax: 619/756-5857

The Marketing to KIDS Report, published by North Shore Communications since 1987, is an international monthly newsletter covering news, trends, and developments in all youth market segments, ages 2 to 18. The Marketing to KIDS Report Annual Fall and Spring Conferences feature expert speakers and interactive workshops for senior-level corporate executives, advertising agencies, and marketing firms.

MarketLine International

Keywords: business to business; consumer segmentation; international; market research; online

Jeff Howard, Sales Executive
41 Madison Avenue, 5th Floor
New York, NY 10010

Phone: 212/661-2525
Fax: 212/661-5551

MarketLine International is an independent market analysis company that publishes more than 500 market reports each year with an emphasis on business-to-business, industrial, and consumer markets. Its reports are also available online and cover markets in Europe, Asia Pacific, Latin America, the U.S., and Japan. Diverse topics include global car rental, European soft drink and food markets, and Latin-American cosmetics and toiletries trends.

Marketplace Information Corporation

Keywords: business to business; consumer segmentation; database marketing; market research

Kristy Martin,New Business Manager
460 Totten Pond Road
Waltham, MA 02154

Phone: 800/590-0065
Fax: 617/672-9290
E-mail: leads@mktplace.com

MarketPlace Information Corporation provides D & B MarketPlace, a business-to-business marketing tool on CD-ROM, with information on more than 10 million businesses. Each record includes an executive contact, address, phone number, industry sector, number of employees, annual revenue, and more. The software can perform sophisticated market analysis to determine the potential of a specific market segment. Users can then generate lists of potential customers for direct mail, telemarketing, or sales prospecting. D&B MarketPlace bases its business information on Dun & Bradstreet data and updates the CD on a quarterly basis.

Marshall Marketing & Communications, Inc.

Keywords: buying behavior; computer services; demographics; lifestyles; local and market information; media research

Richard Kinzler, Vice President - Operations
2000 Oxford Drive, Suite 400
Bethel Park, PA 15102-1841

Phone: 412/854-4500
Fax: 412/854-5030

Marshall Marketing & Communications, Inc. is a marketing consultancy for television stations. It provides local, market-specific consumer information, demographics, psychographics, shopping habits, and media usage. MM&C's annual surveys are conducted via telephone and scheduled throughout the year. Data are supplied to the client on a customized, Windows-based crosstabulation and analysis system.

MatchWare Technologies, Inc.

Keywords: computer services; database marketing; geocoding; health care

Max Eveleth
15212 Dino Drive
Burtonsville, MD 20866

Phone: 301/384-3997
Fax: 301/384-8095
E-mail: matchware@delphi.com

MatchWare Technologies, Inc. publishes generalized intelligent pattern-recognition-parsing and probabilistic record-linkage software for popular computer environments. AutoStan and AutoMatch manage data file content inconsistencies and anomolies, and create standarized and matchable fixed field formats from free-form text. Each linked-record set is individually weight-scored, allowing analysis of "almost" or suspect matches. AutoStan and AutoMatch ensure optimum record linkage results for any kind of data with statistically justifiable accuracy for geocoding (address matching), database integrity, and health data registry applications.

Maturing Marketplace Institute

Keywords: attitudes and opinions; baby boomers; consumer segmentation; market research; mature market

Carol M. Morgan, President
Suite 311, 119 N. Fourth Street
Minneapolis, MN 55401

Phone: 612/341-4244
Fax: 612/341-4127

Maturing Marketplace Institute, a division of Strategic Directions Group, Inc., has surveyed 15,000 U.S. consumers aged 40 and older since 1989 in annual and semi-annual industry-specific shared-cost studies covering purchase behavior, media, and attitudes, and including clients' proprietary questions as well as shared data. The Institute has created and tracked five separate segmentation strategies based on attitudes and motivations, pinpointing best customers for specific products and services. It also provides custom analysis and creates database and software applications based on its studies.

May & Speh

Keywords: computer services;
database marketing; mailing lists

Mike Loeffler, Sr. V.P., Direct Marketing Services
1501 Opus Place
Downers Grove, IL 60515-5713

Phone: 708/964-1501
Fax: 708/719-0447

May & Speh provides information management services for the direct-marketing industry. The company specializes in marketing database system design and implementation; modeling and analysis; data enhancement services; and list processing services.

MBS/Multimode, Inc.

Keywords: analytical services; customer profiling;
database marketing; geocoding; market research

Elisa Krause, Senior Statistician
7 Norden Lane
Huntington Station, NY 11746-2139

Phone: 516/673-5600
Fax: 516/673-6746

MBS/Multimode, Inc. provides database systems and tools to the direct-marketing industry. It develops integrated predictor models with which clients can implement database marketing strategies. Areas of specialization include database creation and maintenance, predictor modeling, customer profiling, trade area analysis, prospect modeling, database segmentation analysis, customer lifetime value models, site selection, survey design and analysis, advertising media analysis, geocoding with multi-level U.S. census demographic data appended, and geodemographic mapping.

McCollum Spielman Worldwide (MSW)

Keywords: advertising research;
brand equity; international

Peter R. Klein, President/C.O.O.
235 Great Neck Road
Great Neck, NY 11021

Phone: 516/482-0310
Fax: 516/482-5180 or 3228

McCollum Spielman Worldwide (MSW) provides marketing communications research services. MSW conducts research via a global network of full-service research companies in 28 countries in Europe, Canada, Japan, Asia/Pacific, Australia, and Latin America. The AD*VANTAGE/ACT TV copy evaluation system offers internationally sales-validated measurements of awareness and persuasion with diagnostics; AD*MAP analysis; central location and mall intercept modalities; MSW-NPD BrandBuilder–brand equity model; and MSW/GFK Advertising Response Model.

Other MSW services include PROLOG/TV–early stage diagnostic copy evaluation; PRINT*CHEK–print advertising evaluation; ACCU*TRACK–advertising recognition tracking system; custom services, and the Child Research Services Division (see separate listing).

Media Market Resources

Keywords: advertising research; media research

Amy Konikowski, Account Executive
322 East 50th Street
New York, NY 10022

Phone: 800/242-9618
Fax: 212/826-3169

Media Market Resources provides cost-per-point projections by market for spot TV, radio, cable, newspapers, magazines, and outdoor. It covers 31 demographics such as age and sex for 1970 to 1996.

Mediamark Research, Inc.

Keywords: buying behavior; consumer segmentation; market research; media research

Ken Wollenberg, Senior Vice President, Sales and Marketing Phone: 212/599-0444
708 Third Avenue
New York, NY 10017

Fax: 212/682-6284
E-mail: info@mediamark.com

Mediamark Research, Inc. conducts an annual syndicated survey of 20,000 adults in the 48 continental states, collecting data on demographic and socioeconomic characteristics, media usage, and purchase behavior. Data are available in printed reports and online. MEMRI is a PC-based system that allows custom analysis of survey data. MRI also combines its media and product data with all four U.S. geodemographic (cluster) systems for lifestyle analysis at the local level.

Mendelsohn Media Research Inc.

Keywords: affluent markets; market research; media research

Mitch Lurin, President
841 Broadway
New York, NY 10003

Phone: 212/677-8100
Fax: 212/677-8833

Mendelsohn Media Research (MMR) conducts an annual survey of the affluent population, and collects marketing, media, and demographic information. In addition, MMR conducts custom media research studies for all aspects of the advertising industry.

Mercator Corporation

Keywords: statistical software; survey software

D. MacDonald, Marketing & Media Relations
172 State Street
Newburyport, MA 01950

Phone: 508/463-4093
Fax: 508/463-9375

Mercator Corporation offers SNAP Professional PC-based survey design and analysis software. Facilities include questionnaire design and printing, and three modes of data entry for applications including CATI and CAPI. Analysis incorporates crosstabulations, frequency, holecount and grid tables, 2D and 3D bar, line and pie charts, and a full range of descriptive statistics. Manipulation of results is provided through percentages, weights, scores, zero suppression, and the use of filters to analyze subsets of data.

Metromail

Keywords: database marketing; demographics; housing and real estate; lifestyles; mailing lists

Julie Springer, Marketing Analyst
360 E. 22nd Street
Lombard, IL 60148

Phone: 708/932-2627
Fax: 708/620-3014
E-mail: jspring@interaccess.com

Metromail provides direct-marketing products and services, including targeted demographic and psychographic lists, list enhancement, database, modeling, and mail-production services. Its National Consumer Data Base (NCDB) provides household and individual demographic information for more than 142 million individuals. Metromail offers specialty lifestyle business and realty lists, including families with children, new movers, and new homeowners. Metromail also compiles BehaviorBank, a 28-million-name database of psychographic and lifestyle information.

Metron, Inc.

Keywords: analytical services; desktop mapping/GIS; employees/labor force; sales and marketing

Steve Hanlin, Business Analyst
11911 Freedom Drive, Suite 800
Reston, VA 22090-5602

Phone: 800/437-9601 or 703/787-8700
Fax: 703/787-9163
E-mail: terralignmi@metsci.com

Metron, Inc.'s TerrAlign Services Group offers a wide range of expertise in sales force management issues such as sales force sizing, call planning, prospect modeling, and territory alignments. Metron's TerrAlign software products feature OptAlign technology, which automatically assigns customers and geography, balances territories, optimizes driving time, and recommends territory locations. TerrAlign also produces maps and reports.

Metropolitan Life Statistical Bulletin

Keywords: demographics; health care; projections

Margaret Moshinski, Deputy Editor
1 Madison Avenue, Area 2C
New York, NY 10010

Phone: 212/578-5014
Fax: 212/213-0577

Metropolitan Life's quarterly *Statistical Bulletin* provides proprietary life expectancy projections and interpretation of government-produced population projections, health-care cost analyses, survey results, common surgical procedure costs, and geographic variations.

Microtab, Incorporated

Keywords: computer services; statistical software

Larry Hills, Managing Director
380 Market Place, Suite 100
Roswell, CA 30075-3943

Phone: 404/552-7856
Fax: 404/552-7719

Microtab's crosstabulation software comes in three editions, each designed with a specific range of needs in mind. Also available is MT/stat, statistical analysis software that performs Chi-Square contingency table analysis, one or two-tailed tests for independent means, and one or two-tailed tests for independent proportions. Microtab also offers full-service data processing from data entry to presentation-quality tables. Comprehensive statistical testing and graphing services are also available.

Millward Brown International

Keywords: advertising research; consulting; international; sales and marketing

Peter Maloney, Executive Vice President
1245 E. Diehl Road
Naperville, IL 60563-9349

Phone: 708/505-0066
Fax: 708/505-0077

Millward Brown International is a full-service marketing research consulting company with particular expertise in tracking research, copy testing, and sales response modeling. Millward Brown also conducts segmentation studies, product tests, and concept tests. It operates throughout the world and maintains wholly owned or affiliate companies in 25 countries.

MORI (Market Opinion Research International) Ltd.

Keywords: attitudes and opinions; business to business; environmental research; financial services; health care; international; market research

Brian Gosschalk, Managing Director
32 Old Queen Street
London, ENGLAND SW1H 9HP

Phone: 011-44-171-222-0232
Fax: 011-44-171-222-1653

Market Opinion Research International (MORI) has areas of research expertise, including business-to-business, consumer behavior, corporate communications, environment, financial, health, human resource, media, qualitative measurement, and social issues. Particular expertise involves international research, opinion leader research, and customer care research. In addition, MORI has a series of research packages designed to provide a cost-effective source of information for clients. "The MORI Communications Programme" is a program of research among key opinion formers in government, the financial community, business, the media, and the public; "MFS" (MORI Financial Services) continuously monitors customer usage of, and attitudes toward, financial services; "EuroImage" studies communications among key opinion formers in Europe; and "SOCIOCONSULT" is a research-based consultancy examining the commercial implications of social trends in Britain and Europe.

MRCA Information Services

Keywords: buying behavior; market research

Ken Murphy, Senior Vice President
20 Summer Street
Stamford, CT 06901

Phone: 203/324-9600 x212
Fax: 203/348-4087

MRCA Information Services provides capabilities tracking and analysis of consumer behavior using static sample databases; and purchase, usage, and awareness for all types of industries.

Munro Garrett International

Keywords: computer services; desktop mapping/GIS

Wayne Lafferty
2200 645 Seventh Avenue, SW
Calgary, ALBERTA T2P 4G8

Phone: 403/263-0070
Fax: 403/262-1929

Munro Garrett International provides Argus, desktop mapping software that links directly to external databases, eliminating the need to import or translate data to a proprietary format before mapping and analyzing. Executive Information System offers summary, analysis, and charting capabilities, along with "business dashboard" features such as alarms that can be set to signal changes in revenue forecasts.

National Analysts, Inc.

Keywords: consulting; market research

John A. Berrigan, President
1700 Market Street
Philadelphia, PA 19103

Phone: 215/496-6800
Fax: 215/496-6801

National Analysts, Inc. provides custom marketing research and consulting services with a strategic focus. Its clients include telecommunications, pharmaceutical, utility, consumer products, and financial services industries.

National Association for Senior Living Industries

Keywords: financial services; health care; housing and real estate; mature market

Tricia Weller, Director of Education and Conferences
184 Duke of Gloucester Street
Annapolis, MD 21401

Phone: 410/263-0991
Fax: 410/263-1262

The National Association for Senior Living Industries (NASLI) is a nonprofit trade association serving all areas of the mature market. The primary benefit of NASLI membership is networking. NASLI connects senior housing and health-care providers, consumer product manufacturers, financial service companies, advertisers, marketers, educators, and aging advocates. Through NASLI, members have instant access to industry leaders whose businesses focus on the mature market. It publishes the *Senior Living Industries Wage, Compensation, and Benefits Report* as well as other bulletins.

National Association of Realtors

Keywords: housing and real estate

Chris Rau, Marketing Research Analyst
700 11th Street, NW
Washington, DC 20001

Phone: 202/383-1000
Fax: 202/383-7568
E-mail: crau.nar@notes@compuserve.com

The National Association of Realtors (NAR) represents more than 700,000 realtors. Its research group conducts qualitative and quantitative research on realtor demographics and needs as well as trends in the real-estate industry. NAR publishes *Real Estate Outlook: Market Trends & Insights*, which provides monthly forecasts for the real-estate industry and excerpts from current research. This monthly publication is also the source for monthly existing-home sales statistics nationally recognized as a leading economic indicator. Other industry reports published by NAR include: *Real Estate Brokerage: Income, Expenses and Profits; The Home Buying and Selling Process; Profile of Real Estate Firms; Membership Profile; Real Estate Agent Profitability; Value of a Real Estate Brokerage Firm; National Real Estate Review; Market Conditions Report; Economic Profiles: The Fifty States;* and *Real Estate Horizons: A Look Towards the 21st Century.*

National Management Services

Keywords: demographics; mailing lists; market research; Texas

Larry Bell
P.O. Box 861964
Plano, TX 75086

Phone: 214/424-8869
Fax: 214/424-8934
E-mail: natman@dallas.net

National Management Services is a full-service marketing and promotional firm. It specializes in providing consumer household demographics, databases, and mailing lists for metropolitan and suburban Dallas. It has an Internet home page at http://www.dallas.net/homes/natman/.

National Opinion Research Center

Keywords: attitudes and opinions; lifestyles; political polling; religion; trends

Tom W. Smith, Director, GSS
1155 East 60th Street
Chicago, IL 60637

Phone: 312/753-7877
Fax: 312/753-7886
E-mail: nnrtws1@uchimvs1.uchicago.edu

The National Opinion Research Center (NORC) has been conducting the General Social Survey (GSS) since 1972. This annual survey covers a wide variety of social, familial, and political topics. Some questions are asked year after year; others are added as deemed relevant. For example, the 1988 survey included a set of questions on AIDS and a topical module on religious background and beliefs. The cumulative database is available on computer tape from The Roper Center, University of Connecticut, Storrs, CT 06268; (203) 486-4882. NORC publishes *GSSNEWS*, an annual newsletter, and other survey reports, including a bibliography of research published using GSS data. All materials are in the public domain, and there are no restrictions on data use.

National Research Bureau

Keywords: database marketing; housing and real estate; media research; retailing

Eric Cohen, Vice President
3975 Fair Ridge Drive
Fairfax, VA 22033

Phone: 800/456-4555
Fax: 703/934-9607

The National Research Bureau, a Blackburn Group Company, provides a wide range of shopping center information in formats ranging from publications to CD-ROM.

It provides comprehensive information on more than 34,000 shopping centers in the *Shopping Center Directories* and *Top Contacts* reports, including such information as location, gross leasable area (GLA), anchors, tenants, market positioning strategy, center type, developer, owner, leasing agent, and more. The data are also available as nearly 30 standard reports, electronic databases, and mailing lists. Electronic databases include tenant, facility, location, contact, enclosed, transaction, power, strip, value, and top contacts, among others. *The Shopping Center Directory* on CD-ROM allows users to search the complete database using 10 different indexes and print up to 11 of its most popular reports.

National Restaurant Association

Keywords: attitudes and opinions; food; trends

Information Service and Library
1200 Seventeenth Street, NW
Washington, DC 20036

Phone: 202/331-5900
Fax: 202/331-2429
E-mail: bitesite@capcon.net

The National Restaurant Association (NRA) is the trade association for food-service companies and restaurants. It publishes a number of reports, all of which are available to nonmembers. *Restaurants USA* and *Foodservice Economic Trends* are monthly publications, and Foodservice Information Abstracts is biweekly. The NRA also publishes the annual reports *Foodservice in Review, Restaurant Industry Operations Report,* and *Foodservice Industry Forecast.* Other studies examine tableservice restaurant trends and consumer attitudes, behavior, and expenditures on food away from home. The NRA has an annual trade show and holds seminars on various aspects of food service and restaurant management. Members have free access to the library and reference service; nonmembers may utilize the service on a fee basis.

National Sporting Goods Association

Keywords: fitness and sports

Thomas B. Doyle, Director of Information and Research
1699 Wall Street
Mt. Prospect, IL 60056

Phone: 708/439-4000
Fax: 708/439-0111

The National Sporting Goods Assocation produces annual studies on sports participation covering 50 sports, as well as consumer purchases of sports equipment and footwear. Its reports provide standard demographics for both participants (1985-94) and purchasers (1980-94).

Neodata Services, Inc.

Keywords: analytical services; database marketing; demographics; lifestyles; mailing lists

Peter Sidwell, Database Marketing Services
6707 Winchester Circle
Boulder, CO 80301-3598

Phone: 303/530-6766
Fax: 303/530-7495

Neodata Services, Inc. compiles demographic, lifestyle, and geodemographic data. It offers a full range of database marketing services. DMS, a division of Neodata, provides integrated direct-marketing services.

New Hope Communications

Keywords: health care; packaged goods; retailing

Marge Gammon, Director of Marketing
1301 Spruce Street
Boulder, CO 80503

Phone: 303/939-8440
Fax: 303/939-9886
E-mail: http://www.newhope.com

New Hope Communications provides national sales data on natural and organic products, vitamins, supplements, herbs, and natural products industry trends by region, store size, and category.

New Mexico State University Border Research Institute

Keywords: demographics; desktop mapping/GIS;

Mexico; sales and marketing
Maria Telles-McGeagh, Director
Box 3001, Dept. 3BRI
Las Cruces, NM 88003-0001

Phone: 505/646-3524
Fax: 505/646-5474
E-mail: bri@dante.nmsu.edu

The New Mexico State University Border Research Institute provides information on all aspects of the U.S.-Mexico border region. This information includes demographics, population projections, marketing data, and trade statistics. The Institute also maintains GIS data, commercial registries (including directories of Maquiladoras), and other business-related information, with an emphasis on New Mexico, West Texas, and Chihuahua.

New Strategist Publications, Inc.

Keywords: baby boomers; consumer spending; demographics; ethnic markets

Penelope Wickham, President
P.O. Box 242
Ithaca, NY 14851

Phone: 607/273-0913
Fax: 607/277-5009

New Strategist publishes reference books on demographics and consumer spending. *The Official Guide to the American Marketplace,* now in its second edition, is an analysis of demographic trends among U.S. consumers–their race and ethnicity, incomes, spending patterns, health, education, living arrangements, population characteristics, and much more. *The Official Guide to the Generations* looks at the demographics and attitudes of four generations of American adults–Generation X, the Baby Boom, the Swing Generation, and the World War II Generation. *The Official Guide to Household Spending,* now in its third edition, is an exploration into the buying habits of the nation's consumers according to age, income, household type, and region. Spending data are given for more than 1,000 products and services. *The Official Guide to American Incomes* explores the purchasing power of hundreds of market segments. It includes a chapter on discretionary household income broken out by age, income, household type and size, number of earners, education, and race.

NewsNet, Inc.

Keywords: business to business; international; online

Ellen S. Keech, Marketing Communications Specialist
945 Haverford Road
Bryn Mawr, PA 19010

Phone: 610/527-8030
Fax: 610/527-0338

NewsNet is an online database providing direct access to current awareness business news. NewsNet features more than 800 industry-specific newsletters, trade publications, and magazines in more than 30 industries. NewsNet also offers more than a dozen worldwide newswires. Information is keyword searchable and is delivered in full text and in many cases is available online before it is in print. Searches can be conducted using traditional Boolean logic or plain-English concepts with relevance-ranked output. NewsFlash is an electronic clipping service that allows for continuous monitoring of unlimited keyword phrases.

NewsNet also provides commercial credit and company background reports from two leading suppliers: Dun & Bradstreet and TRW. D&B supplies background and credit information on more than 9.5 million U.S. companies; TRW reports on more than 13 million U.S. business locations. Both services are available on NewsNet on a pay-as-you-go basis; the usual annual contract fees associated with D&B and TRW do not apply. NewsNet customers also have access to company and industry reports compiled by market analysts like Standard & Poor's and stock and commodity quotes.

Newspaper Association of America (The)

Keywords: media research

Paul Luthringer
11600 Sunrise Valley Drive
Reston, VA 22091

Phone: 703/648-1000
Fax: 703/648-4577

The Newspaper Association of America is a nonprofit group serving more than 1,500 newspapers in the United States and Canada that account for more than 85 percent of daily circulation. The association focuses on five strategic priorities that affect the newspaper industry: marketing, public policy, diversity, industry development, and newspaper operations. It produces several publications, including *Presstime,* and holds several major annual meetings.

NFO Research, Inc.

Keywords: market research

Lawrence D. White, Executive Vice President, Marketing
2 Pickwick Plaza
Greenwich, CT 06830

Phone: 203/629-8888
Fax: 419/661-8595

NFO Research conducts research through its 475,000-plus household panel, which is balanced for a variety of demographic characteristics within the nine census divisions. This allows researchers to select samples that match their requirements. NFO conducts virtually any type of data collection for a wide variety of industries, the results of which can be combined with major psychographic and cluster systems.

NPA Data Services, Inc.

Keywords: economic data; housing and real estate; local and market information; projections; trends

Nestor E. Terleckyj
1424 16th Street, NW, Suite 700
Washington, DC 20036

Phone: 202/884-7634/7638
Fax: 202/797-5516
E-mail: npadsi@dgsys.com

NPA Data Services publishes the annual Regional Economic Projections Series, with long-range projections for regions, states, metropolitan areas, and counties, including population by age, sex, and race; employment; personal income; and earnings by industry. Annual historic and projected data cover 1967 to 2015. Data are available in printed reports and on diskettes, magnetic tapes, and CD-ROM.

The Economic and Construction Projections Service includes historical data and ten-year projections for major categories of residential and nonresidential construction and relevant economic and demographic variables for U.S. metropolitan areas for 1980 to 2005. Data are available as printouts with graphics for specific metropolitan areas or on disk with complete database and model listings. The firm also offers historical building permits data back to 1980 for counties, states, and metropolitan areas. Databases for all services are updated twice a year.

NPD Group, Inc. (The)

Keywords: analytical services; international; market research

Tod Johnson, CEO
900 West Shore Road
Port Washington, NY 11050

Phone: 516/625-0700
Fax: 516/625-2444
E-mail: info@npd.com

The NPD Group is a diversified marketing information company specializing in consumer market research. Its data collection/analytic techniques include diary panels, consumer mail panels, CATI telephone interviewing, and statistical modeling. The company's research capabilities are available throughout the U.S. and in Europe, Asia, Latin America, Australia, and Canada.

Opinion Research Corporation

Keywords: market research

Judi Lescher, Vice President, CARAVAN Services
P.O. Box 183
Princeton, NJ 08542

Phone: 800/999-0213
Fax: 800/759-5786

Opinion Research Corporation provides CARAVAN, a weekly national consumer telephone omnibus survey of 1,000 adults aged 18 and older. Results are available within a week. Opinion Research also offers low-cost supplemental market areas and special audience participation.

Organization for Economic Cooperation & Development (OECD)

Keywords: economic data; environmental research; health care; housing and real estate; international

Suzanne Edam, Marketing Officer
2001 L Street, NW, Suite 650
Washington, DC 20036-4910

Phone: 202/785-6323
Fax: 202/785-0350

The Organization for Economic Cooperation and Development (OECD) provides data on 25 member countries, including the U.S., Canada, Mexico, Japan, New Zealand, Australia, and Western Europe. Data include economics, environmental information, energy statistics, health-care data, tax expenditures and rates, and more.

ORS Publishing

Keywords: attitudes and opinions; buying behavior; international

Dennis Gilbert, President
7200 Wisconsin Avenue
Bethesda, MD 20814

Phone: 301/656-8611
Fax: 301/656-8640

ORS Publishing compiles data from more than 6,000 national, state, local, and special consumer and public opinion surveys conducted from 1986 through 1994, in the United States and more than 50 other countries. Polling the Nations is a CD-ROM that allows full-text and field-based searching of 120,000 questions and responses from nearly 500 sources.

Oryx Press

Keywords: academic research; health care

Shauna Obergfell, Publicist
4041 North Central at Indian School Road
Phoenix, AZ 85012   E-mail: info@oryxpress.com or http://www.oryxpress.com

Phone: 602/265-2651
Fax: 602/265-6350

Oryx Press publishes books on consumer health information and the medical/health-care marketplace. Recent publications include *Consumer Health Information Source Book*, a guide to health books and magazines; *Consumer Health USA: Essential Information from the Federal Health Network*, covering topics for which information is most actively sought by consumers; *Consumer Health & Nutrition Index*, a quarterly publication that indexes more than 2,000 articles in more than 70 periodicals; *Medical & Healthcare Marketplace Guide*, a directory to the worldwide medical and health-care industry, supplying detailed information on products and services; and *The Detwiler Directory of Medical and Market Sources*, profiles of medical market information providers.

Outdoor Advertising Association of America

Keywords: billboards

Diane Cimine, Executive Vice President
12 East 49th Street, 22nd Floor
New York, NY 10017

Phone: 212/688-3667
Fax: 212/752-1687

The Outdoor Advertising Association of America (OAAA) is a trade association of more than 600 out-of-home communication companies that represents its members to the advertising community, public, and government. The OAAA guides itself by the needs of advertisers and communities in developing responsible controls, policies, and better product and service standards. The primary focus of the headquarters office (in Washington, D.C.) is on legislative issues and membership development. The organization's marketing operations function as a resource for advertisers and agencies by providing education about the out-of-home medium.

P-STAT, Inc.

Keywords: statistical software

Sebbie Buhler, Marketing Manager
230 Lambertville-Hopewell Road
Hopewell, NJ 08525-2809

Phone: 609/466-9200
Fax: 609/466-1688
E-mail: sales@pstat.com

P-STAT is a software system for market research/survey analysis, data entry, statistical analysis, data and file management, and report writing. P-STAT is available on PCs, UNIX workstations/servers, and mini/mainframes. It features a front-end MENU system, 4GL command/programming language, macros, and interfaces with SPSS/export, SAS Data Step, ASCII, Informix, dBase, and column-binary data formats.

Packaged Facts (FIND/SVP Published Products Group, Inc.)

Keywords: ethnic markets; market research; mature market; retailing; women; youth and children

Lynn Christie, Vice President
625 Avenue of the Americas
New York, NY 10011

Phone: 212/627-3228
Fax: 212/627-9312
E-mail: http://www.findsvp.com/

Packaged Facts publishes approximately 50 syndicated market studies each year, most of which cover consumer products, such as skincare, Mexican food, energy drinks, and pet food. The company also publishes demographic reports, which include studies of kids, grandparents, African Americans, Hispanics, the over-50 market, and women. Other studies cover retailing trends, such as super centers, electronic shopping, and value retailing.

Palo Alto Software

Keywords: analytical services

Lisa McReynolds, Director, Sales and Marketing
144 E. 14th Avenue
Eugene, OR 97401

Phone: 503/683-6162
Fax: 503/683-6250

Palo Alto Software publishes Marketing Plan Pro, which allows users to develop business marketing plans, set budgets and forecasts, and track results. It prints a complete plan with text, tables, and charts.

Partners in Marketing, Inc.

Keywords: consulting; health care; international; market research; utilities

Harry Leibowitz, PhD, President
879 High Street
Worthington, OH 43085

Phone: 614/844-5600
Fax: 614/844-5811

Partners in Marketing, Inc. (PIM) is a full-service marketing consulting firm offering a range of marketing capabilities, from strategic planning and market research to sales training and market expansion. Specialties include proprietary research and targeting of difficult-to-reach markets such as physicians, attorneys, and CEOs. Specific expertise is available in international business, health care, and utilities. PIM also conducts a quarterly Community Awareness and Preference (CAP) Study in several major U.S. markets that allows companies operating in the region to track consumer purchase trends and advertising awareness.

Pattern Discovery

Keywords: analytical services; customer satisfaction; market research

Steven Hokanson, President
314 Fitzwater Street
Philadelphia, PA 19147

Phone: 215/928-1619
Fax: 215/928-1301
E-mail: 73700.1212@compuserve.com

Pattern Discovery provides analysis of quantitative surveys and datasets using Pattern Discovery NP (Non-Parametric). Pattern Discovery NP uncovers rules, such as: "if a customer orders pancakes, then he/she is likely to want syrup." Rule-based models are valuable in market research because they are robust and capable of modeling complex problems in the area of customer satisfaction and public opinion.

Payment Systems, Inc.

Keywords: business to business; financial services

Maria Erickson, Director
3030 Rocky Point Drive, W., #800
Tampa, FL 33602

Phone: 813/287-2774
Fax: 813/286-7377
E-mail: maria@smarcrd.smartcard.com

Payment Systems, Inc. offers the Corporate Services Research Program, a syndicated program containing comprehensive data and analysis on the financial behavior and attitudes of small business and corporations in the U.S.

Percept

Keywords: attitudes and opinions; religion

Tom Hoyt
151 Kalmus Drive, Suite A104
Costa Mesa, CA 92626

Phone: 714/957-1282
Fax: 714/957-1924
E-mail: perceptInc@aol.com

Percept provides religious data for small-area geography. Ethos2000 is Percept's survey of Americans' religious preferences, attitudes, and concerns. The nationally representative survey is projectable to the block-group level using Percept's LocalLink technology. Data are available on disk and other formats.

PlanGraphics, Inc.

Keywords: consulting; desktop mapping/GIS

Dennis Kunkle, Executive Consultant
202 W. Main Street, Suite 200
Frankfort, KY 40601

Phone: 502/223-1501
Fax: 502/223-1235

PlanGraphics is a consulting firm specializing in the design and implementation of geographic information systems (GIS) and related technologies. Founded in 1979, PlanGraphics has assisted hundreds of clients in the deployment of tools for spatial information management and analysis. The firm's staff is experienced in cost-effectively applying the technology to applications that meet client needs.

Point-of-Purchase Advertising Institute

Keywords: advertising research; attitudes and opinions; buying behavior; packaged goods; retailing

Michael Wolff, Research Assistant
66 North Van Brunt Street
Englewood, NJ 07631

Phone: 201/894-8899
Fax: 201/894-0622/0529

The Point-of-Purchase Advertising Institute (POPAI) is the only international nonprofit trade association dedicated to serving the interests of brand marketers, retailers, and producers/suppliers of point-of-purchase advertising and in-store marketing. POPAI conducts research in the areas of display effectiveness, industry economics, retailer attitudes toward P-O-P, and consumer buying habits. Its

Consumer Buying Habits Study measures the impact of point-of-purchase advertising, consumer buying decisions, and attitudes toward the shopping experience in supermarkets and mass merchandisers.

Polk Company (formerly R.L. Polk)

Keywords: business to business; customer profiling; database marketing; lifestyles; mailing lists; market research

Art Nolan, Corporate Communications
1155 Brewery Park Boulevard
Detroit, MI 48207-2697

Phone: 800/637-7655
Fax: 313/393-2860
E-mail: anolan@rlpolk.com

The Polk Company recently implemented a reorganization that incorporated subsidiaries National Demographics & Lifestyles, Inc. and Polk Direct. It provides business-to-business mailing lists, consumer mailing lists, database development and management of client direct-marketing programs, data enhancement (enhance client databases with lifestyles and behavioral data), and consumer modeling and profiling (analyze consumer trends and recommend name acquisition strategies). The Lifestyle Selector list offers 10 demographic selects and more than 50 self-reported lifestyle selections, and covers 35 million households. TotaList represents 86 million households, more than 100 demographic selects, and 11 distance categories.

Population Association of America

Keywords: academic research; demographics

Jennifer Kilroy, Executive Administrator
721 Ellsworth Drive, Suite 303
Silver Spring, MD 20910

Phone: 301/565-6710
Fax: 301/565-7850

The Population Association of America (PAA) is the professional organization of demographers and others interested in population data. Membership includes a flagship quarterly journal *Demography*, which covers the full range of demographic topics, including population estimates and projections, regional shifts, changing lifestyles, ethnic diversity, and international comparisons. The PAA holds an annual meeting at which the world's premier demographers present research and studies on a wide variety of topics. The Business and Applied Demography committee of the PAA conducts at least one session in which the business aspects of demography are explored. The committee also publishes an occasional newsletter to keep members informed of its activities.

Population Council (The)

Keywords: academic research; demographics; health care

Sandra Waldman, Director, Office of Public Information
One Dag Hammarskjold Plaza
New York, NY 10017

Phone: 212/339-0500
Fax: 212/755-6052
E-mail: pubInfo@popcouncil.org
or www: http://www.popcouncil.org

The Population Council, an international nonprofit, nongovernmental organization established in 1952, conducts research on three fronts–biomedicine, social science, and public health–to improve people's reproductive health, safely reduce unwanted pregnancies, and clarify the causes and consequences of population growth. The council participates in a uniquely wide scope of activities in these areas ranging from molecular biology to demography, contraceptive development, and on-site analyses of family planning programs and clinical trials. The council publishes and disseminates a wide range of written materials to varied audiences, including two peer-reviewed journals, newsletters, working papers, conference proceedings, guideline for research, pamphlets, and project summaries.

Population Index

Keywords: academic research; demographics; international

Richard Hankinson, Editor
21 Prospect Avenue
Princeton, NJ 08544-2091

Phone: 609/258-4949
Fax: 609/258-1039
E-mail: popindex@princeton.edu

The Population Index contains bibliographic citations and abstracts to the world literature on population and demography, including fertility, mortality, migration, marriage and divorce, family planning, abortion, censuses, surveys, and population statistics. Hard copy is available for entries dating from 1933 and machine-readable format for these dating from 1985.

Population Information Program, Center for Communications Program, Johns Hopkins University

Keywords: academic research; demographics; health care; international

Elizabeth Duverlie, Assistant to the Director
111 Market Place, Suite 310
Baltimore, MD 21202

Phone: 410/659-6300
Fax: 410/659-6266

The Population Information Program (PIP) provides up-to-date and extensive information on a broad range of family planning, population, and related health issues. As the publishing and research arm of the Center for Communications Programs (CCP), PIP operates the computerized POPLINE database, containing more than 225,000 citations and abstracts of scientific articles, reports, books, and papers (published and unpublished) in all languages. Topics include family-planning technology and programs, fertility, population law and policy, demography, AIDS and other

STDs, maternal and child health, primary health-care communication, and population and environment issues. Information is searchable by subject, author, country, year of publication, and other data fields. It is available online from the U.S. National Library of Medicine, by mail from PIP, and on compact disc. POPLINE also publishes a User's Guide to POPLINE Keywords, POPLINE on Disc, and POPLINE CD-ROM User's Manual.

Population Reference Bureau, Inc.

Keywords: demographics; international

Arthur Haupt
1875 Connecticut Avenue, NW, Suite 520
Washington, DC 20009

Phone: 202/483-1100
Fax: 202/328-3937
E-mail: prb@popref.org

Founded in 1929, the Population Reference Bureau (PRB) is the oldest private educational and research organization in the population field. PRB's goal is to increase public awareness of the facts and implications of population trends. To that end, it supplies U.S. and international data with which individuals, groups, or government can tackle these issues.

PRB puts out a wide variety of publications. Members receive quarterly *Population Bulletins* and a monthly newsletter, *Population Today*, which summarizes new demographic research and reports on population policies, trends, and data gathering around the world. Two of PRB's four annual *Population Bulletins* analyze American demographics; the other two focus on international trends. Members also receive the annual U.S. and World Population Data Sheets. These poster-sized wall charts provide current population estimates and projections, vital statistics, GNP, and other useful data-at-a-glance for all 50 U.S. states and all but the world's smallest nations. Annual membership ranges from $25 for students to $55 for libraries.

PRB members also receive discounts on other publications, such as the regularly updated *Population Handbook*–an introduction to the basics of demographic analysis, published in American English, as well as in "international" English, Spanish, French, Arabic, and Thai editions. PRB's policy studies department produces a series of reports on the policy implications of U.S. population trends, such as poverty, immigration, and internal migration. Recent titles from the Population Trends and Public Policy series include *Homicide in the U.S.: Who's At Risk?* Members also have access to PRB's extensive library, online bibliographic retrieval service, and the research services of its professional demographers. All publications are also available to nonmembers, and a free publications catalog is available on request.

Prevention Magazine

Keywords: fitness and sports; food; health care; lifestyles; youth and children

Ed Slaughter, Director, Market Research
33 East Minor Street
Emmaus, PA 18098

Phone: 610/967-5171

Prevention magazine publishes The Prevention Index, whch tracks Americans' health and safety habits. The Index provides data on general health, diet, exercise, auto safety, and toy safety. The Children's Health Index is a similar measure geared to kids. The magazine also publishes Shopping for Health, an annual survey of consumer knowledge of nutrition and good health practices, and how this knowledge affects food-shopping habits. The 1996 report contains special sections on consumer acceptance of low-fat foods, produce, and organic food products.

PRI Associates, Inc.

Keywords: African Americans; census data; employees/labor force; local and market information

Harold Thompson, Director of Marketing
1905 Chapel Hill Road
Durham, NC 27707

Phone: 919/493-7534
Fax: 919/493-2935

PRI Associates provides 1990 census race and gender counts for 512 occupations for the nation, states, counties, metropolitan areas, and places with more than 50,000 people. The data are used to prepare affirmative action plans and corporate relocation studies. Special tabulations by salary, education, and industry are also available.

Primelife

Keywords: consulting; database marketing; focus groups; mature market

Frank L. Conaway, President/CEO
127 S. Olive Street
Orange, CA 92666

Phone: 714/744-1291
Fax: 714/744-5221

Primelife is a marketing communications consulting firm that specializes in targeting mature consumers aged 50 and older. The firm analyzes and augments advertising, public relations, research, and direct-marketing services. It also conducts proprietary research for clients, including focus groups, personal interviews, and surveys.

Princeton Religion Research Center

Keywords: attitudes and opinions; religion

George Gallup, IV
P.O. Box 389
Princeton, NJ 08542

Phone: 609/921-8112
Fax: 609/924-0228

The Princeton Religion Research Center (PRRC) reports and interprets trends in religion and values from surveys conducted by the Gallup Poll, The George H. Gallup International Institute, the Gallup Youth Survey, and other organizations. It focuses on survey information that can be put to practical use by churches and other faith communities. PRRC publishes *Emerging Trends*, a monthly publication now in its 16th year, and the annual report *Religion in America*, started 30 years ago.

Princeton University Computer Center

Keywords: census data; computer services; demographics

Judith S. Rowe, Princeton-Rutgers Census Data Project
87 Prospect Avenue
Princeton, NJ 08540

Phone: 609/452-6052

The Princeton-Rutgers Project provides a full range of demographic data services, including creating extracts, printing data from computer tapes, merging files, creating custom disks, and providing statistical analysis using mainframe and microcomputers.

Principia Products, Inc.

Keywords: survey software

Victor Berutti, Vice President, Imaging Products
1506 McDaniel Drive
West Chester, PA 19380

Phone: 610/429-1359
Fax: 610/430-3316

Principia Products offers Remark Office OMR, a forms-processing software package for Windows that scans and performs data entry from surveys, tests, and office forms. Users can create survey forms with word processors and then scan them. The output is compatible with any database or spreadsheet.

Prodigy

Keywords: online

Paul Lewis
445 Hamilton Avenue
White Plains, NY 10601

Phone: 914/448-8117
Fax: 914/448-4752
E-mail: lewisp@prodigy.com

Progidy is a consumer online service with more than 2 million members. It has more than 700 features and was the first company to offer WEB browser to permit members to search the World Wide Web. It offers a full range of communication services including e-mail.

Productive Access, Inc.

Keywords: computer services; statistical software

Bradley T. Hontz, President
19851 Yorba Linda Boulevard, Suite 203
Yorba Linda, CA 92686

Phone: 800/693-3110
Fax: 714/693-8747
E-mail: bhontz@paiwhq.com

Productive Access, Inc. (PAI) offers the mTAB Research Analysis System, which can handle large research datasets and analyze data across time and across studies. mTAB's MS-Windows-based interface is readily mastered by users familiar with spreadsheet and presentation software. PAI's complete service includes data processing, on-site system installation and training, and ongoing support.

Professional Research Consultants

Keywords: health care; market research

Kyle Tonniges, Director of Marketing
11326 P Street
Omaha, NE 68137-2316

Phone: 800/428-7455
Fax: 402/592-3019
E-mail: ktonniges@prof-rsrch.com

Professional Research Consultants is a national health-care marketing firm that has conducted thousands of studies for hospitals and health-care systems such as Johns Hopkins, Duke, and UCLA.

PROGIS Corporation

Keywords: demographics; desktop mapping/GIS; geographic boundary files

Oswin Slade, President
750 E. Holly Street
Bellingham, WA 98225

Phone: 360/738-2449
Fax: 360/738-2798
E-mail: 72733.707@compuserve.com

PROGIS Corporation provides mapping tools, and demographic and business data. The PROGIS line of products, WinGIS, WinMAP, and WinMAP LT, allows users and developers to integrate their own data with those provided by PROGIS. Datasets available include roads, cities, state boundaries, zip codes, etc. Many functions available in the PROGIS Graphic Editors can be driven from another application using MS-Windows Dynamic Data Exchange (DDE).

Program on Population, East-West Center

Keywords: academic research; Asia/Pacific; demographics

Andrew Mason, Director
1777 East-West Road
Honolulu, HI 96848

Phone: 808/944-7471
Fax: 808/944-7490
E-mail: pop@ewc.bitnet

The Program on Population was established in 1969 as a unit of the East-West Center. It conducts research and professional education activities focusing on population issues, with emphasis on the analysis of demographic and human resource trends, their social and economic causes and consequences, and their policy implications in Asia, the Pacific, and the United States. The Program cooperates with government agencies, universities, and other organizations throughout the Asia/Pacific region and the U.S.

Project Market Decisions

Keywords: consulting; desktop mapping/GIS; mature market

Monica C. Weinert, Vice President
635 West Seventh Street, Suite 305
Cincinnati, OH 45220

Phone: 513/651-4567
Fax: 513/651-4586
E-mail: mcwatpmd@aol.com

Project Market Decisions provides the Senior Market Report proprietary database along with SrMART (senior smart) software for segmenting 65-plus markets by household type, age, income, and housing tenure. Geographic areas are client-defined.

Promotion Marketing Association of America, Inc.

Keywords: advertising research; business to business

Emilie Lion, Manager, Education/Programs
257 Park Avenue South, Suite 1102
New York, NY 10010

Phone: 212/420-1100
Fax: 212/533-7622

Promotion Marketing Association of America, Inc., is a trade association representing the multi-billion-dollar promotion marketing industry. The organization provides products and services appropriate to industry needs and promotes better understanding of the importance of promotion in the marketing mix.

PSI

Keywords: affluent market; business to business; financial services; international; market research; retailing

Allen R. DeCotiis, President
3030 N. Rocky Point Drive W., Suite 800
Tampa, FL 33607

Phone: 813/287-2774
Fax: 813/286-7377

PSI specializes in consumer and corporate financial services analysis in the U.S. and internationally. Ongoing membership programs focus on local market share analysis, retail financial services, the affluent market, retirement services, card services, credit-card market-share analysis, delivery system strategies, mutual-fund analysis, corporate services, and corporate market-share analysis.

Public Policy Research Centers of the University of Missouri–St. Louis

Keywords: attitudes and opinions; census data

Mark Tranel, Senior Research Analyst
8001 Natural Bridge Road, 362 SSB
St. Louis, MO 63137

Phone: 314/516-5273
Fax: 314/516-5268
E-mail: smtrane@umslvma.ums.edu

The Public Policy Research Centers play a key role in achieving the urban mission of the University of Missouri-St. Louis through basic and applied public policy research. The Centers conduct public opinion surveys, programs, and analyzes significant public issues. The UMSL Urban Information Center provides decennial census data.

Qualitative Research Consultants Association, Inc.

Keywords: consulting; focus groups

Patricia Sabena, 1995-96 President
P.O. Box 6767, FDR Station
New York, NY 10022

Phone: 212/315-0632; or 203/454-1225
Fax: 607/699-3269; 203/221-0180
E-mail: cis 72640,2312

Qualitative Research Consultants Association, Inc. (QRCA) is an association of independent qualitative research professionals (505 members in 35 states and on 5 continents) committed to the highest professional standards and advancement of the discipline. QRCA holds an annual conference and publishes a member newsletter five times a year.

Quality Controlled Services

Keywords: computer-assisted surveys; focus groups; market research

Phil Wiseman, Marketing Director
1297 North Highway Drive
Fenton, MO 63099

Phone: 800/446-1690
Fax: 314/827-6014

Quality Controlled Services, a part of Maritz Marketing Research, is a data collection firm. Its nationwide services include telephone interviewing, project management, mall intercepts, pre-recruits, focus groups, central location tests, mystery shopping, taste tests, executive interviews, mail surveys, and in-home placement studies. The firm also offers FocusVision, a teleconferencing service, in several U.S. locations.

Quality Education Data, Inc.

Keywords: database marketing; education; market research

Jeanne A. Hayes, President/CEO
1600 Broadway, 12th Floor
Denver, CO 80202-4912

Phone: 303/860-1832
Fax: 303/860-0238
E-mail: jhayes@qeddata.com

Quality Education Data, Inc. is an education research company that specializes in American schools, from kindergarten through college, focusing on the U.S., Canada, and Puerto Rico. The company offers market research and strategic planning; database design and marketing programs, including mailing lists; directories of school district buyers and influencers in a variety of specialized areas; and research reports on technology, enrollment, and demographic trends. Trend data are available back to 1981.

Raosoft, Inc.

Keywords: survey software

Catherine McDole Rao, President
6645 NE Windermere Road
Seattle, WA 98115

Phone: 206/525-4025
Fax: 206/525-4947
E-mail: raosoft@raosoft.com

Raosoft, Inc. offers Raosoft SURVEY, a user-friendly data-handling system for gathering and analyzing data. It provides form design, data entry, import/export, data analysis, and reports. Optional electronic entry is available for network pop-up, mail-out, kiosk, notebook, bulletin boards, and phone-out data collection.

Response Analysis Corporation

Keywords: advertising research; customer satisfaction; employees/labor force; financial services; health care; market research; telecommunications

Diane S. Linck, Executive Vice President
377 Wall Street, P.O. Box 158
Princeton, NJ 08542

Phone: 609/921-3333
Fax: 609/921-2611

Response Analysis Corporation is a full-service market and survey research company. The company provides research design, data collection, and advanced statistical analysis. Response Analysis has groups that specialize in advertising and marketing tracking research, corporate reputations and communications, financial services, health care, litigation support, customer satisfaction and employee studies, and telecommunications and interactive media. In addition, the company carries out social and policy research for government agencies and other nonprofit organizations.

Rivendell Marketing Company, Inc.

Keywords: gay and lesbian market

Todd Evans, President
P.O. Box 518
Westfield, NJ 07090

Phone: 908/232-2021
Fax: 908/232-0521

Rivendell Marketing has been securing national advertisers for the gay press since 1979, and serves as advertising representative for more than 175 gay and lesbian newspapers, magazines, and entertainment guides. It can develop strategies and make recommendations as well as design national and local campaigns.

RONIN Corporation

Keywords: survey software

James C. Weber, Vice President
103 Carnegie Center, Suite 303
Princeton, NJ 08540

Phone: 609/452-0060
Fax: 609/452-0091
E-mail: sales@ronincorp.com

RONIN Corporation produces Results for Research, a fully integrated CATI software program for PC-LANs. Results provides features critical for conducting business-to-business, international, multi-mode, or otherwise complex telephone research surveys. Analysis tools are included, with export capabilities to SPSS, SAS, P-STAT, Mentor, Quantime, Uncle, Excel, 123, Foxpro, and dBase.

Roper Center for Public Opinion Research (The)

Keywords: attitudes and opinions; elections; trends

Lois Timms-Ferrara
P.O. Box 440
Storrs, CT 06268-0440

Phone: 203/486-4440
Fax: 203/486-6308

The Roper Center maintains a record of publicly released polls and surveys for the U.S. and a growing collection of data compiled outside the U.S. The center's holdings are historic–containing data from as early as 1936–and contemporary. It disseminates this material in paper and electronic form to academic social scientists, government researchers, and policy professionals.

Roper Starch Worldwide

Keywords: advertising research; business to business; international; market research; youth and children

Philip W. Sawyer, Senior Vice President
566 E. Boston Post Road
Mamaroneck, NY 10543

Phone: 914/698-0800
Fax: 914/698-0485

Roper Starch Worldwide (formerly Starch INRA Hooper and The Roper Organization) provides marketing, media, advertising, and public opinion research. It has expertise in corporate image, legal evidence, and business-to-business research, both quantitative and qualitative. In addition to custom research, it offers syndicated services (Roper Reports, Roper CollegeTrack, Roper High School Report, and Roper Youth Report), a national omnibus survey, and two newsletters, *Public Pulse* and *Tested Copy*. Roper Starch Worldwide operates the world's largest print ad database, Starch Ad Readership, and the most complete database on Americans' attitudes and buying habits. It is also the coordinator of International Research Associates (INRA - see separate listing), a global research network.

Roper Starch Worldwide - International Division
Keywords: international

Thomas A.W. Miller, Group Senior Vice President
205 East 42nd Street
New York, NY 10017

Phone: 212/599-0700
Fax: 212/867-7008

Roper Starch Worldwide's International Division performs consumer, business-to-business, services, media, and public opinion research on a global basis. It conducts custom and syndicated market research services including customer satisfaction and retail/trade channel model.

Roslow Research Group, Inc.
Keywords: Hispanics

Peter Roslow, President
16 Derby Road
Port Washington, NY 11050

Phone: 516/883-1100
Fax: 516/883-4130

Roslow Research Group, Inc. (RRG) is a full-service research and consulting firm serving Hispanic marketing and media industries in the U.S. and Latin America. Founded in 1984, RRG provides methodological designs and adapts general market methods to Hispanic marketing and media problem-solving.

Runzheimer International
Keywords: automotive; cost of living; employees/labor force; international; travel and tourism

Peter Packer, Vice President, Communication
Runzheimer Park
Rochester, WI 53167

Phone: 414/767-2224
Fax: 414/767-2254

Runzheimer International provides geographically adjusted-per-mile vehicle costs, including fixed and operating costs, for every make and model sold in the U.S. It also analyzes costs of living for more than 300 U.S. metropolitan areas and hundreds of international locations, for any income level and family size. Runzheimer also provides business travel and employee relocation costs for 200 U.S. and 100 international destinations.

Rx Remedy, Inc.

Keywords: database marketing; health care; market research; mature market

William G. Wyman, Executive Vice President
120 Post Road West
Westport, CT 06880

Phone: 203/221-4910
Fax: 203/221-4913

Rx Remedy, Inc. is an information-based direct-marketing services company that provides targeted access to 55-plus consumers with regard to health/wellness issues: illness/health concerns, prescription and OTC drug usage, food and drug purchase habits, dietary considerations, as well as standard demographics. In-depth profiles are available on specific topics, such as arthritis and heartburn. RxEMEDY Health Graphics provides a quantifiable look at an issue/topic and how it relates to the mature population. Services include magazine advertising, couponing, solo direct mail, polybagging with RxEMEDY magazine, and custom market research.

S.M. Detwiler & Associates, Inc.

Keywords: health care; online

Susan Detwiler, President
P.O. Box 15308
Ft. Wayne, IN 46885

Phone: 219/749-6534; 800/861-6715 information line
Fax: 219/493-6717
E-mail: 76670.2211@compuserve.com

S.M. Detwiler & Associates, Inc. specializes in secondary research for the health-care, pharmaceutical, and medical industries. The firm maintains a proprietary database of health-care and medical information sources published as the *Detwiler Directory of Medical Market Sources*, available in print or electronically. The company assists in market planning, new-product development, and acquisition studies, as well as identifying trends in medical markets.

Sachs Group

Keywords: health care; local and market information

Laurie Potter, Director of Sales
1800 Sherman Avenue, Suite 609
Evanston, IL 60201

Phone: 708/475-7526 or 800/366-PLAN
Fax: 708/475-7830
E-mail: info@sachs.com

The Sachs Group provides information and data for the health-care industry. The company supplies health-care organizations with information through databases, reports, maps, graphs, and the Market Planner PC-workstation, integrating proprietary research with publicly available data. Products include market profiles, managed-care inpatient and outpatient utilization models, information for network development and provider contracting, comparative quality data, consumer attitude and behavior research, and information for medical management and utilization.

Sage Publications

Keywords: academic research; demographics; health care; Hispanics; mature market

Phone: 805/499-0721
Fax: 805/499-0871

2455 Teller Road
Thousand Oaks, CA 91320

Sage Publications is a leading publisher of social research journals. *Family and Consumer Sciences Journal* offers original research concerned with the general well-being of families and individuals and focuses on current issues such as consumer studies and family economics. *The Hispanic Journal of Behavior Sciences* publishes research articles and case histories that deal with methodological issues related to Hispanic populations. Other topics include research on aging, qualitative health research, work and occupations, and youth and society.

Sammamish Data Systems, Inc.

Keywords: desktop mapping/GIS; geographic boundary files; local and market information

Richard Schweitzer, President
2889 152nd Avenue, NE, Suite A
Redmond, WA 98052-5514

Phone: 206/867-1485
Fax: 206/861-0184
E-mail: sammdata@aol.com

Sammamish Data Systems has Geosight, a geographic information system for marketing research and target marketing. Users can import their own data, commercial data, or public domain information. The GeoSight Professional system adds interactive territory-management manipulation to the basic GeoSight capabilities. Users can interactively define and modify sales territories, marketing regions, or franchise territories and receive instantaneous reports of the distribution of one or more key marketing indicators.

Sammamish Data has also developed national geographic databases and polygons of postal areas. Detailed postal carrier route polygons are available with quarterly updates. A national file of ZIP+4 Centroids is also available. This file is also updated quarterly using the most recent Postal Service Address Management System (AMS II) files.

SAS Institute, Inc.

Keywords: desktop mapping/GIS; statistical software

Software Sales & Marketing Department
SAS Campus Drive
Cary, NC 27513

Phone: 919/677-8000
Fax: 919/677-8123
E-mail: software@sas.sas.com

SAS Institute, Inc. offers the SAS System, an integrated suite of information delivery software for business decision making that provides the tools to access, manage, analyze, and present data. Capabilities include client/server computing, database access, data analysis, report writing, decision support, and more. The software also allows users to create, analyze, and alter maps representing major roads, business locations, county boundaries, and other map features.

Sawtooth Technologies, Inc.

Keywords: survey software

Brett Jarvis, Marketing Manager
1007 Church Street, Suite 402
Evanston, IL 60201

Phone: 708/866-0870
Fax: 708/866-0876
E-mail: info@sawtooth.com

Sawtooth Technologies offers software for market research, survey research, and data analysis. It offers the C:3 CATI System for computer-aided telephone Interviewing, the C:3 System for computer interviewing, and Knowledge SEEK-ER, which finds significant relationships among variables.

Scan/US, Inc.

Keywords: business to business; demographics; desktop mapping/GIS; geocoding

Michael Kim, Product Manager
2032 Armacost Avenue
Los Angeles, CA 90025

Phone: 800/272-2687
Fax: 310/826-6863
E-mail: ggirton@ix.netcom.com

Scan/US, Inc. offers a variety of demographic, consumer, business, lifestyle, and industry-specific data for use in Scan/US, its Windows-based desktop market analysis and mapping system. Scan/US comes on a CD-ROM, preloaded with extensive maps, incuding detailed streets, and demographic data for the entire U.S. Scan/US includes MicroGrids showing map detail and population density down to 1/16 of a square mile. Data are also available for census tracts, block groups, MicroGrids, rings, polygons, and other user-defined trade areas. Users can analyze data, produce maps and reports, and import/export data for any location in the U.S. Scan/US Geocoder, a sister product to Scan/US, assigns street-level lat/long coordinates to addresses so that they can be displayed on a map.

Scarborough Research

Keywords: buying behavior; local and market information; media research; retailing

Robert Cohen, President
11 West 42nd Street
New York, NY 10036

Phone: 212/789-3560
Fax: 212/789-3577

Scarborough Research conducts comprehensive local market measurement of media usage, retail shopping, consumer behavior, demographics, and leisure activities. It measures the top-50 DMAs plus 8 other major markets.

SchoolMatch by Public Priority Systems, Inc.

Keywords: education; local and market information

Steven M. Sundre
Blendonview Office Park, 5027 Pine Creek Drive
Westerville, OH 43081

Phone: 614/890-1573
Fax: 614/890-3294
E-mail: schools@schoolmatch.com
or http://ppshost/schoolmatch/com/

SchoolMatch by Public Priority Systems is a research and database services firm that collects, audits, integrates, and manages information about public and private, elementary and secondary schools. The SchoolMatch database is used in site selection, corporate relocation, executive recruitment, WorkLife programs, marketing to schools, and school litigation. Audits of school-business partnerships help corporations and foundations analyze their support. The firm also conducts customized research studies.

Scientific Software International, Inc.

Keywords: consulting; statistical software

Stephanie Robinson, Office Manager
1525 East 53rd Street, Suite 530
Chicago, IL 60615-4530

Phone: 312/684-4920
Fax: 312/684-4979
E-mail: info@ssi-inc.com

Scientific Software International, Inc. provides LISREL, a statistical computer software package for structural equation modeling (by Professors Karl G. Jöreskog and Dag Sörbom).

Senecio Software, Inc.

Keywords: computer services; statistical software; survey software

Connie Black-Postl, Marketing Director
525 Ridge Street
Bowling Green, OH 43402

Phone: 419/352-4371
Fax: 419/352-4281

Senecio Software offers three Macintosh platform products: MaCATI (Macintosh-assisted telephone interviewing), IPSS (interactive population statistical system), and Flo Stat (an elementary statistics, mapping, and graphing package). In addition to the CATI version of the MaCATI, it offers a CAPI/DMS version (personal interviewing and Disk-by-Mail). Survey programming is available.

Simmons Market Research Bureau, Inc.

Keywords: buying behavior; consumer segmentation; Hispanics; media research; youth and children

Rebecca McPheters, President & CEO
420 Lexington Avenue
New York, NY 10170

Phone: 212/916-8900
Fax: 212/916-8918

Simmons Market Research Bureau supplies consumer media (TV, magazine, radio, newspaper, outdoor, cable TV, Yellow Pages) and marketing information. Databases include: The Study of Media and Markets, The Survey of American Readership, Simmons Teenage Research Study (STARS), The Kids Study, CompPro, The Hispanic Study, Top Management Insights, and the Food Service Industry Study. Custom media studies are also available.

Slater Hall Information Products

Keywords: census data; demographics; economic data; employees/labor force; local and market information

George Hall, President
1301 Pennsylvania Avenue, NW, Suite 507
Washington, DC 20004

Phone: 202/393-2666
Fax: 202/638-2248
E-mail: slaterco@netcom.com

Slater Hall Information Products provides demographic and economic statistics on CD-ROM for the U.S., states, metropolitan areas, counties, cities, zip codes, and congressional districts. It offers comprehensive census data for 1980 and 1990, plus updated data for population, employment, income, and more. Each CD comes with proprietary retrieval software.

Social Development Center

Keywords: academic research; demographics; local and market information; projections

Donald T. Bogue, Director
1313 East 60th Street
Chicago, IL 60637

Phone: 312/947-2010
Fax: 312/947-2012

The Social Development Center provides methods of demographic research including development, training, consulting, and publications, such as Readings in the Methodology of Demographic Research, a manual distributed worldwide. It also conducts small-area data analysis by census tract and provides population estimates and projections by race, sex, and age.

Sophisticated Data Research (SDR)

Keywords: survey samples

Rick Hunter, Manager
2251 Perimeter Park Drive
Atlanta, GA 30341

Phone: 404/451-5100
Fax: 404/451-5096

SDR Sampling Services provides RDD and listed residential samples for telephone and mail surveys. Using GENESYS Sampling Software, it generates samples defined by virtually any geographic or demographic criteria. It offers a complete array of targeted samples to reach low-incidence populations. SDR also offers services to clean RDD samples of nonproductive numbers, as well as full demographic reporting capabilities and radius mapping.

Spatial Insights, Inc.

Keywords: demographics; desktop mapping/GIS; geocoding; local and market information

Lynn Marie Fasciano, Vice President
8221 Old Courthouse Road, Suite 203
Vienna, VA 22182

Phone: 703/827-7031
Fax: 703/827-7037

Spatial Insights is a geographic information services company that provides spatial analysis services, data products, and custom mapping applications for commercial clients. The company offers a full range of GIS services including site selection, territory optimization, geocoding, demographic profiling, and more.

Spectra/Market Metrics

Keywords: consumer segmentation; demographics; local and market information; market research; packaged goods

John Larkin, President and CEO
333 W. Wacker Drive, Suite 650
Chicago, IL 60606

Phone: 312/263-0606
Fax: 312/263-7022

Spectra/Market Metrics provides micromarketing and consumer segmentation products and services to the consumer packaged-goods industry. Spectra/Market Metrics customizes pictures of consumer behavior at the national, market, key account, neighborhood, and household level. It uses an integrated marketing platform that links household-level-panel purchase data with geographic locations and stores to identify targeted sales and marketing opportunities.

Sprint Integrated Marketing Services

Keywords: business to business; database marketing; market research

Dave Cramer
7015 College Boulevard
Overland Park, KS 66211

Phone: 800/829-2955
Fax: 913/491-7300

Sprint Integrated Marketing Services (IMS) provides a range of marketing services, including market research, database design and modeling, teleservices, and direct-response advertising. Market research services encompass complete in-house capabilities for qualitative and quantitative studies, with expertise in customer satisfaction. Sprint IMS specializes in developing customized database solutions and business-to-business marketing models. Teleservice applications include outbound lead qualification and verification, inbound lead fulfillment and after-hours/overflow. Direct-response expertise includes lead generation, customer retention, and loyalty programs. Sprint IMS has also developed proprietary models that combine employment data, input/output statistics, and county business pattern data for enhancing/scoring prospecting lists and market analysis.

SRDS

Keywords: demographics; lifestyles; local and market information; market research; media research

Jane Long, Marketing Manager
1700 Higgins Road
Des Plaines, IL 60018

Phone: 800/851-SRDS
Fax: 708/375-5001

SRDS publishes *The Lifestyle Market Analyst*, an annual sourcebook of market-by-market information and profiles of more than 19 million households providing a mix of demographic and lifestyle information. Seventy-five consumer interests, hobbies, and activities are measured in 211 Designated Market Areas. SRDS also provides media and marketing information products. *Lifestyle Market Analyst* is published jointly with the former National Demographics & Lifestyles, now the Polk Company.

SRG International

Keywords: consulting; international; market research

Mark Stapylton-Smith, Managing Director
427 Bedford Road
Pleasantville, NY 10570

Phone: 914/769-4444
Fax: 914/769-7760
E-mail: mstapylton@aol.com

SRG International, part of the Survey Research Group (SRG) of market research companies, Asia's largest market research organization, is a wholly owned subsidiary of A.C. Nielsen. SRG International provides research support services to companies with global research needs from consultation in research design to analysis and presentation of the research findings. It routinely conducts research in more than 40 countries in Asia/Pacific, Eastern and Western Europe, Latin America, and the Middle East.

SRI International

Keywords: attitudes and opinions; buying behavior; consumer segmentation; international; market research

John Garrett, Director of Marketing
333 Ravenswood Avenue
Menlo Park, CA 94025

Phone: 415/859-4600
Fax: 415/859-4544
E-mail: vals@sri.com

SRI International provides VALS2, a psychographic consumer segmentation system of U.S. adults that links consumers' psychological attributes and their buying behavior. It also provides GeoVALS, which estimates the number of each VALS type at the zip code and block group level. National product, service, and media data by VALS-type are provided through a link-up with the Simmons Market Research Bureau. VALS/Simmons data are available from 1989 through the current year. The VALS questionnaire can also be used in custom survey research or as a screener for focus groups. Other VALS program products include Japan-VALS, for Japanese consumers; UK VALS, for United Kingdom consumers; and iVALS for segmenting users of interactive media such as the Internet.

Statistics Canada

Keywords: Canada

Daniel Scott, Chief, Communications & Public Relations
R.H. Coats Bldg., Holland Avenue, Tunney's Pasture
Ottawa, ONTARIO K1A 0T6

Phone: 800/263-1136
Fax: 613/951-0581
E-mail: http://www.statcan.ca

Statistics Canada is Canada's central statistical agency. It presents a comprehensive picture of the national economy through statistics on manufacturing, agriculture, exports and imports, retail services, prices, trade, transportation, employment, and aggregate measures such as gross domestic product and consumer price index. It also presents social conditions through statistics on demography, health, education, justice, culture, and household incomes and expenditures. This information is produced at the national, provincial, and regional levels.

Statistics Canada collects statistics through surveys and censuses and by consulting administrative records. The Canadian Census of Population, held every five years, collects basic information such as age, sex, marital status, and family composition, as well as additional information that varies from one census to another. The next census will be held in May 1996. Annual and quarterly estimates of the population, households, and families are also produced.

The Statistics Catalogue, available in print, CD-ROM, and through the Internet, contains information about the wide range of print and electronic information sources and services offered by Statistics Canada. The most popular print titles are the *Canada Year Book* and *Canada: A Portrait*. Electronic services include The Daily, the official release bulletin, and an extensive international trade database, as well as Infohort, which provides information on horticulture commodities. Other databases include CANSIM, which contains socioeconomic statistics, and TIERS, a trade information recovery system.

Regional Reference Centres:

Halifax, Nova Scotia:	902/426-5331
Montreal, Quebec:	514/283-5725
National Capital Region:	613/951-8116 or 800/263-1136
Toronto, Ontario:	416/973-6586
Winnepeg, Manitoba:	204/983-4020
Regina, Saskatchewan:	306/780-5405
Calgary, Alberta:	403/292-6717
Edmonton, Alberta:	403/495-3027
Vancouver, British Columbia:	604/666-3691

StatPac Inc.

Keywords: statistical

David Walonick, President
4532 France Avenue South
Minneapolis, MN 55410

Phone: 612/925-0159
Fax: 612/925-0851
E-mail: statpac@aol.com

StatPac's Gold IV software is designed for survey analysis and marketing research. It features survey design, sample selection, data entry and management, CRT and telephone interviewing, basic analyses, and presentation-quality graphics. The software includes frequencies, tabs and banners, open-ended response coding, multiple response, descriptives, breakdowns, correlations, and t-tests. Advanced analyses are also available as separate modules.

Strategic Directions Group, Inc.

Keywords: attitudes and opinions; business to business; consumer segmentation; market research

Doran J. Levy, Ph.D.
Suite 311, 119 N. Fourth Street
Minneapolis, MN 55401

Phone: 612/341-4244
Fax: 612/341-4127

Strategic Directions Group has over 25 years experience doing custom studies using Marketer proprietary segmentation and targeting methodologies. Using attitudinal and psychographic research, it identifies customer segments having the greatest profit potential and then creates applications, including computer software, for reaching them. Marketer provides insights for prospecting, new-product design, advertising, customer satisfaction, and pricing for both business-to-business and consumer applications.

Strategic Leadership Forum

Keywords: education; market research

Robert E. Becker
435 N. Michigan Avenue, #17000
Chicago, IL 60611-4067

Phone: 312/644-0829
Fax: 312/644-8557
E-mail: 102615.1076@compuserve.com

The Strategic Leadership Forum (formerly The Planning Forum) is a membership organization that monitors new developments in planning and strategic management, conducts research and evaluates complementary and conflicting information, and disseminates information and viewpoints on issues and tools related to corporate performance.

Strategic Marketing Communications, Inc.

Keywords: education;
media research;
youth and children

Eric R. Weil
550 North Maple Avenue
Ridgewood, NJ 07450

Phone: 800/383-2060
Fax: 201/612-1444
E-mail: trnds@aol.com

Strategic Marketing Communications (SMC) provides marketing plan design, analysis, and implementation to marketers targeting the college student market. SMC publishes two syndicated college market studies, as well as a quarterly newsletter. *The College Marketing Annual* is a strategic marketing and media guide to the college market published annually in hard copy and magnetic media formats. *The College Media Advertiser Spending Tracking Report* monitors advertiser spending in college-student-specific media. *Collegiate Trends* is a quarterly newsletter monitoring college student demographic, lifestyle, and consumer trends. The newsletter also provides in-depth coverage and analysis of student-targeted media and promotion tools and techniques.

Strategy Research Corporation

Keywords: focus groups; Hispanics; international;
Latin America; market research

Richard W. Tobin, President
100 NW 37th Avenue
Miami, FL 33125

Phone: 305/649-5400
Fax: 305/649-6312

Strategy Research Corporation is a full-service marketing research company, conducting domestic and international qualitative and quantitative research, survey studies, attitude, usage, tracking, distribution studies, and focus groups studies. The company also has Hispanic research capabilities, providing custom marketing research studies, syndicated market profiles, and television audience estimates. It conducts multi-country studies with its own personnel in many Latin-American and Caribbean countries, providing comparable results on a country-to-country or market-to-market basis. Survey Research Corporation publishes the annual *U.S. Hispanic Market Study* and the *1995 Latin American Market Planning Handbook*.

Survey Sampling, Inc.
Keywords: consulting; survey samples

Terrence Coen, Vice President, Sales & Marketing
One Post Road
Fairfield, CT 06430

Phone: 203/255-4200
Fax: 203/254-0372
E-mail: info@ssisamples.com

Survey Sampling, Inc. (SSI) provides a complete line of samples for survey research. SSI's new software, SSI-SNAP, lets clients place sample orders using their own PC and modem. Its Sample Screening Service removes disconnects from RDD samples. Subgroups are targested based on income (high, low, range), age (children, teenagers, adults, mature), and race/ethnic origin (black, Hispanic, Asian). SSI-LITe (Low Incidence Targeting) reaches low-incidence groups. Business-to-business samples can be selected by SIC code, employee size, sales volume, and other criteria. SSI's Account Team provides consulting on sample type, size, geographic definition, and cost efficiencies.

Surveys of Consumers - University of Michigan
Keywords: attitudes and opinions; consumer confidence; economic data; projections and forecasts

Richard T. Curtin
426 Thompson Street
Ann Arbor, MI 48106

Phone: 313/763-5224
Fax: 313/764-3488
E-mail: curtin@umich.edu

Surveys of Consumers produces the Index of Consumer Sentiment based on Americans' responses to three economic topics: personal finances, business conditions, and buying conditions. The monthly surveys track consumer confidence on a national level as well as for census regions dating back to 1947. Demographics include age, sex, income, education, marital status, and geographic region.

Tactician Corporation

Keywords: demographics; desktop mapping/GIS; sales and marketing

Dave Donelan, Director of Sales
16 Haverhill Street
Andover, MA 01810

Phone: 508/475-4475, 800/927-7666
Fax: 508/475-2136

Tactician Corporation supplies mapping software and data. It offers a compatible range of products for sales, marketing, and business planning used to analyze sales and market trends, optimize sales territories, study customer demographics, evaluate advertising and promotion campaigns, select retail sites, do risk analysis, and demonstrate regulatory compliance. Platforms supported are Macintosh, MS-Windows, and Windows-NT for Intel and Alpha AXP.

Teenage Research Unlimited

Keywords: market research; youth and children

Peter Zollo, President
707 Skokie Boulevard, Suite 450
Northbrook, IL 60062

Phone: 708/564-3440
Fax: 708/564-0825

Teenage Research Unlimited (TRU) is a full-service marketing research firm specializing in the youth market. TRU's syndicated Teenage Marketing & Lifestyle Study includes attitudes and lifestyles, being "cool," activities, product and brand preferences, what's "in," what's "out," rules for advertisers, celebrities, media, and Teen/Types–TRU's lifestyle segmentation system. More than 2,000 nationally representative teens are included in each study, which is released twice a year. Data are available from 1982. TRU also offers custom-research capabilities through focus groups, in-depth personal interviews, mall intercepts, and its teen phone and mail panels. Kids Research Unlimited, TRU's youngest division, extends the firm's research into the children's market.

Telematch

Keywords: database marketing; demographics; geocoding; mailing lists

Jane Kressel, Sales Manager
6883 Commercial Drive
Springfield, VA 22159

Phone: 800/523-7346
Fax: 703/658-8301

Telematch provides computer and database marketing services, specializing in computerized telephone number appending, data enhancement, and data processing. In addition to computerized telephone and name-and-address appending services, Telematch provides demographics, list maintenance, list rental, and laser printing. Telematch's line of appending services includes Electronic Directory Assistance (EDA). EDA provides the most current telephone numbers available from the Regional Bell Operating Companies. Telematch accepts and returns data on magnetic tape/cartridge, diskette, and via modem.

Temple University Press

Keywords: academic research; ethnic markets; women

Ann-Marie Anderson, Marketing Director
Broad and Oxford Streets, USB Room 305
Philadelphia, PA 19122

Phone: 215/204-8787
Fax: 215/204-4719
E-mail: tempress@astro.ocis.temple.edu

Temple University Press is a nationally recognized university press that sustains a dedication to political and social ideals. Projects include books in the following areas: American studies, sociology, photography, political science, urban studies, women's studies, ethnic studies, and the Philadelphia region.

Terra Research & Computing

Keywords: computer services; market research

Nick Stoyanoff, President
261 E. Maple
Birmingham, MI 48009

Phone: 810/258-9657
Fax: 810/258-9668

Terra Research & Computing develops neural-network software for marketing and advertising applications. It has experience conducting both qualitative and quantitative research. Terra is a full-service market research supplier.

Tetrad Computer Applications Limited

Keywords: Canada; computer services; consumer segmentation; consumer spending; employees/labor force; local and market information; projections and forecasts

Wilson Baker, President
3873 Airport Way, Box 9754
Bellingham, WA 98227-9754

Phone: 800/663-1334
Fax: 360/734-4005
E-mail: email@tetrad.com

Tetrad Computer Applications' PCensus provides demographics for user-defined study areas (circles/polygons). Sources include the 1990 census, as well as Equifax's current-year estimates and five-year projections, Business-Facts with daytime population, Consumer-Facts with household spending on 400 items, and MicroVision market segments. PCensus also works with MapInfo mapping sofware. In addition, Tetrad provides 1991 2-A and 2-B census data as collected by Statistics Canada.

TGE Demographics, Inc.

Keywords: consulting; consumer spending; desktop mapping/GIS; market research; projections and forecasts

Thomas G. Exter, President
61 North Main Street
Honeoye Falls, NY 14472

Phone: 716/624-7390
Fax: 716/624-7394

TGE Demographics provides strategic research and consulting services in consumer market demography, specializing in demographic trends and projections for national and international markets. For an annual subscription fee, members of the Center for Consumer Market Demography receive four reports: Consumer Income, Consumer Households, Consumer Spending, and Consumer Geography. The first three reports contain national-level information; the fourth contains projections for U.S. regions, states, and metropolitan areas. Each report covers current data and five- and ten-year projections. As an independent data broker, TGE assists clients with demographic data purchases.

Total Research Corporation (TRC)

Keywords: brand equity; business to business; consulting; customer satisfaction; financial services; health care; market research; telecommunications

James Alleborn, Senior Vice President
5 Independence Way -- CN 5305
Princeton, NJ 08543-5305

Phone: 609/520-9100
Fax: 609/987-8839
E-mail: trc@totalres.com

Total Research provides a full range of marketing research and consulting services: custom qualitative and quantitative studies using advanced research and analytical techniques, syndicated consumer brand and media equity/quality data (EquiTrend 1990-1995), and a customer-loyalty management process for measuring and managing customer satisfaction. It has industry expertise in consumer products, business-to-business, health care, telecommunications/information technology, and financial services.

Trade Dimensions

Keywords: retailing

Garrett Van Siclen, Senior Vice President
263 Tresser Boulevard
Stamford, CT 06901

Phone: 203/977-7600
Fax: 203/977-7645

Trade Dimensions offers retail store databases of supermarkets, mass merchandisers, chain drug, wholesale clubs, and convenience stores. Extensive physical facts about each store including estimated retail sales volume indicators are available. Comprehensive directories covering each of the above industries are also available.

Traffic Audit Bureau for Media Measurement, Inc.

Keywords: billboards; circulation data

Anna Fountas, President
420 Lexington Avenue, Suite 2520
New York, NY 10170

Phone: 212/972-8075
Fax: 212/972-8928

The Traffic Audit Bureau for Media Measurement's (TAB) primary purpose is to authenticate circulation data for out-of-home media such as billboards. It seeks to inform and educate the advertising community regarding the quantitative and qualitative values of all forms of out-of-home media. In special instances, TAB also audits visibility values and certifies advertising placement. The TAB membership consists of outdoor plant operators, advertising agencies, major advertisers, and suppliers to the outdoor industry. The Summary of Audited Markets Book lists information for all audited markets.

Training Technologies

Keywords: survey software

Renée Reed, Creative Director
11449 Lebanon Road
Cincinnati, OH 45241

Phone: 513/769-4121
Fax: 513/769-5950

Training Technologies, Inc., offers Survey Tracker for Windows. Survey Tracker can design surveys and maintain large or small audience lists with automatic sampling. Response data can be collected using Survey Tracker E-Mail version, by scanning responses, or by manual data entry. The software also offers analytical and reporting capabilities in three-dimensional charts and graphs.

Trans Union Corporation

Keywords: analytical services; computer services; consumer segmentation; database marketing; housing and real estate; risk assessment

Dolly Duplantier, Corporate Communications Manager
555 West Adams Street
Chicago, IL 60661-3601

Phone: 800/899-7132
Fax: 312/466-7990

Trans Union Corporation provides credit-based (Silouette) and demographic-based segmentation systems (Solo and Portrait), an individual-level income estimator (TIE), and a home value estimator (Reveal). Data are available down to the individual level (note: data are subject to the Fair Credit Reporting Act according to end use). Also available are market analysis tools, custom response modeling, generic revenue predictors (RPM), and risk models.

Travel Industry Association of America

Keywords: travel and tourism

Publications Ordering
1100 New York Avenue, NW, Suite 450
Washington, DC 20005-3934

Phone: 202/408-8422
Fax: 202/408-1255

The Travel Industry Association of America (TIA) is a national, nonprofit association representing the common concerns of all components of the U.S. travel industry. TIA includes both private and public sector members. Its primary role is to take a leadership position with major industry developments and initiatives in marketing, government policy, research and analysis, and public education. Through its research department, the U.S. Travel Data Center (see separate listing), TIA provides aggregate statistical information for the industry. Subscribers to the annual research subscription package receive publications that examine U.S. domestic travel trends and the economic impact of the travel industry. Publications include *1995 Outlook for Travel and Tourism* and *The 55+ Traveler*. Members can also buy individual research publications.

Trends Research Institute

Keywords: market research; projections; trends

Mary Ann Martinson, Vice President, Professional Services
P.O. Box 660
Rhinebeck, NY 12572-0660

Phone: 914/876-6700
Fax: 914/758-5252

The Trends Research Institute analyzes more than 300 trend categories such as social, political, media, health, family, education, and other domestic and international trends, and forecasts their direction and life cycle. Services include commissioned trend studies, in-house trend-tracking systems, Tracking Trends for Profit Workshops, and *The Trends Journal* newsletter.

TRW Target Marketing Services

Keywords: affluent market; automotive; computer services; database marketing; ethnic markets; financial services; housing and real estate; mailing lists

Raelyn Wade, Sales Director
701 TRW Parkway
Allen, TX 75013

Phone: 214/390-5229
Fax: 214/390-5195

TRW Target Marketing Services, a business unit of TRW Information Systems and Services based in Allen, Texas, provides information services to the direct marketing, financial services, real estate, and automotive industries. It helps marketers locate consumers most likely to respond to offers. Its PerformanceData System (PDS) allows marketers to reach 183 million consumers in 98 million households nationwide. The PDS is compiled from consumer names and addresses from TRW's consumer credit database, public record information and data from questionnaires, publications, direct mail, real estate deed recordings, birth records, tax assessor

files, telephone White Pages, and other sources. TRW list selections include the Consumer Database, Highly Affluent Database, Ethnic Markets, New Movers, HomeownersPlus Smart Targeting Tools, Credit Card Markets, and Buyers' Response. TRW also offers radius marketing capabilities and behavior-based segmentation tools. The company provides database marketing services, including data enhancement, address cleaning, National Change of Address (NCOA)* file processing, merge/purge and postal qualification services.
TRW Inc. is a nonexclusive licensee of the U.S. Postal Service.

U.S. Travel Data Center (Research Department of The Travel Industry Association of America)

Keywords: travel and tourism

Suzanne D. Cook, Ph.D., Senior Vice President, Research
1100 New York Avenue, NW, Suite 450
Washington, DC 20005-3934

Phone: 202/408-1832
Fax: 202/408-1255

The U.S. Travel Data Center provides U.S. domestic travel volume and trip characteristics based on a national monthly survey of 1,500 U.S. resident adults. The National Travel Survey covers travel in the past month, purpose of trip, mode of transportation, other members of the household traveling, as well as basic demographic information.

United Nations

Keywords: census data; demographics; international

Alice Clague, Officer-in-Charge, Demographic Section
Statistical Division DC2-1514 United Nations
New York, NY 10017

Phone: 212/963-4972
Fax: 212/963-1940
E-mail: demostat@un.org

The annual *United Nations Demographic Yearbook* includes the latest available demographic data on population structure and change, fertility, mortality, international migration, and family formation in cooperating countries. Its Demographic and Social Statistics Database is a microcomputer database containing 40-year trends covering the same subjects. A storage and retrieval system is also available on diskette.

Unitrac Software Corporation

Keywords: analytical services; computer services; database marketing; sales and marketing

Rori L. Gammons, Manager, Marketing Services
141 E. Michigan Avenue
Kalamazoo, MI 49007

Phone: 800-UNITRAC
Fax: 616/344-2027

Unitrac Software Corporation develops UNITRAC–The Enterprise Information Manager, a sales/marketing software package for Windows. Unitrac supports sales force automation, account management, telemarketing, customer service, client/prospect surveys, and more.

University of South Carolina Survey Research Laboratory

Keywords: attitudes and opinions; elections; market research

Robert W. Oldendick, Director
Institute of Public Affairs, 1503 Carolina Plaza
Columbia, SC 29208

Phone: 803/777-8157
Fax: 803/777-4575
E-mail: oldendick@iopa.scarolina.edu

The University of South Carolina Survey Research Laboratory is a full-service research organization providing all aspects of survey research, evaluation, and public policy research. It conducts national, regional, and local computer-assisted telephone surveys, mail surveys, as well as data management, processing, and analysis.

Urban Decision Systems

Keywords: business to business; census data; crime; demographics; desktop mapping/GIS; local and market information; projections and forecasts; retailing

Eric Cohen, Executive Vice President
4676 Admiralty Way
Marina del Rey, CA 90292

Phone: 800/633-9568
Fax: 310/827-2339

Urban Decision Systems, a Blackburn Group Company, provides a variety of demographic and business data in formats ranging from printed reports to data-on-disk to reporting systems. Its Data On Call product line offers more than 50 standardized reports including 1970, 1980, and 1990 census data; current-year estimates; five- and ten-year projections; merchandise potential data for 185 lines of products; daytime census/business data; PRIZM Lifestyles information; traffic volumes; data for 34,000 shopping centers and 375,000 restaurants; crime data; environmental data; and more. Reports, maps, and consumer and business mailing lists can be customized. Data are available on disk or CD-ROM through the MarketBase and MarketBase product lines. MarketReporter software allows users to select from more than 30 different reports to evaluate current or potential sites.

Urban Institute (The)

Keywords: demographics; health care; housing and real estate; immigration; projections and forecasts

Susan Brown, Director, Office of Public Affairs
2100 M Street, NW
Washington, DC 20037

Phone: 202/833-7200
Fax: 202/429-0687

The Urban Institute conducts economic and social research on key domestic and some international issues. It follows demographic trends relating to immigration, population size and characteristics, health-care costs, housing, public finance, and welfare reform.

Urban Science

Keywords: analytical services; consulting; database marketing; local and market information

David Sheeran, Account Manager
200 Renaissance Center, 19th Floor
Detroit, MI 48243

Phone: 800/321-6900
Fax: 313/259-1362

Urban Science utilizes scientific problem-solving methods and computer technology to provide customized marketing services. Applications include GIS, database management, consulting services, advanced computer modeling, and statistical and quantitative analysis.

US WEST Market Information Products

Keywords: analytical services; database marketing; mailing lists; market research

Phone: 800/431-9000
Fax: 303/889-2687

8200 East Belleview, Suite 500
Englewood, CO 80111

US WEST Market Information Products offers a complete line of products and services to help businesses find customers, sell to them, and keep them coming back. Products include direct-marketing lists updated daily and available by 40 demographic qualifiers, as well as a wide range of customized and packaged database marketing tools such as database design, predictive modeling, statistical analysis, and consulting services.

Vista Information Solutions, Inc.

Keywords: demographics; desktop mapping/GIS; local and market information

Richard Byers
7525 Mitchell Road
Eden Prairie, MN 55344

Phone: 800/533-7742
Fax: 612/934-8727

Vista Information Solutions, Inc. provides geodemographic services and software, including customer profiling, site selection, and target marketing. Geographic coverage includes counties, MSAs, zip codes, postal carrier routes, census tracts, and census block groups.

W.E.R. The Information Connection, Inc.

Keywords: demographics; desktop mapping/GIS; geographic boundary files

C. Michael Long, President
P.O. Box 107
Mill City, OR 97360

Phone: 503/897-2300
Fax: 503/897-2335
E-mail: wer@teleport.com

W.E.R. The Information Connection, Inc., provides five-digit zip code outline maps. It provides demographic data, such as age and ethnicity, and digital boundary files, and nationwide coverage for 1980 to 2000 for zip codes, census tract, and more.

W-Two Publications, Inc.

Keywords: demographics; international; trends

Doris Walsh, President
202 The Commons, Suite 401
Ithaca, NY 14850

Phone: 607/277-0934
Fax: 607/277-0935
E-mail: 76500.1504@compuserve

W-Two Publications focuses on consumers outside the United States. Monthly newsletters cover the attitudes and lifestyles, demographics, consumer behavior, media behavior, and other related factors of consumers in Asia-Pacific, Europe, Latin America, and Mideast/Africa. Subscribers get automatic, free access to a Quick Query service for answers to specific questions. Subscribers include large consumer-goods companies worldwide and the advertising, consulting, accounting, and market research firms that supply them with customer and marketing information.

Walker Information

Keywords: customer satisfaction; database marketing; health care; market research

Connie Burking
3939 Priority Way, South Drive
Indianapolis, IN 46280-0432

Phone: 317/843-3939
Fax: 317/843-8997

Walker Information is a global firm that measures and manages stakeholder relationships. The Corporate Reputation and Stakeholder Assessment product examines how companies are perceived by stakeholders, helping to formulate plans for action and deployment. Walker Information's Customer Satisfaction Measurement and CSM Worldwide help businesses develop information-based strategies for achieving customer loyalty. The Organizational Culture Assessment identifies internal barriers that prevent employee commitment. Healthcare Product Research combines clincial and consumer research to offer pharmaceutical, medical device, and consumer-product manufacturers an opportunity to understand both clinical profiles and patient customers. Database Marketing offers methods to build relationships with customers and clients through lead generation, tele-sales, tele-service, telephone account measurement, and other direct-marketing tactics. Marketing Research is a custom-designed service that provides tools for implementing marketing, sales, and service strategies. Design and execution of data collection and data processing phases of survey research and customer satisfaction measurement are provided by Walker Information's Data Management.

Walsh America/PMSI

Keywords: computer services; consulting; database marketing; health care; market research

John Meyers, Director of Marketing
2394 E. Camelback Road
Phoenix, AZ 85016

Phone: 602/381-9500
Fax: 602/381-9717

Walsh America/PMSI provides a broad range of proprietary database-driven pharmaceutical marketing services, including Source, which accesses information from more than 34,000 pharmacies to build a 2.6 billion prescription database by prescriber, form of payment, payer, and product; Premiere ClientServer; PMSI research and consulting services; PMSI direct relationship marketing programs; and PRECISE electronic territory management systems.

WEFA Group (The)

Keywords: computer services; consulting; economic data; international

401 City Avenue, Suite 300
Bala Cynwyd, PA 19004

Phone: 610/667-6000
Fax: 610/660-6477

The WEFA Group operates throughout North America and Europe and has affiliates in Latin America and the Far East, resulting from the 1987 merger of two international consulting firms, Wharton Econometric Forecasting Associates (WEFA) and Chase Econometrics. Its U.S. Economic Services cover the U.S. economy, with particular emphasis on monetary and fiscal policy, financial markets, industrial and consumer markets, and demographics. Its Regional Services focuses on economic activity at the state, county, metropolitan, and zip code levels. In addition, WEFA offers international, industry-specific consulting, data, and software services.

Wessex, Inc.

Keywords: demographics; desktop mapping/GIS; geographic boundary files

Bob Ruschman, Vice President, Public Affairs
1015 Tower Road
Winnetka, IL 60093

Phone: 708/501-3662
Fax: 708/501-3691

Wessex, Inc. provides national geographic and demographic data products that work with ArcView, MapInfo, and other leading GIS mapping products. It offers complete results of the 1990 census summarized by state, county, tract, block group, place, and zip code in its Pro/Filer for SAS/Windows format and Pro/Filer for SPSS/Windows/Unix format.

Windham International

Keywords: employees/labor force; international

Michael S. Schell, President
55 Fifth Avenue
New York, NY 10003

Phone: 212/647-0555
Fax: 212/647-0494
E-mail: 102015.204@compuserv.com

Windham International provides international relocation services for corporations and their expatriates and families in 60 countries through the Global Relocation Partnership (GRP). The program begins with cross-cultural preparation and continues with destination home-finding and settling.

Wirthlin Group (The)

Keywords: attitudes and opinions; desktop mapping/GIS; elections; international

Bryce Bassett, Director, Marketing Support
1998 South Columbia Lane
Orem, UT 84058-8052

Phone: 801/226-1524
Fax: 801/226-3483

The Wirthlin Group conducts custom public opinion surveys at the national, state, zip, and congressional district level. It also provides geodemographic mapping, political polling for 1980 through 1995, and community surveys.

Woods & Poole Economics, Inc.

Keywords: economic data; local and market information; market research; projections and forecasts

Martin K. Holdrich
1794 Columbia Road, NW, Suite 4
Washington, DC 20009-2805

Phone: 800/786-1915

Woods & Poole Economics specializes in long-range projections for counties and metropolitan areas. The Woods & Poole database contains more than 550 economic and demographic variables for every state, region, county, MSA, and Designated Market Area (DMA) in the U.S. for every year from 1970 to 2020. This database includes population by age, sex, and race; employment and earnings by industry; personal income; retail sales by kind of business; and households by size and income. Special forecasts are available using Woods & Poole's regional model. Products come with an explanation of the forecast methods, data definitions, and data sources. Forecasts are available in printed reports, tape, disk, or CD-ROM.

World Bank (The)

Keywords: academic research; economic data; international; projections and forecasts

Publications Department
Box 7247-7956
Philadelphia, PA 19170-7956

Phone: 202/473-1155
Fax: 202/522-2627
E-mail: books@worldbank.org

The World Bank publishes the *World Population Projections* (biannually), *World Bank Atlas* (annually), *World Data: World Bank Indicators on CD-ROM* (annually), *World Debt Tables* (annually), and *Trends in Developing Economies* (annually).

World Future Society

Keywords: projections and forecasts; trends

Jefferson Cornish, Business Manager
7910 Woodmont Avenue, Suite 450
Bethesda, MD 20814

Phone: 301/656-8274
Fax: 301/951-0394

The World Future Society (WFS) is a nonprofit, nonpartisan scientific and educational association of people interested in the social and technological developments shaping the future. WFS publishes three journals: *The Futurist* (a full-color bimonthly magazine), *Futures Research Quarterly*, and *Future Survey* (monthly journal of abstracts of relevant publications). WFS also sponsors meetings ranging from small seminars and Professional Members' Forums to large general assemblies.

World Health Organization

Keywords: health care; international

Distribution and Sales
1211 Geneva 27
SWITZERLAND

Phone: 011-41-22-791-21-11
Fax: 011-41-22-791-07-46
E-mail: library@who.ch

The World Health Organization (WHO) is a specialized agency of the United Nations charged to act as the world's directing and coordinating authority on questions of human health. WHO provided the first truly global framework for setting international standards to promote and protect health. It produces health statistics on cases of morbidity and mortality from all member countries.

Yankelovich Partners Inc.

Keywords: attitudes and opinions; brand equity; consulting; ethnic markets; market research; youth and children

John Struck, CEO
101 Merritt 7 Corporate Park
Norwalk, CT 06851

Phone: 203/846-0100
Fax: 203/845-8200

Yankelovich Partners Inc. is an international marketing research and consulting firm featuring models, methodologies, and proprietary databases designed to provide marketing intelligence and prescriptive guidance for solutions to consumer issues such as market targeting, positioning, product design, brand equity, customer satisfaction, and new-product forecasting. Syndicated products include MONITOR; Hispanic, Asian, African-American, and Youth MONITOR; Yankelovich CnXn; Viewpoint Series (business-to-business studies); and public opinion surveys.

Zandl Group (The)

Keywords: consulting; projections and forecasts; youth and children

Irma Zandl, President
270 Lafayette Street, Suite 612
New York, NY 10012

Phone: 212/274-1222
Fax: 212/274-1352
E-mail: princest1@aol.com

The Zandl Group is a marketing consulting firm specializing in young consumers in the United States–tweens, teens, and young adults. It provides qualitative consumer insights and trend forecasts. The Zandl Group also maintains a nationwide database of 3,000 8-to-29-year-olds.

Chapter 5: Federal Government Sources

Bureau of Economic Analysis

Public Information Office   Phone: 202/606-9900
U.S. Department of Commerce, 1441 L Street, NW
Washington, DC 20230   E-mail: REIS.REMD@BEA.DOC.GOV

The Bureau of Economic Analysis (BEA) provides the only ongoing annual measure of economic activity at regional and local levels, as well as national and international economic analysis. It examines principal sources of personal income, including transfer payments and rental income, dividend and interest income, wages and salaries, and the industries that supply them. The BEA also produces an important economic indicator—per capita personal income.

BEA data differ from those of the Census Bureau in that the later surveys people to learn their income, while the BEA works down from the macro-level, determining the total personal income of a county or state. For more information, see the "User's Guide to BEA Information," which appears each year in the January issue of the Survey of Current Business (see below). The publication is available free from BEA's Public Information Office.

Telephone contacts

Public Information Office, ... 202/606-9900
Economic Projections, State and Metropolitan Areas, George Downey 606-5341
Personal Income and Employment, State, MSA and County Data
  Requests, Regional Economic Information Staff 606-5360

What You Can Get From the Bureau of Economic Analysis

Survey of Current Business

This monthly publication provides four valuable series of income data:

1. Quarterly estimates of personal income for states appear in the February, May, September, and November issues.
2. Preliminary annual estimates of personal income and disposable personal income for states appear in the May issue; revised estimates appear in September.

3. Preliminary annual estimates of per capita personal and disposable personal income for states are in the May issue; revised estimates appear in September.
4. Estimates of personal income for counties for two years earlier appear in the May issue.

The Survey of Current Business is $41 a year from the Government Printing Office; 202/512-1800.

REIS CD-ROM

The Regional Economic Information System (REIS) CD-ROM contains over 25 years of economic data for all U.S. states, counties, and metropolitan areas. Estimates include annual personal income by major source, per capita personal income, earnings by two-digit SIC industry code, full- and part-time employment by one-digit SIC industry, regional economic profiles, transfer payments by major program, and farm income and expenses. The data include BEA estimates of quarterly personal income by state, Gross State product, and projections to 2040 of income and employment for states and metropolitan areas. Data are updated annually. The CD-ROM for 1969-93 costs $35. For more information or to order, call 202/606-5360.

BEA Regional Projections

Published every five years, these projections forecast demographic and economic characteristics for regions, states, metropolitan areas, and BEA Economic Areas, for population by three age groups: 0 to 14, 15 to 64, and 65 and older; personal income by source; employment and gross state product for 56 industrial sectors; and earnings for 14 industries. The projections are available as publication, disk, on the Internet through STAT-USA, and the Department of Commerce's electronic Bulletin Board (EBB). Data are also included on REIS CD-ROM (see above). For more information, call the BEA at 202/606-5341.

Tabulations

Tabulations can be requested for counties or combinations of counties, and can be ordered on disk or hard copy. For this service, which the BEA provides relatively quickly, call 202/606-5360.

Bureau of Justice Statistics

633 Indiana Avenue, NW
Washington, DC 20531

Phone: 202/307-0765
E-mail: http://www.ojp.usdoj.gov/bjs

As the statistical arm of the U.S. Department of Justice, the Bureau of Justice Statistics (BJS) provides data on crime, criminal offenders, victims of crime, and the operation of justice systems at all levels of government. BJS reports can be ordered free of charge from the BJS Clearinghouse, Box 6000, Rockville, MD 20850. Outside of Maryland and Washington, D.C., call 800/732-3277. In Maryland and Washington, D.C., call 301/251-5500.

The Drugs & Crime Clearinghouse is a resource for current data about illegal drugs, drug law violations, drug-related crime, and the effect of drugs and drug-using offenders on the criminal justice system. Call 800/666-3332 for reports and information.

BJS sponsors the National Archive of Criminal Justice Data at the Inter-university Consortium of Political and Social Research at the University of Michigan. All BJS data tapes and other high-quality data are stored at the archive and disseminated via magnetic tapes, CD-ROM, and diskettes compatible with the user's computing environment. To order machine-readable data files, call the archive staff at 800/999-0960; or write NACJD, P.O. Box 1248, Ann Arbor, MI 48106.

Telephone contacts

National Corrections Statistics, Allen J. Beck 202/616-3277
National Crime Victimization Statistics, Michael R. Rand 616-3494
Prosecution & Adjudication Statistics, Steven K. Smith 616-3485
Law Enforcement & Pretrial Statistics, Brian A. Reaves 616-3287
Federal Justice Statistics, Steven K. Smith 616-3485

What You Can Get From BJS

National Corrections Statistics

Consists of a number of separate data collection and analysis efforts designed to obtain detailed information on offenders under correctional care, custody, or control, and the agencies and facilities responsible for administering the supervision of offenders.

National Crime Victimization Statistics

This is the second-largest ongoing household survey undertaken by the federal government and the only national forum for victims to describe outcomes of crime and offender characteristics. The survey produces annual estimates of the amount of crime against persons and experienced by households, victimization rates, the characteristics of victims, criminal events and offenders, the reporting of crime to police, and victims' reasons for not reporting. Data on topical issues such as elderly victims, police response time, and domestic violence are also analyzed and reported.

Prosecution and Adjudication Statistics

This program provides data on prosecutorial policies and practices, felony sentencing in state courts, the nation's state court systems, and civil case load data.

Law Enforcement and Pretrial Statistics

This program provides data and information on the organization and administrative practices of the nation's law enforcement agencies, pretrial status of persons charged with felonies, and incident-based crime data.

Federal Justice Statistics

Provides data on the movement of accused offenders through the federal criminal process, beginning with the number of suspects investigated, prosecution, adjudication, sentencing of defendants, and concluding with the types and durations of sanctions received and served.

Bureau of Labor Statistics

Veola Kittrell   Phone: 202/606-7828
2 Massachusetts Avenue, NE   E-mail: stats.bls.gov/blshome.html
Washington, DC 20212

The BLS is known for employment and unemployment information, but it also provides some of the best consumer spending data around.

Many of the statistics that people need to assess what is going on in the economy—trends in prices, earning, employment, unemployment, consumer spending, wages, and productivity—come from the Bureau of Labor Statistics. The following reports are free and may be obtained from the Office of Inquiries and Correspondence, U.S. Bureau of Labor Statistics, 2 Massachusetts Avenue, NE, Room 2860, Washington, DC 20212; telephone 202/606-7828: Major Programs of the Bureau of Labor Statistics describes each of the agency's activities in detail and lists relevant publications; BLS Update is a quarterly publication that lists all new publications and tells how to get them; and Telephone Contacts for Data Users lists names and telephone numbers of all subject-matter specialists.

What You Can Get From the Bureau of Labor Statistics

Employment and Unemployment Statistics

The Bureau of Labor Statistics analyzes and publishes data from the monthly Current Population Survey (CPS) on the labor force, employment, unemployment, and persons not in the labor force. Studies based on CPS data cover a broad range of topics, including analyses of the nation's overall labor market situation, as well as special worker groups such as minorities, women, school-age youth, older workers, disabled veterans, persons living in poverty, and displaced workers.

The bureau also collects, analyzes, and publishes detailed industry data on employment, wages, hours, and earnings of workers on payrolls of nonfarm business establishments. It publishes monthly estimates of state and local unemployment for use by federal agencies in allocating funds as required by various federal laws. In addition, the bureau provides current data on the occupational employment of most industries for economic analysis, vocational guidance, and education planning. Data collection and preparation are carried out under federal-state cooperative programs by state agencies using methods and procedures prescribed by the bureau.

Program Information

Business Establishment List, Michael Searson 202/606-6469
Employment and Earnings, Gloria P. Green 606-6373
Employment and Wages (ES 202), Staff 606-6567
Data Diskettes and Tapes, Staff 606-6567

Employment Situation

News Release, Staff . . . . 606-6378 or 606-6373
Recorded Messages, 24-Hour Hotline 606-7828

Establishment Survey Employment, Hours, Earnings

National Data, Staff 606-6555
    Benchmarks, Patricia Getz 606-6521
    Data Diskettes, David Hiles 606-6551
    Real Earnings-News Release, David Hiles 606-6551
    State and Area Data, Kenneth Shipp 606-6559
    Data Diskettes, Guy Podgornik 606-6559

Foreign Direct Investment Data, Staff 606-6568
    Occupational Employment Statistics Survey, Staff 606-6569

National Labor Force Data: 606-6378
    Concepts and Definitions, Staff 606-6373
    Employment and Unemployment Trends, Staff 606-6378
    Machine-Readable Data and Diskettes, Gloria P. Green 606-6373
    Microdata Tapes, Rowena Johnson 606-6345

Occupational Data

Current Population Survey, Staff 606-6378
Occupational Mobility, Lawrence Leith 606-6378

State and Area Labor Force Data

Demographic Characteristics, Edna Biederman 606-6392
Data Diskettes and Tapes, Jessie Marcus 606-6392

Weekly and Annual Earnings

Current Population Survey, Staff 606-6378

Special Topics

Absences from Work, Staff 606-6378
Contingent Workers, Staff 606-6378
Discouraged Workers, Harvey Hamel 606-6378
Displaced Workers, Jennifer Gardner 606-6378
Educational Attainment, Staff 606-6378
Flextime and Shift Work, Staff 606-6378
Home-Based Work, William Deming 606-6378
Job Tenure, Joseph Meisenheimer 606-6378
Longitudinal Data/Gross Flows, Francis Horvath 606-6345
Marital and Family Characteristics, Howard Hayghe 606-6378
Mass Layoff Statistics, Lewis Siegel 606-6404
Minimum Wage Data, Steven Haugen 606-6378

Minority Workers, Peter Cattan 606-6378
Multiple Jobholders, John Stinson 606-6373
Older Workers, Diane Herz 606-6378
Part-Time Workers, Staff 606-6378
Seasonal Adjustment Methodology, Robert McIntire 606-6345
Standard Industrial Classification System, Mary Anne Phillips 606-6473
Standard Occupational Classification System, Michael McElroy 606-6516
Veterans, Sharon Cohany 606-6378
Women in the Labor Force, Howard Hayghe 606-6378
Work Experience, Staff 606-6378
Working Poor, Monica Castillo 606-6378
Youth, Students, and Dropouts, Randy Ilg 606-6378
Topics Not Specifically Mentioned, Staff 606-6378

Prices and Living Conditions

Consumer Price Indexes

The Consumer Price Index (CPI) is a measure of the average change in prices paid by urban consumers for a fixed market basket of goods and services. The CPI is based on prices of food, clothing, shelter, fuel, drugs, transportation fares, doctors' and dentists' fees, and other goods and services that people buy for day-to-day living. The CPI-U is the designation for the CPI for All Urban Consumers and covers about 80 percent of the total civilian noninstitutional population, including wage earners and clerical workers; professional, managerial, and technical workers; short-term workers; the self-employed; the unemployed; retirees; and others not in the labor force. The CPI-W is the designation for the CPI for Urban Wage Earners and Clerical Workers and covers about 32 percent of the total civilian noninstitutional population. U.S. data are published monthly. Aggregate data are available for some areas on a monthly, bimonthly, semiannual, or annual basis.

Current and Historical Data, Information staff 202/606-5886
Recorded CPI Detail, 24-Hour Hotline 606-7828
Recorded CPI Summary, 24-Hour Quickline 606-6994
General Information and Analysis, Staff 606-7000
Data Diskettes, Karin Smedley 606-6968
Methodology, Patrick Jackman 606-6952

Special Topics

Average Retail Food Prices, William Cook 606-6988
Average Retail Prices and Indexes:
    Motor Fuels, Joseph Chelena 606-6982
    Fuels and Utilities, Robert Adkins 606-6985
    Department Store Inventory Indexes (LIFO), Sharon Gibson 606-6968

Consumer Expenditure Survey

The Consumer Expenditure Survey (CE) provides quarterly data on the buying habits of American consumers by socioeconomic characteristics. The data are used to update the Consumer Price Index market basket every ten years and for research by government, business, labor, and academic analysts. The survey has two components, an interview survey and a diary survey. Diary data offer detailed expenditure information on small, frequently purchased items. Interview data provide information on relatively large or recurring expenditures. Integrated data are available in bulletins, quarterly and annual reports, and on disk. Microdata are available on public-use tape files.

General Information and Analysis, Staff 202/606-6900

Compensation and Working Conditions

The BLS conducts an extensive program of occupational compensation surveys and provides information on average weekly and hourly earnings for selected occupations for specific metropolitan and nonmetropolitan areas. The Employee Benefits Survey provides comprehensive data on the incidence and characteristics of employee benefit plans. The Employment Cost Index measures changes in total compensation, in wages and salaries only, and in benefit costs only. All private nonagricultural industries except households are covered, as well as state and local governments; minimum employment size is 50 workers. Bulletins are published throughout the year to present the results of Occupational Pay Surveys in metropolitan areas.

Employee Benefits Survey, Staff 202/606-6222
    Child Care/Parental Leave/Family Benefits
    Employee Benefits
    Paid Leave and Disability Benefits
    Retirement Benefits
    Health Benefits

Employment Cost Index

Recorded ECI Detail, 24-Hour Hotline 202/606-7828
Current and Historical Data, Wayne Shelly 606-6199

Occupational Compensation Surveys (Locality Pay)

Current and Historical Data, Information staff 202/606-5886
General Information and Analysis, Staff 606-6220

Area Data

National Data

Data Diskettes and Methodology, Staff 202/606-6245

Special Topics

Collective Bargaining:
    General Information 202/606-6282

Safety, Health, and Working Conditions

The Bureau conducts an annual survey of occupational illness and injuries using employer records of job-related injuries and illnesses to provide information about the injured/ill worker and circumstances of the injury or illness. The Census of Fatal Occupational Injuries provides information about fatally injured workers and events leading to the fatality.

Current and Historical Data, Information staff 202/606-5886
Annual Survey of Occupation Injuries, Ethel Jackson 606-6179
Data Disk, Staff 606-6179
Data Tapes, Staff 606-6179
Census of Fatal Occupational Injuries, Guy Toscano 606-6165
Data Disk, Blaine Derstine 606-6175

Industry Injuries and Illnesses

Estimates and Incidence

Rates, Staff 202/606-6180
Characteristics, Elyce Biddle 606-6170

Employment Projections

The bureau develops and publishes long-term economic projections. These are based upon certain specific assumptions that lead to projections of aggregate labor force, potential gross domestic product, industrial output, and employment by industry and occupational detail. These projections provide a comprehensive and integrated framework for analyzing the implications of likely economic growth trends for the national economy and employment in specific industries and occupations. Occupational projections and descriptive information are developed for use in career guidance and educational planning. Bureau projections are based upon extensive analysis of current and past economic and employment relationships and on special occupational studies. This work provides the basis for a variety of reports on employment needs generated by major categories of expenditures such as defense, health care, and infrastructure.

Current and Historical Data, Information staff 202/606-5886

Data Tapes and Disk

Industry-Occuption Matrix, Delores Turner 606-5730
Input-Output and Employment Requirements, Art Andreassen 606-5689
Industry Output and Employment Time Series, James Franklin 606-5709

Special Topics

Industry-Occupation Matrix, Delores Turner 606-5730
Occupational Outlook Handbook, Michael Pilot 606-5703
Occupational Outlook Quarterly, Neale Baxter 606-5691

Projections

Economic Growth and Industry, Charles Bowman 606-5702
Economic, Norman Saunders 606-5723
Final Demand, Betty Su 606-5729
Industry Employment, James Franklin 606-5709
Intermediate Demand, Art Andreassen 606-5689
Labor Force, Howard Fullerton 606-5711
Occupational, Neal Rosenthal 606-5701

Bureau of the Census

Customer Service
Data User Services Division
Washington, DC 20233

Phone: 301/457-4100
E-mail: http://www.census.gov

Frequently called numbers (Use area code 301 unless otherwise noted)

Census Customer Services (Data product and ordering
information for computer tapes, CD-ROMs, microfiche, and some publications) . . . 457-4100
FAX (general information) 457-4714
(orders only) 457-3842
TDD 457-4611
Agriculture Information 800/523-3215
Business Information 800/541-8345
Census-BEA Bulletin Board 457-2310
Census Job Information (Recording) 457-4449
Census Personnel Locator 457-4608
Congressional Affairs 457-2171
Data Centers (DUSD) 457-1305
FastFax (DUSD) 900/555-2FAX
Foreign Trade Information 457-3041/2311
Internet (General Information) - (DUSD) 457-1242
Library 457-2511
Population Information . . . . 457-2422/2435 (TTY)
Public Information Office (Press) 457-2794
Technical Support (CD-ROM Products) 457-1324

Census regional offices (information services, data product information)

Regional Office Liaison - FLD 457-2032
Atlanta . . . . 404-730-3833/3964 (TDD)
Boston . . . . 617-424-0510/0565 (TDD)
Charlotte . . . . 704-344-6144/6548 (TDD)
Chicago . . . . 708-562-1740/1791 (TDD)
Dallas . . . . 214-767-7105/7181 (TDD)
Denver . . . . 303-969-7750/6769 (TDD)
Detroit . . . . 313-259-1875/5169 (TDD)
Kansas City . . . . 913-551-6711/5839 (TDD)
Los Angeles 818-904-6339/6249 . . . . (TDD)
New York 212-264-4730/3863 . . . . (TDD)
Philadelphia 215-597-8313/8864 . . . . (TDD)
Seattle 206-728-5314/5321 . . . . (TDD)

Key to Office Abbreviations

AGFS - Agriculture & Financial Statistics Division
CAO - Congressional Affairs Office
DMD - Decennial Management Division
DPD - Data Preparation Division
DSD - Demographic Surveys Division
DSMD - Demographic Statistical Methods Division
DSSD - Decennial Statistical Studies Division
DUSD - Data User Services Division
EPCD - Economic Planning & Coordination Division

ESMPD - Economic Statistical Methods & Programming Division
FLD - Field Division
FTD - Foreign Trade Division
GEO - Geography Division
GOVS - Governments Division
HHES - Housing & Housing Economic Statistics Division
MCD - Manufacturing and Construction Division
PIO - Public Information Office
POP - Population Division
PPDO - Program & Policy Development Office
SRD - Statistical Research Division
SVSD - Services Division
TCO - Telecommunications Office
TMO - CASIC Technologies Management Office
2KS - Year 2000 Research and Development Staff

Other key contacts

1990 Census Tabulations and Publications -
    U.S.: Gloria Porter (DMD) 457-4019
    Puerto Rico and Outlying Areas: Lourdes Flaim (DMD) 457-4023
1992 Economic Census - Paul Zeisset/Robert Marske (EPCD) 457-4151
2000 Census Plans - Catherine Keeley (DIR) 457-4036
Bulletin Board (Technical assistance) - DUSD 457-1242
CENDATA (Online service) - DUSD 457-1214
Census & You (newsletter) - Neil Tillman (DUSD) 457-1221
Census Catalog - John McCall (DUSD) 457-1221
Census History - Les Solomon (DUSD) 457-1167
Census Records (Age search) - DPD 812-285-5314
Conferences/Exhibits - Joanne Dickinson (DUSD) 457-1191
Confidentiality and Privacy - Jerry Gates (PPDO) 457-2516
County and City, State and Metropolitan Area Data Books - Wanda Cevis (DUSD) . . 457-1166
Economic Studies - Arnold Reznek (CES) 457-1856
Education Support - Dorothy Jackson (DUSD) 457-1210
FastFax (General Information) - DUSD 457-1242
Freedom of Information Act - Gary Austin (PPDO) 457-2532
Historical Statistics - DUSD 457-1166
Legislation - Thomas Jones (PPDO) 457-2512
Litigation - Nick Birnbaum (PPDO) 457-2490
Microdata Files - Carmen Campbell (DUSD) 457-1139
Monthly Product Announcement (Newsletter) - Mary Kilbride (DUSD) 457-1221
Statistical Abstract - Glenn King (DUSD) 457-1171
Statistical Briefs - Robert Bernstein (DUSD) 457-1221
Statistical Research - C. Easley Hoy (SRD) 457-4978
User Training - DUSD 457-1210

Internet

Census - BEA Bulletin Board (Telnet) . . . . cenbbs.census.gov
Gopher . . . . gopher gopher.census.gov
FTP . . . . ftp.census.gov
World Wide Web . . . . http://www.census.gov

BUSINESS ECONOMICS

Agriculture

Crops & Livestock Statistics - Linda Hutton (AGFS) 763-8569
Farm Economics - James Liefer (AGFS) 763-8514
General Information - Sharon Powers (AGFS) 800-523-3215
Irrigation Statistics - John Blackledge (AGFS) 763-8560
Laboratory - Dave Peterson (AGFS) 763-8260
Outreach - Quentin Coleman (AGFS) 763-8561
Puerto Rico, Virgin Islands, Guam, Northern Marianas,
& American Samoa - Kent Hoover (AGFS) 763-8564

Communications and Utilities

Census - Dennis Shoemaker (SVSD) 457-2786
Current Programs - Tom Zabelsky (SVSD) 457-2766

Construction

Building Permits - Linda Hoyle (MCD) 457-1321
Census - Pat Horning (MCD) 457-4680
Construction in Metro Areas - Joseph Gilvary (MCD) 457-4666
Housing Starts & Completions - David Fondelier (MCD) 457-4703
Residential Characteristics, Price Index, Sales - Steve Berman (MCD) 457-4666
Residential Improvements and Repairs - Joe Huesman (MCD) 457-1605
Value of New Construction - George Roff (MCD) 457-1605

Finance, Insurance, and Real Estate

Census - SVSD 457-2777

Foreign Trade

Data Services - Reba Higbee (FTD) 457-3041/2227
Shipper's Declaration - Hal Blyweiss (FTD) 457-1086

Manufacturing

Concentration - Andy Hait (MCD) 457-4769
Exports From Manufacturing Establishments - Philippe Morris (MCD) 457-4761
Financial Statistics (Quarterly Financial Report) - Ronald Lee (AGFS) 763-5435
Fuels and Electric Energy Consumer, and Production Index - Pat Horning (MCD) ... 457-4680

Industries

Electrical and Transportation Equipment, Instruments, and Miscellaneous -
Bruce Goldhirsch (MCD) 457-4817
Food, Textiles, and Apparel - Judy Dodds (MCD) 457-4651
Metals and Industrial Machinery - Kenneth Hansen (MCD) 457-4755
Wood, Furniture, Paper, Printing, Chemicals, Petroleum Products,
Rubber, and Plastics - Michael Zampogna (MCD) 457-4810
Monthly Shipments, Inventories, and Orders - Kathy Menth (MCD) 457-4832
Technology, Innovation, Research and Development, Capacity,
and Pollution Abatement - Elinor Champion (MCD) 457-4701

Retail Trade

Advance Monthly - Ronald Piencykoski (SVSD) 457-2713
Census - .... SVSD 457-2687
Monthly Report - Irving True (SVSD) 457-2706
Monthly Sales (24-hour recording) 457-1089
Quarterly Financial Report - Ronald Lee (AGFS) 763-5435

Services

Census - Jack Moody (SVSD) 457-2689
Current Reports - Thomas Zabelsky (SVSD) 457-2766

Transportation:

Census - Dennis Shoemaker (SVSD) 457-2786
Commodity Flow Survey - John Fowler (SVSD) 457-2108
Truck Inventory and Use - Bill Bostic (SVSD) 457-2797
Warehousing and Trucking - Tom Zabelsky (SVSD) 457-2766

Wholesale Trade

Census - John Trimble (SVSD) 457-2694
Current Sales and Inventories - Nancy Piesto (SVSD) 457-2779
Quarterly Financial Report - Ronald Lee (AGFS) 763-5435

Special Topics

Assets/Expenditures - Sheldon Ziman (AGFS) 800/541-8345
Business Investment - Charles Funk (AGFS) 763-2542
Census Products - Robert Marske/Paul Zeisset (EPCD) 457-4151
Characteristics of Business Owners - Valerie Strang (AGFS) 763-5726
County Business Patterns - Paul Hanczaryk (EPCD) 457-2580
Enterprise Statistics - Eddie Salyers (AGFS) 763-7234
Industry and Commodity Classification - James Kristoff (EPCD) 457-2813
Mineral Industries - Patricia Horning (MCD) 457-4680
Minority- and Women-Owned Businesses - Valerie Strang (AGFS) 763-5726
Puerto Rico and Outlying Areas - Kent Hoover (AGFS) 763-8564
Quarterly Financial Report - Ronald Lee (AGFS) 763-5435

Demographics and Population

Aging Population, U.S. (POP) 457-2378
Ancestry (POP) 457-2403
Apportionment (POP) 457-2381
Child Care - Martin O'Connell/Lynne Casper (POP) 457-2416
Children - Donald Hernandez (POP) 457-2465
Citizenship (POP) 457-2403
Commuting, Means of Transportation, and Place of Work -
   Phil Salopek/Celia Boertlein (POP) 457-2454
Crime - Gail Hoff (DSD) 457-3925

Current Population Survey

General Information (DUSD) 457-4100
Questionnaire Content - Ron Tucker (DSD) 457-3806
Sampling Methods - Preston Waite (DSMD) 457-4287
   Demographic Surveys (General Information DSD) 457-3811

Disability - Jack McNeil/Bob Bennefield (HHES) 763-8300/8578
Education (POP) 457-2464
Education Surveys - Richard Schwartz (DSD) 457-3800
Equal Employment Opportunity Data - Tom Schopp (HHES) 763-8199
Fertility and Births - Martin O'Connell/Amara Bachu (POP) 457-2416
Foreign Born (POP) 457-2403
Group Quarters Population - Denise Smith (POP) 457-2378
Health Surveys - Robert Mangold (DSD) 457-3879
Hispanic and Ethnic Statistics (POP) 457-2403
Homeless - Annetta Clark (POP) 457-2378
Household Estimates (POP) 457-2465
Household and Families - Steve Rawlings (POP) 457-2465
Immigration (Legal/Undocumented) and Emigration - Edward Fernandez (POP) . 457-2103
Journey to Work - Phil Salopek/Gloria Swieczkowski (POP) 457-2454
Language (POP) 457-2464
Longitudinal Surveys - Sarah Higgins (DSD) 457-3801
Marital Status and Living Arrangements - Arlene Saluter (POP) 457-2465

Metropolitan Areas (MAs)

Population (POP) 457-2422
Standards - James Fitzsimmons (POP) 457-2419
Migration - Kristin Hansen (POP) 457-2454
National Estimates and Projections (POP) 457-2422
Outlying Areas - Michael Levin (POP) 457-2327
Place of Birth - Kristin Hansen (POP) 457-2454
Population Information (POP) .... 457-2422/2435 (TTY)
Prisoner Surveys - Gail Hoff (DSD) 457-3925
Puerto Rico - Lourdes Flaim (DMD) 457-4023
Race Statistics (POP) 457-2453/2402
Reapportionment and Redistricting - Marshall Turner, Jr. (DIR) 457-4039
Sampling Methods, Decennial Census - Henry Woltman (DSSD) 457-4199
School District Data - Jane Ingold (POP) 457-2408
Special Demographic Surveys - Sarah Higgins (DSD) 457-3801
Special Population Censuses - Elaine Csellar (FLD) 457-1429
Special Tabulations - Rose Cowan (POP) 457-2408
State and County Estimates (POP) 457-2422
State Projections (POP) 457-2422
Undercount, Demographic Analysis - Gregg Robinson (POP) 457-2103
Veterans' Status - Thomas Palumbo (HHES) 763-8574
Women - Denise Smith (POP) 457-2378

Geographic Concepts

1980 Census Map Orders - Ann Devore (DPD) 812-288-3192
1990 Census Maps (DUSD) 457-4100
Annexations and Boundary Changes - Joseph Marinucci (GEO) 457-1099
Area Measurement (GEO) 457-1099
Census County Divisions - Cathy McCully (GEO) 457-1099
Census Designated Places - Nancy Torrieri (GEO) 457-1099
Census Geographic Concepts (GEO) 457-1099
Census Tracts - Cathy Miller (GEO) 457-1099
Centers of Population - Lourdes Ramirez (GEO) 457-1073

Congressional Districts

Address Allocations (GEO) 457-1050
Boundaries - Cathy McCully (GEO) 457-1099
   Federal Geographic Data Committee - Fred Broome (GEO) 457-1056
   Fee-Paid Block Splits - Joel Miller (GEO) 457-1099
   FIPS Codes - Virgeline Davis (GEO) 457-1099
   Internal Points - Tony Costanzo (GEO) 457-1073
   Master Address File - Dan Sweeney (GEO) 457-1106
   Metropolitan Areas - James Fitzsimmons (POP) 457-2419
   Outlying Areas - Virgeline Davis (GEO) 457-1099
   Population Circles (Radii) - Rick Hartgen (GEO) 457-1128
   Postal Geography - Rose Quarato (GEO) 457-1128
   School Districts - Dave Aultman (GEO) 457-1099
   State Boundary Certification - Louise Stewart (GEO) 457-1099

TIGER System

Future Plans and Products (GEO) 457-1100
Products - Larry Carbaugh (DUSD) 457-1242
Thematic Mapping - Tim Trainor (GEO) 457-1101
   Urban/Rural Residence (POP) 457-2381
   Urbanized Areas and Urban/Rural Concepts - Nancy Torrieri (GEO) 457-1099
   Voting Districts - Cathy McCully (GEO) 457-1099

ZIP Codes

Demographic Data (DUSD) 457-4100
Economic Data - Anne Russell (SVSD) 457-2687
Geographic Relationships - Rose Quarato (GEO) 457-1128

Governments

Criminal Justice - Alan Stevens (GOVS) 457-1550
Education:
   Elementary-Secondary - Larry MacDonald (GOVS) 457-1563
   Post-Secondary - John Monaco (GOVS) 457-1106
   Federal Expenditure Data - Robert McArthur (GOVS) 457-1565
Finance and Employment:
   General - Henry Wulf (GOVS) 457-1486
   Eastern States - George Beaven (GOVS) 457-1529
   Western States - Russell Price (GOVS) 457-1488
   Governmental Organization - David Kellerman (GOVS) 457-1586
   Taxation - Henry Wulf (GOVS) 457-1486

Housing

American Housing Survey
   Edward Montfort (HHES) 763-8551
   John Cannon (DSD) 457-3877
Census - Robert Bonnette (HHES) 763-8553
Components of Inventory Change Survey - Barbara Williams (HHES) 763-8551
Housing Affordability - Peter Fronczek/Howard Savage (HHES) 763-8165
Market Absorption/Residential Finance - Anne Smoler/Ellen Wilson (HHES) 763-8165
New York City Housing and Vacancy Survey - Peter Fronczek (HHES) 763-8165
Vacancy Data - Alan Friedman/Robert Callis (HHES) 763-8165

Income, Poverty, and Wealth

Consumer Expenditures - Ron Dopkowski (DSD) 457-3914
Household Wealth - T.J. Eller/Wallace Fraser (HHES) 763-8578
Income Statistics (HHES) 763-8578
Poverty Statistics (HHES) 763-8576
Survey of Income and Program Participation (SIPP) - Judy Eargle (HHES) 763-8375
General Information - Enrique Lamas (DSD) 457-3819
Microdata Files - Carmen Campbell (DUSD) 457-1139
Statistical Methods - Vicki Huggins (DSMD) 457-4192

International Statistics

Africa, Asia, Latin America, North America, and Oceania - Patricia Rowe (POP) 457-1358
Aging Population - Kevin Kinsella (POP) 457-1371
China, People's Republic - Loraine West/Christina Harbaugh (POP) 457-1360
Europe, Former Soviet Union - Marc Rubin (POP) 457-1362
Health - Karen Stanecki (POP) 457-1406
International Data Base - Peter Johnson (POP) 457-1403
International Visitors - Gene Vandrovec (PIO) 457-2816
Women in Development - Patricia Rowe (POP) 457-1358

Labor Force

Commuting, Means of Transportation, & Place of Work -
    Phil Salopek/Celia Boertlein (POP) 457-2454
Employment and Unemployment - Thomas Palumbo (HHES) 763-8574
Journey to Work - Phil Salopek/Gloria Swieczkowski (POP) 457-2454
Occupation and Industry Statistics (HHES) 763-8574

National, State, and Local Data Centers

Business/Industry Data Centers (DUSD) 457-1305
Clearinghouse for Census Data Services - Larry Carbaugh (DUSD) 457-1242
National Census Information Centers - Barbara Harris (DUSD) 457-1305
State Data Center Program - Tim Jones (DUSD) 457-1305

National Census Information Centers

National Census Information Centers, in partnership with the Census Bureau, coordinate information networks that disseminate census data on the black, Hispanic, Asian and Pacific Islander, and American Indian/Alaska Native populations.

Asian American Health Forum, Inc., San Francisco - Clarissa Tom 415-541-0866
IndianNet Information Center, Arkadelphia, AR - George Baldwin 501-230-5294
National Council of La Raza, Washington, DC - Sonia Perez 202-289-1380
National Urban League, Washington, DC - Billy Tidwell 202-898-1604
Southwest Voter Research Institute, San Antonio, TX - Robert Brischetto 210-222-8014

U.S. Bureau of the Census Management

Director - Martha Farnsworth Riche 457-2135
Deputy Director - Harry A. Scarr 457-2138
Special Assistant to Deputy Director - Peter A. Bounpane 457-2879
Principal Associate Director for Programs - Paula J. Schneider 457-2092
Chief Financial Officer - Harry A. Scarr (Acting) 457-2138

Associate Directors

Administration - Charles V. St. Lawrence 457-2182
Decennial Census - Robert W. Marx 457-2131
Demographic Programs - William P. Butz 457-2126
Econ. Programs - Thomas L. Mesenbourg (Acting) 457-2112
Field Operations - Bryant Benton 457-2072
Information Technology - Arnold A. Jackson 457-2168
Planning and Organization Development - Stanley D. Matchett 457-2118
Statistical Design, Methodology, and Standards - Robert D. Tortora 457-2160

Assistant Directors

Communications - Jane A. Callen 457-2158
Decennial Census - Susan M. Miskura 457-2933
Economic Programs - Thomas L. Mesenbourg 457-2932

Bureau of Transportation Statistics, U.S. Department of Transportation

Kathleen Bradley, Customer Service Manager   Phone: 202/366-8925
400 Seventh Street, SW, Room 3430   Fax: 202/366-3640
Washington, DC 20590   E-mail: info@bts.gov or http://www.bts.gov

The Bureau of Transportation Statistics (BTS) provides data for each transportation mode. Information and services offered by BTS include descriptive analyses of
the nation's transportation system; commodity flow and passenger travel surveys;
network facilities; geographic mapping displays; data source and telephone directories; safety, financial, and performance statistics; journey-to-work data; toll-free
statistical information and bulletin board access; and Internet connection. Most
information is national in scope, although some data are provided for counties, zip
codes, and states. Historic and current data are available on CD-ROM, diskette,
print, the Internet, and bulletin board system.

What You Can Get from the Bureau of Transportation Statistics

The Directory of Transportation Data Sources 1995

This is an inventory of transportation statistical databases and publications within
the federal government, as well as in private industry, and in Canada and Mexico.
The directory provides users of transportation statistics with a comprehensive catalog of data sources. The directory is also available on diskette in a dBase viewer format. To obtain a copy, contact the BTS at 202/366-DATA or fax 202/366-3640

TIGER/Line Files, 1994 on CD-ROM

TIGER/Line Files, 1994 are extracts of selected geographic and cartographic information from the Census Bureau's TIGER System. The files define Traffic Analysis
Zones as recognized in the Census Transportation Planning Package (CTPP). The
files reflect an increase in the editing of address ranges and new ZIP+4 Codes
derived from the latest matching with the Address Control File and the USPS files.

The files are available by region on a set of six CD-ROMs. These files are in limited supply and may no longer be available. Call 202/366-DATA, fax 202/366-3640, or e-mail info@bts.gov for more information.

CEMR, University of South Florida

Maria Angelou
4202 E. Fowler Avenue
Tampa, FL 33620

Phone: 813/974-4266

Center for Remote Sensing Michigan State University

Bill Enslin
115 Manly Miles, 1405 S. Harrison
East Lansing, MI 48823-5243

Phone: 517/353-7195

E-mail: bill.enslin.msu.edu

City University of New York CUNY Data Center

Marta Fisch
33 West 42nd Street, Room 1446
New York, NY 10036-8003

Phone: 212/642-2085
Fax: 212/642-2642

Concordia University

Peter M. Becker
7400 Augusta Street
River Forest, IL 60305-1499

Phone: 708/209-3021
Fax: 708/209-3176
E-mail: beckerpm@crf.cuis.edu

Energy Information Administration

Sandra Wilkins, National Energy Information Center
Forrestal Building, 1000 Independence Avenue, SW
Washington, DC 20585   E-mail: infoctr@eia.doe.gov or http://www.eia.doe.gov

Phone: 202/586-1173

As we enter a new era of environmental awareness, the Energy Information Administration (EIA) tells us how Americans use energy. The EIA is an independent statistical agency of the U.S. Department of Energy, serving as the government's collector, processor, interpreter, analyst, and disseminator of energy information. In 1994, EIA conducted more than 77 surveys to collect information on supply, consumption, and cost of all major forms of energy. It also maintained approximately 37 forecasting models to provide analyses of possible future trends in energy use.

What You Can Get From the EIA

Monthly Energy Review

The most widely read of its 86 periodicals and reports, the Monthly Energy Review presents current EIA data on production, consumption, stocks, imports, exports, and prices of the principal energy commodities in the U.S. These data are also available on disk, as are state data, grouped by census regions.

Housing Characteristics 1993

Housing Characteristics 1993 is based on data from the 1993 Residential Energy Consumption Survey (RECS) and provides information on energy use in residential housing units in the United States. This information includes the physical characteristics of the residential housing units, the appliances used, the number and characteristics of occupants, the fuels being used, and other energy-related characteristics.

Other Publications

Certain publications, such as EIA directories, are available free of charge, but most must be purchased by subscription or as individual copies. All publications are free to government agencies and repositories as well as academic institutions.

Equal Employment Opportunity Commission

James S. Neal, EEOC Survey Division
Office of Program Research   Phone: 202/663-4920
1801 L Street, NW, Room 9608
Washington, DC 20507

Women and minorities will account for five in six net additions to the labor force in the 1990s. The EEOC tracks the status of these workers. It surveys employment in private industry categorized by sex, race, ethnic group, and broad job categories. Results are published for metropolitan areas and larger geographical areas.

What You Can Get From the EEOC

Job Patterns for Minorities and Women

Current reports in this series are: Job Patterns for Minorities and Women in Private Industry, 1993; and Minorities and Women in State and Local Government, 1993. Single copies are available free of charge from the EEOC Survey Division.

Federal Bureau of Investigation
Criminal Justice Information Services Division

Nancy Carnes, Kristine Waskiewicz
Programs Support Section   Phone: 202/324-5015
Gallery Row Building
10th & Pennsylvania Avenue, NW, Suite 3R
Washington, DC 20535

The U.S. Department of Justice administers two statistical programs to measure the magnitude, nature, and impact of crime in the nation: The Uniform Crime Reporting (UCR) Program, conducted by the Federal Bureau of Investigation, and the National Crime Victimization Survey, conducted by the Bureau of Justice Statistics (see separate entry).

The FBI's UCR program collects information on the following crimes reported to law enforcement agencies: homicide, forcible rape, robbery, aggravated assault, burglary, larceny-theft, motor vehicle theft, and arson. Arrests are reported for 21 additional crime categories.

The UCR data are compiled from monthly law enforcement reports or individual crime incident records transmitted directly to the FBI or to centralized state agencies that report to the FBI. In 1994, law enforcement agencies active in the UCR Program represented approximately 249 million U.S. residents, or 96 percent of the total population.

The UCR Program provides crime counts for the nation as a whole, as well as for regions, states, counties, cities, and towns. This permits studies among neighboring jurisdictions and among those with similar populations and other common characteristics.

What You Can Get From the Federal Bureau of Investigation

UCR findings for each calendar year are published in a preliminary spring release, followed by a detailed annual report, Crime in the United States, issued in the next calendar year. In addition to crime counts and trends, this report includes data on crimes cleared, persons arrested (age, sex, and race), law enforcement personnel (including the number of sworn officers killed or assaulted), and the characteristics of homicides (including age, sex, and race of victims and offenders, victim-offender relationships, weapons used, and circumstances surrounding the homicides). Other special reports are also available from the UCR Program.

The UCR is currently being converted to a more comprehensive and detailed National Incident-Based Reporting System (NIBRS). NIBRS will provide detailed information about each criminal incident in 22 broad categories of offenses.

Idaho State University Center for Business Research and Services

Paul Zelus   Phone: 208/236-2504
Campus Box 8450
Pocatello, ID 83209

Immigration and Naturalization Service

Statistics Division   Phone: 202/376-3066
425 I Street, NW, Tariff Building, Room 235
Washington, DC 20536

By the year 2028, 100 percent of U.S. population growth may come from immigration. The Immigration and Naturalization Service (INS) tracks the multitudes who enter the U.S. each year. Part of the Department of Justice, the INS gathers a wide array of data about immigrants, nonimmigrants, refugees, people becoming naturalized citizens, and children claiming citizenship through the naturalization of their parents.

Telephone Contacts:

Deportations, Required Departures, and Exclusions, John Bjerke 202/376-3015
Emigration, Robert Warren 376-3008
Immigrants, Michael Hoefer 376-3066
Nonimmigrants, Mark Herrenbruck 376-3066
Refugees, Naturalization, and Derivative Citizenship, Linda Gordon 376-3015

What You Can Get From the INS

The Statistical Yearbook

This annual yearbook provides data about population change due to international migration. Characteristics include age, country of birth, occupation, country of last permanent residence, marital status, sex, nationality, and zip code of intended residence. The data also include when, where, and under what status the individual entered the country. Order from the National Technical Information Service, 5285 Port Royal Road, Springfield, VA 22161; 703/487-4650.

Tapes Available

The division provides public-use tapes that go back ten years, making it easy to analyze trends. The tapes are available from the National Technical Information Service (see separate listing).

Indiana University of Pennsylvania Department of Geography

Robert Sechrist
212 Whitmyre Hall
Indiana, PA 15705

Phone: 412/357-2251

International Programs Center, Population Division

James Gibbs, Project Development Coordinator
U.S. Bureau of the Census
Washington, DC 20233

Phone: 301/457-1390
Fax: 301/457-3033
E-mail: ipc@census.gov

International Programs Center (IPC) is the international arm of the U.S. Census Bureau, conducting specialized demographic and economic studies and providing training and technical assistance in statistics around the world. IPC has provided technical assistance to more than 100 countries on planning, conducting, and analyzing statistical activities and has trained more than 11,000 demographers, statisticians, and programmers.

What You Can Get From the International Programs Center

IPC maintains an international demographic database and an HIV/AIDS surveillance database, both available through the Internet. It issues a biennial report, World Population Profile (latest issue is 1994 and covers all countries in the world), Population Trends reports on selected countries, and staff papers. In addition, IPC has developed several software packages to assist in the planning, processing, and analysis of census and survey data. The Integrated Microcomputer Processing System (IMPS) performs major tasks in survey and census processing. IPC's Population Analysis Spreadsheets provide tools for analyzing and projecting age structure, fertility and mortality, internal migration and urbanization, and rural-urban population projections. IPC products are available on request. In addition, IPC provides training, technical assistance, and research services on a reimbursable basis.

Mississippi State University Department of Sociology and Anthropology

Mohamed Ed-Attar
P.O. Drawer C
Mississippi State, MS 39762

Phone: 601/325-7886

National Center for Health Statistics, U.S. Department of Health and Human Services

Rob Weinzimer, Data Dissemination   Phone: 301/436-8500
6525 Belcrest Road, Room 1064
Hyattsville, MD 20782   E-mail: http://www.cdc.gov NCHSWWW.nchshome.htm

The National Center for Health Statistics (NCHS) provides data on Americans' health. It is also the place to go for national vital statistics. The NCHS was founded in 1960 to collect and disseminate data on health in the United States. Some of the center's statistics come from local registrations of births, deaths, marriages, and divorces, but most come out of an extensive program of national surveys, usually conducted for the center by the Census Bureau or private survey firms.

Two main types of data are available from the NCHS. The first covers vital statistics. Most of these data are compiled from administrative records, such as certificates. Others are collected through surveys. Most NCHS data are published in its series of Vital and Health Statistics reports.

What You Can Get From the National Center for Health Statistics

Vital Statistics

The Monthly Vital Statistics Report provides monthly and cumulative data, with brief analyses of births, deaths, marriages, divorces, and infant deaths for states and the U.S. Final statistics are released about a year later in Advanced Reports, available from the center at no charge.

Annual Volumes, Vital Statistics of the United States contain final figures tabulated by natality, mortality, marriage, and divorce for states, counties, metropolitan areas, and cities with populations of 10,000 or more. The data, which are published four years after they are collected, can be ordered from the Government Printing Office; telephone 202/512-1800.

Additional Vital Statistics Publications

Since the information contained on a birth, death, or marriage certificate is necessarily limited, the center supplements it by taking four broad surveys, the results of which are published in Vital and Health Statistics:

1986 National Mortality Followback Survey - Covers risk factors associated with premature death, health services received and their cost during the last year of life, and lifestyles: diet, exercise, etc. Data from this survey became available in late 1988. For more information, call the center at 301/436-7464.

National Mortality Survey (Series 20) - Mortality surveys, conducted annually from 1961 through 1968 and again in 1986, collected data on such topics as the smoking habits of people who died between the ages of 35 and 84. Call the center at 301/436-8884 for more information.

National Natality Survey (Series 21) - The birth survey periodically studies pregnancy history, birth expectations, family composition, employment status, health insurance coverage, and related topics. Data from 1993 are currently available.

National Survey on Family Growth (Series 23) - This survey gathers statistics about the dynamics of population change, family planning, and maternal and child health. Data on birth expectations and a range of demographic and economic variables are also reported. For more information, call 301/436-8731.

Health

The NCHS also conducts surveys regarding Americans' health and publishes the results in several series of Vital and Health Statistics publications:

Health Interview Survey (Series 10) - This annual survey is the principal source of information on the health of Americans. It obtains statistics on health and demographic factors related to illness, injuries, and disability, and the costs and uses of medical services.

Health and Nutrition Examination Survey (Series 11) - The data in this survey are collected by means of physical examinations, as well as through interviews. The center sends out a mobile examination unit made up of specially constructed truck-drawn rooms. This ensures that all examinations are uniform in temperature and humidity control for exercise tests, and in noise levels for hearing tests.

Hispanic Health and Nutritional Examination Survey (Series 11) - This one-time survey of a sample of 16,000 Hispanics was conducted in 1982-84, and information was released in separate reports. Because the information published is so diverse, it is organized by topic such as "cholesterol levels" and "periodontal disease."

Hospital Discharge Survey (Series 13) - This survey collects information annually on hospital patients' demographic characteristics, how long they stayed in the hospital, and the purpose of their visits.

National Ambulatory Medical Care Survey (Series 13) - A complement to the Hospital Discharge Survey, this survey is a continuous sample of patients' visits to doctors' offices. Doctors fill out forms for a sample of their patients, including their age, race, sex, principal problem, diagnosis, and prescribed treatment.

Nursing Home Series (Series 13) - This national, intermittent survey collects data on nursing-home residents, staff, and facilities. The information is used for evaluating present legislation, such as Medicare and Medicaid, and for planning new legislation. The 1985-86 survey was updated in 1995.

Computer Tapes Available

Computer tapes containing detailed data are available. The center will also answer requests for unpublished data if it has already made the tabulations or, for a fee, it will make special tabulations. For further information, call the Data Dissemination

Branch at 301/436-8500. To order tapes, contact the National Technical Information Service, 5285 Port Royal Road, Springfield, VA 22161; telephone 703/487-4650. Most tapes are available at an average cost of $160.

National Park Service

Kenneth E. Hornback, Ph.D.   Phone: 303/969-6977
Denver Service Center, T-N-T, P.O. Box 25287
Denver, CO 80225   E-mail: kenhornback@nps.gov.

Millions enjoy the parks and other sites maintained by the National Park Service (NPS)—which also keeps tabs on its visitors. The NPS, part of the Department of the Interior, administers national parks; memorials; monuments; battlefields; historic, recreation, and other areas designated by the U.S. Congress. The NPS collects, edits, and publishes data about public use of the areas—recreation visits, backcountry use, tent camping, recreational vehicle use, and concession lodging.

What You Can Get From the NPS

The audit-controlled data collection efforts by parks are unique in the realm of federal data in that they are edited and available within three weeks of the close of each month. Data are available in preliminary monthly reports showing volume of use by park and by NPS region, and final data are published in the annual National Park Service Statistical Abstract.

National Technical Information Service (NTIS)

Stuart M. Weisman, Product Manager   Phone: 703/487-4650
5285 Port Royal Road   Fax: 703/321-8547
Springfield, VA 22161   E-mail: orders@ntis.fedworld.gov or telnet to fedworld.gov

As information becomes an important business resource, establishments are tapping into NTIS's treasury of information products and services. For 50 years, NTIS, as part of the U.S. Department of Commerce, has served as the nation's clearinghouse for business and management studies, training tools, computer and telecommunications standards, international market reports, mail lists, and much more.

For an introduction to the vast array of publications and electronic products available from NTIS, call or write for its free 1995-96 Catalog of Products and Services, PR-827. For a sampling of the most recent research and statistical information available in the business fields, ask for the free Business Highlights, PR-985. For free information available by fax, call 703/487-4142. For free dial-up and Internet access to information available at NTIS, connect to the FedWorld Information Network either by modem at 703/321-3339 or by Internet:telnet to fedworld.gov. For File Transfer Protocol services, connect to ftp.fedworld.gov; for World Wide Web services, point your browser to http://www.fedworld.gov. The FedWorld help desk can be reached at 703/487-4608.

Northern Ohio Data and Information Service, Cleveland State University

Mark Salling   Phone: 216/687-2209
College of Urban Affairs
Cleveland, OH 44115

Public Data Resources Virginia Commonwealth University

Robert D. Rugg   Phone: 804/367-1134
P.O. Box 2008
Richmond, VA 23284-2008

Social Security Administration (SSA)

Helen Kearney, Office of Research and Statistics   Phone: 202/282-7137
4301 Connecticut Avenue, NW, Room 209
Washington, DC 20008

Social Security isn't just for retired people. SSA programs and data cover a broader audience. One of the best sources of data on America's growing elderly population is the Social Security Administration, which puts out regular reports on the Old Age, Survivors, and Disability Insurance Program (OASDI-Social Security), as well as the Supplemental Security Income (SSI) and Aid to Families with dependent children (AFDC) programs. The SSA Research and Statistics Publications Catalog and single copies of all documents in the catalog are available from the Office of Research and Statistics Publication staff.

What You Can Get From the Social Security Administration

Biennial Reports
The following reports are available from the Government Printing Office; telephone 202/512-1800.

Social Security Programs in the United States

Issued biennially, this is a layman's guide to the nation's network of publicly funded cash and in-kind income-maintenance programs provided by the Social Security Act. It discusses the history and current provisions of the OASDI program, Medicare, unemployment insurance, workers' compensation, and the temporary disability program.

Social Security Programs Throughout the World

This biennial publication describes in chart format the Social Security systems of 165 countries. It provides perspectives on methods used by different countries in designing and applying income-maintenance measures.

Income of the Population 55 or Older

This biennial publication presents a broad economic picture of a cross-section of the population aged 55 and older. The major focus is on sources of income and amounts received from various sources.

Income of the Aged Chartbook

This chartbook presents a picture of the economic status of the aged. Information includes amount, sources, and shares of income, as well as how these have changed over time.

Annual Reports

The following annual reports are available from the Social Security Administration by calling 202/282-7138.

OASDI Beneficiaries by State and County

This report has information on the number of persons receiving OASDI benefits by type and amount.

Supplemental Security Income State and County Data

This report contains statistical data on the distribution of federally administered SSI payments to aged, blind, and disabled adults; and disabled children.

Earnings and Employment Data for Wage and Salary Workers Covered Under Social Security by State and County

This report presents data on employment for wage and salary workers, including number of persons, amount of taxable wages, amount of Social Security contributions, as well as age, sex, and race of worker. The population includes those in the armed forces and in U.S. territories.

Fast Facts and Figures About Social Security

This chartbook is an easy-to-use reference with answers to the most frequently asked questions about Social Security, SSI, Medicare, Medicaid, and AFDC.

Annual Statistical Supplement to the Social Security Bulletin

This data-packed compilation of more than 230 detailed statistical tables covers virtually all aspects of the OASDI and SSI programs. It also provides data for related social insurance and welfare programs, such as veterans' benefits, workers' compensation, AFDC, Medicare, and Medicaid.

Statistics of Income Division, U.S. Internal Revenue Service

John Kozielec, Sandra Byberg, Statisticians
CP:R:S, P.O. Box 2608
Washington, DC 20013-2608

Phone: 202/874-0410
Fax: 202/874-0964
E-mail: electronic bulletin board 202/874-9574
or http://www.irs.ustreas.gov

IRS data are useful for more than tax and income information. They can be used to examine migration and population trends between censuses. Income-by-income source, tax deductions, and tax exemptions are all reported by marital status of the taxpayer. Researchers can infer household composition based on marital status and the number of exemptions claimed. Exemption data can also be used in making population inferences for years between censuses; researchers can also obtain exemption data from matched tax returns for adjacent years to track annual migration by county and state, based on changes in mailing address.

What You Can Get From the Internal Revenue Service

Statistics of Income (SOI) Bulletin

This quarterly report publishes the most current, preliminary statistics based on individual income tax returns. Selected income and tax data are also shown by state by size of taxpayer income. For some years, the Bulletin also provides estimates of the personal wealth of the nation's top wealthholders derived from estate tax returns, by age, sex, and marital status. SOI Bulletin (Publication 1136) is available for $26 per year from the Superintendent of Documents, Government Printing Office, P.O. Box 371954, Pittsburgh, PA 15250-1954; telephone 202/512-1800 or fax 202/512-2250.

Statistics of Income —Individual Income Tax Returns

This annual report presents the final statistics for a given income year. It includes data (at the national level only) on income sources, tax deductions, personal exemptions, and income tax, in considerably more detail than that offered by the preliminary estimates presented in the SOI Bulletin. The data are presented by several classifications, including taxpayer marital state and size of income. Statistics of Income (Publication 1304) can be purchased for $14, also from the Superintendent of Documents, Government Printing Office, P.O. Box 371954, Pittsburgh, PA 15250-1954; telephone 202/512-1800 or fax 202/512-2250.

Individual Income Tax Return File

The microdata available in the public-use tapes often provide more detailed information than the printed publication, based on the same sample used for the final statistics. However, some data are edited to protect the identity of individual taxpayers. Individuals can buy annual files from the IRS for $2,150.

Migration Data

IRS sells summaries of migration patterns, presenting origins and destinations, by county and state, based on year-to-year changes in taxpayer addresses. Income data for migrants are also available for the most recent year. Prices vary.

County Income Data

IRS sells county-level income tables showing types of income, number of returns, and personal exemptions. Data are also summarized by state. Prices vary.

U.S. Department of Agriculture

14th and Independence Avenue, SW
Washington, DC 20250

Phone: 202/720-5192
Fax: 202/690-3611

Four groups in the Department of Agriculture are of interest to marketers. The Population Group provides information about the population of farms, rural areas, and small towns; the Center for Nutrition Policy and Promotion provides direction and coordination for USDA's nutrition education research and policy activities; the Agricultural Research Service conducts Nationwide Food Surveys to see whether the nutritional needs of the population are being met; and the Economic Research Service's Food and Consumer Economics Division provides economic analyses and data on the choices society makes regarding food and marketing issues, and the impact of these choices on social welfare. Each group provides a wealth of data in its respective area. The Center for Nutrition Policy and Promotion publishes the Family Economics and Nutrition Review and Expenditures on Children by Families, and, in conjunction with the Department of Health and Human Services, develops and publishes Dietary Guidelines for Americans and the Food Guide Pyramid.

For more information, see Agricultural Statistics, available from the Government Printing Office, 202/512-1800; and ERS-NASS Reports, which lists new publications from the Economic Research Service. To get on the free mailing list, call 800/999-6779.

Telephone Contacts

Family Economics Research, Betsy Kuhn 202/219-0880
Nationwide Food Surveys, Katherine Tippett 301/734-8457
Childraising Costs, John Webster 202/418-3139
Center for Nutrition Policy and Promotion, John Webster 202/418-3139
Population Group, Calvin Beale 202/219-0482

What You Can Get From the Department of Agriculture

Continuing Survey of Food Intakes by Individuals/Diet and Health Knowledge Survey

These surveys measure what Americans eat and their attitudes about diet and health. Data are tabulated by sex, age, race, income, and other demographic variables. Reports from the 1989-91 surveys, as well as microdata from a more recent survey, are available. Call Katherine Tippett at 301/734-8457.

Food Review

This journal of the Economic Research Service covers economic issues of the food sector, including food consumption, prices, spending, assistance, nutrition, marketing, and safety. It usually profiles sociodemographic trends. Call 800/999-6799 for subscription information.

Family Economics and Nutrition Review

This quarterly journal of the Center for Nutrition Policy and Promotion covers factors that affect the decisions people make about life's big events—getting married, having children, buying a house, deciding to retire. It also reports on such topics as child and adult nutrition and nutrition education and promotion, how much it costs to raise a child, and household savings and credit use. An annual subscription is $8 and can be ordered from the Government Printing Office; 202/512-1800.

Rural Development Perspectives

Rural Development Perspectives, published three times a year by the Economic Research Service, contains nontechnical articles by both the Economic Research Service staff and outside authors on the results of new rural research and what those results mean. It covers a wide range of rural economic and social topics, such as employment, development, education, population trends, banking and investment, health, and income. The subscription rate is $14 annually. Call 800/999-6779 for subscription information.

Rural Conditions and Trends

Rural Conditions and Trends, issued three times annually by the Economic Research Service, tracks recent economic trends such as income, employment, industrial structure, earnings, poverty, and population in nonmetropolitan America. The subscription rate is $15 annually. Call 800/999-6799 for subscription information.

U.S. Department of Education, National Center for Education Statistics

Suellen Mauchamer, Office of Educational
Research and Improvement   Phone: 202/219-1828
555 New Jersey Avenue, NW   Fax: 202/219-1736
Washington, DC 20208   E-mail: smauchamer@ed.gov or http://www.ed.gov

One in four Americans is involved in the educational process as a student or teacher.
The Office of Educational Research and Improvement (OERI) covers all aspects of
this huge industry. Since 1867, the Department of Education has been responsible
for information on the "condition and progress of education." It provides a wealth of
statistical and research information through its Office of Educational Research and
Improvement. The National Center for Education Statistics (NCES), OERI's statistical unit, conducts a wide variety of surveys covering all levels of education.

For more information, see the OERI Publications Catalog, which lists the wide
range of statistical reports that are available, many of them free. The catalog is
available by writing or calling the address and/or number above.

Telephone contacts

General information	800/424-1616
in metro Washington area	202/219-1651
Norman Brandt	
Vance Grant	
Richard Whalen	
Common Core of Data, John Sietsema	219-1335
Data Tapes/Computer Products, Joyce Robertson	219-1547
Jack Dusatko	219-1522
Elementary and Secondary Education, Joanell Porter	219-1614
Longitudinal Studies, Aurora M. D'Amico	219-1365
International Education, Eugene Owen	219-1746
Library Surveys, Carrol Kindel	219-1371
Postsecondary Education, Bill Freund	219-1373
Projections, Debra Gerald	219-1581
School District Tabulation, Ted Drews	219-1731

What You Can Get From NCES

Digest of Education Statistics and Condition of Education

These annual publications contain a wide range of education statistics gathered
from the National Center for Education Statistics' own surveys and a variety of other sources. They are available from the Government Printing Office; telephone
202/512-1800. The 1995 edition of the Digest was released in October 1995.

Longitudinal Surveys

The Center has been tracking the accomplishments of high school students, beginning with seniors in 1972, for the National Longitudinal Study (NLS-72); sopho-
mores and seniors in 1980, for the High School and Beyond (HS&B) Study; eighth
graders in 1988, for the National Education Longitudinal Survey (NELS:88); institutions, students, and parents of students who began their postsecondary education

in 1989-90 in the Beginning Postsecondary Student Longitudinal Study (BPS); and baccalaureate degree completers for a 12-year period after degree completion in academic year 1992-93 in the Baccalaureate and Beyond Longitudinal Study (B&B). These surveys follow up on the education and labor force experience of individuals over time. Publications are produced periodically, and data are available on tape and CD-ROM.

National Assessment of Educational Progress (NAEP)

NAEP is popularly known as the Nation's Report Card. It tracks the achievement levels of children aged 9, 13, and 17 in a variety of academic subjects.

Integrated Postsecondary Education Data Systems (IPEDS)

The Center conducts an annual survey of all colleges and universities, gathering data on enrollment, faculty, faculty salaries and tenure, degrees conferred, financing, and student costs. Annual reports and the database on CD-ROM are available from the NCES National Data Resource Center. Call Carl Schmitt at 202/219-1642.

Projections of Education Statistics

The Center periodically issues ten-year projections of enrollment, graduates, teachers, and expenditures for elementary, secondary, and higher education institutions. Projections of Education Statistics to 2005 was released in December 1995.

Computer Tapes and Other Products

The Center provides access to more detailed data than its publications contain via 3.5 inch diskettes and CD-ROM. Special tabulations can be made for any database through the NCES National Data Resource Center. Contact Carl Schmitt at 202/219-1642. Data are also available via the Internet at gopher.ed.gov or on the Education Web Site at http://www.ed.gov.

U.S. Fish and Wildlife Service

Sylvia Cabrera, Richard Aiken, David Waddington   Phone: 703/358-2156
4401 N. Fairfax Drive, Room 140
Arlington, VA 22203   E-mail: http://www.fws.gov/

The Fish and Wildlife Service concerns itself not only with wildlife populations, but the human populations that enjoy wildlife-related recreation.

What You Can Get From the U.S. Fish and Wildlife Service

The 1991 National Survey of Fishing, Hunting, and Wildlife-Associated Recreation provides estimates of the number and length of trips, number of participants, and expenditures for hunting, fishing, and nonconsumptive wildlife-related recreation in the U.S. The survey also covers geographic and socio-demographic information about wildlife recreation participants. A printed report of survey results is available from the U.S. Fish and Wildlife Service; telephone 703/358-2156. A new survey will be conducted in 1996 with results available in 1997. Analysis of specific results are also available: 1980-90 Fishing, Hunting, and Wildlife-Associated Recreation Trends; 1991 Net Economic Values for Bass and Trout Fishing, Deer Hunting, and Wildlife Watching; and Participation and Expenditure Patterns of Black, Hispanic, and Women Hunters and Anglers.

United States Postal Service

475 L'Enfant Plaza, SW   Phone: 202/268-2000
Washington, DC 20260

The United States Postal Service sorts and delivers more than 177 billion pieces of mail each year, has 745,000 career employees, and operates 39,372 post offices, stations, and branches throughout the country.

What You Can Get From the United States Postal Service

Household Diary Study

The Postal Service's Household Diary Study offers information on and analysis of mail sent and received by households. A 34-page executive summary or the complete 700-page study is available. Both include information, tables, and graphs on mail sent and received by mail class, sector, and industry; factors influencing the response to advertising mail; household demographics, including mail volume by age, household size, education, and income; newspapers and magazines received through the mail and by other means; bill payment practices; and the use of electronic alternatives to mail. The executive summary costs $20 per copy; the complete study is $50. Contact Jay Lewis, Finance, Room 8016; telephone 202/268-2672.

University of Missouri-St.Louis Urban Information Center

John G. Blodgett   Phone: 314/553-6014
8001 Natural Bridge Road   Fax: 314/516-6014
St. Louis, MO 63121-4499   E-mail: c192@umslvma.umsl.edu

Veterans Affairs, Department of

A. J. Singh, National Center for Veteran
Analysis and Statistics (008C)   Phone: 202/273-5036
810 Vermont Avenue, NW
Washington, DC 20420   E-mail: http://www.va.gov or kleinr@mail.va.gov

The U.S. has 27 million living veterans. VA tracks the status of this special group, especially its health status. The National Center for Veteran Analysis and Statistics within the Office of the Assistant Secretary for Policy and Planning produces and maintains a wealth of statistical data on the veteran population, including demographic, socioeconomic, and medical care information. Publications from the Statistical Service describe the many reports that are available from VA. All reports are free and can be ordered by writing to the above address.

Telephone contacts

Secretary of Veterans Affairs Annual Report, Hazel Briston 202/273-5123
Patient Treatment File and Annual Patient Census, Susan Gee Krumhaus 273-5108
Population Estimates and Projections, Kathleen Sorensen 273-5104
Surveys of Veterans, Susan Gee Krumhaus 273-5108
Veterans Receiving Compensation or Pension and Veterans
Receiving Educational Benefits, Mike Wells 273-5106
Veterans Unemployment, Labor Force Status, Income,
Dr. Robert E. Klein 273-5101
Census Data Products, Steve Schwartz 273-5103

What You Can Get From the Department of Veterans Affairs

The following are examples of some of the reports and data available from VA.

Veteran Population Estimates and Projections

This is an annual report with estimates of the number of living veterans by period of military service, state of residence, sex, and age. Projections are made to the year 2020. A summary report of the veteran population projected to the year 2010 is available.

State and County Veteran Population

This annual report presents county-level estimates and forecasts of the veteran population.

National Survey of Veterans

This 1992 survey collected data from some 11,645 veterans nationwide on their income, assets, and liabilities, as well as their health status, medical condition, and use of veteran programs.

Projections of Veterans Receiving VA Compensation

This analysis uses demographic projection methods and regression analysis to estimate the number of veterans receiving VA compensation by age and degree of disability to the year 2010.

Disability, VA Programs, and Labor Force Status Among Vietman Era Veterans

This report examines the relationships among disability, labor force status, employment characteristics, and use of VA job programs.

Secretary of Veterans Affairs Annual Report

Every key subject area on veterans is discussed in this report, and data are included on population, health care, compensation and pension, education benefits, cemeteries and memorials, and veterans assistance.

Annual Patient Census

The National Center collects and disseminates information on VA hospital inpatients, residents of domiciliaries, and patients in VA nursing homes. The data collected pertain to the numbers of patients and their characteristics as of one particular day in the year. Standard data items collected include date of birth, compensation and pension status, disability rating, period of service, date of admission, sex, marital status, race/ethnicity, and principal diagnosis.

1990 Census Data Products

VA maintains state and county demographic and socioeconomic data on veterans from the 1990 census. Some exist on diskette and in hard copy, while others may be accessed through VA's data-processing system. Several subject reports using decennial census data are available.

Patient Treatment File

The PTF contains information on all incidences of patient discharge from VA medical centers, nursing homes, and domiciliaries during a given fiscal year. The file includes detailed data on patient characteristics as well as clinical data.

Chapter 6: State and Local Sources

ALABAMA

State Data Center

Center for Business & Economic Research
University of Alabama, P.O. Box 870221
Tuscaloosa, AL 35487-0221
Annette Watters
Phone: 205/348-6191
Fax: 205/348-2951
E-mail: awatters@ualvm.ua.edu

Labor

Alabama Department of Industrial Relations
649 Monroe Street, Room 422
Montgomery, AL 36131-2279
Douglas Dyer, Chief, Research and Statistics Division
Phone: 334/242-8855
Fax: 334/242-2543

Health

Alabama State Department of Public Health
Center for Health Statistics
Statistical Analysis Division, P.O. Box 5625
Montgomery, AL 36103-5625
Dale E. Quinney
Phone: 334/613-5429
Fax: 334/613-5407

Education

Alabama Commission on Higher Education
100 North Union Street
Montgomery, AL 36104-3702

Debbie Boyd
Phone: 334/242-1998

Education

State Department of Education
50 North Ripley Street, Office #5301
Montgomery, AL 36103
Dean R. Argo, Director, Information & Communications
Phone: 334/242-9700
Fax: 334/242-9708

ALASKA

State Data Center

Census and Geographic Information Service
P.O. Box 25504
Juneau, AK 99802-5504
Kathryn Lizik
Phone: 907/465-2437
Fax: 907/465-4506

Labor

Alaska Department of Labor, Research & Analysis
P.O. Box 25501
Juneau, AK 99802-5501
Gregory Williams, State Demographer
Ingrid Zaruba, Statistical Technician
907/465-4500
Phone: 907/465-6029
Fax: 907/465-4506
E-mail: greg_williams%labor@state.ak.us

Health

Alaska Bureau of Vital Statistics
P.O. Box 22566
Juneau, AK 99811-0675
Anthony Zenk
Phone: 907/465-3392
Fax: 907/465-3618

Education

Alaska Department of Education
School of Finance & Data Management
801 West 10th Street, Suite 200
Juneau, AK 99801-1894
Phone: 907/465-8681

ARIZONA

State Data Center

Arizona Department of Economic Security
DES 045Z, First Floor, Southeast Wing
1789 West Jefferson Street
Phoenix, AZ 85007
Betty Jeffries
Phone: 602/542-5984
Fax: 602/542-6474

Labor

Arizona Department of Economic Security
1789 W. Jefferson, P.O. Box 6123,
Site Code 733A
Phoenix, AZ 85005
Research Administration
Phone: 602/542-3871
Fax: 602/542-6474

Health

Arizona Department of Health Services
1740 W. Adams, Suite 312
Phoenix, AZ 85007
Joe Brennan, Economist
Phone: 602/542-2960
Fax: 602/542-1244
E-mail: jbrenna@hs.STATE.AZ.US

Education

Arizona Department of Education
1535 West Jefferson
Phoenix, AZ 85007
Kelly Powell, Director, Research and
Development Unit
Phone: 602/542-5031
Fax: 602/542-5467

Local Information

The Arizona Republic/The Phoenix Gazette Newspaper
120 E. Van Buren Street
Phoenix, AZ 85004
Ellen Jacobs, Market Research
Phone: 602/271-8870
Fax: 602/271-8325

ARKANSAS

State Data Center

State Data Center
University of Arkansas-Little Rock
2801 South University
Little Rock, AR 72204
Sarah Breshears
Phone: 501/569-8530
Fax: 501/569-8538
E-mail: sgbreshears@.ualr.edu

Labor

Arkansas Employment Security Department
P.O. Box 2981
Little Rock, AR 72203
Alma Holbrook, Manager, Labor Market
Information Section
Phone: 501/682-3198

Health

Arkansas Department of Health
Center for Health Statistics
4815 West Markham, Slot 19
Little Rock, AR 72205
Phone: 501/661-2368

Education

Arkansas State Department of Education
4 Capitol Mall, Room 202A
Little Rock, AR 72201
John Kunkel, Coordinator, Local Fiscal
Services
Phone: 501/682-4258

CALIFORNIA

State Data Center

State Census Data Center
Department of Finance, 915 L Street
Sacramento, CA 95814
Linda Gage, Director
Phone: 916/322-4651
Fax: 916/327-0222
E-mail: cfl.filgage@ts3.teale.ca.gov

Labor

**Employment Development Department -
Labor Market Information Division**
Publications and Information Unit
7000 Franklin Boulevard, Building 1100
Sacramento, CA 95823
Phone: 916/262-2162
Fax: 916/262-2443

Health

**Department of Health Services
Vital Statistics Section**
714 P Street, Room 1494
Sacramento, CA 95814
Anthony Oreglia, Research Manager I
Phone: 916/657-2967
Fax: 916/324-5599

Education

California Department of Education
Bureau of Publications
515 L Street, Suite 250
Sacramento, CA 95814
Curt Robinson, Editor in Chief
Phone: 916/445-7608
Fax: 916/322-3257
E-mail: crobinso@cde.ca.gov

COLORADO

State Data Center

Colorado Department of Local Affairs
Division of Local Government
1313 Sherman Street, Room 521
Denver, CO 80203
Rebecca Picaso
Phone: 303/866-2156
Fax: 303/866-2803

Labor

**Colorado Department of Labor and
Employment**
Labor Market Information
1515 Arapahoe Street, Tower 2, Suite 300
Denver, CO 80202
Phone: 303/620-4856

Health

Colorado State Department of Health
Vital Records
4300 Cherry Creek Drive South, Room A1
Denver, CO 80222-1530
Phone: 303/692-2200

Education

Colorado Department of Education
Research and Evaluation Unit
201 East Colfax Avenue
Denver, CO 80203-1799
Jan Rose Petro
Phone: 303/866-6840
Fax: 303/830-0793
E-mail: petro-J@cde.state.co.us

Local Information

Rocky Mountain News
400 W. Colfax Avenue
Denver, CO 80204
Matt Baldwin, Research Director
Phone: 303/892-5253
Fax: 303/892-2784

CONNECTICUT

State Data Center

Connecticut Office of Policy and Mgmt.
Policy Development and Planning Division
80 Washington Street
Hartford, CT 06106-4459
Bill Kraynak
Phone: 203/566-8285
Fax: 203/566-1589

Labor

Connecticut Department of Labor
200 Folly Brook Boulevard
Wethersfield, CT 06109
Roger Therrien, Director, Office of Research
Phone: 860/566-7823
Fax: 860/566-7963

Health

Connecticut State Department of Public Health
Vital Statistics
150 Washington Street
Hartford, CT 06106
Lloyd Mueller
Phone: 203/566-2038

Education

Connecticut State Department of Education
State Office Building
165 Capitol Street, Room 304
Hartford, CT 06106
Tom Murphy, Assistant to the Commissioner for Public Information
Phone: 203/566-5061

Local Information

The New Haven Register
40 Sargent Drive
New Haven, CT 06511
Tina Goodwin, Research Manager
Phone: 203/789-5437
Fax: 203/865-8360

DC

State Data Center

Mayor's Office of Planning
Data Services Division, Presidential Building
415 12th Street, NW, Room 570
Washington, DC 20004
Herb Bixhorn
Phone: 202/727-6533
Fax: 202/727-6964

Labor

Department of Employment Services, LMI
500 C Street, NW, Suite 201
Washington, DC 20001
Eileen Dent, Economist
Phone: 202/724-7213
Fax: 202/724-7216

Health

State Center for Health Statistics

DC Commission of Public Health
613 G Street, NW, 9th Floor
Washington, DC 20001
Carl W. Wilson
Phone: 202/727-0682
Fax: 202/727-3396

Education

DC Department of Education Office of Education Research and Improvement
Statistics Department
CP 555 New Jersey Avenue, NW
Washington, DC 20208
Jeanne Griffin
Phone: 202/219-1828

DELAWARE

State Data Center

Delaware Development Office
99 Kings Highway, P.O. Box 1401
Dover, DE 19903
Mike Mahaffie
Phone: 302/739-4271
Fax: 302/739-5749
E-mail: mmahaffie@state.de.us

Labor

Delaware Department of Labor
P.O. Box 9029
Newark, DE 19714
Bob Schulz, Senior Labor Market Analyst
Phone: 302/368-6962

Health

Bureau of Health Planning and Resources Management
P.O. Box 637, Federal and Water Streets
Dover, DE 19903
Donald E. Berry, Manager, Health Statistics and Research
Phone: 302/739-4776
Fax: 302/739-3008

Education

Delaware Department of Public Instruction
P.O. Box 1402
Dover, DE 19903-1402
Robert F. Boozer

Phone: 302/739-4583
Fax: 302/739-4221

FLORIDA

State Data Center

Florida State Data Center
Executive Office of the Governor
REA/OPB, The Capitol, Room 1604
Tallahassee, FL 32399-0001
Valerie Jugger
Phone: 904/487-2814
Fax: 904/488-9005
E-mail: juggerv@eog.mail.ufl.edu

Labor

Bureau of Labor Market Information
200 Hartman Building
2012 Capitol Circle, SE
Tallahassee, FL 32399-2151
Pamela Schenker, Economist Supervisor
Phone: 904/488-1048
Fax: 904/488-2558

Health

**Florida Health and Rehabilitative
Services, Vital Statistics**
P.O. Box 210
Jacksonville, FL 32231
Kenneth T. Jones, Vital Statistics
Administrator
Phone: 904/359-6929
Fax: 904/359-6993

Education

Florida Department of Education
722 Florida Education Center
325 West Gaines Street
Tallahassee, FL 32399-0400
Lavan Dukes, Administrator, Education
Information and Accountability Services
Phone: 904/487-2280
Fax: 904/922-8041
E-mail: dukesl@mail.doe.state.fl.us

Local Information

Tampa Tribune
P.O. Box 191, 202 S. Parker Street
Tampa, FL 33601
Research Analyst
Phone: 813/259-7765
Fax: 813/259-8909

GEORGIA

State Data Center

Georgia Office of Planning and Budget
Division of Demographic and Statistical
Services
254 Washington Street, SW, Room 640
Atlanta, GA 30334
Marty Sik
Phone: 404/656-0911
Fax: 404/656-3828

Labor

**Georgia Department of Labor, Labor
Information Systems**
CWC Building, Room 300
148 International Boulevard
Atlanta, GA 30303
Jim Liesendahl, Research Unit Supervisor
Phone: 404/656-3177
Fax: 404/651-9568

Health

**Georgia Division of Public Health, Center
for Health Information**
2 Peachtree Street, Room 3-522
Atlanta, GA 30303-3186
Susan Deaver, Statistician
Phone: 404/657-6321
Fax: 404/657-6282

Education

Georgia State Department of Education
Information Management Services
1654 Twin Towers East, 205 Butler Street
Atlanta, GA 30334
Phone: 404/656-2400

HAWAII

State Data Center

Hawaii State Data Center
Department of Business, Economic
Development and Tourism
220 S. King Street, Suite 400
Honolulu, HI 96813
Jan Nakamoto
Phone: 808/586-2493
Fax: 808/586-2452
E-mail: jann@uhunix.uhcc.hawaii.edu

Labor

Hawaii Department of Labor and Industrial Relations
830 Punchbowl Street, Room 304
Honolulu, HI 96813
Naomi Harada, Chief, Research and Statistics Office
Phone: 808/586-8999
Fax: 808/586-9022

Health

State Department of Health
State Registrar, Office of Health Status Monitoring
P.O. Box 3378
Honolulu, HI 96801
Alvin Onaka
Phone: 808/586-4539

Education

Hawaii State Department of Education
Information Resource Management
1505 Dillingham Boulevard, Room 216
Honolulu, HI 96817
Phone: 808/832-5880

IDAHO

State Data Center

Idaho Department of Commerce
700 West State Street
Boise, ID 83720
Alan Porter
Phone: 208/334-2470
Fax: 208/334-2631

Labor

Idaho Department of Employment, Research and Analysis
317 Main Street
Boise, ID 83735
James C. Adams, Chief
Phone: 208/334-6168
Fax: 208/334-6455

Health

Idaho Department of Health
Vital Statistics
P.O. Box 83720
Boise, ID 83720-0036
Phone: 208/334-5979

Education

Idaho State Department of Education
650 West State Street, P.O.Box 83720
Boise, ID 83720-0027
James A. Smith, Deputy State Superintendent/Finance and Administration
Phone: 208/334-2203
Fax: 208/334-2228

ILLINOIS

State Data Center

Illinois Bureau of the Budget
William Stratton Building, Room 605
Springfield, IL 62706
Suzanne Ebetsch
Phone: 217/782-1381
Fax: 217/524-4876

Labor

Illinois Department of Employment Security
401 S. State Street, Room 215
Chicago, IL 60605
Henry L. Jackson, Labor Market Information Director
Phone: 312/793-2316
Fax: 312/793-5723

Health

Illinois Department of Public Health
Illinois Center for Health Statistics
525 West Jefferson Street, 2nd Floor
Springfield, IL 62761
Merwyn Nelson, PhD
Phone: 217/785-1064
Fax: 217/785-4308

Education

Illinois State Board of Education
Research and Policy Division
100 North 1st Street
Springfield, IL 62777
Phone: 217/782-3950

Local Information

The Pantagraph
301 Washington Street, P.O. Box 2907
Bloomington, IL 61702-2907
Cathy A. Oloffson, Market Research Analyst
Phone: 309/829-9411

Fax: 309/829-8497
E-mail: pantagra@pantagraph.com

INDIANA

State Data Center

Indiana State Data Center
Indiana State Library
140 North Senate Avenue
Indianapolis, IN 46204
Laurence Hathaway
Phone: 317/232-3733
Fax: 317/232-3728
E-mail: lhathaway@statelib.lib.in.us

Labor

Indiana Workforce Development
10 North Senate Avenue
Indianapolis, IN 46204
Charles Mazza, Director, Labor Force
Statistics
Phone: 317/232-7670

Health

Indiana State Department of Health
Vital Records Section
1330 W. Michigan Street
Indianapolis, IN 46206-7125
Phone: 317/383-6701

Education

Indiana State Department of Education
Educational Information Services
State House, Room 229, 251 East Ohio
Street
Indianapolis, IN 46204-2798
Phone: 317/232-0808

IOWA

State Data Center

State Library of Iowa
East 12th and Grand Avenue
Des Moines, IA 50319
Beth Henning
Phone: 515/281-4350
Fax: 515/281-3384
E-mail: bh1211s@acad.drake.edu

Labor

Iowa Department of Employment Services
1000 East Grand Avenue
Des Moines, IA 50319-0209
Stephen C. Smith, Chief, Staff Services
Bureau
Phone: 515/281-8181
Fax: 515/281-8195

Health

Iowa Department of Public Health
321 E. 12th, Lucas Building, 4th Floor
Des Moines, IA 50319-0075
Phyllis Blood, Director, Center for Health
Statistics
Phone: 515/281-4435
Fax: 515/281-4958

Education

Iowa Department of Education
Bureau of Planning, Research and
Evaluation
Grimes State Office Building
Des Moines, IA 50319
Phone: 515/281-3757

KANSAS

State Data Center

State Library, Kansas State Data Center
State Capitol Building, Room 343-N
Topeka, KS 66612
Marc Galbraith
Phone: 913/296-3296
Fax: 913/296-6650

Labor

Kansas Department of Human Resources
401 Topeka Avenue
Topeka, KS 66603
William H. Layes, Chief, Labor Market
Information Services
Phone: 913/296-5058

Health

Kansas State Department of Health
109 SW 9th Street, Mills Building, Ste 400A
Topeka, KS 66612
Lou Saadi, Director, Office of Health-Care

Information
Phone: 913/296-5639

Education

Kansas State Board of Education - LEA Finance Division
120 SE 10th Street
Topeka, KS 66612-1182
Gary Watson, Research Analyst
Phone: 913/296-3871
Fax: 913/296-0459
E-mail: gwatson@smtpgw.ksbe.state.ks.us

KENTUCKY

State Data Center

College of Business and Public Administration
Center for Urban and Economic Research
University of Louisville
Louisville, KY 40292
Ron Crouch
Phone: 502/852-7990
Fax: 502/852-7386
E-mail: rtcrou01@ulkyvm.louisville.edu

Labor

Research and Statistics Branch
Department for Employment Services
275 East Main Street, 2nd Floor
Frankfort, KY 40621
Carlos H. Cracraft, State Labor Market Analyst
Phone: 502/564-7976
Fax: 502/564-7799

Health

Vital Statistics Branch
Department for Health Services
275 East Main Street
Frankfort, KY 40621-0001
Barbara F. White
Phone: 502/564-4212
Fax: 502/227-0032

Education

Kentucky State Department of Education
Office of Education Technology
15 Fountain Place
Frankfort, KY 40601
Paula Kinsolving
Phone: 502/564-2020 ext. 222

Local Information

The Courier-Journal
525 West Broadway, P.O. Box 740031
Louisville, KY 40201-7431
Mark Schneider, Research Manager
Phone: 502/582-4351
Fax: 502/582-4753
E-mail: mschneid@louisvil.gannett.com

LOUISIANA

State Data Center

Louisiana Office of Planning and Budget
Division of Administration
1051 N. 3rd Street, P.O. Box 94095
Baton Rouge, LA 70804
Karen Paterson
Phone: 504/342-7410
Fax: 504/342-1057
E-mail: kpaters@kpaters.doa.state.la.us

Labor

Louisiana Department of Labor
P.O. Box 94094
Baton Rouge, LA 70804-9094
Patty Lopez, Labor Market Analyst
Phone: 504/342-3141
Fax: 504/342-9193

Health

Louisiana Public Health Statistics
P.O. Box 60630, Room 106, DHH/OPH
New Orleans, LA 70160
Janet Reed
Phone: 504/568-5337

Education

Louisiana State Department of Education
Research and Development (Statistics)
P.O. Box 94064
Baton Rouge, LA 70804-9064
Phone: 504/342-3736

MAINE

State Data Center

Maine Department of Labor
Division of Economic Analysis and Research

20 Union Street
Augusta, ME 04330
Jean Martin
Phone: 207/287-2271
Fax: 207/287-5292

Labor

Maine Department of Labor
Division of Economic Analysis and
Research
20 Union Street
Augusta, ME 04333
Ray Fongemie, Director
Phone: 207/287-2271
Fax: 207/287-5292

Health

Maine Department of Human Services
Office of Data, Research and Vital
Statistics
State House Station #11
35 Anthony Avenue
Augusta, ME 04333-0011
Donald R. Lemieux, Director, Statistical
Services
Phone: 207/624-5445
Fax: 207/624-5470

Education

Maine Department of Education
Management Information
Statehouse Station #23
Augusta, ME 04333
Phone: 207/287-5841

MARYLAND

State Data Center

Maryland Office of Planning
301 West Preston Street
Baltimore, MD 21201
Robert Dadd
Phone: 410/225-4450
Fax: 410/225-4480

Labor

Maryland Department of Labor,
Licensing, and Regulation
11 N. Eutaw Street
Baltimore, MD 21201
Patrick Arnold, Director, Office of Labor

Market Analysis and Information
Phone: 410/767-2250

Health

Maryland Department of Health and
Mental Hygiene
Health Statistics
201 West Preston Street
Baltimore, MD 21201
Phone: 410/225-5950

Education

Maryland State Department of Education
200 West Baltimore Street
Baltimore, MD 21201
Ricka Markowitz, Chief, Research,
Evaluation, and Statistical Svcs.
Phone: 410/767-0026
Fax: 410/333-2017

MASSACHUSETTS

State Data Center

Massachusetts Institute for Social and
Economic Research
128 Thompson Hall, University of
Massachusetts
Amherst, MA 01003
Valerie Conti
Phone: 413/545-3460
Fax: 413/545-3686
E-mail: miser@miser.umass.edu

Labor

Massachusetts Department of
Employment and Training
19 Staniford Street
Boston, MA 02114
Rena Kottcamp, Director of Research
Phone: 617/626-6600

Health

Massachusetts State Department of
Health
Bureau of Health Statistics, Research and
Evaluation
150 Tremont Street, 8th Floor
Boston, MA 02111
Phone: 617/727-3282

Education

Massachusetts Department of Education

Statistics and Evaluation
350 Main Street
Malden, MA 02148
Phone: 617/388-3300 ext. 327

MICHIGAN

State Data Center

Michigan Information Center
Department of Management and Budget
Demographic Research and Statistics
P.O. Box 30026
Lansing, MI 48909
Carolyn Lauer
Phone: 517/373-7910
Fax: 517/373-2939
E-mail: eswansdon@mail.msen.com

Labor

Michigan Employment Security Commission
Research and Statistics Department
7310 Woodward Avenue, Room 520
Detroit, MI 48202
Phone: 313/876-5480

Health

Michigan Department of Public Health
Vital Records
3423 North Logan Street
Lansing, MI 48909
Phone: 517/335-8666

Education

Michigan Department of Education - Elementary/Secondary
Administrative Services and Information
Division
P.O. Box 30106
Lansing, MI 48909
Phone: 517/373-3352

Education

Michigan Office of Higher Education Management
P.O. Box 30008
Lansing, MI 48909
Phone: 517/373-3820

Local Information

Detroit Newspapers
615 West Lafayette Boulevard

Detroit, MI 48226
Kris McKean, Research Director
Phone: 313/222-2227
Fax: 313/222-2190

MINNESOTA

State Data Center

Minnesota Planning
State Demographer's Office
300 Centennial Office Building
658 Cedar Street
St. Paul, MN 55155
David Birkholz
Phone: 612/296-2557
Fax: 612/296-3698
E-mail: birkholz@lmic.state.mn.us

Labor

Minnesota Department of Economic Security
390 North Robert Street, 5th Floor
St. Paul, MN 55101
Med Chottepanda, Director, Research and
Statistical Services
Phone: 612/296-6546

Health

Minneapolis Department of Health
717 Delaware Street, SE, P.O. Box 9441
Minneapolis, MN 55440-9441
Sue Johnson
Phone: 612/623-5353
Fax: 612/623-5264
E-mail: johnson@mdh-admin.health.state.mn

Education

Minnesota State Department of Children, Families and Learning
District Data, Capitol Square Building
550 Cedar Street, 7th Floor
St. Paul, MN 55101
Patricia Tupper
Phone: 612/296-6104

Local Information

Saint Paul Pioneer Press
345 Cedar Street
St. Paul, MN 55101
Jeanine Pearson, Director/Information
Services

Phone: 612/228-5306
Fax: 612/228-5382

MISSISSIPPI

State Data Center

Center for Population Studies
The University of Mississippi
Bondurant Building, Room 3W
University, MS 38677
Rachel McNeely, Manager
Phone: 601/232-7288
Fax: 601/232-7736
E-mail: urmaxwms@vm.cc.olemiss.edu

Labor

Mississippi Employment Security Commission
Labor Market Information Department
P.O. Box 1699
Jackson, MS 39215-1699
Raiford G. Crews, Chief, Labor Market Information
Phone: 601/961-7424
Fax: 601/961-7448

Health

Mississippi State Department of Health
Public Health Statistics
P.O. Box 1700
Jackson, MS 39215-1700
Phone: 601/960-7960

Education

State Department of Education
P.O. Box 771
Jackson, MS 39205
Nathan Slater, Director, Management Information Services
Phone: 601/359-3487

MISSOURI

State Data Center

Missouri State Library
P.O. Box 387, 600 W. Main Street
Jefferson City, MO 65102
Kate Graf
Phone: 314/751-1823
Fax: 314/526-1142
E-mail: kgrafl@mail.more.net

Labor

Missouri Department of Labor
P.O. Box 59
Jefferson City, MO 65104
William C. Niblack, Chief, Research and Analysis
Phone: 314/751-3591

Health

Missouri State Department of Health
State Center for Health Statistics
P.O. Box 570
Jefferson City, MO 65102
Phone: 314/751-6278

Education

Missouri Coordinating Board for Higher Education
3515 Amazonas Drive
Jefferson City, MO 65109
Phone: 314/751-2361
Fax: 314/751-6635

Education

Missouri Department of Elementary and Secondary Education
School Data
P.O. Box 480
Jefferson City, MO 65102-0480
Phone: 314/751-2569

MONTANA

State Data Center

Montana Department of Commerce
Census and Economic Information Center
1424 Ninth Avenue, P.O. Box 200501
Helena, MT 59620-0501
Patricia Roberts
Phone: 406/444-2896
Fax: 406/444-1518
E-mail: proberts@win.com

Labor

Montana Department of Labor and Industry
P.O. Box 1728, 1301 Lockey Street
Helena, MT 59624-1728
Bob Rafferty, Chief, Research and Analysis Bureau

Phone: 406/444-2430
Fax: 406/444-2638

Health

Montana State Department of Health
Bureau of Records and Statistics
1400 Broadway
Helena, MT 59620
Phone: 406/444-2614

Education

Montana Commissioner of Higher Education
2500 Broadway
Helena, MT 59620
Patty Davis, Director of Student and Employee Research
Phone: 406/444-6570

Education

Montana Office of Public Instruction
P.O. Box 202501, State Capitol Building
Helena, MT 59620-2501
Dori Nielson
Phone: 406/444-3656
Fax: 406/444-3924
E-mail: dnielson@opi.mt.gov

NEBRASKA

State Data Center

Nebraska State Data Center
Center for Public Affairs Research
Peter Kiewit Conference Center, #232
University of Nebraska at Omaha
Omaha, NE 68182
Jerome Deichert
Phone: 402/595-2311
Fax: 402/595-2366
E-mail: nparjd@unomalia.edu

Labor

Nebraska Department of Labor
550 South 16th Street, P.O. Box 94600
Lincoln, NE 68509
Phillip Baker, Research Administrator, Bureau of Labor Statistics
Phone: 402/471-9964

Health

Nebraska Department of Health
P.O. Box 95007, State Office Building

Lincoln, NE 68509-5007
Stanley Cooper, Director, Bureau of Vital Statistics
Phone: 402/471-2872

Education

Nebraska State Department of Education
Data Center
P.O. Box 94987
Lincoln, NE 68509-4987
Phone: 402/471-2367

NEVADA

State Data Center

Nevada State Library
Capitol Complex, 100 Stewart Street
Carson City, NV 89710
Laura Witschi
Phone: 702/687-8327
Fax: 702/687-8330

Labor

Research and Analysis, DETR
500 East Third Street
Carson City, NV 89713
Zina Turney, Chief Research and Analysis
Phone: 702/687-4550
Fax: 702/687-1063

Health

Nevada Division of Health - Vital Statistics
Capitol Complex, 505 East King Street
Carson City, NV 89710
Phone: 702/687-4481

Education

Nevada Department of Education
700 East 7th, Capitol Complex
Carson City, NV 89710
Douglas C. Thunder, Director, Fiscal Services
Phone: 702/687-3125
Fax: 702/687-5660

NEW HAMPSHIRE

State Data Center

New Hampshire Office of State Planning
2 1/2 Beacon Street

Concord, NH 03301
Tom Duffy
Phone: 603/271-2155
Fax: 603/271-1728

Labor

New Hampshire Department of Employment Security
32 South Main Street
Concord, NH 03301
George E. Nazer, Jr., Director, Economic and Labor Market Information Bureau
Phone: 603/228-4124
Fax: 603/228-4172

Health

New Hampshire Department of Health and Human Services
Bureau of Vital Records
6 Hazen Drive
Concord, NH 03301
Phone: 603/271-4654

Education

New Hampshire State Department of Education
Information Services
State Office Park South, 101 Pleasant Street
Concord, NH 03301
Phone: 603/271-2778

NEW JERSEY

State Data Center

New Jersey State Data Center
Division of Labor Market and Demographic Research
New Jersey Department of Labor, CN 388
Trenton, NJ 08625-0388
Doug Moore
Phone: 609/984-2595
Fax: 609/984-6833

Labor

New Jersey State Data Center
New Jersey Department of Labor
Trenton, NJ 08625
Connie O. Hughes
Phone: 609/984-2595
Fax: 609/984-2593

Health

New Jersey State Department of Health
Center for Health Statistics
CN 360, John Fitch Plaza
Trenton, NJ 08625-0360
Mark C. Fulcomer, PhD
Phone: 609/984-6702
Fax: 609/984-7633

Education

New Jersey State Department of Education
Public Information Office
225 East State Street, CN 500
Trenton, NJ 08625-0500
Phone: 609/292-4041
Fax: 609/984-6756

Local Information

The Press of Atlantic City
1000 W. Washington Avenue
Pleasantville, NJ 08232
Kelly Hasson, Promotion and Research Supervisor
Phone: 609/272-7000
Fax: 609/272-7059

NEW MEXICO

State Data Center

University of New Mexico
Bureau of Business and Economic Research
1920 Lomas, NE
Albuquerque, NM 87131-6021
Kevin Kargacin
Phone: 505/277-6626
Fax: 505/277-7066
E-mail: kargacin@unm.edu

Labor

New Mexico Department of Labor
401 Broadway Boulevard, NE
P.O. Box 1928
Albuquerque, NM 87103
Larry Blackwell, Chief, Economic Research and Analysis Bureau
Phone: 505/841-8645

Health

Bureau of Vital Records and Health Statistics

P.O. Box 26110
Santa Fe, NM 87505
Betty Hileman
Phone: 505/827-2342

Education

New Mexico State Department of Education
Education Building
Santa Fe, NM 87501-2786
Carroll (Bud) L. Hall
Phone: 505/827-6524
Fax: 505/827-6696

NEW YORK

State Data Center

Department of Economic Development
Division of Policy and Research
1 Commerce Plaza
99 Washington Avenue, Room 905
Albany, NY 12245
Phone: 518/474-1141
Fax: 518/473-9748
E-mail: roberts355@aol.com

Labor

New York Department of Labor
State Campus, Building 12, Room 400
Albany, NY 12240-0020
Thomas A. Rodick, Director, Division of
Research and Statistics
Phone: 518/457-6181

Health

New York State Department of Health
Concourse
Empire State Plaza, Room C-144
Albany, NY 12237-0044
Gene D. Therriault, Director, Bureau of
Biometrics
Phone: 518/474-3189
Fax: 518/486-1630
E-mail: gdt01@health.state.ny.us

Education

New York State Department of Education
Information Reporting and Technology
State Education Building Annex, Room 962
Albany, NY 12234
Phone: 518/474-7965

Local Information

**Gannett Rochester Newspapers
(Democrat and Chronicle/Times-Union)**
55 Exchange Boulevard
Rochester, NY 14614-2001
Susan Lindsay, or Jay Peak
Phone: 716/258-2740
Fax: 716/258-2742

NEW YORK CITY

Health

New York City Department of Health
Division of Vital Records
125 Worth Street
New York, NY 10013
Phone: 212/788-4520

NORTH CAROLINA

State Data Center

North Carolina Office of State Planning
116 West Jones Street
Raleigh, NC 27603-8003
Francine Stephenson
Phone: 919/733-3270
Fax: 919/733-5679
E-mail: francine@cgia.state.nc.us

Labor

**Employment Security Commission of
North Carolina**
P.O. Box 25903
Raleigh, NC 27611
Tim Parker
Phone: 919/733-2936
Fax: 919/733-8662
E-mail: parker.tim@esc.state.nc.us

Health

North Carolina Vital Records
P.O. Box 29537
Raleigh, NC 27626-0537
A. Torrey McLean, State Registrar
Phone: 919/733-3000
Fax: 919/733-1511

Education

North Carolina Public Schools
301 N. Wilmington Street

Raleigh, NC 27601-2825
Engin Konanc, Chief Consultant, Statistical
Research
Phone: 919/715-1609
Fax: 919/715-1611
E-mail: ekonanc@dpi1.dpi.nov.gov

NORTH DAKOTA

State Data Center

North Dakota State University
Department of Agricultural Economics
Morrill Hall, Room 217, P.O. Box 5636
Fargo, ND 58105
Richard Rathge
Phone: 701/231-8621
Fax: 701/231-7400
E-mail: rathge@plains.nodak.edu

Labor

**Job Service North Dakota/Labor Market
Advisor**
P.O. Box 5507
Bismarck, ND 58506-5507
Tom Pederson, Director of Research and
Statistics
Phone: 701/328-2868

Health

**Division of Vital Records, North Dakota
Department of Health**
State Capitol, 600 East Boulevard Avenue
Bismarck, ND 58505-0200
Beverly Wittman, Director
Phone: 701/328-2360
Fax: 701/328-4727

Education

**North Dakota Department of Public
Instruction**
600 East Boulevard Avenue
Bismarck, ND 58505
Addy Schmaltz, Fiscal Management
Phone: 701/328-2260

OHIO

State Data Center

Ohio Department of Development
Office of Strategic Research
P.O. Box 1001, 77 High Street, 27th Floor

Columbus, OH 43266-0101
Barry Bennett
Phone: 614/466-2115
Fax: 614/644-5167
E-mail: bbennett@odod.ohio.gov

Labor

Ohio Bureau of Employment Services
145 South Front Street
Columbus, OH 43215
Keith Ewald, Director, Labor Market
Information Division
Phone: 614/752-9494

Health

Ohio Department of Health
Vital Statistics
P.O. Box 15098
Columbus, OH 43215-0098
Phone: 614/466-2531

Education

Ohio State Department of Education
Information Management Services
2151 Carmack Road
Columbus, OH 43221-3595
Phone: 614/466-7000

Local Information

The Cincinnati Enquirer
312 Elm Street
Cincinnati, OH 45202
Gerald T. Silvers, Vice President/Market
Development
Phone: 513/721-2700
Fax: 513/768-8150

OKLAHOMA

State Data Center

Oklahoma State Data Center
Oklahoma Department of Commerce
P.O. Box 26980
Oklahoma City, OK 73126-0980
Jeff Wallace
Phone: 405/841-5184
Fax: 405/841-5199
E-mail: jeff_wallace.odoc@notes.com-
puserve.com

Labor

Oklahoma Employment Security Commission
2401 North Lincoln Blvd., P.O. Box 52003
Oklahoma City, OK 73152-2003
Lisa Schuman
Phone: 405/557-7261
Fax: 405/525-0139

Health

Oklahoma State Department of Health
Vital Records Sections
1000 NE 10th Street, P.O. Box 53551
Oklahoma City, OK 73152
Phone: 405/271-4040

Education

Oklahoma State Department of Education
Data Research Services
2500 North Lincoln
Oklahoma City, OK 73105
Phone: 405/521-3354

Local Information

The Daily Oklahoman
9000 North Broadway
Oklahoma City, OK 73114
Loni Shropshire, Marketing Research Manager
Phone: 405/475-3644
Fax: 405/475-3817

OREGON

State Data Center

School of Urban and Public Affairs, Portland State University
Center for Population Research and Census
P.O. Box 751
Portland, OR 97207-0751
George Hough
Phone: 503/725-5159; 800/547-8887
Fax: 503/725-5199
E-mail: george@upa.pdx.edu

Labor

Oregon Employment Department
Research, Tax and Analysis
875 Union Street, NE
Salem, OR 97311
Phone: 503/378-3220

Health

Center for Health Statistics
P.O. Box 14050
Portland, OR 97214-0050
Joyce Grant-Worley, Supervising Research Analyst
Phone: 503/731-4354
Fax: 503/731-4084

Education

Oregon State Department of Education
Data Information Services
255 Capitol Street, NE
Salem, OR 97310-0203
Phone: 503/378-3569

PENNSYLVANIA

State Data Center

Pennsylvania State Data Center
Institute of State and Regional Affairs, Penn State Harrisburg, 777 W. Harrisburg Pike
Middletown, PA 17057-4898
Diane Shoop, Assistant Director
Phone: 717/948-6336
Fax: 717/948-6306
E-mail: des102@psuvm.psu.edu

Labor

Bureau of Research and Statistics
Department of Labor and Industry
300 Capitol Associates Building
Harrisburg, PA 17120-0034
Phone: 717/787-6466

Health

Pennsylvania State Department of Health
Division of Vital Records
Health and Welfare Building, Room 516
Harrisburg, PA 17108
Phone: 717/772-3481

Education

Pennsylvania State Department of Education
Division of Data Services
333 Market Street, 14th Floor
Harrisburg, PA 17126-0333
Phone: 717/787-2644

Local Information

The Morning Call
101 N. 6th Street
Allentown, PA 18101
Linda Pearse, Research Supervisor
Phone: 610/820-6729
Fax: 610/820-6617

PUERTO RICO

State Data Center

Junta de Planificacion
Centro Gubernamental Minillas
P.O. Box 41119
San Juan, PR 00940-1119
Sra. Irmgard Gonzalez Segarra
Phone: 809/728-4430
Fax: 809/268-0506

Labor

**Puerto Rico Department of Labor -
Research and Statistics**
Munoz Rivera Avenue, #505
San Juan (H.R.), PR 00918
Phone: 809/754-5385
Fax: 809/751-7934

Health

**Department of Health - Demographic
Registry**
P.O. Box 11854, Fernandez Juncos Station
San Juan, PR 00910
Jose A. Torrado, State Registrar
Phone: 809/767-9120
Fax: 809/751-5003

Education

Department of Education
P.O. Box 190759
San Juan, PR 00919-0759
Aida I. Rodriguez Roig, Assistant Secretary
Area for Planning and Educational
Development
Phone: 809/759-2000 ext. 3291, 3290
Fax: 809/751-2874

RHODE ISLAND

State Data Center

Rhode Island Department of

Administration

Office of Municipal Affairs
One Capitol Hill
Providence, RI 02903-5873
Paul Egan
Phone: 401/277-6493
Fax: 401/277-3809

Labor

**Rhode Island Department of Employment
and Training**
101 Friendship Street
Providence, RI 02903
Robert Langlais, Assistant Director, LMI
Phone: 401/277-3730
Fax: 401/277-2731

Health

Rhode Island State Department of Health
Health Statistics
407 Cannon Building, 3 Capitol Hill
Providence, RI 02908-5097
Phone: 401/277-2550

Education

**Rhode Island Department of Elementary
and Secondary Education**
22 Hayes Street
Providence, RI 02908
Peter McWalters, Commissioner
Phone: 401/277-4600 ext. 2001
Fax: 401/277-6178

Education

**Rhode Island Department of Higher
Education**
301 Promenade Street
Providence, RI 02908
Phone: 401/277-6560

SOUTH CAROLINA

State Data Center

**South Carolina Budget and Control
Board**
Division of Research and Statistical Services
Rembert Dennis Building, Room 425
Columbia, SC 29201
Mike MacFarlane
Phone: 803/734-3780
Fax: 803/734-3619

Labor

South Carolina Employment Security Commission
P.O. Box 995
Columbia, SC 29202
David L. Laird, Director, Labor Market Information
Phone: 803/737-2660

Health

Biostatistics/Office of Vital Records and Public Health Statistics
2600 Bull Street
Columbia, SC 29201
Mary Hill Glover, Data Management and Research Analysis
Phone: 803/734-4860
Fax: 803/734-5131

Education

South Carolina State Department of Education
Research
Rutledge Building, 1429 Senate Street
Columbia, SC 29201
Phone: 803/734-8262

SOUTH DAKOTA

State Data Center

School of Business, University of South Dakota
Business Research Bureau
414 East Clark
Vermillion, SD 57069
DeVee Dykstra
Phone: 605/677-5287
Fax: 605/677-5427

Labor

South Dakota Department of Labor
420 South Roosevelt, P.O. Box 4730
Aberdeen, SD 57402-4730
Phillip George, Director, Labor Market Information Center
Phone: 605/626-2314

Health

South Dakota Department of Health
Statistics and Research
445 East Capitol Avenue

Pierre, SD 57501-3185
Phone: 605/773-3361
Fax: 605/773-5683

Education

Department of Education and Cultural Affairs
700 Governors Drive
Pierre, SD 57501
John Cummings, Director, Centralized Data Collection
Phone: 605/773-4638
Fax: 605/773-6139
E-mail: johnc@deca.state.sd.us

TENNESSEE

State Data Center

Tennessee State Planning Office
John Sevier State Building
500 Charlotte, Suite 307
Nashville, TN 37243-0001
Charles Brown
Phone: 615/741-1676
Fax: 615/532-7918

Labor

Tennessee State Dept. of Employment Security
500 James Robertson Parkway, 11th Fl.
Nashville, TN 37245-1000
Joe Cummings, Director, Research and Statistics Division
Phone: 615/741-2284

Health

Tennessee State Department of Health
Tennessee Tower, Health Statistics and Information
312 8th Avenue, N, 8th Floor
Nashville, TN 37247
Phone: 615/741-1954

Education

Tennessee Department of Education
Office of Education and Technology
Gateway Plaza Building, 7th Floor
710 James Roberston Parkway
Nashville, TN 37243-0381
Phone: 615/741-0728

TEXAS

State Data Center

Texas A&M University System
Department of Rural Sociology
Special Services Building
College Station, TX 77843-2125
Steve Murdock
Phone: 409/845-5115 or 5332
Fax: 409/845-8529

Labor

Texas Employment Commission
15th and Congress Avenue, Room 208T
Austin, TX 78778
Mark Hughes, Director, Economic Research
and Analysis
Phone: 512/463-2616

Health

Texas State Department of Health
Bureau of Vital Statistics
P.O. Box 12040
Austin, TX 78711-2040
Phone: 512/458-7383

Education

Texas Education Agency
Division of Communications and Public
Information
1701 N. Congress Avenue, Room 2-180
Austin, TX 78701
Phone: 512/463-9000

UTAH

State Data Center

Utah Office of Planning and Budget
Room 116, State Capitol Building
Salt Lake City, UT 84114
Brenda Weaver
Phone: 801/538-1036
Fax: 801/538-1547
E-mail: bweaver@email.ut.us

Labor

Utah Labor Market Report
P.O. Box 45249
Salt Lake City, UT 84145-0249
Lecia Parks Langston
Phone: 801/536-7810

Fax: 801/536-7869
E-mail: eslmia.llangst@email.state.ut.us

Health

Utah Department of Health/Bureau of Vital Records
288 North 1460 West
Salt Lake City, UT 84114-2855
John E. Brockert, Director
Phone: 801/538-6186
Fax: 801/538-7012

Education

Utah State Department of Education
School of Finance and Statistics
250 East, 500 South
Salt Lake City, UT 84111
Deanna Timothy
Phone: 801/538-7674

VERMONT

State Data Center

Vermont Department of Libraries
109 State Street
Montpelier, VT 05609-0601
Sybil McShane
Phone: 802/828-3261
Fax: 802/828-2199

Labor

Vermont Department of Employment and Training
5 Green Mountain Drive, P.O. Box 488
Montpelier, VT 05601
Mike Griffin, Chief, Research and Analysis
Phone: 802/828-4153
Fax: 802/828-4050

Health

Vermont State Department of Health
Vital Records
P.O. Box 70, 108 Cherry Street
Burlington, VT 05402
Phone: 802/863-7275

Education

Vermont Department of Education
School Finance Operations Workgroup
Leader
120 State Street
Montpelier, VT 05620

Paul Rousseau
Phone: 802/828-3151
Fax: 802/828-3140

VIRGIN ISLANDS

State Data Center

University of the Virgin Islands, Eastern Caribbean Center
N. 2 John Brewer's Bay, Charlotte Amalie
St. Thomas, VI 00802
Frank Mills
Phone: 809/693-1027
Fax: 809/693-1025

Labor

Virgin Islands Department of Labor/Labor Market Review
P.O. Box 303359
St. Thomas, VI 00803-3359
David J. Barber, Chief, Bureau of Labor Statistics
Phone: 809/776-3700 ext. 2034
Fax: 809/774-5908

Health

Department of Health
Charles Harwood Memorial Complex, 3500 Richmond
Christiansted, St. Croix, VI 00820-4370
Noreen Michael, PhD, Director, Health Statistics and Acting Director, Health Planning
Phone: 809/773-4050
Fax: 809/773-0850

VIRGINIA

State Data Center

Virginia Employment Commission
703 East Main Street
Richmond, VA 23219
Dan Jones
Phone: 804/786-8308
Fax: 804/786-7844

Labor

Virginia Employment Commission
P.O. Box 1358
Richmond, VA 23211
Dolores A. Esser, Director, Economic

Information Services
Phone: 804/786-7496
Fax: 804/786-7844

Health

Virginia State Department of Health
Health Commissioner's Office
Main Street Station, Room 214, P.O. Box 2448
Richmond, VA 23219
Phone: 804/786-3561

Education

Virginia Department of Education
101 N. 14th Street, James Monroe Building, 21th Floor
Richmond, VA 23219
Kay Brown, Specialist, Marketing Education
Phone: 804/225-2057
Fax: 804/371-2456

WASHINGTON

State Data Center

Office of Financial Management
Forecasting Division
450 Insurance Building, Box 43113
Olympia, WA 98504-3113
David Lamphere
Phone: 206/586-2504
Fax: 206/664-8941
E-mail: david@ofm.wa.gov

Labor

ESD Labor Market and Economic Analysis Branch
P.O. Box 9046
Olympia, WA 98507-9046
Ivars Graudins, Research Supervisor
Phone: 360/438-4800
Fax: 360/438-4846
E-mail: Klausies@wln.com

Health

Washington State Department of Health
Center for Health Statistics
P.O. Box 47814
Olympia, WA 98504-7814
Katrina Wynjoop Simmons
Phone: 360/586-0408

Education

State Superintendent of Public Instruction
Information Services
P.O. Box 47200
Olympia, WA 98504-7200
Phone: 360/753-1700

WEST VIRGINIA

State Data Center

West Virginia Development Office
Capitol Complex, Building 6, Room 553
Charleston, WV 25305
Mary C. Harless, Research and Strategic
Planning Division
Phone: 304/558-4010
Fax: 304/558-3248

Labor

West Virginia Economic Summary, WV Bureau of Employment Programs
Office of Labor and Economic Research
112 California Avenue
Charleston, WV 25305-0112
Rita Wiseman
Phone: 304/558-2660
Fax: 304/558-0301

Health

West Virginia Health Statistics Center
1900 Washington Street, E
Charleston, WV 25305
Eugenia Thoenen
Phone: 304/558-9100
Fax: 304/558-1553

Education

West Virginia State Department of Education
Office of School Finance - Statistics
State Capitol Complex, Room B215,
Building 6
Charleston, WV 25305
Sharon Lewis
Phone: 304/558-6300

WISCONSIN

State Data Center

Wisconsin Department of Administration
Demographic Services Center
101 E. Wilson Street, 6th Floor
P.O. Box 7868
Madison, WI 53707-7868
Robert Naylor
Phone: 608/266-1927
Fax: 608/267-6931

Labor

Wisconsin Department of Industry, Labor and Human Relations
Employment and Training Library
P. O. Box 7944
Madison, WI 53707-7944
Janet Pugh
Phone: 608/266-2832
Fax: 606/266-5887
E-mail: pughja@mail.state.wi.us

Health

Wisconsin State Department of Health
Center for Health Statistics and Vital
Records
1 West Wilson Street, Room 165
P.O. Box 309
Madison, WI 53701
Phone: 608/266-1372

Education

Wisconsin Center for Educational Statistics
State Office of Public Instruction
P.O. Box 7841
Madison, WI 53707
Phone: 608/266-1746

Local Information

Milwaukee Journal Sentinel
333 West State Street
Milwaukee, WI 53203
Paul Dyer, Research Manager
Phone: 414/224-2115
Fax: 414/224-7690

WYOMING

State Data Center

Wyoming Economic Analysis Division
Department of Administration and
Information
Emerson Building, Room 327E
Cheyenne, WY 82002-0060
Wenlin Liu
Phone: 307/777-7504
Fax: 307/777-6725

Labor

Wyoming Department of Employment
Division of Administration, P.O. Box 2760
Casper, WY 82602
Tom Gallagher, Manager, Research and
Planning
Phone: 307/235-3200

Health

**Wyoming Department of Health, Vital
Records Services**
Hathaway Building
Cheyenne, WY 82002
Lucinda McCaffrey, Deputy State Registrar
Phone: 307/777-7591

Education

Wyoming State Department of Education
Accounting Data and School Finance Unit
Hathaway Building, 2nd Floor,
2300 Capitol Avenue
Cheyenne, WY 82002
Shirley Winter
Phone: 307/777-7623

Demographic Dictionary

Compiled by Jacqueline Lurie

adolescent: An individual in the stage of life between puberty and maturity.

adult: An individual older than a certain age—usually 18—or an individual who has reached the legal age of majority. The age marking adulthood varies widely among surveys.

affluent market: Usually households with incomes of at least $60,000. Definitions may vary from study to study.

African American: *See* black.

aggregation: A concept of market segmentation that assumes all consumers are alike. Retailers that adhere to this concept focus on the broadest possible number of buyers, using mass advertising, mass distribution, and the theme of low price.

aging of the population: A gradual increase in the median age of a population that results from declining fertility rates and/or increasing life expectancy.

agriculture: The production of crops and raising of livestock.

Alaskan Native or American Indian: A person having origins in any of the original peoples of North America, and who maintains cultural identification through tribal affiliations or community recognition.

ancestry: National origin or culture with which a person identifies, such as Danish or Armenian. Persons may have a single or multiple (mixed) ancestry.

Asian or Pacific Islander: One of four racial groups defined by the Office of Management and Budget for the purposes of federal data collection. Members of this group have origins in any of the original peoples of the Far East, Southeast Asia, the Indian subcontinent, or the Pacific Islands.

attitude: A positive or negative feeling about an object that influences motivational and behavioral tendencies.

audience: The individuals or households exposed to a message.

baby boom: The large generation of Americans born between 1946 and 1964.

baby boomlet: The generation of American children born primarily to the baby boomers between 1977 and 1994. Also called echo boom.

baby bust: The small generation of Americans born between 1965 and 1976. Also called Generation X.

belief: The emotionally neutral pattern of meanings an individual constructs to organize some aspect of the world.

benchmark: An area or group with which a smaller or narrower group is compared. For example, the U.S. may be used as the benchmark for an individual state.

birth rate: Annual number of births per 1,000 population. *See also* fertility rate.

black: One of four racial groups as defined by the Office of Management and Budget for the purposes of federal data collection. Members of this group have origins in any of the black racial groups of Africa. Also called African American.

block: A census administrative area, generally equivalent to a city block.

block group: A group of blocks that has an average population of between 1,000 and 1,200. More data are available for block groups than for blocks.

blue-collar: A category of occupations that includes precision production/craft/repair, and operator/fabricator/laborer.

boomerangers: Young adults who, in a short period of time, sample many of the career, marriage, and living options available to them.

borough: The largest administrative district of local government in the state of Alaska. The Census Bureau treats Alaska's boroughs like the counties of other states. Also a division of New York City government.

boundary: The borders around a government, geographic, or market area.

boundary file: Geographic information including streets, blocks, and census tracts, described in a computer file.

buyer's market: An economic climate in which the buyer's demands are more likely to be met than the seller's.

CAPI: Computer-assisted personal interviewing.

career: The general nature of an individual's employment experiences.

carrying capacity: The maximum population that can be sustained by a given ecosystem.

CATI: Computer-assisted telephone interviewing.

CD-ROM (Compact Disk with Read-Only Memory): A technique of data storage and delivery introduced in the 1980s.

census: The official collection of information about the demographic, social, and economic situation of all people residing in a specific area at a certain time. In the U.S., a census is conducted every ten years.

census area: A geographic study area whose boundaries are defined by the Census Bureau; for example, MSAs, census tracts, block groups, and enumeration districts.

census division: One of the nine smaller census statistical areas. Census divisions are smaller than census regions. The nine census divisions and the states they include are:

1. Pacific: Alaska, California, Hawaii, Oregon, Washington

2. Mountain: Arizona, Colorado, Idaho, Montana, Nevada, New Mexico, Utah, and Wyoming

3. West North Central: Iowa, Kansas, Minnesota, Missouri, Nebraska, North Dakota, and South Dakota

4. East North Central: Illinois, Indiana, Michigan, Ohio, and Wisconsin

5. West South Central: Arkansas, Louisiana, Oklahoma, and Texas

6. East South Central: Alabama, Kentucky, Mississippi, and Tennessee

7. South Atlantic: Delaware, District of Columbia, Florida, Georgia, Maryland, North Carolina, South Carolina, Virginia, and West Virginia

8. Middle Atlantic: New Jersey, New York, and Pennsylvania

9. New England: Connecticut, Maine, Massachusetts, New Hampshire, Rhode Island, and Vermont.

census region: One of the four larger census statistical areas. The four census regions and the states they include are:

1. West: Alaska, Arizona, California, Colorado, Hawaii, Idaho, Montana, Nevada, New Mexico, Oregon, Utah, Washington, and Wyoming

2. Midwest: Illinois, Indiana, Iowa, Kansas, Michigan, Minnesota, Missouri, Nebraska, North Dakota, Ohio, South Dakota, and Wisconsin

3. South: Alabama, Arkansas, Delaware, Florida, District of Columbia, Georgia, Kentucky, Louisiana, Maryland, Mississippi, North Carolina, Oklahoma, South Carolina, Tennessee, Texas, Virginia, and West Virginia

4. Northeast: Connecticut, Maine, Massachusetts, New Hampshire, New Jersey, New York, Pennsylvania, Rhode Island, and Vermont.

Also called region.

census statistical area: One of the four census regions or nine census divisions. Also a group of census county divisions in states where minor civil division boundaries are not satisfactory for statistical purposes, census designated places, urbanized areas, census tracts and subdivisions of counties averaging about 4,000 people, census blocks, enumeration districts, and block groups.

census tract: A small, relatively permanent area into which metropolitan and certain other areas are divided for the purpose of providing statistics for small areas. When census tracts are established, they are designed to be homogeneous with respect to population characteristics, economic status, and living conditions. Tracts generally have between 2,500 and 8,000 residents.

census undercount: The number of Americans who do not respond to or otherwise are not included in the decennial census.

central city: The largest city in an MSA and other cities of central character to an MSA.

centroid: Geographic points marking the approximate centers of population of the 260,000 block groups and enumeration districts in the U.S.

childbearing years: The age range during which women are reproductive, which in the U.S. is generally assumed to be ages 15 to 44.

children: Usually refers to people under age 18. Sometimes refers to offspring of any age. In household surveys, may refer to own children or any related children of householders, such as grandchildren.

city: A division of municipal government.

cluster: A category assigned to a neighborhood based on the assumption that the households share certain demographic, social, and economic characteristics.

cluster system: In marketing, the categorization of neighborhoods using such characteristics as income, age, types of housing, education, and occupation. Cluster analysis is based on the assumption that averages describe the households in a neighborhood. Also called geodemographic segmentation system.

CMSA: *See* Consolidated Metropolitan Statistical Area.

cohabitation: The act of living together, frequently refers to unmarried couples.

cohort: A group of people who experience the same significant demographic event such as birth or marriage during a specific time period, usually a year, and can thus be identified as a group in subsequent analysis.

cohort analysis: Observation of a cohort's demographic behavior through life or through many periods. An example would be the examination of the fertility rate of the cohort born in a particular time period throughout its childbearing years. Rates derived from cohort analysis are cohort measures.

cohort measures: *See* cohort analysis.

computer mapping: The use of computer software to analyze information in map form.

Congressional district: A subdivision of a state, created solely for the purpose of determining Congressional representation. The Census Bureau does not treat Congressional districts as governmental divisions.

consensual union: An extended period of cohabitation by an unmarried couple.

Consolidated Metropolitan Statistical Area (CMSA): Two or more adjacent primary metropolitan statistical areas, such as Miami-Fort Lauderdale.

consumer: A person who buys or uses a specific product or service.

consumer expenditure: The money consumers spend on goods and services.

Consumer Expenditure Survey (CE): Data about the expenditures of consumer units gathered in an ongoing survey by the Bureau of Labor Statistics.

consumer information system: A database that links information about consumer demographics, lifestyles, media preferences, and purchase behaviors. By linking this information together, companies can build a complete picture of consumers to analyze products, define markets, target advertising, and plan marketing strategies.

Consumer Price Index (CPI): A comparison of the current cost of purchasing a fixed set of goods and services with the cost of purchasing the same set in a previous time period.

consumer unit: The related members of a particular household, a financially independent person living alone or as a roomer or sharing a houshold with others, or two or more persons living together who pool their incomes to make joint purchases, as defined by the Consumer Expenditure Survey.

consumption: The actual use of a product or service to satisfy a want or need of its ultimate consumer.

cost of living: The money required to buy the products and services necessary to maintain a particular standard of living.

county: The largest administrative unit of local government. A.C. Nielsen has labeled counties A, B, C, or D according to population size, in order of decreasing population size. They are: (A) counties with the 25 largest U.S. cities or their metropolitan areas; (B) counties in other major urban or suburban areas; (C) and (D) counties in rural areas.

CPI: *See* Consumer Price Index.

CPS: *See* Current Population Survey.

culture: The totality of learned values and behaviors shared by a society, including shared beliefs, norms, and mores.

Current Population Survey (CPS): A Census Bureau survey conducted for the Bureau of Labor Statistics to monitor employment. Each month, interviewers ask people in about 60,000 households about their employment-related activities during the preceding week. The results provide up-to-date estimates of population characteristics.

customer: Someone who has purchased or is likely to purchase a product or service.

database: A collection of information on the attributes of units of analysis, such as patients or customers.

database marketing: A technique whereby customer databases are enhanced with demographic and other information for the purpose of improving direct-marketing efforts.

daytime population: An area's population during the daytime, which usually differs from the residential population. Daytime-oriented businesses need to know where a given population is during the day in order to locate or expand most effectively.

decennial census: The census conducted by the Census Bureau every ten years in those years ending in "0."

demographics: *See* demography.

demography: A social science concerned with the size, distribution, structure, and change of populations. Also called demographics.

Designated Marketing Area (DMA): A television market as defined by A.C. Nielsen.

desktop marketing system: A personal computer system that combines multiple databases with software for use in market analysis and other tasks.

diary panel: A survey in which respondents keep a diary of what they watch, listen to, do, or buy over a period of time.

direct marketing: A technique in which a sale is completed without face-to-face contact, as by telephone or mail.

discretionary income: Money left over after taxes, housing, food, and other necessities have been paid for. A measure of the market for luxury goods.

disposable income: *See* disposable personal income.

disposable personal income (DPI): The money remaining after an individual's or household's taxes have been paid. Also called disposable income, Effective Buying Income.

divorce: The legal dissolution of a marriage.

divorce rate: The number of divorces per 1,000 population at a given point in time.

DMA: *See* Designated Marketing Area.

downscale: Low-income individuals or households.

dual earners: The members of a married or cohabitating couple in which both partners are employed.

dwelling: The place where a household resides. Also called residence.

earned income: Income from work or services performed; income from investments, rent, or benefits is not included.

echo boom: *See* baby boomlet.

ED: *See* Enumeration District.

education: Knowledge gained through formal schooling.

educational attainment: A measure of the number of years of school completed or degrees obtained, typically presented for the population aged 25 and older.

Effective Buying Income (EBI): *See* disposable personal income.

elderly: The population aged 65 and older. *See also* mature market.

emigration: The process of leaving one country to live in another.

employed: Currently working as a paid employee in a business, profession, or on a farm, or temporarily absent from such a job or business. Does not include unpaid family workers, such as on a farm.

empty nesters: A married couple typically aged 45 to 64 with no children living in their household.

Enumeration District (ED): A census area with an average of 500 inhabitants.

environmental analysis: The evaluation of the political, social, and economic environments in which a company operates to identify trends and how they will affect the company.

environmental monitoring: The activities used to gather data about changes in the political, social, and economic environments that will affect the markets for a company's products or services. Also called environmental scanning.

environmental scanning: *See* environmental monitoring.

estimate: An inference about the size of a population group or demographic characteristic, based on a sample or other statistical method.

ethnicity: The cultural characteristics, such as language, that a person shares with a population. Often refers to those of Hispanic origin.

fad: A short-lived trend in attitude or behavior.

family: A group of two or more persons related by birth, marriage, or adoption who reside together.

family group: Two or more persons related by birth, marriage, or adoption who reside together. *See also* subfamily.

family household: A household consisting of a householder and at least one other member related to the householder by blood, marriage, or adoption. In 1995, 70 percent of U.S. households were family households.

family life cycle: The pattern of changes a family goes through across time that affect their needs, values, and behaviors.

fecundity: The physiological ability of a man or woman to reproduce.

female-headed household: A household, which may or may not be a family household, in which the householder is a female with no spouse present.

fertility: Actual reproduction by an individual, couple, group, or population.

fertility rate: The number of live births per 1,000 women aged 15 to 44 in a given year. *See also* birth rate, total fertility rate.

focus group: A qualitative market research method in which a topic is discussed by a group of people led by a trained moderator.

forecast: A projection believed to be likely to occur.

fragmentation: The tendency of markets to diverge into distinct consumer subgroups with similar needs or behaviors.

general fertility rate: *See* fertility rate.

generation: People born within a specific time period. *See also* cohort.

Generation X: *See* baby bust.

geocoding: The process whereby addresses are segmented by county, MSA, postal route, or other criteria in order to compare them with information about the demographics and psychographics of those geographies. Geocoding is integral to demographically enhanced mailing lists and cluster analysis. Also called geographic encoding.

geodemographic segmentation system: *See* cluster system.

geographic encoding: *See* cluster system.

geographic information system (GIS): A type of computer software that identifies relationships between database information and geographic data, and displays the results in map form.

geography: The physical characteristics of a study area. There are many types of geographic divisions, including postal areas, political areas, census areas, telephone areas, and marketing areas.

geometric study area: A market site in the shape of a concentric circle or polygon. Private data companies use the data available from standard political and census geography to approximate the data for geometric study areas.

GIS: *See* geographic information system.

good: *See* product.

gross income: The total amount of money available to an individual or other unit before taxes are paid and necessities purchased.

group quarters population: Residents of institutional organizations who dwell in facilities such as military barracks, college dormitories, prisons, long-term-care hospitals, boarding houses, and nursing homes.

head of household: *See* householder.

Hispanic: Of Spanish or Latin origin. Hispanic is an ethnic group; as currently defined, its members may be of any race.

homemaker: The individual in a household with primary responsibility for management of the dwelling. A homemaker may or may not be a householder.

homeowner: An individual who owns a housing unit, even one that is not fully paid for.

household: All the persons who occupy a housing unit.

householder: The first person whose name is listed as the homeowner or renter; called the head of household or head of family before the 1980 census. Also called head of family, head of household, and reference person.

housing unit: A house, apartment, group of rooms, or single room occupied as separate living quarters.

illegal alien: A foreigner who is in a country illegally due to lack of proper documentation or violation of the terms of legal admission. Also called undocumented alien.

immigration: Movement of people from one country to another country.

income: As defined by the Census Bureau, money received from any of the following sources: wages or salary; farm or nonfarm self-employment; interest; dividend or rental properties; Social Security; public assistance; or any other source, including unemployment compensation, veterans' payment, pensions, and alimony.

industry: A sector of employment. There are three major types of industry: agriculture; goods-producing, which includes construction, manufacturing, and mining; and service-producing, which includes services, wholesale and retail trade, transportation and public utilities, financial services, insurance, real estate, and public administration.

infertility: The inability of a couple to conceive after one year or more of intercourse without contraception.

information-based economy: An economic system in which a dominant form of employment and a significant portion of wealth created is through the production, distribution, and use of information. In the 1990s, the U.S. is undergoing the transition from a service-based to an information-based economy.

labor force: All civilians who are working or actively looking for work, plus members of the armed forces stationed in the U.S.

labor force participation rate: The ratio of any segment of the population working or looking for work to the total population in that segment.

leisure: All activities engaged in that are not work, sleep, or other things people have to do. The activities people pursue when they are free from the demands of work and other duties.

life cycle: A series of stages through which an individual, group, culture, product, or organization passes during its lifetime.

life expectancy: The average number of expected years of life that remain at a given age, usually measured from birth.

life span: The maximum attainable age for a human being under optimal conditions.

life stage: The point of life an individual is in, such as married with children or empty nest.

lifestyle: The way in which an individual goes about his daily life. Lifestyle choices include an individual's activities, interests, and opinions.

long-form questionnaire: The detailed decennial census questionnaire answered by a sample (one in seven U.S. households in 1990) of the population. Data from this form are not available for the smallest geographic areas in order to protect the anonymity of individual respondents.

longitudinal survey: A long-term survey based on repeated analysis of the same sample.

male-headed household: A household, which may or may not be a family household, where the householder is a male with no spouse present.

manufacture: To produce goods from raw materials.

manufacturing-based economy: An economic system in which a dominant form of employment and a significant portion of wealth created is through the production, distribution, and consumption of manufactured goods. In the 1800s, the U.S. underwent the transition from agriculture-based to a manufacturing-based economy.

marital status: A measure of the occurrence of marriage in the population, typically for people aged 15 and older. An individual may fall into one of four categories: never-married (or single); married, which includes those who are separated and with a spouse absent for other reasons; divorced; or widowed.

market: The geographic area in which products or services are sold. Markets are also classified by the type of customers served, as in the teen market; and the types of products offered, as in the music market.

marketing: The aggregate of functions involved in moving goods and services from producer to consumer. Those functions include pricing, promotion, advertising, and distribution.

market research: The scientific study of the wants and needs of actual or potential consumers in relation to actual or proposed products or services.

marketing research: The process of designating, collecting, and analyzing data about consumers in a given market for the purpose of generating or improving marketing efforts.

market segmentation: The process of dividing customer markets into distinct subgroups, each consisting of customers with similar needs or behaviors. Marketing strategies can then be tailored to appeal to each individual market segment. Also called segmentation.

marriage: The legal union of two partners.

marriage rate: The number of marriages per 1,000 population in a given period of time.

married-couple household: A household headed by a married man or woman whose spouse is also present. By definition, all married-couple households are family households. They may or may not have children of any age living with them. In 1995, 54 percent of U.S. households were headed by married couples.

married with children: Typically refers to married couples with children under age 18 living in their household.

married without children: Typically refers to married couples without children under age 18 living in their household. May include those with adult children, present or absent.

mass market: An undifferentiated market that consists of the population in general.

mass marketing: The direction of sales efforts for a product or service to as many customers as possible rather than to a specific target market.

mature market: Usually the population aged 50 and older or 55 and older. *See also* elderly.

MCD: *See* minor civil division.

mean: An average calculated by dividing the total number of incidences by the number of individuals exhibiting the characteristic.

media: All vehicles, such as television, radio, magazines, newspapers, and direct mail, that convey advertising messages.

media marketing area: A geographic study area, like a DMA, whose boundaries are defined by the reach of media consumed by its residents.

median: The middle value that divides a distribution into two equal parts, one-half above the median and one-half below.

merchandising: Typically refers to promotion of a product or service at the point of purchase, such as display advertising, but can also mean sales promotion as a comprehensive function, including market research, new-product development, and effective advertising and selling.

metropolitan area: A large concentration of population consisting of a central city with a population of at least 50,000 and the surrounding suburbs and cities that are economically and socially linked to the central city. A metropolitan area has a minimum total population of 100,000. In 1990, 78 percent of the U.S. population lived in metropolitan areas. *See also* Metropolitan Statistical Area, Consolidated Metropolitan Statistical Area, Primary Metropolitan Statistical Area, Standard Metropolitan Statistical Area, and New England County Metropolitan Area.

Metropolitan Statistical Area (MSA): A free-standing metropolitan area surrounded by nonmetropolitan counties and not closely associated with any other metropolitan area. MSAs are grouped by population size as follows: (A) population of 1 million or more, (B) population of 250,000 to 1 million, (C) population of 100,000 to 250,000, (D) population of less than 100,000.

microdata: The census or survey records of individual respondents stripped of identifying information.

micromarketing: *See* target marketing.

middle class: Those with an income, standard of living, or lifestyle neither upscale nor downscale.

migration: Movement of persons from one part of a country to another part of the same country. *See also* mobility, immigration, emigration, net migration, outmigration.

minor civil division (MCD): A political and administrative subdivision of a county, generally a township.

minority: A racial, religious, ethnic, or political group that comprises a smaller portion of the population than the dominant group or groups.

mobility: Geographic movement involving a change of residence. *See also* migration.

modeling: The formulation of mathematically expressed variables to simulate a business or other decision environment.

morbidity: Illness.

more: A cultural standard of behavior that encourages conformity to societal moral values. The prohibition against bigamy in many societies is a more.

mortality: Death.

motivational research: The study of the reasons consumers make purchases or respond to products and advertising. It typically attempts to identify the desire, impulse, or stimulated need that drives a consumer to make a purchase.

MSA: *See* Metropolitan Statistical Area.

municipal government: The general-purpose government within a county that serves the population concentration of a defined area.

North American Industrial Classification System (NAICS): *See* Standard Industrial Classification.

natality: Birth.

natural decrease: The excess of deaths over births in a population.

natural increase: The excess of births over deaths in a population.

NECMA: *See* New England County Metropolitan Area.

net migration: The sum total of migration minus outmigration for a given area.

New England County Metropolitan Area (NECMA): A New England metropolitan area similar to an MSA.

niche market: A specialized segment of a market with specific demographic, geographic, or usage characteristics. Aerobic exercisers, for example, are a niche market for athletic shoes.

niche marketing: The direction of sales efforts for a product or service to a niche market.

noncash benefits: Government assistance, like food stamps and subsidized housing, that are not in cash form.

nonfamily household: A household made up of a householder living alone or with nonrelatives.

nonmetropolitan: Refers to the geographic area or population located outside a metropolitan area.

norm: A standard of behavior that specifies appropriate and inappropriate actions in a group.

occupation: Type of job. The Census Bureau defines six major groups of occupations: managerial and professional specialty; technical, sales, and administrative support; service; farming, forestry, and fishing; precision production, craft, and repair; and operators, fabricators, and laborers.

outmigration: Movement out of a given area to another area within the same country.

owner-occupied: A housing unit that is lived in by its owner or co-owner, even if it is not fully paid for.

panel survey: *See* longitudinal survey.

parent: Any person who is biologically or legally responsible for a child of any age.

parish: The largest administrative district of local government in the state of Louisiana. The U.S. Census Bureau treats parishes like counties in other states.

perception: An impression of reality based on an individual's attitudes, beliefs, needs, and situational factors. Perceptions influence behavior.

PMSA: *See* Primary Metropolitan Statistical Area.

point-of-purchase advertising:
Advertising within an establishment
where a product is sold to its ultimate
consumer. Such advertising usually is in
the form of window or interior displays.

political area: A geographic study
area with government-determined
boundaries, such as a state, county, or
city.

population: The number of people in a
certain place at a specific time.

population density: A measure com-
puted by dividing the total population
of a geographic area by its land area
measured in square miles or square
kilometers.

population growth rate: The increase
in a population during a given period,
divided by population at the beginning
of the period. If the population has
declined, this number is negative.

population pyramid: The graphic representation of a population's age-sex
composition in the form of a horizontal
bar graph.

postal area: A geographic study area
whose boundaries are defined by zip
codes or carrier routes.

poverty: The state of having income
below the federally determined poverty
threshold.

poverty level: The measure of a family's money income that reflects its ability to meet minimum consumption
requirements. A family is classified as
either above or below the poverty level.

poverty threshold: The income cut-offs
used by the government to determine
the poverty status of families and unrelated individuals based on family size.
Poverty thresholds are revised annually
to allow for changes in the cost of living.

**Primary Metropolitan Statistical
Area (PMSA):** A metropolitan area
that is adjacent to another; a component of a Consolidated Metropolitan
Statistical Area.

product: A tangible item made or sold
by a company. Also called a good.

profession: An occupation that
requires advanced education. Medicine
and law are examples of professions.

projection: An estimate based on
assumptions about future trends of the
incidence of a demographic characteristic such as age or household type.
Population projections usually make
assumptions about births, deaths, and
migration trends.

promotion: Any technique that persua-
sively communicates favorable information about a product to potential buyers.

psychographics: Lifestyle and attitude
research and data.

public: A group of people that may
affect or be affected by a government's
or other organization's policies and
efforts.

**Public-Use Microdata Samples
(PUMS):** Census microdata available
to the public, stripped of individual
identifiers.

qualitative research: Research charac-
terized by an interest in subjective
evaluations and the absence of empirical measurements; for instance, focus
groups.

quality of life: A measure of an individual's or society's well-being as reflected in social indicators.

quantitative research: Research conducted for the purpose of obtaining empirical evaluations of attitudes, behavior, or performance; for example, consumer expenditure surveys. Most quantitative research is based on information supplied by a relatively small group that is representative of a larger population.

race: The U.S. government classifies four major racial groups for the purpose of data collection—whites, blacks, Asians and Pacific Islanders, and American Indians and Alaskan Natives. This system is currently under review.

random digit dialing (RDD): A method of selecting phone numbers for telephone interviews with the intent of ensuring an unbiased sample.

random sampling: A sample in which each unit has an equal and independent chance of selection.

rate: A measure of a portion or number of events with respect to a whole, such as a divorce rate per 1,000 population.

ratio: A numerical relationship between two things, such as the male:female ratio of the population.

real income: The extent to which an individual's income can be used to obtain products and services in the marketplace.

recreation: Leisure activities that allows people to relax, recharge, and enjoy.

reference person: *See* householder.

region: *See* census region.

regional marketing: Marketing aimed at local rather than national markets.

renter: An individual who does not own the housing unit in which he lives, even if no cash rent is paid to the unit's owner.

renter-occupied: A housing unit that is not lived in by its owner, even if the occupant does not pay cash rent to the owner.

residence: *See* dwelling.

residential population: The number of people who live in a given area. May or may not be citizens. *See also* daytime population.

retail: The environment in which a product or service is sold to its ultimate consumer.

retired: An individual of any age who is receiving retirement income and who may or may not be employed.

rural: Any population not classified as urban.

sample: A representative group of members of a population used to approximate the characteristics of the entire population within acceptable limits of statistical error.

sampling: The method of selecting a specified portion of a population from which information concerning the whole can be inferred.

sampling error: The estimated inaccuracy of the results of a study when a population sample is used to explain the behavior of the total population.

scanner data: Purchase and other data collected through the use of scanner devices, either in retail stores or at home.

segmentation: *See* market segmentation.

selective marketing: *See* target marketing.

seller's market: An economic climate in which the seller's demands are more likely than the buyer's to be met.

separate living quarters: Dwellings in which occupants live and eat separately from other occupants in the building and have direct access from the outside of the building or through a common hall.

service: An intangible item that assists or benefits its consumer.

service-based economy: An economic system in which a dominant form of employment and a significant portion or wealth created is through the production, distribution, and consumption of services. Between the 1950s and 1970s, the U.S. shifted from a manufacturing-based to a service-based economy.

sex ratio: The number of males per 100 females in a population.

short-form questionnaire: The brief decennial census questionnaire sent to all U.S. households.

SIC: *See* Standard Industrial Classification.

single-parent family: A family household headed by a man or woman with no spouse present and with children under age 18.

single-person household: A person living alone in a housing unit.

single-source data: Integrated data on demographic characteristics, media use, and purchase behavior collected from the same individuals.

site evaluation: The process of determining through an analysis of a given area's demographic and economic characteristics whether that area offers a good market for a product or service.

SMSA: *See* Standard Metropolitan Statistical Area.

snowbird: A northern person who is a temporary resident of a southern area; for example, retirees who spend the winter in Florida but maintain a summer residence in Michigan.

social class: A hierarchy that classifies individuals and groups on the basis of esteem and prestige.

social indicator: A numerical measure of the quality of life in a particular area, such as wealth, health, safety, education, profession, income, and leisure.

socioeconomic: Refers to social and economic characteristics like social class, education, profession, income, and wealth.

Standard Industrial Classification (SIC): A system used by the Commerce Department to classify businesses and their products into specific categories. The major categories are construction, manufacture, mineral industries, retail, service, transportation, and wholesale. The system is being revised to include product classifications for the service sector of the economies of the U.S., Canada, and Mexico, to be called the North American Industrial Classification System (NAICS).

Standard Metropolitan Statistical Area (SMSA): An obsolete designation used to describe a metropolitan market, replaced by MSA.

standard of living: A measure of the relative distribution of wealth and material goods among people.

state data center: An organization within a state, generally a planning agency, university, or library to which the Census Bureau furnishes products, training in data access and use, technical assistance, and consultation. The data center in turn disseminates the products to the public and provides assistance with their use in the state.

STFs: *See* Summary Tape Files.

subculture: Segments within a culture that have values and behaviors that are different from those of the culture in general.

subfamily: A family group that does not include a householder. For example, a single mother and her child who live with the child's grandparents are a subfamily within a married-couple family household.

suburb: Any part of a metropolitan area that is not designated as a central city.

Summary Tape Files (STFs): Census computer tapes, organized according to subject and geography, that contain a broad range of population and housing data from the short and long decennial census forms.

target market: A market segment or group of consumers to whom marketing efforts are directed and whose needs a product or service is designed to meet.

target marketing: A strategy aimed at a particular audience, rather than at a broad or mass audience. Also called micromarketing, selective marketing.

teenager: An individual aged 13 to 19.

telephone area: A geographic study area whose boundaries are defined by area codes and three-digit prefix calling areas.

telephone sample: A group of randomly or otherwise-selected people who are surveyed by telephone.

temporary population: Tourists, commuters, snowbirds, and other nonpermanent residents of an area.

tenure: The ownership or renter status of a housing unit.

thematic map: A computer-generated map that combines geography with demographic data or other information.

TIGER: *See* Topologically Integrated Geographic and Encoding Reference File.

time-use survey: A survey that determines how people use their time by asking people to record what they do and how they do it in a diary over several days or weeks.

Topologically Integrated Geographic and Encoding Reference File (TIGER): A geographic information system developed for use with the 1990 census that provides a complete boundary file of the U.S.

total fertility rate: Expected number of live births per 1,000 women in their lifetime given current age-specific rates. An approximation of complete family size.

total money income: *See* income.

town: A division of local government, granted municipal powers in some states.

township: A division of local government in some northeastern, midwestern, and southern states.

trade area: A geographic area of any size from which the customers of a business are drawn.

traditional family: A married-couple family with their own children under age 18 living with them. In 1994, 36 percent of all families, or 26 percent of all households, were traditional families.

trend: A pattern of attitudes and behaviors that emerges over a period of time.

tween: An individual aged 10 to 12.

ultimate consumer: An individual who buys a product or service for personal or household use.

undocumented alien: *See* illegal alien.

unemployed: Currently not working as a paid employee but available for work and actively seeking work.

upscale: *See* affluent market.

urban: Places with 25,000 or more inhabitants and urbanized zones around cities with 50,000 or more inhabitants.

urbanization: An increase in the proportion of the population living in urban areas, typically viewed as a measure of development.

urbanized area: A central city or cities and the surrounding closely settled territory or "urban fringe."

usage: The purposes, methods, and frequency of use of a particular product or service.

VALS: *See* Values Attitudes and Lifestyles Survey.

value: A culturally shared belief about the goodness or badness of an attitude or activity. For example, U.S. culture values free speech but not arson.

Values Attitudes and Lifestyle Survey (VALS2): A psychographic segmentation technique used by market researchers to measure audience quality. Developed by SRI International, it divides the U.S. population into nine lifestyle groups.

variance: The statistical measure of how similar groups are by specific characteristics.

vernacular region: A self-identified place of any size, as defined by those who live in or are familiar with it, such as the Sunbelt.

village: A division of local government granted municipal powers in some states.

vital statistics: Information about the basic life events of birth, death, marriage, and divorce.

wealth: Net worth that includes all assets and accumulates over time.

white: One of four racial groups used in federal data collection. Members of this group have origins in any of the original peoples of Europe, North Africa, or the Middle East.

white-collar: A category of occupations that includes professional specialty; managerial and executive; and technical, sales, and administrative support.

wholesale: The sale of a product or service in large quantities, usually for resale to the ultimate consumer.

young adult: An individual aged 18 to 24.

youth market: Usually the population aged 18 to 24; sometimes includes younger teenagers.

zip-code demographics: The demographic characteristics of a population living in a particular zip-code area.

SOURCES

Dictionary of Marketing Terms, American Marketing Association, 1988

Population Handbook, Population Reference Bureau, 1991

The Vest-Pocket Marketer, by Alexander Hiam, Prentice Hall Inc., 1991

Webster's New Collegiate Dictionary, G. & C. Merriam Co., 1979

Webster's New World Dictionary of Media and Communications, by Richard Weiner, Simon & Schuster Inc., 1990

Key Word Index to Sources

African Americans

analytical services

Asia

Asia/Pacific

Asian-American market

attitudes and opinions

business to business

buying behavior

California

Canada

census data

China

circulation data

computer services

computer-assisted surveys

consulting

consumer confidence

consumer segmentation

consumer spending

demographics

desktop mapping/GIS

direct marketing

(see also: database marketing,
mailing lists)

mature market

media research

Mexico

New York

online

risk assessment

Russia

sales and marketing

statistical software

survey samples

survey software

Source Name/Telephone Index:

**AMERICAN
DEMOGRAPHICS BOOKS**

Targeting Transitions: Marketing to Consumers During Life Changes

Millions of Americans go through major life transitions each year, including getting married or remarried, becoming parents and grandparents, changing careers, getting divorced, moving, becoming caregivers, and retiring. Once you understand the characteristics of people in transition, you can begin to discover the marketing opportunities created by these events.

Everybody Eats: Supermarket Consumers in the 1990s

This is the first book to focus exclusively on supermarket shoppers and factors that influence their food purchasing decisions. It divides shoppers into four age segments: mature consumers, baby boomers, baby busters, and hidden influencers (young children and teenagers). It further divides consumers in terms of region, race and ethnicity, and economic groups. Learn how different groups of consumers respond to new products and how you can help consumers manage the sea of product information they face every time they enter the supermarket.

Marketing Health Care to Women: Meeting New Demands for Products and Services

Visit any general hospital or the waiting room of any physician, and you're likely to see more women than men. Women buy more over-the-counter and prescription drugs and spend more money per person than men on health care. Women tend to be the primary decisionmakers for family health care, and often it is women who prompt men to see a physician. This book is must-reading for marketers linked to drug companies, hospitals, health-insurance plans, and medical-supply companies. It also discusses the potential for nonmedical health products, such as comfort pillows for breast feeding, diet supplements, and vitamins.

The Baby Bust: A Generation Comes of Age

As a generation, busters are unique in their experiences, beliefs, politics, and preferences. This is the first statistical biography of this generation. It tells the baby bust's story through demographics, opinion polls, expert analysis, anecdotes, and the indispensable comments and experiences of busters themselves.

Segmenting the Mature Market

People over age 50 account for 43 percent of all U.S. households and half of all quantitative discretionary income. Learn how and where seniors spend their money, what cars they drive and where they go, who is retiring, and who is returning to work. Find out about their media preferences, health-care concerns, and enormous political influence.

Targeting Families: Marketing To and Through the New Family

Word-of-mouth product recommendations made from one family member to another are significantly more effective than those made between friends or colleagues. Learn how to get family members on your sales force and how to implement a "Full Family Marketing" approach that attracts youths, spouses, and seniors.

Beyond Mind Games: The Marketing Power of Psychographics

The first book that details what psychographics is, where it came from, and how you can use it.

Selling the Story: The Layman's Guide to Collecting and Communicating Demographic Information

A handbook offering a crash course in demography and solid instruction in writing about numbers. Learn how to use numbers carefully, how to avoid misusing them, and how to bring cold numbers to life by relating them to real people.

The Seasons of Business: The Marketer's Guide to Consumer Behavior

Learn which demographic groups are the principal players and which consumer concerns are most pressing in each marketing season.

About the Author

Peter Francese is president and founder of American Demographics, Inc., a Dow Jones company which publishes *American Demographics* and *Marketing Tools* magazines, *The Numbers News* newsletter, and books on related topics. As the nation's leading expert on consumer trends, Mr. Francese has written numerous magazine and newspaper articles and is the creator of the column, "People Patterns," which appears exclusively in *The Wall Street Journal*. He frequently speaks to business audiences on consumer trends and the market information industry. He is a recipient of the Silver Bell Award for distinguished public service from the Advertising Council, and has a graduate degree from Cornell University.

His preceding book, *Capturing Customers*, is a handbook of information-based marketing techniques.